THE BOOK OF DANIEL

VOLUME 23

THE ANCHOR BIBLE is a fresh approach to the world's greatest classic. Its object is to make the Bible accessible to the modern reader; its method is to arrive at the meaning of biblical literature through exact translation and extended exposition, and to reconstruct the ancient setting of the biblical story, as well as the circumstances of its transcription and the characteristics of its transcribers.

THE ANCHOR BIBLE is a project of international and interfaith scope. Protestant, Catholic, and Jewish scholars from many countries contribute individual volumes. The project is not sponsored by any ecclesiastical organization and is not intended to reflect any particular theological doctrine. Prepared under our joint supervision, THE ANCHOR BIBLE is an effort to make available all the significant historical and linguistic knowledge which bears on the interpretation of the biblical record.

THE ANCHOR BIBLE is aimed at the general reader with no special formal training in biblical studies; yet, it is written with the most exacting standards of scholarship, reflecting the highest technical accomplishment.

This project marks the beginning of a new era of co-operation among scholars in biblical research, thus forming a common body of knowledge to be shared by all.

William Foxwell Albright
David Noel Freedman
GENERAL EDITORS

THE BOOK OF DANIEL

A New Translation with Notes
and Commentary on Chapters 1–9
by † LOUIS F. HARTMAN, C.SS.R.

Introduction, and Commentary
on Chapters 10–12
by ALEXANDER A. Di LELLA, O.F.M.

DOUBLEDAY & COMPANY, INC.
GARDEN CITY, NEW YORK
1978

NIHIL OBSTAT
Cassian F. Corcoran, O.F.M., *Censor Deputatus*

IMPRIMI POTEST
Charles V. Finnegan, O.F.M., *Minister Provincial*

IMPRIMATUR
✠ William Cardinal Baum,
Archbishop of Washington

6 April 1977

Library of Congress Cataloging in Publication Data

Bible. O.T. Daniel, I–XII. English. Hartman. 1978.
The Book of Daniel.

(The Anchor Bible; 23)
Bibliography: p. 111.
Includes indexes.
1. Bible. O.T. Daniel—Commentaries. I. Hartman, Louis Francis, 1901–1970. II. Di Lella, Alexander A. III. Title. IV. Series.
BS192.2.A1 1964.G3 vol. 23 [BS1554.E] 220.6′6s
[224′.5′077]
ISBN: 0-385-01322-1
Library of Congress Catalog Card Number 77–82762

Printed in the United States of America
First Edition

PREFACE

The division of labor and coauthorship indicated on the title page of the present volume were not originally intended by the editors of the Anchor Bible. Many years ago, they had asked the Rev. Louis F. Hartman, C.SS.R., to be sole author of this work. As in many other situations, however, "man proposes but God disposes" (Thomas à Kempis, *Imitation of Christ* i 19). Father Hartman, a highly esteemed and widely revered teacher and later colleague of mine at The Catholic University of America, Washington, D.C., died unexpectedly in his sleep during the early morning hours of 22 August 1970 following a typically busy and fruitful day in the loving service of God and neighbor. Father Hartman was also a cherished friend whose accomplishments as an eminent scholar and superlative human being it was my privilege to describe in a memorial tribute published in *CBQ* 32 (1970), 497–500. It is a distinct honor for me to be associated with him in the production of the present commentary. And I dedicate my portion of this work to his hallowed memory.

Before his death, Hartman completed the translation, text-critical apparatus, and explanatory notes of all twelve chapters of the Book of Daniel as well as the commentary on chapters 1–9. After his death, the Anchor Bible editors, the late William F. Albright and David Noel Freedman, asked me to finish the volume. I wrote the commentary on chapters 10–12 and the whole Introduction, and I am also responsible for the Bibliography. Hartman's portion of the work is published here in generally the exact form in which he had left it in 1970 at the time of his death; I merely did some copy editing of this material. In a few instances, however, I also made slight revisions and added some updated information; these small bits and pieces I have enclosed in square brackets so that the gentle reader may see at a glance that I am responsible for them.

The Book of Daniel is one of the most fascinating portions of the Bible, and one of the most difficult as well. It is earnestly hoped that Father Hartman and I have provided reasonable explanations and sufficient background necessary for one to understand the book in its historical context, and to appreciate the enduring relevance the book can have for the believer today. Scholars and students of Daniel will find here much that is familiar, some that is original, and little, I pray, that is pointless. Undoubtedly, critics will not agree with all of the positions and judgments expressed, and they will propose alternative opinions and solutions. All of which is as it should be, for such is the way that progress is made in biblical studies and in other disciplines.

This volume was composed with two principal groups of people in mind: the biblical scholar and the interested lay reader. The linguistic discussions and other technical details found in the Introduction and throughout the rest of the volume will be of concern chiefly to the scholar. The lay reader can skip such matters and still follow the general argument being advanced. I have been particularly sensitive to the often heard complaint that specialists in biblical studies generally talk to and write for one another with little or no regard for the vast majority of the non-scholarly public who read and study Holy Scripture regularly and take it seriously. Sad to say, that complaint is quite legitimate. As partial redress for this state of affairs, I have written as conclusion to the Introduction a special section entitled "The Book of Daniel Today." I trust that lay readers will see at once that this section is addressed specifically to them and to their questions, though it may be of some interest to my professional colleagues as well. Other parts of the Introduction are also meant primarily for the general reading public. It is hoped that the Introduction, translation, notes, and commentary strike a happy balance between the rightful concerns both of Scripture scholars and of non-professional students and other readers of the Bible.

In the Introduction and Commentary on chapters 10–12 I have used the *New American Bible* (*NAB*) for Scripture quotations outside the Book of Daniel. Father Hartman apparently made some of his own translations of the biblical texts he cited in his NOTES and COMMENTS on chapters 1–9; these I have left unchanged. Doubtless, the reader will notice other differences in Hartman's materials and my own as regards style and manner of presentation. I trust that these differences will not detract from the value of the present volume but may even add some interest and variety.

I am grateful to General Editor David Noel Freedman for carefully reading the entire manuscript; he corrected my mistakes and made many worthwhile suggestions. Sincere thanks are due also to William J. Parker, C.SS.R., one of my graduate students, who generously gave of his time to compile all the indexes. Finally I express my thanks to Robert Hewetson and Eve Roshevsky of Doubleday for overseeing the publication of the work.

27 December 1976 ALEXANDER A. DI LELLA, O.F.M.

CONTENTS

PRINCIPAL ABBREVIATIONS

AB	The Anchor Bible
Abel	F.-M. Abel, *Histoire de la Palestine depuis la conquête d'Alexandre jusqu'à l'invasion arabe**
AJSL	*American Journal of Semitic Languages and Literature*
ALBO	Analecta lovaniensia biblica et orientalia
AnBib	Analecta biblica
ANET	*Ancient Near Eastern Texts,** ed. J. B. Pritchard
AnOr	Analecta orientalia
APOT	*Apocrypha and Pseudepigrapha of the Old Testament,** ed. R. H. Charles
Aq.	Aquila
ASTI	*Annual of the Swedish Theological Institute*
BA	*Biblical Archaeologist*
BASOR	*Bulletin of the American Schools of Oriental Research*
Bentzen	A. Bentzen, *Daniel**
Bevan	A. A. Bevan, *A Short Commentary on the Book of Daniel**
Bib	*Biblica*
BibOr	Biblica et orientalia
BibS	Biblische Studien
BJRL	*Bulletin of the John Rylands Library, University of Manchester*
BKAT	Biblischer Kommentar: Altes Testament
BR	*Biblical Research*
BZ	*Biblische Zeitschrift*
BZAW	Beihefte zur *ZAW*
CAD	*The* [*Chicago*] *Assyrian Dictionary,** eds. I. J. Gelb et al.
CAT	Commentaire de l'Ancien Testament
CBQ	*Catholic Biblical Quarterly*
ch(s).	chapter(s)
Charles	R. H. Charles, *A Critical and Exegetical Commentary on the Book of Daniel**
ConB	Coniectanea biblica
DBSup	*Dictionnaire de la Bible, Supplément*
Delcor	M. Delcor, *Le livre de Daniel**
DJD	Discoveries in the Judaean Desert of Jordan

* For the full reference, see the Selected Bibliography.

Driver	S. R. Driver, *The Book of Daniel**
Driver, *Introduction*	S. R. Driver, *An Introduction to the Literature of the Old Testament**
EBib	Etudes bibliques
EncJud	*Encyclopaedia judaica* (1971)
ETL	*Ephemerides theologicae lovanienses*
FBBS	Facet Books, Biblical Series
FRLANT	Forschungen zur Religion und Literatur des Alten und Neuen Testaments
Ginsberg	H. L. Ginsberg, *Studies in Daniel**
HAT	Handbuch zum Alten Testament
Heaton	E. W. Heaton, *The Book of Daniel**
hend.	hendiadys
HKAT	Handkommentar zum Alten Testament
HR	*History of Religions*
HSM	Harvard Semitic Monographs
HTR	*Harvard Theological Review*
HTS	Harvard Theological Studies
HUCA	*Hebrew Union College Annual*
IB	*Interpreter's Bible*
ICC	International Critical Commentary
IDB	*Interpreter's Dictionary of the Bible,* ed. G. A. Buttrick
IDBSup	*Interpreter's Dictionary of the Bible,* Supplementary volume (1976)
IEJ	*Israel Exploration Journal*
Int	*Interpretation*
ITQ	*Irish Theological Quarterly*
JAOS	*Journal of the American Oriental Society*
JB	*Jerusalem Bible*
JBL	*Journal of Biblical Literature*
Jeffery	A. Jeffery, "The Book of Daniel"*
JPS	*Jewish Publication Society* translation of the Old Testament (1916)
JQR	*Jewish Quarterly Review*
JQRMS	Jewish Quarterly Review Monograph Series
JSS	*Journal of Semitic Studies*
JTC	Journal for Theology and the Church
JTS	*Journal of Theological Studies*
KAT	Kommentar zum Alten Testament
Keil	C. F. Keil, *The Book of the Prophet Daniel**
KJV	*King James Version*
Lacocque	A. Lacocque, *Le livre de Daniel**
Lattey	C. Lattey, *The Book of Daniel**
LCL	Loeb Classical Library
LD	Lectio divina

* For the full reference, see the Selected Bibliography.

Linder	J. Linder, *Commentarius in Librum Daniel**
LXX	Septuagint
LXX967	Papyrus 967 (third century) of the LXX
Montgomery	J. A. Montgomery, *The Book of Daniel**
MT	Masoretic Text: R. Kittel, *Biblia Hebraica,* 3d ed.
NAB	*New American Bible*
NCE	*New Catholic Encyclopedia,* eds. M. R. P. McGuire et al.
NEB	*New English Bible*
NovT	*Novum Testamentum*
NovTSup	Novum Testamentum, Supplements
NTS	*New Testament Studies*
OTS	*Oudtestamentische Studiën*
PG	*Patrologia graeca,* ed. J. Migne
PL	*Patrologia latina,* ed. J. Migne
Plöger	O. Plöger, *Das Buch Daniel**
Porteous	N. Porteous, *Daniel**
RB	*Revue biblique*
RevQ	*Revue de Qumrân*
Rinaldi	G. Rinaldi, *Daniele**
Rosenthal, *Grammar*	F. Rosenthal, *A Grammar of Biblical Aramaic**
Rosenthal, *Handbook*	F. Rosenthal, ed., *An Aramaic Handbook**
RSV	*Revised Standard Version*
RTL	*Revue théologique de Louvain*
Sam.	Samaritan Pentateuch
SB	*Sources bibliques*
SBJ	*La sainte bible de Jérusalem*
SBM	Stuttgarter biblische Monographien
SBS	Stuttgarter Bibelstudien
SBT	Studies in Biblical Theology
Schürer	E. Schürer, *History of the Jewish People**
Sem	*Semitica*
SNT	Studien zum Neuen Testament
ST	*Studia theologica*
Steinmann	J. Steinmann, *Daniel: Texte français, introduction et commentaires**
Syh.	Syrohexaplar
Sym.	Symmachus
Syr.	Syriac Peshiṭta
Targ.	Targum
Tcherikover	V. Tcherikover, *Hellenistic Civilization and the Jews**
TDNT	*Theological Dictionary of the New Testament*
TDOT	*Theological Dictionary of the Old Testament*
Test.	Testament
TEV	*Today's English Version* (1976)

* For the full reference, see the Selected Bibliography.

Theod.	Theodotion-Daniel
TRu	*Theologische Rundschau*
TSK	*Theologische Studien und Kritiken*
vs(s).	verse(s)
UF	*Ugaritische Forschungen*
Vet. Lat.	Vetus Latina (Old Latin translation)
VT	*Vetus Testamentum*
VTSup	Vetus Testamentum, Supplements
Vulg.	Vulgate
ZAW	*Zeitschrift für die alttestamentliche Wissenschaft*
1QapGen	*Genesis Apocryphon* from Qumran Cave 1
1QDan[a,b]	Fragments of Daniel from Qumran Cave 1
1QH	*Hôdāyôt* (Thanksgiving Hymns) from Qumran Cave 1
1QIsa[a]	First copy of Isaiah from Qumran Cave 1
1QpHab	*Pesher* on *Habakkuk* from Qumran Cave 1
1QM	*Milḥāmāh* (War Scroll) from Qumran Cave 1
4QDan[a,b,c]	Fragments of Daniel from Qumran Cave 4
4QDeut	Fragments of Deuteronomy from Qumran Cave 4
4QDibHam	Prayer of intercession from Qumran Cave 4
4QFlor	*Florilegium* from Qumran Cave 4
4QpNah	*Pesher* on *Nahum* from Qumran Cave 4
4QPrNab	Prayer of Nabonidus from Qumran Cave 4
6QDan	Fragments of Daniel from Qumran Cave 6
11QPs[a]	The Psalms Scroll from Qumran Cave 11

INTRODUCTION

I. CONTENTS OF THE BOOK

The Book of Daniel in its protocanonical form appearing in the Masoretic Text (MT) exists in two languages: Aramaic (2:4b–7:28) and Hebrew (1:1–2:4a and chs. 8–12). The book also contained in its pre-Christian Greek forms other materials (the prayers in Greek 3:24–90, and the narratives of Susanna, Bel, and the Dragon) which are considered apocryphal by Jews and Protestants, but deuterocanonical by Roman Catholics. The present work is concerned primarily with the MT-form of the book; the deuterocanonical sections are handled in Vol. 44 of the Anchor Bible.

In terms of content the book is divided into two roughly equal parts: (*a*) chs. 1–6 are six midrashic or edifying stories, narrated in the third person, about an ancient worthy named Daniel and his three fellow believers who undergo various trials because of their piety and strict observance of Jewish customs and practices; (*b*) chs. 7–12 contain, in first-person form, four apocalypses or visions granted to the same Daniel for the purpose of sustaining faith and loyalty during the perilous times to come.

Chapter 1 is set in the third year of Jehoiakim king of Judah (606 B.C.) when Nebuchadnezzar king of Babylon takes the people of Judah into exile. Among them are Daniel, Hananiah, Mishael, and Azariah—flawless and handsome young men who are then put into training for royal service. They are provided with a sumptuous diet and good wine to ensure vigorous health, but Daniel and his companions refuse to defile themselves with the king's rich food and wine and partake instead only of vegetables and water. Rather than lose weight as one would expect, they look healthier and better fed than their classmates. God also gives them such impressive knowledge and skill that they become far more effective than all the other officials of the realm.

Chapter 2 tells of an unpleasant apocalyptic dream Nebuchadnezzar had during the second year of his reign (603 B.C.). None of the Chaldean dream experts who are summoned can tell the king his dream or its meaning. Furious, the king orders all the wise men of the kingdom to be executed. Daniel too is to be included, but he asks for and is granted a stay of execution. Daniel and his three companions then pray earnestly to God to inform them of the dream and its intrepretation. Their prayer is answered. Daniel tells the king that in his dream he saw a colossal statue symbolizing four successive pagan kingdoms—the Babylonian, Median, Persian, and

Greek or Hellenistic. Finally, a stone, symbolizing the People of God, was cut from the mountain with no human aid and crushed the monstrous statue. The stone grew into a great mountain and filled the earth forever. Nebuchadnezzar acknowledges God as the true revealer of mysteries and appoints Daniel and his companions to positions of high rank in the realm.

Chapter 3 describes the gigantic golden idol which Nebuchadnezzar set up and decreed to be worshipped by all on pain of being summarily cast into a white-hot furnace. All comply, except of course Daniel's three pious companions, who are called by their Babylonian names, Shadrach, Meshach, and Abednego. Daniel does not appear at all in this chapter. When charged with violating the king's law, the three stalwart Jews fearlessly proclaim their faith in the power of their God to save them from the royal wrath. Enraged, the king orders the furnace to be heated seven times its usual temperature. Bound and cast into the inferno, the three Jews remain unharmed and walk about in the flames accompanied by a fourth person who looks like a divine being. The three emerge from the furnace with not a single hair singed and not even the smell of fire on their clothes. The king, duly impressed, blesses the God of Israel and grants the three men a promotion.

Chapter 4 (the story begins in 3:31) contains Nebuchadnezzar's autobiographical epistle to all the peoples of the world. In it he recounts his frightening dream about a huge tree that was cut down to the stump and how he summoned Daniel to give him the true interpretation of the dream. Daniel explains that the king is the tree, and that because of arrogance he would become insane for seven years. But the king's sanity and kingdom would be restored because of his repentance and conversion to the true God. Everything Daniel had predicted came to pass, and Nebuchadnezzar addresses a hymn of praise to the King of heaven.

Chapter 5 (ending at 6:1) is the narrative of Belshazzar's banquet. Under the influence of wine King Belshazzar of Babylon brings in the sacred vessels which his father Nebuchadnezzar had taken from the Jerusalem Temple. He and his thousand grandees drink wine from these vessels in praise of their false gods. Suddenly a mysterious hand appears and inscribes three words, the now proverbial handwriting on the wall. None of the pagan wise men can understand the strange words. At the queen's urging, Daniel is brought in; he sternly lectures the king and then reads and explains the words: *Mene* means the king's days are numbered; *Teqel,* the king has been weighed and been found wanting; and *Peres,* the kingdom has been divided up. For his labors Daniel receives royal honors, but that same night the king is slain and replaced by Darius the Mede.

Chapter 6 details the jealousy of Daniel's fellow ministers and satraps who plot his downfall. They induce Darius the Mede to issue a decree forbidding anyone from petitioning for thirty days any god or man except the king. Ignoring the wicked law, Daniel prays to the God of Israel three times a day as was the custom for Jews. The schemers catch Daniel at prayer and constrain the reluctant king to order the holy man to be cast into the lions' den as punishment. The next morning Darius is pleased to find that Daniel was preserved safe and sound of limb from the jaws of the hungry lions. Thereupon the king commands that Daniel's accusers, together with their wives and children, be thrown to the lions who then tear them to pieces. Darius orders all his subjects to reverence and fear the God of Daniel. Daniel prospers in the reigns of Darius the Mede and Cyrus.

Chapter 7, an apocalyptic vision, takes place in the first year of King Belshazzar of Babylon. The chapter opens in the third person and immediately switches to a first-person autobiographical account. Seeing four immense beasts coming up out of the sea, Daniel becomes duly horrified. Now it is Daniel's turn to seek enlightenment as to the meaning of the vision, as the pagans did of him in the earlier narratives of the book. An angel explains that the lion symbolizes the Babylonian kingdom; the bear, the Median; the leopard, the Persian; and the terrifying monster with the ten horns, the Hellenistic (Seleucid). Three of the horns are uprooted by a small horn which sprouts up and speaks arrogantly (Antiochus IV Epiphanes). The Ancient One, symbol of God, appears in glory and judgment. The four beasts are slain, and finally everlasting dominion is given to "one in human likeness," symbolizing the holy ones of the Most High, or the faithful Jews who had been devastated by the wicked Antiochus for three and a half years.

Chapter 8 is dated in the third year of King Belshazzar. This apocalyptic vision is also told in the first person. Daniel sees a ram with two long horns butting toward the west, the north, and the south; no other beast could withstand it. Then a he-goat with one big horn appears from the west and breaks the ram's horns and totally subdues it. The he-goat's big horn eventually breaks off to be replaced by four conspicuous horns, from one of which a small horn grows up toward the south and the east. This small horn blasphemes God and defiles the sanctuary of the pious ones, setting up in it an appalling offense and interrupting for twenty-three hundred evenings and mornings the prescribed daily sacrifice of the Jews. Daniel, again at a loss as to the meaning of the vision, is enlightened by the angel Gabriel: the two-horned ram represents the kingdom of the Medes and Persians; the he-goat, the Greek kingdoms, the big horn being the kingdom of Alexander the Great and the four later horns the kingdoms of Cassander (Macedonia), Lysimachus (Thrace), Ptolemy I (Egypt), and Seleucus I (Syria). The small horn is Antiochus IV.

Chapter 9, also autobiographical, is set in the first year of Darius the Mede. Here the apocalyptic vision is preceded by prayer and fasting as

Daniel seeks to learn the meaning of the seventy years of Jerusalem's devastation predicted by Jeremiah the prophet (Jer 25:11–12; 29:10). The angel Gabriel again appears and reveals that the seventy years are in reality seventy weeks of years upon the completion of which justice will be done and the temple reconsecrated. The accuracy of Gabriel's mathematics is apparently of little concern, Daniel's true interest being the last week of years, from the death of Onias III in 171 B.C. to the inauguration of the Kingdom of God in 164, which followed the roughly half week of years during which Antiochus IV abolished sacrifices and defiled the temple by placing on the altar the "appalling abomination" (or "abomination of desolation").

Chapters 10–12 contain the last and by far the longest apocalypse, and is dated in the third year of Cyrus. It describes the course of events from Cyrus the Great in 538 B.C. to the death of the vicious tyrant Antiochus IV in 164 B.C. The opening verse is told in the third person about Daniel; the rest in the first person by Daniel himself. After three weeks of fasting and other forms of mortification, Daniel experiences a vision of an angel who (as in ch. 9) acts as revealer of the future, and not (as in chs. 7 and 8) as interpreter of what Daniel saw. The angel provides a panoramic vista of history that includes: four Persian monarchs; Alexander the Great; the four kingdoms following the breakup of Alexander's empire; the battles, intrigues, and alliances that took place among the Seleucids and Ptolemies (or Lagids); the rise and career of the infamous Antiochus IV who brutally victimized the Jews and desecrated their temple; and the final vindication of the Ḥasidim who are the Israel of faith. Before a concluding word of comfort, the angel admonishes Daniel to keep the words secret and sealed till "the final phase."

It is to be noted that the historical outlook in both the midrashic and the apocalyptic parts of the book is essentially the same. What is being followed is a mistaken Jewish tradition as to the sequence of kingdoms and kings. Thus, in the midrashic Part One, the sequence of monarchs is: Nebuchadnezzar (chs. 1–4), Belshazzar (ch. 5), and Darius the Mede and Cyrus (ch. 6). In the apocalyptic Part Two, the sequence is: Belshazzar (chs. 7–8), Darius the Mede (ch. 9), and Cyrus (chs. 10–12). For a discussion of this peculiar historical tradition see Part VI, "The Historical Background."

II. ATTRIBUTION TO DANIEL

The Aramaic and Hebrew form of the name Daniel is *dānîy'ēl,* which means "God (or El) has judged," or "My judge is God." According to the Chronicler, one of David's sons was named Daniel (I Chron 3:1= Chileab of II Sam 3:3); and one of the Jews who returned from the Babylonian exile in the days of Ezra and Nehemiah (second half of the fifth century B.C.) also bore the same name (Ezra 8:2; Neh 10:7). Neither of these two gentlemen, however, can be identified with the protagonist of the Book of Daniel. In Ezek 14:14,20, the name also occurs, but in slightly different form (Hebrew *qᵉrē dānī'ēl, kᵉtîb dān'ēl*), between two other heroes of hoary antiquity, Noah and Job. All three holy men are not Israelite but belong to foreign nations; and each is an idealized figure belonging to a wider sphere of ancient Near Eastern tradition. The prophet Ezekiel speaks of these three embodiments of righteousness in order to refute the idea that Yahweh will be kind to guilty children out of consideration for the virtues of their fathers.[1] In Ezek 28:3, the same Daniel is mentioned as a proverbial figure of wisdom in a context in which the prince of Tyre is being castigated for his blasphemous arrogance. This Daniel must be some figure who was widely recognized throughout Syria-Palestine.

W. Eichrodt[2] thinks it very probable that this Daniel is to be identified with the king bearing the same name in the Ugaritic literature. In "The Tale of Aqhat"[3] (the extant fragments of which from Ras Shamra-Ugarit can be dated to about the second quarter of the fourteenth century B.C.) appears a King Dnil, a name that can be vocalized "Danel" or "Daniel." In *2 Aqhat,* V:7–8, is found this couplet regarding the activity of this Dnil:

ydn dn almnt	He judges the cause of the widow,
yṯpṭ ṯpṭ ytm	He tries the case of the orphan.[4]

When publication data (place, publisher, year) is not included in footnote, it may be found in the Selected Bibliography. Ed.

1 W. Eichrodt, *Ezekiel* (tr. C. Quinn), pp. 188–189.

2 Ibid., p. 391.

3 A translation of the extant fragments of "The Tale of Aqhat" can be found in *ANET,* pp. 149–155.

4 Possibly a distant echo of these words is found in the brilliant cross-examination of the wise young judge in the deuterocanonical Susanna narrative in the LXX and

Thus from very early times in Syria-Palestine the name Daniel must have been associated with outstanding righteousness and surpassing wisdom. Presumably for this reason the name is given to Enoch's father-in-law in the Book of Jubilees 4:20.[5]

Whatever the exact link between this idealized hero and the protagonist of the Book of Daniel, there is sufficient reason to believe that the authors of the book knew of such an ancient worthy and were familiar with certain stories in which he played a leading role. Thus scriptural narratives of the kind found in the Book of Daniel, including also the deuterocanonical portions extant in the Greek and Syriac forms of the book (3:24–90, and the stories of Susanna, Bel, and the Dragon), as well as non-scriptural accounts dealing with an Israelite seer who was noted for his heaven-sent gifts of dream interpretation, general sagacity, and unimpeachable integrity (e.g. the pseudo-Daniel fragments and Prayer of Nabonidus from Qumran Cave 4 which will be discussed in the next section) were attributed to a character named Daniel in much the same way that Torah (the Law) had been traditionally assigned to Moses, Psalms to David, and Wisdom Literature to Solomon. Whether Daniel in these stories represents a historical figure or a legendary literary creation cannot be determined with certainty. In a Jewish composition, however, the absence of a genealogy, contrary to custom, gives probability to the suggestion that the characters of Daniel and his pious companions are legendary.

Theodotion-Daniel forms of the book. On the Greek forms of Daniel, cf. below. As regards the special concern for the cause of the widow and orphan in the Old Testament, cf. Deut 10:18; 24:17; Isa 1:17; Jer 22:3; Zech 7:9–10; Ps 68:6; Sir 4:9–10.

[5] According to O. Eissfeldt, *The Old Testament: An Introduction* (tr. P. R. Ackroyd), pp. 607–608, the Book of Jubilees was composed ca. 100 B.C.

III. UNITY OF THE BOOK AND DATE

The Book of Daniel is logically divided into ten sections. The first nine correspond almost exactly to the chapter divisions of the book, except for the fourth section (3:31 – 4:34) and the fifth (5:1 – 6:1), while the tenth goes from 10:1 to 12:13. This book is unique among all the books of the Bible, Old and New Testament, in that each of these sections forms a distinct unit separable from the rest. Any one of the ten sections could have existed independently of any of the others and would have been virtually as intelligible, or unintelligible, as it now stands in the Book of Daniel. Or put differently, any one or more of the sections could have been lost, and the remaining sections would not have suffered in any significant way at all. Superficially, the book seems to be a collection of once isolated mini-works brought together by some unknown editor or redactor who despite his work as compiler could hardly claim the title of author of the whole book.

1. *The Problems*

Yet there are certain features in the book which seem to point to one author or at most two for the whole work. Every section of the book lays special emphasis on the belief that the God of Israel is master and guide of human history; that he knows the future and reveals its secrets to his chosen ones; and that under his rule the kingdom of his holy people will ultimately supplant the pagan empires of the world. In some parts of the book there are also literary links that join one section to another; for example, ch. 7 with ch. 2, ch. 6 with ch. 3, and ch. 5 with ch. 4. These features, however, do not necessarily prove that a single author is responsible for the whole book. The general orientation and horizon pervading the book could be due simply to the commonly shared ideas of the Jews of the second century B.C., or possibly to a certain group or school of Jewish writers of the time. The literary links between some of the sections may be merely the work of an editor or redactor who put together the ten originally independent sections.

From the literary point of view the book may be divided into two parts: (*a*) six midrashic or edifying stories (chs. 1–6; 2:13–45 is an apocalypse), and (*b*) four apocalyptic visions (chs. 7, 8, 9, and 10–12). This division seems to be *prima facie* evidence that one author composed the first part, another the second. This theory receives support from a consideration of some other factors. The first part of the book contains simple, easily remembered and repeatable stories about Daniel and his faithful companions. No pretense is made in the book that Daniel wrote the stories himself; in fact, he is referred to in the third person. The second part recounts four visions seen by Daniel and apparently written by him since he is referred to in the first person. These visions become progressively more detailed and complicated and virtually impossible to be remembered easily or repeated.[6] But there are difficulties in assuming a separate author for each of the two parts. The second edifying story (ch. 2), in which Nebuchadnezzar has an apocalyptic dream of the colossal statue with its four different metals symbolizing four successive empires, cannot be entirely dissociated from the first of the apocalyptic visions (ch. 7), in which Daniel sees four strange beasts symbolizing the same four successive empires. There are similar relationships between chs. 3 and 6 and between chs. 4 and 5, as was pointed out above. Moreover, the last four apocalyptic sections may not be treated on a par. In the second and third apocalypses (chs. 7 and 8), Daniel sees certain symbolic visions of monstrous beasts, etc., which are then explained to him by the angel who acts as interpreter, the *angelus interpres*. In the last two apocalypses (chs. 9 and 10–12), Daniel sees only the *angelus revelator* who conveys revelations to him directly and without the aid of any symbolic visions.

Another feature that makes the Book of Daniel different from every other book of the Bible is its *peculiar* bilingual character (Aramaic and Hebrew) and if the deuterocanonical (or, in Protestant and Jewish terminology, apocryphal) parts in Greek are included, the book is trilingual—the only such book in the Old Testament. There are, to be sure, a few Aramaic documents quoted in the Hebrew Book of Ezra (4:8–6:18; 7:1–26), and one Aramaic verse appears in Jer 10:11 and two Aramaic words in Gen 31:47. But the situation in Daniel is quite different. About half the book is in Hebrew and half in Aramaic. To complicate matters, the linguistic division between the Hebrew (1:1–2:4a; 8:1–12:13) and Aramaic parts (2:4b–7:28) does not correspond to the literary division between the midrashic stories (chs. 1–6) and the apocalyptic narratives (chs. 7–12). If the six edifying stories of chs. 1–6 (including the first apocalypse, 2:13–45) had been all in Aramaic, and the last four apocalypses of chs. 7–12 all in Hebrew, then there would have been no difficulty in finding a persuasive explanation. One would have said that the compiler of the midrashic stories left them in the Aramaic language in which they were composed, and then added his own original work in Hebrew, viz. the last four apocalyptic visions.

Aramaic is certainly the original of 2:4b–7:28 as they now appear in

[6] Cf. H. H. Rowley, "The Unity of the Book of Daniel," in *The Servant of the Lord and Other Essays on the Old Testament,* 2d ed. rev., p. 250.

the MT. There is not the slightest indication that any part of these chapters is "translation Aramaic" of a Hebrew original. But is the Hebrew of the Hebrew parts the original language, or is this Hebrew a translation from an assumed Aramaic original which is no longer extant? If the latter alternative be correct, can a retroversion or retranslation back into Aramaic be used for clarifying obscure passages which the Hebrew translator may have misunderstood or at least poorly translated?

There are, therefore, two main questions regarding the unity of the Book of Daniel: (a) the question of one or multiple authors; (b) the question of interpreting the Hebrew parts as a translation of an assumed Aramaic original.

2. *One or Multiple Authors*

If the book has more than one author, practical questions of interpretation arise. For if one section was not composed by the author of another section (say, for instance, chs. 2 and 7), the two sections need not necessarily be understood in the same way. And more importantly, if one section was interpolated by another author when he added his section to the book, the interpolated verses may conceivably have a meaning quite different from the original section.

That various stories about Daniel, a Jewish hero of the Babylonian exile, were in circulation during the last few pre-Christian centuries can now be taken for granted. Some of these materials, which are not found in the protocanonical Book of Daniel (=MT) have fortunately been preserved in the book's deuterocanonical parts which are now extant in Greek and Syriac and other ancient versions but are generally believed to have been composed in Hebrew or Aramaic:[7] the Prayer of Azariah (Greek 3:24–45), a connecting narrative (Greek 3:46–51), the Hymn of the Three Jews (Greek 3:52–90), the stories of Susanna, Bel, and the Dragon.[8] The last two stories are altogether distinct, even though the Dragon narrative supposes knowledge of Bel (cf. 14:28). The fact that the story of the Dragon contains an account of Daniel in the lions' den like the narrative in ch. 6, serves to point out that variations of the same elements could be employed in different accounts about Daniel.[9]

Additional evidence has now become available from several Qumran manuscript fragments which show that there were even more Daniel narratives in circulation at that time (ca. 100 B.C.–A.D. 68), though only one of these fragments is of sufficient size to indicate the nature of its contents—a

[7] Cf. M. Delcor, pp. 88–89, 261, 291–292.

[8] For a brief discussion of the narratives of Susanna, Bel, and the Dragon, see Part IV, "Other Daniel Stories."

[9] Aphraat in his "Homily on Prayer" witnesses either to a third story about Daniel in the lions' den, or more likely to an early Christian midrash on Daniel 6. For my translation and comments on the Syriac original of this lovely text, see Part IV, "Other Daniel Stories."

story written in Aramaic of an unnamed Jewish wise man and the sick Nabonidus, which has a broad resemblance to the story of Daniel and the mad Nebuchadnezzar in Daniel 4.[10]

There is also clear evidence that in the time before Daniel was received into the Jewish canon of Sacred Scripture the book was interpolated in at least a few places. In ch. 3, the Prayer of Azariah and the Hymn of the Three Jews (found in the two Greek forms of the book and in the Syriac Peshiṭta and other ancient versions) are certainly additions made to the original Aramaic story. Likewise the fine Hebrew prayer in Dan 9:4b–19, with the words in 9:4a that introduce it and the words in 9:20 that link it with the following verses, is surely an insertion, as is indicated in the GENERAL and DETAILED COMMENTS on ch. 9 below. Not only is its Hebrew much better than the Hebrew of the rest of the book (this prayer at least is in original Hebrew and not in translation Hebrew from an assumed Aramaic *Vorlage*), but the sentiments expressed in the prayer hardly fit the context of the narrative, and the poorly made seams by which it is sewed on like a purple patch to the rest of the chapter betray its secondary nature in ch. 9. The original sequence in ch. 9 was as follows: (vs. 3) "Then I turned to the Lord God, seeking an answer from him by earnest prayer with fasting, sackcloth, and ashes; (vs. 21) and while I was occupied in prayer, the manlike Gabriel whom I had seen before in vision drew near me. . . ." Someone who read this passage thought that this was a good place to put a prayer into Daniel's mouth. So he took an older Hebrew prayer and inserted it here, without being bothered by the fact that this is a prayer not of an individual but of the community, and that it is not a plea for enlightenment as to the meaning of the seventy years foretold by the prophet Jeremiah, as the context would demand, but an acknowledgment of public guilt and a supplication for the restoration of Zion. Not satisfied with the mention of Daniel at prayer in 9:3, the glossator felt he had to introduce the prayer with the repetitious statement, "I prayed to Yahweh, my God, and confessed" (9:4a). The glossator also thought he had to tie the prayer in at the end to the following verses by enlarging the original phrase. "While I was occupied in prayer" (9:21a), to the longer statement, "While I was occupied with these prayers, confessing my sins and the sins of my people Israel, and presenting my petition before Yahweh, my God, on behalf of the holy mountain of my God" (9:20). The presence in the text of both the longer and the shorter forms of this conclusion betrays the hand of the glossator at work. Other instances of interpolations are 2:14–23,29–30,41b–43,49; 7:8,11a,20b–22,

[10] Cf. J. T. Milik, "'Prière de Nabonide' et autres écrits d'un cycle de Daniel," *RB* 63 (1956), 407–415; D. N. Freedman, "The Prayer of Nabonidus," *BASOR* 145 (1957), 31–32. For a translation of this story see COMMENT: DETAILED on ch. 4.

24b–25; 8:13–14,16,18–19,26a,27b; 11:1; 12:5–10,13; 12:11,12; for discussion of these verses, cf. NOTES and COMMENT: DETAILED ad loc.

To account for these glosses or interpolations as well as other problems regarding the unity of the Book of Daniel, scholars have proposed a variety of theories which have been surveyed and competently annotated by H. H. Rowley.[11] There is no need here to repeat that summary. Instead it seems preferable to state briefly the theory proposed as a working hypothesis in the present work, a theory for which the late Father Hartman and I are indebted to H. L. Ginsberg and his perceptive analysis of the book.[12]

The six midrashic folk tales in chs. 1–6, even in their written form, most likely antedate the vicious persecution of the Jews by Antiochus IV Epiphanes, and in oral form these stories may go back to the Persian period, though hardly to the seventh and sixth centuries B.C., the fictional dates given in the narratives. The many correct references to customs and terms used at the Persian court have often been noted by commentators. Yet the Aramaic of chs. 2–6 is of a later stage than that of the Elephantine papyri (end of the fifth century B.C.),[13] and the Greek names for the musical instruments in 3:5 probably do not antedate the reign of Alexander the Great (336–323 B.C.). It is simply impossible on the basis of the evidence currently available to pinpoint with any accuracy when and by whom these narratives were originally composed, and when they were edited in their present form, which shows a secondary strand at least in ch. 2, as indicated above. But the opinion that these stories were written sometime in the third century B.C. seems highly probable, as will be shown in the COMMENT on these chapters. If these narratives were put into their present state during the reign of Antiochus IV, the editor-compiler did not attempt to adapt the stories so as to make the Babylonian kings who appear in them as archetypes of the wicked Seleucid monarch who persecuted the Jews so relentlessly.

The first apocalypse of Part Two of Daniel—ch. 7 but without the later glosses in vss. 8,11a,20b–22,24b–25—was written during the reign of Antiochus IV, but probably before he began his active persecution, i.e. before 168 B.C. The chapter was composed not only in Aramaic (as were also the five midrashic narratives of chs. 2–6) but also as a sort of sequence to them, for its vision of the four beasts symbolizing the four pagan empires is surely a development of the same ideas in ch. 2. Ginsberg states that it was written as an appendix to the midrashic stories, though it also circu-

[11] "Unity of the Book of Daniel," pp. 249–260.

[12] H. L. Ginsberg, *Studies in Daniel;* "The Composition of the Book of Daniel," *VT* 4 (1954), 246–275; and "Daniel, Book of," *EncJud*, vol. 5, cols. 1277–1289.

[13] Cf. K. A. Kitchen, "The Aramaic of Daniel," in *Notes on Some Problems in the Book of Daniel*, pp. 31–79.

lated separately.[14] The second apocalypse—ch. 8 without its later additions which were pointed out above—was composed by another author not long after the desecration of the Temple in December 167 B.C., and was soon joined to the first apocalypse. The third apocalypse (originally only 10:1 – 12:4) was written by a third author shortly before the summer of 165 B.C. when he expected a third campaign of Antiochus against Egypt (cf. Dan 11:40 – 44), which as a matter of fact did not take place, as will be explained in the COMMENT: DETAILED on these verses. When this apocalypse was added to the first two apocalypses in chs. 7 and 8, its author inserted 8:18–19 into the second apocalypse.[15] The fourth and final apocalypse—ch. 9 but without the obviously interpolated Hebrew prayer of vss. 4–20—was written by a fourth author after Antiochus' brilliant victory over Artaxias of Armenia in the autumn of 165, but before the end of the religious persecution toward the close of 164 B.C. This author not only added his work as an appendix to the other three apocalypses in chs. 7, 8, and 10–12, but he revised each of these three by adding explanatory verses. In ch. 7, he added vss. 8,11a,20b–22,24b–25, all of which deal with the "small horn," symbol of Antiochus IV. In ch. 8, he inserted vss. 13–14,16,26a,27b, which deal with the angel Gabriel, speculation on the exact length of time before the end of the persecution, and Daniel's failure to understand what was going on. In chs. 10–12, he added 11:1 and 12:5–10,13, which deal with the same themes as the glosses in ch. 8. Thus the author of the core apocalypse in ch. 9 is the final redactor of the whole book. Two final glosses, 12:11 and 12:12, as well as the beautiful Hebrew prayer in 9:4–20, were added later by either one or more other persons.[16]

3. *Aramaic Original of the Whole Book*

During the following generation, the four apocalypses of the second part of Daniel were added to the six midrashic narratives of the first part to form a single book which began to be regarded as Sacred Scripture. All twelve chapters had originally been composed in Aramaic. But in order to ensure that the book would receive canonical recognition, the beginning (1:1 – 2:4a) and end (chs. 8–12) were translated into Hebrew.[17] Why

[14] Ginsberg, p. 38.

[15] Ibid., pp. 37, 62.

[16] Ibid., pp. 29, 38, 62. J. G. Gammie, "The Classification, Stages of Growth, and Changing Intentions in the Book of Daniel," *JBL* 95 (1976), 191–204, offers a different theory about the composition of the book. He suggests three primary stages in the growth of the book:

2:4b – 7:18 (less 7:7b–8,11a,12);
1:1 – 2:4a; ch. 10; 12:1–4;
7:19–28; chs. 8, 9, and 11; 12:5–13; and 7:7b–8,11a,12.

[17] Ginsberg, pp. 38–39; on pp. 41–61, Ginsberg provides detailed arguments for the theory that the Hebrew parts of the Book of Daniel were translated from an often

the assumed translator did not render into Hebrew the Aramaic section 2:4b – 6:29 can be accounted for by Ginsberg's suggestion that these five narratives could be understood as reporting the dialogue, of which they contain a great deal, in the language in which it was spoken. Support for this suggestion can be seen in the Aramaic gloss *'ărāmît,* "Aramaic," which is the first word of the section.[18] It should be noted, however, that in 1QDan[a] there is simply a space and not the gloss before the beginning of the Aramaic section. Nevertheless Ginsberg's suggestion may be correct, for the Hebrew translator of the assumed Aramaic original perhaps consciously adopted the procedure he already found in the Hebrew Book of Ezra (ca. 400 B.C.), where *'ărāmît,* the last word of 4:7, should probably be considered as the same type of gloss found in Dan 2:4b—"The document was written in Aramaic and was accompanied by a translation [Aramaic:]" (Ezra 4:7).[19] It is more difficult to account for the retention of the Aramaic original of the apocalypse in ch. 7, especially in view of the theory postulated in the present work that the three apocalypses in chs. 8, 9, and 10–12 were translated from Aramaic into Hebrew. A reasonable explanation is that ch. 7 was left untranslated so that the midrashic stories in Part One (chs. 1–6) might be linked to the apocalypses in Part Two (chs. 7–12) by a linguistic bond.[20] It is also probable that ch. 7 was retained in Aramaic because of the concentric arrangement that can be seen between the related chs. 2 and 7, 3 and 6, and 4 and 5, all of which are in Aramaic (except of course 2:1–4a). Despite certain acknowledged difficulties with, and perhaps even *ad hoc* explanations of, the theory that 1:1 – 2:4a and chs. 8–12 were originally composed in Aramaic and later translated into the present Hebrew of the MT, the late Father Hartman postulated this theory in his translation of these sections; and as he has shown in the NOTES, this assumption leads to a better understanding of the Hebrew text which in places failed to render accurately the presumed Aramaic original.

---

imperfectly understood Aramaic original. Cf. also F. Zimmermann, *Biblical Books Translated from the Aramaic.* It should also be observed that Theodotion-Daniel (abbr. Theod.) is an indirect witness to the Aramaic original of a few words that are now extant only in Hebrew. In 1:3, Theod. does not translate Hebrew *partᵉmîm* but merely transliterates the word into Greek letters, *phorthommin,* reflecting the Aramaic masculine plural absolute ending *-în* and not the Hebrew ending *-îm.* The same phenomenon occurs in 10:5 and 12:6–7—Greek *baddin* transcribes Hebrew *baddîm.* In Greek 3:54 (the assumed Aramaic or Hebrew original underlying the Greek is no longer extant), we find *cheroubin* in Theod. where LXX has *cheroubim.* Finally, we should note that the very last word of the book in the MT is *yāmîn,* "days" (12:13), again with the Aramaic masculine plural ending rather than with the usual Hebrew ending *-îm.*

[18] Ginsberg, p. 38.

[19] The *RSV* has a similar translation, but cf. its note.

[20] Ginsberg, pp. 38–39; Delcor, pp. 12–13.

4. *A Proposed Solution*

It is unfortunate that scholars seem constrained to adopt one of two essentially polarized positions with regard to the unity of the Book of Daniel: (*a*) Only one author of Maccabean times, who may have utilized and reworked older traditions and written materials, composed the entire twelve chapters of the MT as we now have them; so, for example, S. R. Driver,[21] S. B. Frost,[22] O. Eissfeldt,[23] and H. H. Rowley.[24] (*b*) Two or more authors from the third and second centuries B.C. and probably a final redactor had their hands in the production of the book; so, for instance, J. A. Montgomery,[25] H. L. Ginsberg,[26] A. Bentzen,[27] and M. Delcor.[28] Here, however, a respectable middle ground hypothesis may be proposed which would avoid the polarization of either the *a* or the *b* position, and at the same time would do justice to the evidence supportive of each position. In this hypothesis, the present book was composed, according to the rather intricate reconstruction I outlined above, by several like-minded authors, the last of whom (the writer of the core apocalypse in ch. 9) acted as final editor-compiler of the whole book—this is the general attitude of the *b* position. Nevertheless, the book in its present form has an overall literary unity centering on the person of Daniel and a central theological purpose, viz. to inculcate courage and fidelity in the persecuted and disheartened Jews of Maccabean times—this is the basic contention of the *a* position. This literary and theological unity derives from the fairly obvious activity of the final editor-compiler and also in part from the assumed translator of 1:1 – 2:4a and chs. 8–12, sections which in our opinion had originally been composed in Aramaic. It was this Hebrew translator who was responsible for publishing the work in its present form as a single book. The date would be ca. 140 B.C.

Such an approach to the question of the unity of the book can best account for the existence of other Daniel stories that were not included in the protocanonical (MT) edition. For the advocates of position *a* could scarcely maintain that the assumed single author of the twelve chapters of the MT also wrote, but decided not to utilize in the Book of Daniel, the originally Semitic (Hebrew or Aramaic) though deuterocanonical Prayer of Azariah and Hymn of the Three Jews (Greek 3:24–90) as well as the

21 Driver, *Introduction*, pp. 497–514; and *The Book of Daniel*, pp. lxv–lxvii.

22 S. B. Frost, "Daniel," *IDB* 1, pp. 764–767.

23 Eissfeldt, *The Old Testament*, p. 527.

24 H. H. Rowley, "Unity of the Book of Daniel," pp. 260–280.

25 Montgomery, pp. 88–99.

26 Ginsberg, pp. 27–40.

27 Bentzen, pp. 5–10.

28 Delcor, pp. 10–13.

stories of Susanna, Bel, and the Dragon,[29] or the non-canonical Aramaic story of Nabonidus and three Aramaic pseudo-Daniel narratives contained in fragments that were recovered from Cave 4 at Qumran.

In the admittedly complex and involved hypothesis I have offered here as a proposed solution, the fourteen-chapter edition of Daniel (now extant in Greek and Syriac and other ancient versions) reflects the complicated history of the book itself. That is to say, diversity of authorship of the underlying Semitic originals coexists with a certain literary and theological unity. Thus, in addition to the several hands postulated here for the protocanonical chs. 1–12 of the MT, there are several other authors who composed the Hebrew or Aramaic originals of the deuterocanonical prayers inserted into ch. 3 and the additional narratives of Susanna, Bel, and the Dragon. Nevertheless the Greek translators responsible for LXX-Daniel and Theodotion-Daniel collected all these Daniel materials, translated them, and finally published them as a unified work which was evidently considered to be sacred by Greek-speaking Jews both in Alexandria (where the LXX was translated) and in Palestine or Asia Minor (where Theodotion-Daniel was translated[30]) at least up to the last decade of the first century A.D. when the Pharisaic rabbis in fixing the so-called Hebrew Canon did not include the "Additions to Daniel." It should be recalled that when the Western Church established the Christian Canon of the Old Testament at the end of the fourth and beginning of the fifth century it declared as canonical the fourteen-chapter (Greek) form of the Book of Daniel.[31]

If the hypothesis detailed here appears unusually intricate and perhaps overly ingenious, if indeed not fully satisfying, based as it is in part on a series of probabilities and conjectures, the reader is reminded that other books of biblical literature also have undergone a similar complicated literary history—books like the Tetrateuch (Genesis, Exodus, Leviticus, and Numbers), the Deuteronomistic history (Deuteronomy, Joshua, Judges, I–II Samuel, and I–II Kings), Isaiah, Second Isaiah, Third Isaiah, Jeremiah (short and long form), Job (short and long form), Proverbs, the Song of Songs, and the four Gospels. To be sure, there are certain objections that have been raised against individual arguments, assumptions, and

[29] In Theodotion-Daniel, the story of Susanna comes immediately before the protocanonical book or the MT, and not after as in the Hexaplaric LXX arrangement. For more on the arrangement of the materials in the Greek forms of Daniel cf. Part V, "Place in Canon."

[30] For particulars regarding LXX-Daniel and Theodotion-Daniel see Part XII, "The Greek Forms of Daniel."

[31] Cf. A. C. Sundberg, Jr., "The Protestant Old Testament Canon: Should It Be Reexamined?" *CBQ* 28 (1966), 194–203; *idem,* "The Bible Canon and the Christian Doctrine of Inspiration," *Int* 29 (1975), 352–371.

conjectures on which this hypothesis is based. But no pretense is made here that every shred of pertinent evidence put forward has equal cogency or is fully convincing. What is suggested is that the hypothesis as a whole explains more of the hard facts as well as the elusive and not completely resolved difficulties than any other theory I have examined. The argument should be seen as cumulative. The hypothesis attempts to render an internally consistent and logically coherent account of enormously involved issues (the three languages found in the longer form of the book, the so-called "Additions," the different literary genres, the unity of outlook, the view of history, etc.), while at the same time I candidly acknowledge an important but unfortunately often forgotten principle in biblical research, viz. that more precise verdicts in matters such as the ones under review are simply not possible from the imprecise and often ambiguous evidence currently available.[32]

[32] Eissfeldt, *The Old Testament,* p. 519, gingerly and appropriately calls to mind this critical principle in his discussion of the lively and somewhat heated dispute that took place between H. H. Rowley and H. L. Ginsberg regarding the unity of the Book of Daniel.

IV. OTHER DANIEL STORIES

As indicated in Part III, "Unity of the Book and Date," there were other Daniel stories in circulation besides the ones found in the MT-form of the book. Among these the deuterocanonical narratives of Susanna, Bel, and the Dragon, which are given in an Appendix to the present work, deserve brief mention even though they are now treated in detail in vol. 44 of the Anchor Bible. Also noteworthy is a paragraph which the early fourth-century Syriac Church father Aphraat wrote about Daniel in the lions' den.

1. *Susanna*

In Roman Catholic editions of the Bible the story of Susanna appears as ch. 13 of the Book of Daniel.

Susanna, very beautiful and pious, is the wife of Joakim, a wealthy and respected Jew in Babylon. Seeing Susanna on her daily walk in the garden, two Jewish elders begin to burn with lust for her. The two old lechers finally conspire to force Susanna to commit adultery with them. On a warm day Susanna decides to take her bath in the garden, completely unaware that the two elders had hidden themselves nearby to watch her bathe. When her maids leave to fetch the soap and bath oil, the two dirty old men surprise Susanna and threaten her if she refuses to have intercourse with them. The virtuous woman courageously repulses their sinful advances and cries out for help. The elders make good their threat, accusing Susanna of adultery. At the trial the two scoundrels falsely testify that Susanna had lain with a young man hidden in the garden. The upright woman protesting her innocence is then led away to execution. A young lad named Daniel is raised up by God to intervene in the matter and rebuke the Israelites for condemning Susanna without sufficient evidence. During a brilliant cross-examination Daniel succeeds in proving that the two old rascals had perjured themselves. The whole assembly thanks God for sparing Susanna who had placed her complete trust in God, and they then inflict on the two elders the death penalty they had wickedly plotted against the holy woman.

This charming and well-constructed short story is one of the earliest examples of a modern literary genre, viz. the detective story, and has even been included in some contemporary anthologies of such stories.[33] The name "Susanna," *šôšannāh* in Hebrew, means "lily," a word that occurs as a name elsewhere in the Bible only in Luke 8:3. But with the meaning of "lily" the word occurs most often in the Song of Songs—2:1,2,16; 4:5; 6:2–3; 7:3—and in only a few other places in the Old Testament. Hence, we may conclude that the heroine of the story is given the name "Lily" to evoke the delightful freshness and surpassing beauty of the beloved woman in the Song of Songs.[34]

2. *Bel*

In Roman Catholic editions of the Book of Daniel, the story of Bel appears as 14:1–22.

During the reign of Cyrus the Persian, Daniel becomes the king's favorite. Now the Babylonians had an idol named Bel, and each day they provided for it "six barrels of fine flour, forty sheep, and six measures of wine" (14:3). Daniel when asked by the king why he did not adore Bel answers that he worships only the living God, the Creator and Lord of all. When the king protests that Bel is a living god since he eats and drinks so much each day, Daniel laughs. Enraged, the king tells the seventy priests of Bel to find out who consumes all these provisions. If Bel does, then Daniel will be put to death for blaspheming the idol. Daniel agrees to help in the investigation. Inside the temple the priests of Bel tell the king to put out on the table the customary food and wine for the idol. After they leave, the king does so. With only the king present, Daniel now orders some fine ashes to be scattered on the floor of the temple. Both men then go outside, and the door is sealed with the king's ring. During the night the priests together with their wives and children enter the temple through a secret entrance they had made under the table of offering, and they eat and drink everything the king had set out. The next morning Daniel and the king find the seals unbroken. Opening the door of the temple, the king cries out: "Great are you, O Bel; there is no trickery in you" (14:18). Again laughing, Daniel prevents the king from entering the temple and asks him to inspect the floor. The king sees the footprints of the priests, their wives, and their children. Furious at the deception, the king puts them all to death and hands Bel over to Daniel who then destroys the idol and its temple.

The story of Bel is another example of a well-written detective story with a theological point, viz. a stinging and entertaining polemic against pagan religion and idolatry. In the Old Testament it is constantly empha-

[33] Cf. R. H. Pfeiffer, *History of New Testament Times, with an Introduction to the Apocrypha,* pp. 448–449.

[34] Cf. Delcor, pp. 262–263. On pp. 260–278, Delcor gives an excellent exegesis of the story of Susanna, date of composition, original language, extant texts, etc.

sized that idols, man-made of wood or stone or metal, cannot eat or drink or perform any other functions of intelligent beings. Greek *Bēl* is *Ba'al* in Hebrew, a name that was given to Marduk, chief god of the Babylonian pantheon.[35]

3. *The Dragon*

In Roman Catholic editions the story of the Dragon is found in Dan 14:23–42.

The king orders Daniel to adore the great dragon which the Babylonians used to worship, for, they say, it is a living god. Daniel answers: "I adore the Lord, my God, for he is the living God" (14:25). He then receives the king's permission to slay the dragon—without sword or club. Daniel boils pitch, fat, and hair, making them into cakes. He feeds these to the dragon which proceeds to burst asunder. Thereupon Daniel proclaims: "This is what you worshipped" (14:27). The angry Babylonians, accusing the king of becoming a Jew, demanded that Daniel be handed over to them. Fearing for his life, the king accedes to their wishes. They then throw Daniel into the lions' den where the seven lions are accustomed to being fed two carcasses and two sheep daily. During Daniel's six days in the den, however, the lions are fed nothing, so that they may find the pious Jew more appetizing. Nothing happens to Daniel. Then an angel of God seizes a prophet named Habakkuk, who had just prepared a good lunch for the reapers in the field, and whisks him and the food from Judea to the lions' den in Babylon. Habakkuk tells Daniel to eat the lunch God has sent. Praising God, Daniel has the tasty meal. On the seventh day the king, coming in sorrow to the den, makes the joyful discovery that Daniel is unharmed. Overwhelmed, the king acknowledges the one true God of Israel, removes Daniel, and throws into the den the men who had tried to destroy the holy Jew. In an instant the famished lions devour the wicked men.

The theological intent of the story of the Dragon, which is not as well written as the stories of Susanna and Bel, is to ridicule the gross idolatry of the Babylonian pagans.[36] It is at once obvious that this story was influenced by Daniel 6 where the Israelite seer was thrown to the lions for the first time.

4. *Aphraat's Account of Daniel in the Lions' Den*

The Syriac father Aphraat (died ca. 345 A.D.) wrote a homily on prayer in the year 337. It is the fourth of his twenty-three extant homilies. In paragraph nine, Aphraat speaks of Daniel's spirit of prayer in the lions' den.

[35] Cf. ibid., pp. 279–285, for a good discussion of the text of Bel in the LXX and in Theod., date, interpretation, etc.

[36] Cf. ibid., pp. 285–292, for details about date of composition, historical background, etc.

Since, as far as I know, no English translation of this homily was ever published, it may be of interest to quote this winsome paragraph in full:

> Daniel prayed, and his prayer shut the mouths of voracious lions which were deprived of the flesh and bones of this righteous man. The lions also stretched out their paws and caught Daniel so that he did not hit the ground. They embraced him with their paws and kissed his feet. When Daniel got up in the den to pray, they followed Daniel's example and stretched out their paws to heaven. It was the offerer of prayers [i.e. Gabriel] who came down into their midst to shut the mouths of the lions. For later Daniel said to Darius: "My God sent his angel to shut the mouths of the lions so that they would not harm me" [Dan 6:23]. Although the pit was completely covered and sealed, a bright light shone inside. And so the lions rejoiced, for they saw this light because of Daniel. When Daniel wanted to lie down and go to sleep, the lions stretched themselves out so that he could sleep on their backs and not on the ground. The pit was much brighter than his upper room that had many windows [cf. Dan 6:11]. In the pit Daniel said more prayers than he did in his own room where he used to pray only three times a day [Dan 6:11]. Daniel emerged from the pit unharmed, but his calumniators were cast down into it instead. The lions' mouths were then released and they devoured these men and crushed their bones. Daniel's prayer also brought back the captives from Babylon at the completion of seventy years [Dan 9:23–24; Jer 25:11]. Every one of our righteous fathers when faced with adversity took up the weapon of prayer and through prayer were delivered from that adversity.[37]

The main story to which Aphraat refers is, of course, Daniel 6. There are seven points of contact between Aphraat and Daniel 6:

a. Daniel is thrown to the lions because of a vicious plot planned by his enemies.

b. The pit is covered and sealed.

c. In Aphraat, Daniel's response to King Darius is exactly the same as the Syriac Peshiṭta text of Dan 6:23.

d. Daniel is said to pray three times a day in his upper room.

e. Daniel is said to live in an upper room which had windows.

f. Daniel emerges from the pit unharmed.

g. Daniel's calumniators are cast into the pit and devoured by the lions.

But, interestingly enough, there are nine details in Aphraat that are not present in Daniel 6:

a. The lions stretch out their paws and catch Daniel so that he does not hit the ground.

[37] My translation. The Syriac text was published by W. Wright, *The Homilies of Aphraates, the Persian Sage*, vol. 1: *The Syriac Text* (London: Williams and Norgate, 1869), pp. 66–67 (vol. 2: *The English Translation* never appeared); and by I. Parisot, *Patrologia syriaca* (ed. R. Graffin), vol. 1, cols. 156–157.

b. The lions embrace Daniel and kiss his feet.

c. When Daniel prays in the pit, the lions follow his example and stretch out their paws to heaven.

d. The angel who is sent to shut the mouths of the lions (Dan 6:23) is explicitly identified as the "offerer of prayers," who in paragraph eight of the same homily is the angel Gabriel.

e. A bright light shines inside the pit which is completely covered and sealed.

f. The lions are happy because they can also enjoy this light thanks to Daniel's presence.

g. When Daniel wants to sleep, the lions stretch out to form a bed so that he does not have to sleep on the ground.

h. The pit is much brighter than his upper room that had many windows (Dan 6:11).

i. Daniel says more prayers in the pit than he did in his own room where he prayed only three times a day (Dan 6:11).

Moreover, in addition to these nine details not found in Daniel 6, there are five other differences between Aphraat and Daniel 6 that should be noticed:

a. In Aphraat, Daniel *gets up* to pray and prays apparently with outstretched arms, for the lions in imitation of Daniel stretch out their paws. In Dan 6:11, Daniel *kneels down on his knees* to pray; nothing is said about his arms.

b. In Aphraat, Daniel prayed in the pit. In Daniel 6, nothing is said about praying there.

c. In Aphraat, Daniel's upper room has *many* windows. In Dan 6:11, windows are mentioned, but nothing is said about their number.

d. In Aphraat, Daniel prays with no reference to Jerusalem. In Dan 6:11, "the windows of his upper room were opened toward Jerusalem" when Daniel prays.

e. In Aphraat, the lions "*ate* (the calumniators) and crushed their bones," presumably at the bottom of the pit; nothing is said about their wives and children. In Dan 6:25, the calumniators together with their wives and children "*did not reach the bottom of the pit* when the lions *overpowered* them and crushed *all* their bones."

In view of these considerations it is possible that Aphraat refers to a third story of Daniel in the lions' den. It is more probable, however, that Aphraat is providing his readers with a very early Christian midrash on Daniel 6, a midrash that is highly imaginative and colorful, somewhat in the manner of Jewish midrashim on the Old Testament.[38]

[38] R. Murray, *Symbols of Church and Kingdom: A Study in Early Syriac Tradition*, p. 288, says that he could not trace any Jewish midrashic parallels to Aphraat's treatment of Daniel in the lions' den. Jewish materials comparable in extent to Aphraat's

I could not find either. The closest echo I could discover is in *Midrash Tehillim* on Psalm 8: "According to R. Simon, God let the angels see Daniel go down into a pit of lions, ride upon their necks, and suffer no injury" (*The Midrash on Psalms,* vol. 1 [tr. W. G. Braude], Yale Judaica Series 13, p. 128). The following are other rabbinic comments on Daniel 6: A stone "rose up out of the Land of Israel, brought itself to the mouth of the den, and laid itself upon it" (*Midr. Teh.* on Psalm 24; Braude, p. 345). R. Huna interpreted the stone as meaning an angel in the likeness of a lion which sat at the mouth of the den (*Midr. Teh.* on Psalm 64; Braude, p. 528). Early the next morning when the king came to the pit and asked the seer if God had been able to deliver him from the lions, Daniel did not answer right away because he was reciting the *Shema* (ibid.). When Daniel's accusers alleged that the lions did not devour the seer because they were not hungry, the king commanded them to spend the night with the ferocious beasts. The result was that these men, 122 in number, were cast into the den together with their 122 wives and 122 children—a total of 366 persons. They were torn to bits by 1,464 lions (ibid., p. 529). L. Ginzberg, "Daniel," *The Jewish Encyclopedia,* vol. 4, p. 428, also records that the lions received Daniel as faithful dogs receive their returning master, wagging their tails and licking him, and that Daniel spent the night in prayer, to which the lions listened in silence (*Yosippon* iii 8b). Josephus *Antiquities* x 11, 6 (vol. 6, pp. 300–303, in the LCL edition) contains a variant on the motif of the lions' not touching Daniel because they were satiated. The king gives the lions a large quantity of meat so that they may eat their fill. The satraps are then thrown into the den and are quickly devoured even though the beasts are not hungry at all. Thus it became evident to the king that it was God who had saved Daniel.

V. PLACE IN CANON

In the Jewish Canon, presumably from the time it was fixed by the rabbis of Pharisaic Judaism near the end of the first century A.D., the Book of Daniel without the so-called "Additions" (Greek 3:24–90, Susanna, Bel, and the Dragon) was situated not among the Prophets (Hebrew *nᵉbîʾîm*) but in the Hagiographa or the Writings (Hebrew *kᵉtûbîm*). The reason for this arrangement is not certain. It is possible that the rabbis did not consider the Book of Daniel as a prophetic writing. More probable, however, is the theory that because the book appeared so late (second quarter of the second century B.C.) it could not be included in the prophetic corpus which the rabbis held to be closed with the death of the fifth-century B.C. prophet Malachi. Support for this view comes from Ben Sira, who wrote his book in Hebrew less than a generation before the publication of the Book of Daniel. He speaks of Isaiah (Sir 48:20), of Jeremiah, Ezekiel, and the Twelve Prophets (Sir 49:6–10) in such a way as to clearly imply that there existed in his day a fixed body of prophetic literature. In the tenth-century A.D. Aleppo Codex of the MT, Daniel is placed between Esther and Ezra in the Writings. In the Talmud and seven MSS, Daniel comes before Esther and Ezra-Nehemiah; in other MSS, the order is Esther, Daniel, Ezra-Nehemiah, as in the Aleppo Codex. In one MS, Daniel appears between Job and Ruth.[39]

In 4Q174, col. ii, line 3, however, we find this expression: . . . *ʾš]r ktwb bspr dnyʾl hnbyʾ*,[40] ". . . a]s it is written in the Book of Daniel the prophet." These words are then followed by quotations of Dan 12:10 and 11:32. This Qumran text is to be dated ca. 30–1 B.C.[41] It seems, from this evidence, that the Essenes of the Qumran community considered Daniel as

[39] N. M. Sarna, "Bible: Canon," *EncJud,* vol. 4, cols. 826, 830.

[40] Published by J. M. Allegro, *Qumrân Cave 4: I (4Q158–4Q186)*, DJD 5, p. 54 and plate xix, fragment 3. Allegro labels this document "Florilegium," but gives this note at the beginning of col. ii: "Quotations from Dan 12^{10} 11^{32} and *pešer*." Actually, as P. W. Skehan has pointed out, this particular text and 4Q177 form a running *pesher* on the opening Psalms of the *psalter;* cf. J. Strugnell, "Notes en marge du volume V des 'Discoveries in the Judaean Desert of Jordan,'" *RevQ* 7/2 (1970), 220, 237. The reference to Daniel is in a comment on Psalm 2.

[41] Strugnell, *RevQ* 7/2 (1970), 177, describes the text as being written in an early Herodian formal hand. That type of script is dated ca. 30–1 B.C. by F. M. Cross, "The Development of the Jewish Scripts," in *The Bible and the Ancient Near East* (ed. G. E. Wright), p. 138.

one of the prophets and presumably placed his book among the prophetic books rather than among the Writings as did the later rabbis. The Gospel of Matthew speaks of our seer as "the prophet Daniel" (24:15); and Josephus *Antiquities* x 11, 7 (vol. 6, pp. 304–307, in the LCL edition) refers to Daniel as a prophet and calls his writings prophecies. L. Ginzberg has shown that Palestinian sources (both tannaitic and amoriac) count Daniel among the prophets, but he then observes that "the writing of a prophet is not necessarily a prophetic book, as may be seen from the Book of Psalms, which belongs to the Hagiographa, though David was a prophet."[42]

In Codex 88 and the Syrohexaplar, the only two fully extant witnesses to the Old Greek or LXX form of the book, Daniel appears among the Major Prophets, but before Ezekiel and Isaiah. In 88, the order of books is: Jeremiah, Baruch, Lamentations, Epistle of Jeremiah, LXX-Daniel, Hippolytus on Daniel, Theodotion-Daniel, Ezekiel, and Isaiah.[43] In 88 and the Syrohexaplar, the order of material in Daniel is: chs. 1–12 (including 3:24–90), Susanna, Bel, and the Dragon. Since 88 and the Syrohexaplar contain a hexaplaric text, however, this order of material undoubtedly derived from Origen. In the Latin Vulgate St. Jerome also followed the hexaplaric order. The original arrangement in LXX-Daniel we now know thanks to the early third-century A.D. Papyrus 967 which contains a pre-hexaplaric text with the following order of material: chs. 1–12, Bel, the Dragon, and Susanna.[44]

All the other MSS of the LXX contain the text of Theodotion-Daniel (cf. Part XII, "The Greek Forms of Daniel"). In these MSS, Theodotion-Daniel is attached to the Major Prophets, but generally after Ezekiel as a fourth member.[45] The order of material in Codex Vaticanus (the oldest of the uncials and the best type of Theodotion-Daniel available[46]) is: Susanna, chs. 1–12 (including 3:24–90), Bel, and the Dragon.

In English Bibles edited by Christians, Daniel is placed among the Major Prophets after Ezekiel, as in the Greek witnesses (except, as noted above, for Codex 88 and the Syrohexaplar) and also in the Latin Vulgate. Jews follow their own ancient tradition, placing Daniel after Esther, as in the Aleppo Codex and other old MSS noted above. Protestants have either

[42] L. Ginzberg, *The Legends of the Jews,* vol. 6, p. 413.

[43] Cf. H. B. Swete, *The Old Testament in Greek,* vol. 3, 4th ed., p. xii. The Syrohexaplar has the same order of books but omits Hippolytus on Daniel and Theodotion-Daniel.

[44] A. Geissen, *Der Septuaginta-Text des Buches Daniel, Kap. 5–12, zusammen mit Susanna, Bel et Draco, nach dem Kölner Teil des Papyrus 967* (Papyrologische Texte und Abhandlungen 5), pp. 33–37, 276–291. In this papyrus, Daniel comes after Ezekiel and before Esther.

[45] In Codex Alexandrinus, Daniel appears before Ezekiel.

[46] Montgomery, p. 39.

completely omitted the translation of Greek 3:24–90 and Susanna, Bel, and the Dragon (the deuterocanonical or apocryphal sections) from their editions of the Bible, or have relegated them to an appendix, as in the *RSV* and the *NEB*. Jewish editions of the Old Testament in English do not contain the deuterocanonical sections at all. Roman Catholics, however, because they believe that these and other deuterocanonical parts of the Old Testament (Tobit, Judith, parts of Esther, Baruch, Sirach, Wisdom, and I–II Maccabees) are also sacred and inspired by God,[47] include the longer form of Daniel in their editions of the Bible, with Susanna appearing as ch. 13 and Bel and the Dragon as ch. 14, the order in which these narratives appear in Codex 88 and the Syrohexaplar as well as the Latin Vulgate, as was noted above.

In the sixth-century A.D. Codex Ambrosianus of the Syriac Peshiṭta,[48] Daniel 1–12, Bel, and the Dragon appear on folios 206b–213a, after "the Book of the Twelve Holy Prophets" (so the colophon) and before Ruth. But curiously, Susanna comes after Ruth on folios 214a–215a. The order of books is: Daniel 1–12 (including 3:24–90), Bel, the Dragon, Ruth, Susanna, Esther, Judith, and Sirach. There are four superscriptions, the first being "Next the Book of Daniel the Prophet"; the second "Bel the Idol"; the third "The Dragon"; and the fourth "The Book of Susanna." There are also four colophons, the first appearing at the end of ch. 12, "Daniel is finished" (folio 212a); the second at the end of the story of Bel, "[The story] about Bel the Idol is finished" (folio 212b); the third at the end of the story of the Dragon, "The end of the writing of the Book of Daniel" (folio 213a); and the fourth at the end of the story of Susanna, "The Book of Susanna is finished" (folio 215a).

It is noteworthy that there is a six-line space left blank between the end of ch. 12 and the beginning of the story of Bel and the story of the Dragon. This layout and the second colophon are sure indications that the manuscript tradition, or at least the Syriac tradition to which the scribe in

[47] A. C. Sundberg, Jr. (a Protestant), *Int* 29 (1975), 352–371, has argued persuasively that Protestants have made a serious error in adopting as their own the Jewish canon of the Old Testament. He writes: "The church inherited scripture from Judaism but not a canon, the Jewish canon not being defined until about A.D. 90. Thus, in view of the Christian doctrine of inspiration, it is no longer possible for Protestant Christians to argue for the validity of the Jewish canon for the Christian Old Testament. . . . It is evident that both in content and doctrine, Protestantism, in its view of the Old Testament canon, has broken away from its spiritual heritage. . . . Any Christian doctrine of canonization that takes seriously the Christian doctrine of inspiration will lead ultimately to the Christian Old Testament as defined in the Western church since that Western church is our spiritual heritage" (pp. 358–359). The Old Testament canon as defined in the Western church includes all the deuterocanonical parts listed above.

[48] Published in a sumptuous facsimile edition by A. M. Ceriani, *Translatio Syra Pescitto veteris testamenti ex codice Ambrosiano sec. fere VI photolithographice edita.*

question belonged, considered the narratives of Bel and the Dragon to be quite distinct. Moreover, as already indicated, each of the stories has its own proper superscription. The wording of the third colophon, however, clearly implies that the stories of Bel and the Dragon were thought to be parts of the canonical Book of Daniel. The reason why the Susanna narrative is detached from the rest of the Book of Daniel and placed after Ruth and before Esther is that the Syriac manuscript tradition tended to place biblical books about women in one sequence.

VI. THE HISTORICAL BACKGROUND

In Daniel 2, King Nebuchadnezzar of Babylon dreams of a colossal and terrifying statue made of gold, silver, bronze, and iron, with feet partly of iron and partly of terra cotta. Not knowing what to make of the dream, the king summons his magicians, enchanters, sorcerers, and Chaldeans to tell him first what he had dreamt and then the meaning of the dream itself. The king threatens them with death if they do not come up with the right answers. Since they have no idea what the king dreamt, they cannot even attempt to interpret his dream. But the king is adamant; in a rage he orders them to be put to death. Daniel, however, appears on the scene and announces that he not only knows the content of the dream but also its interpretation. The Israelite seer explains that the head of gold on the statue symbolizes the Babylonian kingdom which will be replaced by another kingdom symbolized by silver, hence inferior to Nebuchadnezzar's, and then by still another kingdom symbolized by bronze, which in turn will be followed by a fourth kingdom "as strong as iron." In Daniel 8, which is dated in the third year of King Belshazzar of Babylon, Daniel sees a vision of a ram with two long horns, "one longer and more recent than the other" (8:3). He also sees a he-goat come from the west. The angel explains that the two-horned ram "represents the kingdom of the Medes and Persians" and the he-goat represents the Greeks (8:20–21). Because 6:1 and 6:29 make a clear distinction between the reigns of the Medes and Persians, it is quite legitimate to conclude that the Book of Daniel itself suggests a framework of four successive world-kingdoms in this order: the Babylonians, Medes, Persians, and Greeks (or Macedonians). Hence, critical scholarship has been in general agreement that the four metals in ch. 2 symbolize these four kingdoms. There is also common agreement that in ch. 7 the four immense beasts—a lion, a bear, a leopard, and an unidentified monster—likewise represent the same four world-kingdoms. In Daniel 2 and 7, these four kingdoms are to be succeeded by the everlasting kingdom or reign of God.

Daniel's long career is said to span the first three of these kingdoms. In chs. 1–4, Nebuchadnezzar (605/4–562 B.C.) appears as monarch of Babylon. In chs. 5, 7, and 8, Belshazzar is referred to as the Babylonian king. Darius the Mede is the ruler in question in chs. 6 and 9; and Cyrus (550–530 B.C.) king of Persia is mentioned in the last apocalypse (chs. 10–12). The fourth kingdom, the Greek (or Macedonian) is far into the future from the viewpoint of Daniel the seer.

The trouble is this succession of world-empires does not correspond to the facts of history as these are known from reliable sources. Outside the Book of Daniel there is no record of a Median kingdom between the Babylonian and Persian empires. As will be pointed out in Part VIII, "Literary Genres," efforts to establish the historicity of a "Darius the Mede" (6:1 and 9:1) have proved to be notably unsuccessful and singularly unconvincing to students of history and of the Bible. The real history[49] of the four kingdoms and their respective rulers from Nebuchadnezzar to Antiochus IV Epiphanes—the first and the last monarchs alluded to in the Book of Daniel—may be outlined as follows:

BABYLON	MEDIA	PERSIA
Nebuchadnezzar 605/4–562	Cyaxares 625–585	
Amel-marduk 562–560		
Neriglissar 560–556		Cyrus 550–530
Nabonidus 556–539	Astyages 585–550	defeats Astyages 550
(Belshazzar coregent 549–539)	<————————————	Cyrus captures Babylon 539
		Cambyses 530–522
		Darius I Hystaspes 522–486
		Xerxes I 486–465
		Artaxerxes I 465–424
		Xerxes II 423
		Darius II 423–404
		Artaxerxes II 404–358
		Artaxerxes III 358–338
		Arses 338–336
		Darius III 336–331

MACEDONIA

Alexander the Great 336–323

The Ptolemies	*The Seleucids*
Ptolemy I Lagi 323–285	Seleucus I 312/11–280
	Antiochus I 280–261
Ptolemy II Philadelphus 285–246	Antiochus II 261–246
Ptolemy III Euergetes 246–221	Seleucus II 246–226
	Seleucus III 226–223
Ptolemy IV Philopator 221–203	Antiochus III the Great 223–187
Ptolemy V Epiphanes 203–181	Seleucus IV 187–175
Ptolemy VI Philometor 181–146	Antiochus IV Epiphanes 175–164

[49] For a history of these kingdoms particularly insofar as they relate to events in biblical literature, cf. J. Bright, *A History of Israel,* 2d ed., pp. 312–429.

In the Book of Daniel, the first empire is clearly the Babylonian, or more exactly, the Neo-Babylonian; the second is the Median. But as can be seen from the outline history above, the Neo-Babylonian and Median kingdoms were roughly contemporaneous, the former being in the south and the latter in the north. The Median empire, in fact, was older and was destroyed more than a decade earlier than the Neo-Babylonian. Finally, the Persian empire of history follows immediately after the Neo-Babylonian and not after the Median kingdom, as the Book of Daniel would have it. The question naturally arises, therefore: Why does the Book of Daniel present the wrong sequence of these kingdoms? This question becomes all the more pressing because the book places the hero in the Babylonian court in chs. 1–5 and 7–8, and in the Median court in chs. 6 and 9, and in the Persian era in chs. 10–12, in all of which circumstances the seer should have known the correct order of rulers and kingdoms. The obvious answer to this question, which will be discussed more fully in Part VIII, "Literary Genres," is this: the Book of Daniel was not written in the sixth century B.C., nor does it intend to convey real history. Rather the book merely employs a commonly accepted "historical framework" as the setting for its inspired narratives and apocalyptic visions. The further question then crops up: Where did the authors of Daniel get this erroneous "historical framework"? Or did they manufacture it themselves out of whole cloth?

Some years ago J. W. Swain published an important article on these questions.[50] From a careful study particularly of a fragment of Aemilius Sura in the work of the Roman historian Velleius Paterculus (i 6, 6) ca. A.D. 30, Swain has been able to prove that a theory of four successive world-empires was current in Rome at least as early as the first quarter of the second century B.C. The text in question is as follows:

> Aemilius Sura says in his book on the chronology of Rome: "The Assyrians were the first of all races to hold power, then the Medes, after them the Persians, and then the Macedonians. Then, when the two kings, Philip and Antiochus [III], of Macedonian origin, had been completely conquered, soon after the overthrow of Carthage, the supreme command passed to the Roman people. Between this time and the beginning of the reign of Ninus, king of the Assyrians, who was the first to hold power, lies an interval of 1,995 years."[51]

This text is an early witness to the notion that four world-empires—Assyria, Media, Persia, and Macedonia—would precede the fifth and more glorious empire, viz. the Roman. In discussing the problem as to where Sura got his list, Swain observes that, since the list is probably of Asiatic

[50] "The Theory of the Four Monarchies: Opposition History under the Roman Empire," *Classical Philology* 35 (1940), 1–21.

[51] Ibid., p. 2. Swain gives the Latin text in note 3.

origin, the Romans came into contact with this idea of successive empires from Asia Minor.[52] The Greeks before Alexander the Great knew of the succession of the kingdoms of Assyria, Media, and Persia. Those kingdoms are mentioned by Herodotus (i 95, 130), who wrote in the third quarter of the fifth century B.C., and more at length by Ctesias (epitomized by Diodorus Siculus ii 1–34), who wrote in the first quarter of the fourth century B.C.[53] Swain notes that when Alexander put an end to the Persian empire at the battle of Gaugamela in 331 B.C., it was easy to add to the list a fourth name, viz. the Macedonian. Thus, the tradition of four successive world-kingdoms took root, but only in the Asiatic or Seleucid part of Alexander's empire. Quite understandably, we find in Greece and Egypt no reference to these four world-kingdoms. Indeed, such a succession would have been pointless, since it gave no place to either ancient Egypt or pre-Alexandrian Greece.[54]

D. Flusser, who accepts Swain's general conclusions, has produced a careful study[55] in which he shows that political hatred of the Macedonians coupled with the desire for a bright future for the East were the roots of this four-empire theory in ancient literature. He proves quite satisfactorily that the theory of the four monarchies had its origin in Persian sources, apparently in the Avesta itself, of which the *Zands* ("midrashic" explanations of lost material from the Avesta) are extant. One of these *Zands*

> not only spoke about the division of history into four ages, symbolized by four metals [cf. Daniel 2], but also like the *Zand-ī Vohūman Yasn,* it probably spoke about kings and their reigns; it took, however, a further step: its four kings represented the four kingdoms: Assyria, Media, Persia and Macedonia. As the *Zand-ī Vohūman Yasn* speaks about the last and tenth century of the millennium, and as some of our witnesses speak about the division in ten generations, it may be assumed that this theme was more developed in the supposed *Zand,* possibly in a way similar to the ancient source of the fourth Sibyl. By the identification of the Zoroastrian schemes with the four monarchies, Macedonian rule became the period of final wickedness before heavenly vengeance and salvation, and so the new concept became political as well as eschatological and served in the Book of Daniel and probably also in the ancient source of the fourth Sibyl and elsewhere as an ideological weapon of the East against the West.[56]

Thus, the authors of Daniel cannot be regarded as inventors of the philosophy of history inherent in the succession of four world-monarchies to be followed by a fifth.

[52] Ibid., pp. 4–5.
[53] Ibid., pp. 5–7.
[54] Ibid., p. 7.
[55] "The Four Empires in the Fourth Sibyl and in the Book of Daniel," *Israel Oriental Studies* 2 (1972), 148–175.
[56] Ibid., p. 173.

Rather the Book of Daniel merely reflects the oriental tradition about these empires. The author of Daniel 2 (or his source) did, however, alter the original sequence, presumably to associate the first empire with the legendary Daniel living in Babylon. And he badly confused the traditional sequence of successive world-kingdoms by making the Neo-Babylonian the first of the series, thus eliminating the Assyrian empire altogether. But he kept as the second in the apparently chronological series the Median empire, whose sole monarch is later identified as the non-existent "Darius the Mede."[57]

Four kingdoms also appear in the Book of Tobit (14:4–15). In the Sinaiticus recension (the basis of the *NAB*) Tobit tells his son Tobiah to flee from Nineveh into Media, for "it will be safer in Media than in Assyria or Babylon" (14:4). In 14:15, the king of Media destroys Nineveh and leads the Assyrians captive into Media. Thus, the assumed order of kingdoms seems to be: Assyria, Babylon, and Media. The Persian empire is not mentioned explicitly, but 14:5 predicts the return from exile and the rebuilding of Jerusalem—events which took place during the Persian rule.

It should be kept in mind that the rather substantial altering of the traditional series of kingdoms apparently did not bother the authors of Daniel 2 and 7 or the original Jewish audience for whom these chapters were composed. These authors were not interested in ancient history as such but employed and freely adapted for their own literary purposes a commonly accepted scheme of four empires to serve their well-defined theological goal, viz. to emphasize and dramatize the nature of the fifth and final kingdom which God himself would inaugurate to replace the pagan empires that had their origin in the watery chaos opposed to God (cf. Dan 7:2–3). That final kingdom "will never be destroyed, nor will this kingdom ever be delivered up to another people" (2:44). The inheritors of this glorious kingdom will be "the holy ones of the Most High. . . . [whose] royal rule will last forever, and all dominions will serve and obey it" (7:27).

1. *The Babylonian Kingdom*

The Book of Daniel opens in the third year of King Jehoiakim of Judah, i.e. 606 B.C., at which time King Nebuchadnezzar of Babylon is said to have come and besieged Jerusalem (1:1). Together with other Israelites, Daniel and his three companions are then carried off to Babylon. Al-

[57] Swain, *Classical Philology* 35 (1940), 10. Cf. also D. Winston, "The Iranian Component in the Bible, Apocrypha, and Qumran: A Review of the Evidence," *HR* 5 (1965–66), 189–192; and M. Noth, "The Understanding of History in Old Testament Apocalyptic," in *The Laws in the Pentateuch and Other Essays* (tr. D. R. Ap-Thomas), pp. 200–204. These scholars, among many others, are in basic agreement with Swain's argument.

though this apparently historical information is wrong, as will be pointed out in Part VIII, "Literary Genres," the Babylonian kingdom is clearly the setting for the earlier part of Daniel's ministry. Reliable records indicate that Nebuchadnezzar became ruler of the Neo-Babylonian empire in 605/4 B.C. and reigned for forty-three years. He invaded Judah and captured Jerusalem in 597, deporting to Babylon Jehoiakim's son Jehoiachin, the queen mother, many high officials, and other important citizens (II Kings 24:6–17). This was the first deportation. Another large group of people went into exile in 587 after Nebuchadnezzar had given orders to raze Jerusalem to the ground. Only some of the country's poor were left behind as vine-dressers and farmers (II Kings 25:1–12; Jer 52:4–15). According to Jer 52:30, a third deportation took place in 582.

The seer of the Book of Daniel is among the exiles in Babylon. The fact that Daniel and his companions are said in chs. 1–5 to have achieved high position in the Babylonian court may perhaps suggest that life for the Israelites in exile was not all hardship and distress. Doubtless, many followed the advice given by Jeremiah the prophet in his Letter to the Exiles (Jer 29:4–28). They built houses for themselves, took wives, begot children, and prayed for and actively promoted the welfare of the city to which the Lord had exiled them, for upon its well-being depended their own (Jer 29:5–7). Even Nebuchadnezzar, who in Daniel is depicted as being sometimes capricious and even tyrannical (e.g. 2:7–13; 3:12–15), appears as an essentially noble person who piously comes to recognize the one true God after Daniel and his friends, thanks to heaven's intervention, neutralize the various plots against them. So far as we know, and from the many dedicatory inscriptions, Nebuchadnezzar was a pious polytheist, carrying on the traditions of his forebears.[58] Perhaps it is this piety that is reflected at the end of several of the Daniel stories where the pagan monarch praises the God of Israel (2:47; 3:28[*95*]–33[*100*]; 4:31–34).

After Nebuchadnezzar's death, his son Amel-marduk (562–560) became ruler of Babylon. Of this king and his successors, the ancient historian Berosus (ca. 290 B.C.) writes:

> Nabuchodonosor fell sick and died, after a reign of forty-three years, and the realm passed to his son Evilmaraduch. This prince, whose government was arbitrary and licentious, fell a victim to a plot, being assassinated by his sister's husband, Neriglisar, after a reign of two years. On his death Neriglisar, his murderer, succeeded to the throne and reigned four years. His son, Laborosoardoch, a mere boy, occupied it for nine months, when, owing to the depraved disposition which he showed, a conspiracy was formed against him, and he was beaten to death by his friends. After his murder the conspirators held a meeting, and by common consent conferred

[58] Cf. Driver, pp. xxv–xxvi.

> the kingdom upon Nabonnedus, a Babylonian and one of their gang. . . . In the seventeenth year of his reign Cyrus advanced from Persia with a large army, and, after subjugating the rest of the kingdom, marched upon Babylonia.[59]

The Book of Daniel says nothing about these historically verifiable successors of Nebuchadnezzar. Instead it says in 5:2,11,18,22 that King Belshazzar is son of Nebuchadnezzar. As will be shown in the discussion of literary genres, Belshazzar was not Nebuchadnezzar's son but was the son of the usurper Nabonidus (556–539), the last king of Babylon. Nabonidus did not enjoy a peaceful reign. His attempt to elevate the moon god Sin to replace Marduk as supreme deity in the Babylonian pantheon and his transfer of the images of many local gods to Babylon earned for him the displeasure of many, especially the Marduk priests who regarded the king as impious. Then Nabonidus moved the royal residence from Babylon to Teiman, southeast of Edom, leaving his son Belshazzar as crown prince in charge of affairs in the capital for a period of ten years. The king did not even return to Babylon for the celebration of the New Year Festival. This outrage further divided the realm. Although Nabonidus eventually returned to Babylon, the deep rifts that had occurred over the years remained. As a result, when Cyrus entered Babylon in triumph after his general Gobryas had captured the city in 539 B.C., he was greeted as a liberator by the people.[60] Thus the Neo-Babylonian empire came to an unceremonious demise at the hands of the Persians.

2. *"The Median Kingdom"*

As was indicated above, the Book of Daniel erroneously places the Median kingdom not contemporaneous with but subsequent to the Neo-Babylonian. In point of historical fact, however, it was the Persian empire that succeeded the Neo-Babylonian. The authors of Daniel most likely got from Scripture itself the idea of a Median empire that followed after the Neo-Babylonian. Texts like Isa 13:17; 21:2; and Jer 51:11 speak of the destruction of Babylon to come at the hands of the Medes. A passage from Jer 51:28–29 is particularly clear as regards the participation of the king of Media in the destruction of the city. As a matter of historical record, however, Media and the Median king had no part in the overthrow of Babylon. For, as was pointed out earlier, Cyrus put an end to the Median empire several years before he destroyed the Neo-Babylonian kingdom in 539 B.C.

The historically unidentifiable "Darius the Mede" is said to succeed to

[59] Quoted in Josephus *Against Apion* i 20 (vol. 1, pp. 221–223, in the LCL edition), from which the above citation was taken.

[60] For a history of the period, cf. Bright, *History*, pp. 353–354, 360–361.

the kingdom at the age of sixty-two (6:1), and is described as the son of Ahasuerus (Xerxes I), of the race of the Medes (9:1). Finally, 6:29 clearly implies that Cyrus the Persian succeeded Darius. Granting that "Darius the Mede" is a literary fiction in the Book of Daniel,[61] one may go on to ask if there are any historical facts at all that could have formed the basis of the information given about this monarch. Here are some bits and pieces that are pertinent. Cyrus the Persian was about sixty-two years old when he became sovereign over Babylon. In the confused history of the Book of Daniel, this fact may be echoed by the same age being assigned to "Darius the Mede" at the beginning of his reign (6:1).[62] The name of the fictitious Median ruler was almost certainly borrowed from the brilliant Persian monarch Darius I Hystaspes (522–486) who succeeded Cambyses (530–522). In Dan 9:1, "Darius the Mede" is said to be son of Ahasuerus, i.e. Xerxes I. In real history, however, Xerxes I (486–465) was son of Darius I. Two revolts, a year apart, instigated by two pretenders to the Neo-Babylonian throne, both of whom claimed to be sons of Nabonidus, forced Darius I to settle affairs in Babylon. He quelled the rebellions and executed the two leaders, each of whom had taken the name Nebuchadnezzar.[63] It is possible that these military operations caused the name "Darius" to become associated with the initial conquest of Babylon in 539 B.C., so that the name of the real conqueror, Cyrus, who founded the Persian empire but who was often called king of the Medes and the Persians, was replaced by the imaginary "Darius the Mede."[64] Finally, the division of the fictional Median kingdom into one hundred and twenty satrapies in Dan 6:2 is an obvious reminiscence of the fact that Darius Hystaspes was the monarch who divided the Persian empire into satrapies, although according to Herodotus (iii 89) the number was only twenty.[65]

3. *The Persian Kingdom*

The Persian empire which lasted from 539 to 331 B.C. was the greatest the world had seen up to that time. Compared with the Babylonian policy of deporting captive peoples and keeping them in line by harsh and often brutal measures, the Persian rule was benign and tolerant and even enlightened. In his first year as ruler over Babylon (538 B.C.) Cyrus issued the famous Edict of Restoration which allowed the Jewish exiles to

[61] H. H. Rowley, *Darius the Mede and the Four World Empires in the Book of Daniel: A Historical Study of Contemporary Theories,* 2d ed., p. 59, writes of Darius the Mede: "We are compelled to recognize that he is a fictitious creature."

[62] Ibid., pp. 55–56.

[63] Cf. Bright, *History,* pp. 369–370.

[64] E. W. Heaton, p. 65.

[65] Porteous, pp. 88–89. Cf. COMMENT: DETAILED on 6:2–4 for more on the division of the Persian empire into satrapies.

return to Palestine and to revive their religious cult and customs (Ezra 1:1–4). According to Ezra 6:3–5, the edict stipulated that the Temple was to be rebuilt according to certain specifications with costs being paid out of the royal treasury, and that the gold and silver utensils that Nebuchadnezzar plundered from the Temple and carried to Babylon were to be returned to their rightful place in Jerusalem. It may appear astounding that so great a conqueror as Cyrus would be concerned about the religious sensitivities of a politically insignificant group like the Jews. But his edict is merely one of many illustrations of a moderate and wise policy followed also by his successors in dealing with the religion of conquered peoples. To be sure, such a forward-looking policy enabled the Persian rulers to strengthen their political power by reconciling their subjects to their sovereignty.[66] Indeed, Cyrus and his successors kept firm control over the far-flung empire through a complex bureaucracy, the army, and an efficient communications network.[67]

Because of the unusually kind treatment accorded the Jews, there was good cause for Second Isaiah to speak highly of Cyrus. This great unnamed prophet even applied to the Persian king the epithets "shepherd" (Isa 44:28) and "anointed" (Isa 45:1), the latter designation having been originally reserved for kings in Israel. The prophet also calls Cyrus "the champion of justice' (Isa 41:2) and even "Yahweh's friend" (Isa 48:14). Despite permission to return, however, it seems there was no major movement of Jews from Babylon to Judah. Palestine was far away and dangerous to reach, and after all, only the oldest members of the community could remember the place. Moreover, many Jews were well off at this time in Babylon; these people offered to help the returnees financially (cf. Ezra 1:4,6) but did not wish to join them personally. It is probable that after the edict only some of the boldest and most dedicated Jews volunteered to accompany Shesh-bazzar, "the prince of Judah," who had been placed in charge of the restoration project (Ezra 1:8–11; 5:14). Little is known about this first return and what the outcome was. But it seems certain that the initially hopeful venture turned out to be a bitter disappointment. The great promises uttered by Second Isaiah particularly in his Book of Consolation (Isaiah 40–48) began to sound hollow. Morale was low and sinking, but the low point was yet to come.[68]

Cyrus was killed in 530 during a campaign against nomads beyond the Jaxartes River and was succeeded by his eldest son Cambyses (530–522). In 525, Cambyses added Egypt to the sprawling Persian empire which now embraced virtually the whole world known by Old Testament people. This latest victory must have tried the faith of sincere Jews particularly

[66] M. Noth, *The History of Israel,* 2d ed. rev. (tr. P. R. Ackroyd), p. 304.
[67] Bright, *History,* p. 362.
[68] Ibid., pp. 363–364.

when they realized that they were residents of the tiny province (or even sub-province) of Judah in a gigantic pagan empire which was supremely powerful politically, militarily, economically, and culturally. The words of Second Isaiah about Yahweh's overthrow of the Gentiles never sounded so unconvincing. The little work that had been done on the Temple came to a halt.

After the death of Cambyses by his own hand, Darius I Hystaspes (522–486), a member of the royal family by a collateral line, eventually secured the throne for himself thanks to the support of the army. It was in the sixth year of his long and successful reign that Zerubbabel and his party finally completed and joyfully dedicated the Temple in Jerusalem (Ezra 6:13–18). The other rulers of the Persian empire need not concern us here. What is noteworthy, however, is the mission of Ezra in 458 B.C. to reorganize the Jewish community about the Law.[69] J. Bright observes: "Israel's transition from a nation to a law community had been made. As such she would thenceforth exist, and this she could do without statehood and even though scattered all over the world."[70]

The last of the Persian rulers was Darius III Codomannus (336–331), who, unable to stop the advance of Alexander the Great, was seized in flight and assassinated by one of his own satraps. Thus ended the glory of the vast Persian empire.

4. *The Macedonian or Greek Kingdom*

Alexander the Great (336–323), son of Philip II of Macedon, was born in 356 and was taught by the philosopher Aristotle who was himself the star pupil of Plato. It was Alexander's dream and determined effort to create a world-wide empire which would be suffused throughout by the Greek spirit and culture and language. His ambition, however, was never fully realized, for he was felled by a fever at the height of his enormous power and died in Babylon at the age of thirty-three. Shortly after his death, his generals split up the empire among themselves (Dan 11:3–4). For the history of the Jews we need be concerned with only two of these generals, Ptolemy I Lagi and Seleucus I. It was under the dynasties they founded that the Jews were to live for more than two centuries. Ptolemy I seized Egypt, and Seleucus I gained control of Babylon, Iran, and Syria. The two monarchs fought to establish sovereignty over Palestine since it lay between the two rival kingdoms. Finally, as a result of the battle of Ipsos (301 B.C.), Ptolemy came into undisputed possession of the coveted

[69] F. M. Cross, "A Reconstruction of the Judean Restoration," *JBL* 94 (1975), 9–11, argues that the mission of Ezra took place in 458 B.C. and the mission of Nehemiah in 445. Bright, *History*, pp. 392–403, prefers the opinion that Ezra arrived on the scene ca. 428, hence after Nehemiah but while the latter was still around.

[70] Bright, *History*, p. 392.

area which was the land bridge between Egypt and Asia. Palestine remained in the hands of the Ptolemies for the next century.

Meanwhile, the Jews in Egypt were increasing in number and influence. According to the Letter of Aristeas, Ptolemy I had deported to Egypt many Jewish prisoners after one of his Palestinian campaigns (presumably in 312). The Zeno papyri and other contemporary documents prove that the Jews were present all over Egypt. Eventually, Alexandria became a center of world Jewry. There is no question that Diaspora Jews (i.e. those living outside Palestine) far outnumbered those in the Holy Land. It was not long before the Egyptian Jews spoke Greek as their first language. Since most of them (and their converts) did not understand Hebrew, their Scriptures were translated into Greek; the Torah was done first and later the other books. This version is known as the Septuagint (or Old Greek), and it had an incalculable influence because it opened up communication possibilities between Gentile and Jew, and prepared the Jewish mind for the impact of Greek thought.[71]

The rule of the Ptolemies and the Seleucids over Palestine and their many battles and intrigues are given in outline form with references in the COMMENT: DETAILED on ch. 11, and need not be repeated here. What must be emphasized, however, is that Alexander's dream and policy of Hellenization were vigorously and relentlessly pursued by both the Ptolemies and the Seleucids. In this respect, it mattered little who it was that exercised political and military control of the Jews in Palestine. These Jews must have felt the impact of Hellenism in virtually every aspect of their lives, but particularly the religious. In fact, Hellenization was promoted on all fronts—political, social, cultural, and economic as well as religious. Jews who were dazzled by the Greek ways in the first four of these areas of human endeavor could scarcely have been left untainted in religion. Indeed, the ancestral customs and rites that had been held so dear by pious Jews must now have seemed primitive, if not crude, in comparison with the new standards of the "Greek Enlightenment."[72]

Matters came to a head during the reign of Antiochus IV Epiphanes (175–164) who figures prominently as the archvillain in Daniel 7–12.[73] Antiochus was a despot of the worst sort, eccentric and unpredictable, ferocious and tyrannical. Polybius, in a well-known passage (xxvi 1, 1–14),

[71] Ibid., pp. 416–417.

[72] An excellent account of the impact of Hellenism on Palestinian Judaism can be found in M. Hengel, *Judaism and Hellenism: Studies in Their Encounter in Palestine during the Early Hellenistic Period* (tr. J. Bowden), vol. 1, pp. 58–106; notes are located in vol. 2, pp. 42–71.

[73] For a splendid history of the reign of Antiochus IV, cf. Schürer, vol. 1, pp. 137–163. See also Tcherikover, pp. 152–234; J. C. H. Lebram, "König Antiochus im Buch Daniel," *VT* 25 (1975), 737–772; and J. A. Goldstein, *I Maccabees*, AB 41, pp. 104–160.

describes in great detail[74] the erratic behavior of Antiochus—his drinking bouts with the boys, his roaming the streets and shops in disguise, his lavishness to utter strangers, his practical and often cruel jokes in the public baths, and other outrageous escapades. Diodorus and Livy have similar things to say, adding that Antiochus had a penchant for luxury, flashy spectacles, and magnificent buildings. Senseless extremes prompted Polybius[75] to speak of Antiochus as *epimanēs* (Greek for "madman") rather than as (*theos*) *epiphanēs,* "(God) manifest," a title he assumed in 169 B.C.[76] When Antiochus ascended the throne he was faced with many problems—money, a lack of cohesion in his kingdom, and pesty neighbors (the Egyptians, Romans, and Parthians) who kept pressing him. To solve the financial crisis he plundered temples and shrines, including the Jerusalem Temple. To unify his domain he insisted on total Hellenization, even in religion. To keep his neighbors in check he engaged in repeated military operations, many of which are alluded to in Daniel 11.

The tyrant's untiring Hellenization policy was aided and abetted even by some unscrupulous Jews. Onias III, the legitimate high priest at the time of Antiochus IV's accession to the throne, was ousted from office and replaced by his brother Joshua (the Hebrew behind the Greek Jason, a name he preferred to use). To secure this high office Jason offered Antiochus a huge bribe and promised to take an active part in the royal policy. He even agreed to pay an additional sum of money if he were allowed to establish a Greek gymnasium at the foot of the acropolis in Jerusalem and a youth club for it. Antiochus was, of course, delighted by Jason's generous and cooperative spirit, and readily granted the requested permissions. Here was an unexpected opportunity of swelling the coffers and at the same time enlisting the aid of an influential Jew to implement his own designs. Jason introduced Greek sports into Jerusalem with the appropriate customs attached thereto, one of which was the wearing of the wide-brimmed Greek hat. This particular custom was not just a question of prevailing style or fad (like young men today wearing long hair or sporting a mustache) but had religious significance, for this type of hat was the traditional headgear of the pagan god Hermes, patron of young men and their exercises. Even the priests abandoned their duties at the holy altar to take part in "unlawful exercises on the athletic field" (II Macc 4:7–14). "They

[74] Schürer, vol. 1, pp. 146–147, gives in full the passage from Polybius.

[75] Ibid., p. 147.

[76] Such divine epithets were not unusual among monarchs of that day. Alexander the Great, for instance, also had similar titles attached to his name, and in Egypt Ptolemy V (203–181) was also called Epiphanes. In the Jewish mind, however, such arrogance and presumption were utter blasphemy. In the year 166, Antiochus IV added to his name another title, Nicephorus, "victorious, or victory bearer"; this was an equally divine epithet. Cf. Driver, pp. 191–192, for illustrations of coins bearing the head of Antiochus and inscribed with these epithets.

despised what their ancestors had regarded as honors, while they highly prized what the Greeks esteemed as glory" (II Macc 4:15).

Contempt for the Law of Moses went so far that many Jews even had surgery done to cover over "the mark of their circumcision" (I Macc 1:15).[77] The purpose of the operation was to avoid mockery in the public baths and in the gymnasium where participants in sports were expected to be nude. "The outrageous wickedness of the ungodly pseudo-high priest Jason" (II Macc 4:13) reached such a pitch that he even sent a contribution for sacrifices in honor of the god Heracles (Hercules) on the occasion of the quinquennial games at Tyre. But his envoys were so shocked at what they were commissioned to do that they used the money for the construction of ships instead (II Macc 4:18–20).

The unholy Jason was expelled from office when Menelaus (Greek form of the Hebrew name Menahem) bought the High Priesthood from Antiochus for a sum larger than the bribe his predecessor had offered (II Macc 4:23–26). The new high priest, even more unscrupulous than Jason, plundered the Temple treasury to raise the necessary funds to pay his debts. He also treacherously arranged the murder of the legitimate high priest Onias III (II Macc 4:33–38; Dan 9:26; 11:22). Meanwhile, Jason upon hearing a false rumor that Antiochus was dead attacked Jerusalem in hopes of regaining the high priestly office. After initial success he was repulsed and eventually died a fugitive in disgrace (II Macc 5:5–10). When Antiochus learned what was happening in Jerusalem, he seized the city and massacred many faithful Jews. Then with Menelaus as guide, he plundered the Temple (II Macc 5:11–16). The year was 169 B.C.[78]

For orthodox Jews, however, the worst was yet to come. In 167 B.C. Antiochus sent Apollonius, commander of the Mysians, to crush Jerusalem once and for all. The wily general entered the city, pretending to be peaceful. Then on the Sabbath, aware the orthodox would not take up arms to defend themselves, he attacked, slaughtering a large number of men; women and children he enslaved. He put fire to the city and tore down its walls. He built the Akra as a citadel for the Syrian troops and Jewish Hellenizers (mostly wealthy priests and nobles). Now determined to abolish the practice of the Jewish religion completely in his domain, Antiochus strictly forbade the Jews to live according to their ancestral customs. He abolished Jewish sacrifices and festivals, prohibited circumcision and observance of the Sabbath and dietary laws, built pagan shrines and altars, and ordered swine and other unclean animals to be sacrificed. An-

[77] Jerome, *PL* 23, col. 239, denies that such surgery is possible; but he is wrong. In fact, the operation was common during Hadrian's persecution of the Jews. Cf. Schürer, vol. 1, p. 149, n. 28.

[78] Schürer, vol. 1, p. 151.

tiochus perpetrated the ultimate villainy in December 167 when he erected in the Jerusalem Temple a statue of the bearded Olympian Zeus, placing it on an altar built right over the great altar of holocausts. This disgraceful shrine is "the appalling abomination" of Dan 8:13; 9:27; 11:31; and 12:11; cf. COMMENT: DETAILED on 11:31. The Temple was further profaned by debauchery and drunken orgies; prostitutes were brought in so that, in the caustic words of II Macc 6:5, the Gentiles might amuse themselves. Many Jews apostatized; others risked martyrdom because of their fidelity to the Mosaic Law.[79]

Active military resistance was not long in coming. Mattathias, a leader of the Jewish community in Modein, seventeen miles northwest of Jerusalem, refused to comply with the Seleucid injunction to offer heathen sacrifices. Instead he killed the royal official sent to enforce the law. Mattathias together with his five sons and many other followers then fled to the mountains. There they heard the news of the slaughter of a thousand Jews who had refused to take up arms because of the Sabbath. Realizing that such a course could prove disastrous for the rest of the Jews, Mattathias and his group resolved to fight the Syrians even on the Sabbath if necessary. Mattathias was now able to recruit many other like-minded Jews who armed themselves and prepared to defend their lives and their way of life. They began their campaign by relentlessly cutting down apostate Jews, destroying the pagan altars wherever they found them, and enforcing circumcision on any Jewish boys whose parents had capitulated to the Syrian interdict. At the death of Mattathias, his son Judas Maccabeus, a shrewd organizer, took over the leadership of the military resistance party. He now launched full-scale guerrilla warfare against the Seleucid forces. His brilliant tactics in the field won him many victories which made it possible for him to rededicate the Jerusalem Temple in December 164 B.C., a little more than three years after it had been so monstrously defiled.[80]

The *Sitz im Leben,* or historical setting, of Daniel 7–12 is to be located during the stormy years of Antiochus' vicious persecution of the Jews, and the Book of Daniel as a whole is to be dated some time before the rededication of the Temple in December 164 B.C. and the death of the Syrian tyrant about the same time.

[79] I Macc 1:29–63; II Macc 5:23 – 6:11; Josephus *Antiquities* xii 5, 4 (vol. 7, pp. 126–133, in the LCL edition).

[80] I Macc 2:1 – 4:55; II Macc 8:1–36; 10:1–5; Josephus *Antiquities* xii 6–7 (vol. 7, pp. 136–169, in the LCL edition).

VII. THE ḤASIDIC ORIGIN OF THE BOOK

It has been customary to assign the Book of Daniel to Ḥasidic circles in second century B.C. Judaism.[81] The Ḥasidim or the Pious (Hebrew *ḥăsîdîm*) were a group of uncompromisingly devout and loyal Jews who were so called in order to be distinguished from their more worldly minded and lax coreligionists. J. A. Montgomery[82] calls chs. 7–12 of Daniel an authentic monument to primitive Ḥasidism. The Pious (Greek *hasidaioi* which is a transcription of Aramaic *ḥăsîdayyâ*) are explicitly mentioned in I Macc 2:42 and 7:13. The Book of Daniel as a whole may rightly be viewed as a pacifistic manifesto of the Ḥasidim, which was composed and widely circulated to urge and encourage the faithful Jews to remain steadfast in the practice of the religion of their fathers during the brutal persecution of Antiochus IV Epiphanes, particularly in the last years of his reign, from 167 to 164 B.C.

It should be emphasized that the religious outlook of the book is that of only one segment of Judaism in the second century B.C., viz. the Jews whose spokesmen were like the authors and editors of the books of Daniel and I–II Maccabees. Not all Jews agreed with this unbending position. Many, doubtless in good faith, attempted to accommodate their Jewish belief and practice to the spirit and necessities of the day. They did so by becoming Hellenizers. For they were convinced that in this way they could protect, preserve, and make relevant their religion in an age very different from the old days of faith. That the consequences of such updating were disastrous in the long run does not prove that these Jews acted from base motives. Unfortunately, none of their writings has survived. What we know about them derives from such partisan literature as Daniel and I–II Maccabees which portray them as scoundrels and apostates from the faith of their forefathers.

Antiochus IV became ruler of the Holy Land in 175 B.C. and a year later he converted Jerusalem into a Greek city. Striving for unity on all fronts—political, social, cultural, economic, and religious—he threatened and cajoled both Gentiles and Jews to abandon their respective customs

[81] Cf. Montgomery, p. 87; R. H. Pfeiffer, *Introduction to the Old Testament*, pp. 772–781; Tcherikover, pp. 125–126, 196–198; Delcor, pp. 15–19; and Hengel, *Judaism and Hellenism*, vol. 1, pp. 175–180.

[82] Montgomery, p. 87.

and religious practices and to adopt and live the Greek way of life and religion. The Gentiles readily conformed as did many of the Jews who "sacrificed to idols and profaned the sabbath" (I Macc 1:43). The king's orders left little room for doubt as to how a God-fearing Jew would end up:

> The king [Antiochus] sent messengers with letters to Jerusalem and to the cities of Judah, ordering them to follow customs foreign to their land: to prohibit holocausts, sacrifices, and libations in the sanctuary, to profane the sabbaths and feast days, to desecrate the sanctuary and the sacred ministers, to build pagan altars and temples and shrines, to sacrifice swine and unclean animals, to leave their sons uncircumcised, and to let themselves be defiled with every kind of impurity and abomination, so that they might forget the law and change all their observances. Whoever refused to act according to the command of the king should be put to death (I Macc 1:44–50).

To exacerbate even further the plight of the devout Jews, Antiochus erected the pagan idol of Olympian Zeus, "the abomination of desolation," on the holy altar of holocausts in the Jerusalem Temple early in December 167 (I Macc 1:54; cf. II Macc 6:2; Dan 8:13; 9:27; 11:31; 12:11). The Jews who remained faithful—men, women, and children—"preferred to die rather than to be defiled . . . or to profane the holy covenant" (I Macc 1:63). When the persecution started, however, Mattathias rallied a number of loyal Jews together and persuaded them to flee to the mountains and arid wilderness south and east of Jerusalem where they lived in caves. When the king's officers learned about the escape they ordered the troops garrisoned in the citadel of Jerusalem to pursue the Jews. When they located the caves they tried to bargain with the Jews to give up and thus be spared their lives. But the Jews refused to come to terms; yet because it was the Sabbath they offered no active resistance. The soldiers then burned brush at the mouths of the caves, and the smoke quickly did its work; about a thousand died of suffocation. Mattathias and many others managed to escape unharmed (I Macc 2:27–38; Josephus *Antiquities* xii 6, 2 [vol. 7, pp. 140–143, in the LCL edition]). Although the Jews in this episode are not called Ḥasidim, it is quite probable that is what they were. Indeed later when Mattathias and his associates made the decision to fight even on the Sabbath they were joined by the *synagōgē hasidaiōn,* "the congregation (or group) of the Ḥasidim" (I Macc 2:42). Thus there was a segment of the Ḥasidim who felt constrained to join the cause of armed resistance (cf. I Macc 14:6). It seems, however, that the Ḥasidim originally were strict pacifists and meticulous observers of the ancestral laws and traditions of Israel. It is to this primitive form of Ḥasidism that the authors of chs. 7–12 of Daniel and the editor(s) of the older chs. 1–6 belonged.

The Ḥasidic origin of the Book of Daniel is corroborated by some of the Essene literature recovered from the Qumran caves. It is generally admitted that the Essenes had their origin in the Ḥasidic movements that flourished in early second-century B.C. Judaism. The name "Essenes," Greek *Essēnoi* and *Essaioi,* may in fact be derived from the East Aramaic (and later Syriac) *ḥăsên/ḥăsayyâ,* plural forms of *ḥasyâ,* which is the semantic equivalent of Hebrew *ḥāsîd* (plural *ḥăsîdîm*).[83] Certain linguistic affinities between some of the Qumran literature on the one hand and Daniel and I Maccabees on the other are not accidental but point to a certain continuity between the Ḥasidim during the age of Antiochus IV and the later Essenes.[84] In particular, the Qumran "Apostrophe to Zion" (11QPs^{a} Zion),[85] col. xxii, line 6, says of Zion: "In the deeds of your Ḥasidim (Hebrew *ḥăsîdayik*) you shall glory." And in line 8, "Your pure (or perfect) ones (Hebrew *tammayik*) have mourned for you." Finally, in lines 13–14, "May you attain to everlasting justice (Hebrew *ṣedeq 'ôlāmîm*), and may you receive the blessings of the honorable. Accept a vision (Hebrew *ḥāzôn*) that was spoken about you, and may you seek for yourself the dreams of the prophets (Hebrew *n^{e}bî'îm*)." These words show a remarkable relationship to Dan 9:24: "Seventy weeks are decreed for your people and your holy city, until crime is stopped, sins brought to full measure, guilt expiated, everlasting justice (*ṣedeq 'ôlāmîm*) introduced, the prophetic vision (*ḥāzôn w^{e}nābî'*) confirmed, and the Holy of Holies anointed."

[83] F. M. Cross, *The Ancient Library of Qumran and Modern Biblical Studies,* p. 51, calls this derivation "thoroughly suitable." Cf. Cross, *passim,* for a history of the Essenes.

[84] Cf. Delcor, pp. 17–19.

[85] Published by J. A. Sanders, *The Psalms Scroll of Qumrân Cave 11 (11QPs^{a})*, DJD 4, pp. 43, 85–89.

VIII. LITERARY GENRES

Taken at face value, the stories and visions in the Book of Daniel seem to record historical events that occurred in the seventh and sixth centuries B.C., and sixth-century B.C. predictions of events that would take place in the distant future. Even a critical scholar as eminent as S. R. Driver wrote in his famous Introduction to the Old Testament:

> Daniel, it cannot be doubted, was a historical person, one of the Jewish exiles in Babylon, who, with his three companions, was noted for his staunch adherence to the principles of his religion, who attained a position of influence at the court of Babylon, who interpreted Nebuchadnezzar's dreams, and foretold, as a seer, something of the future fate of the Chaldaean and Persian empires.[86]

To be sure, the Book of Daniel cannot be the work of Daniel himself, for a number of literary and other considerations convinced Driver to conclude that the book was written no earlier than ca. 300 B.C. He quickly added, however, that the book as we now have it is probably a work composed during the age of Antiochus IV.[87] Thus, Driver combines the assured critical view that argues for a second-century B.C. date of composition together with the centuries-old Jewish and Christian view, held till the end of the eighteenth century, that maintained the book deals essentially with a historical person, deported from Jerusalem to Babylon in 606 B.C., the third year of Jehoiakim (Dan 1:1), and the experiences and visions he had in Babylon and environs during the reigns of Nebuchadnezzar (605/4–562), Belshazzar, Darius the Mede, and Cyrus (550–530).[88]

But the claim that the book is essentially a sixth-century B.C. production was questioned even in antiquity. The Neo-Platonist heathen philosopher Porphyry (died ca. A.D. 304) in the twelfth book of a polemical treatise entitled "Against the Christians" maintained that the book was not composed by Daniel but by some unknown author who lived during the days of Antiochus IV in the second century B.C., and that the greater part of its so-called prophecies are really nothing more than *vaticinia ex eventu*

[86] Driver, *Introduction,* pp. 510–511.

[87] Ibid., pp. 509–510.

[88] Cyrus captured Babylon in 539 B.C. and thus became ruler of the Israelites in exile there; hence, the dates in Dan 1:21 ("the first year of Cyrus") and 10:1 ("the third year of King Cyrus") are 538 and 536, respectively. But Cyrus had been ruler of Persia from 550 B.C.

(prophecies after the event).[89] Unfortunately, Porphyry's treatise is no longer fully extant, but large quotations from it have been preserved in Jerome's *Commentary on Daniel* (*PL* 25, cols. 491–584).

It is of course possible that Daniel was actually written during the period of the events and visions it narrates and was subsequently hidden away to be published only in the second quarter of the second century B.C. when the book came to be known in Jewish circles, because that time was thought to be the decisive age about which the book attempts to enlighten the Jewish community so as to encourage them to withstand the onslaughts of Antiochus Epiphanes' diabolical persecution. The book itself lends credence to this view: "As for you, Daniel, keep the words secret and seal the book until the time of the final phase. Many will apostatize, and evil will increase" (12:4). A similar exhortation is found in 8:26—"As for you, keep the vision a secret, for it refers to the distant future."

But a closer look at the dates and events described in the book reveals some rather glaring and uncomfortable inconsistencies and oddities which when taken together make an overwhelming case for understanding the book's supposed historical setting and dates as merely literary conventions and nothing more.

1. The setting of the first narrative of the book is "the third year of the reign of Jehoiakim king of Judah," i.e. 606 B.C., when "Nebuchadnezzar king of Babylon came and besieged Jerusalem" (1:1). But in 606, Nebuchadnezzar was not even on the scene in Judah, and Jehoiakim was, according to II Kings 23:34–35, a vassal of Egypt's Pharaoh Neco II (610–594 B.C.). Moreover, Nebuchadnezzar did not become king of Babylon till September 605, shortly after the death of his father Nabopolassar. But the first official year of his reign did not begin until the following New Year, April 604. Jehoiakim transferred his allegiance from Egypt and became vassal of Nebuchadnezzar in 603/2 (II Kings 24:1). Jehoiakim did not prove to be a compliant subordinate but rebelled against Babylon in 600 (II Kings 24:1). Jehoiakim died in December 598 before Nebuchadnezzar had a chance to punish him, and was succeeded by his son Jehoiachin (II Kings 24:8) who surrendered Jerusalem within three months.

> [Nebuchadnezzar] deported Jehoiachin to Babylon, and also led captive from Jerusalem to Babylon the king's mother and wives, his functionaries, and the chief men of the land (II Kings 24:15).

[89] Jerome's Prologue *In Danielem prophetam, PL* 25, col. 491: "Contra prophetam Danielem duodecimum librum scripsit Porphyrius, nolens eum ab ipso cujus inscriptus est nomine, esse compositum: sed a quodam qui temporibus Antiochi qui appellatus est Epiphanes, fuerit in Judaea, et non tam Danielem ventura dixisse, quam illum narrasse praeterita. Denique quidquid usque ad Antiochum dixerit veram historiam continere: si quid autem ultra opinatus sit, quia futura nescierit, esse mentitum."

This was the first deportation of Judah, and it took place in 597.[90] The supposed deportation of Jehoiakim to Babylon in Dan 1:2 is undoubtedly based on II Chron 36:5–7:

> Jehoiakim was twenty-five years old when he became king, and he reigned eleven years in Jerusalem. He did evil in the sight of the LORD, his God. Nebuchadnezzar, king of Babylon, came up against him and bound him with chains to take him to Babylon. Nebuchadnezzar also carried away to Babylon some of the vessels of the house of the LORD and put them in his palace in Babylon.

J. M. Myers writes:

> Neither story is clear about what actually happened to Jehoiakim. Both distinctly indicate that the temple vessels were brought to Babylon, but they do not say explicitly that Jehoiakim was taken to Babylon. He may only have been threatened by Nebuchadnezzar and frightened into submission by being put into chains.[91]

Whatever the case, Nebuchadnezzar did not besiege Jerusalem in 606 B.C., as Dan 1:1 would have us believe, for, as pointed out above, he did not become king of Babylon till the following year.

2. The date given in Dan 2:1, "the second year of the reign of Nebuchadnezzar," is the year 603 B.C., a date that is consistent with Dan 1:1 (606) only insofar as it allows for the three-year schooling of Daniel and his three companions. Trouble is, however, that in the story of ch. 1, Nebuchadnezzar put Daniel and his companions into a three-year training period for service in the royal palace (1:3–5), at the end of which time (i.e. 603) the monarch himself conducted the final oral examination which Daniel, Hananiah, Mishael, and Azariah passed with honors at the top of their class. They then entered the king's service (1:18–19). But in 2:1, as indicated already, the date given is the *second year* of Nebuchadnezzar, i.e. 603, the year Daniel completed his *three-year* study program according to 1:18–19. Thus the year 603 turns out to be both the third year (1:5,18–19) and the second year (2:1) of Nebuchadnezzar.

3. Some scholars[92] have seen a discrepancy, if not a contradiction, between 1:21 ("Daniel was there until the first year of King Cyrus") and 10:1 ("In the third year of King Cyrus of Persia an oracle was revealed to Daniel"). But there is no inconsistency in these dates, if, as explained in the present commentary ad loc., Daniel is said in 1:21 to have remained in the Babylonian court until its capture by Cyrus in 539 B.C. Nothing is said or directly implied about the end of Daniel's life or career. In fact, the

[90] Cf. Bright, *A History of Israel*, pp. 324–327.

[91] J. M. Myers, *II Chronicles*, AB 13 (Garden City, N.Y.: Doubleday, 1965), p. 218.

[92] For example, Montgomery, pp. 137–138; Frost, "Daniel," *IDB* 1, p. 766.

statement in 6:29 that "Daniel fared well in the reign of Darius and in the reign of Cyrus the Persian," clearly affirms that Daniel was alive and prospering also during the days of Cyrus, and presumably beyond the monarch's first year mentioned in 1:21. Thus the date in 1:21 may merely imply that Daniel was released from exile in the royal court of Babylon when Cyrus during the first year of his hegemony over the Jews issued his edict freeing the exiles (Ezra 1:1–4). Then in Cyrus' third year Daniel experiences his final apocalyptic vision (10:1). Nevertheless, it is truly surprising in chs. 1 and 10 and elsewhere that the book shows so little interest in this long awaited return from exile which receives only passing mention in 9:25. In fact, if the alleged seventh- and sixth-century B.C. author of Daniel had lived from the time of Nebuchadnezzar to Cyrus, he is remarkable for his amazing lack of concern for the momentous events which were of enormous importance to every faithful Judahite. The Book of Daniel contrasts sharply with the basically eyewitness descriptions of contemporary affairs given by Jeremiah and Ezekiel. Then if we consider that the Book of Daniel does provide detailed information about the events and characters of the second century B.C., the conclusion seems inescapable that what we are dealing with is essentially a second-century B.C. literary production.[93]

4. The duration of Antiochus IV's desecration of the Jerusalem Temple and of the suspension of the Jewish daily sacrifice is given variously in Daniel. In 7:25 and 12:7, the time is three and a half years, the same as in 9:27 ("half a week," i.e. of years).[94] But in 8:14, the duration given is "two thousand and three hundred evenings and mornings," i.e. 1,150 days which equal three solar years plus fifty-five days, or three lunar years plus seventy days (a weak approximation of the three and a half years of the other chapters). Finally, in 12:11, the period will last 1,290 days; in 12:12, 1,335 days. Many commentators, however, rightly hold that 12:11 and 12:12 are later interpolations by an unknown hand. Nevertheless, the point can be made fairly that an alleged sixth-century B.C. book by a single inspired author who wrote inerrant predictions of genuinely historical events would hardly contain such conflicting data regarding a rather crucial event in the religious history of the Jews.

5. According to 1:19–21, Daniel became a high official in the Babylonian court under Nebuchadnezzar and remained in that office till the first year of Cyrus, a period of slightly less than seventy years. If Daniel were a real person whose actual exploits are detailed without error in the book bearing his name, then it would appear astounding and incredible that he

[93] This argument was suggested by A. Jeffery, pp. 371–372.

[94] According to the hypothesis argued for in the present commentary, the author of ch. 9 is responsible for interpolating the time in 7:25 and 12:7; hence, the duration is identical in all three places.

did not know, or at least present, the true order of the Babylonian monarchs and their successors. In 5:2,11,18,22, it is said that King Belshazzar is the son of Nebuchadnezzar (605/4–562 B.C.). This information is wrong on two counts: (1) Belshazzar was not the son of Nebuchadnezzar but of Nabonidus (556–539) who himself was not a descendant of Nebuchadnezzar but a usurper of the Babylonian throne;[95] (2) for a period of ten years of Nabonidus' reign Belshazzar was appointed crown prince or coregent with his father, but he never became king in the strict sense because he could not preside at the celebration of the New Year Festival, which was the climax of the Babylonian cultic year.

6. In 6:1, the concluding verse of the narrative in ch. 5, it is stated that after King Belshazzar was slain, "Darius the Mede succeeded to the kingdom." The same Darius appears in the story of ch. 6 and in the apocalypse of ch. 9 where he is called "son of Ahasuerus [Xerxes], of the race of the Medes" (9:1). But there are no historical records at all that speak of a Darius the Mede or of a Median empire or kingdom between the reigns of the last Babylonian King Nabonidus and the Persian King Cyrus. Moreover, Xerxes is given as the father of Darius (9:1) who is then succeeded by Cyrus (6:29; 10:1), whereas the real historical order is Cyrus (550–530), Cambyses (530–522), Darius I the Great (522–486), and Xerxes (486–465). Well-intentioned and often scholarly and elaborate efforts on the part of fundamentalists and others[96] who hold to the absolutely historical character of the Book of Daniel have been singularly unsuccessful in establishing satisfactory evidence for the existence of a "Darius the Mede." For more on this character see Part VI, "The Historical Background."

7. The fourth story (3:31 – 4:34) tells of Nebuchadnezzar's madness which lasted seven years during which time he was deprived of his throne. If this episode did in fact happen, it seems most unusual that the historical

[95] Nebuchadnezzar's successors were: his son Amel-marduk (562–560 B.C.), the Evil-merodach who freed Jehoiachin from prison in II Kings 25:27–30; Nergal-sharuṣur or Neriglissar (560–556), brother-in-law of Amel-marduk; a minor son of Neriglissar, named Labashi-Marduk, who was quickly removed by Nabonidus who usurped the throne. For a brief history of the period, cf. Bright, *History of Israel,* pp. 353–354.

[96] A typical example is C. Boutflower, *In and around the Book of Daniel,* pp. 142–167. For some comments on this book shortly after its initial appearance (1923), cf. H. H. Rowley, "The Belshazzar of Daniel and of History," *Expositor* 9/2 (Sept./Oct. 1924), 269–272. More recently (1973), C. Schedl, *History of the Old Testament,* vol. 5, pp. 51–86, has proposed a series of highly improbable and ultimately unconvincing arguments regarding many of the complex issues in Daniel, including the question of "Darius the Mede." Schedl alleges that this monarch is none other than Darius the Great who had marched from Babylon to Kurundi in Media to quell the revolt of Fravartis. Darius was so successful in battle that, Schedl concludes, his contemporaries gave him the honorific epithet "the Mede."

records say nothing at all about it or of a seven-year interruption of the monarch's reign.[97] Indeed enough is known of Nebuchadnezzar's career to preclude such an interregnum and sojourn among the animals of the field. Moreover, the Nebuchadnezzar of this narrative speaks and acts like a pious Jew who is quite familiar with Old Testament rubrics and forms of prayer:

How great are his miracles,	They speak of the splendor of your glorious majesty
how mighty his wonders!	and tell of your wondrous works.
His reign is an everlasting reign:	Your kingdom is a kingdom for all ages,
his dominion endures for ages and ages (Dan 3:33).	and your dominion endures through all generations (Ps 145:5,13).
There is no one who can stay his hand	Woe to him who contends with his Maker;
or say to him, "What have you done?" (Dan 4:32).	a potsherd among potsherds of the earth!
	Dare the clay say to its modeler, "What are you doing?" (Isa 45:9).
All his deeds are right (lit. truth)	The works of his hands are faithful (lit. truth) and just (Ps 111:7).
and his ways are just;	
Those who walk in pride	The man of haughty eyes and puffed-up heart
he is able to humble (Dan 4:34).	I will not endure (Ps 101:5).

8. After discovering that the lions in the den did not devour Daniel, Darius the Mede addresses himself "to all the people of every nation, tribe, and tongue, wherever they lived on earth," and decrees "that throughout my realm the God of Daniel shall be reverenced and feared" (6:27). Here is the account of another stupendous conversion of a heathen monarch who acts in a way similar to Nebuchadnezzar in ch. 4. The case for an alleged historical "Darius the Mede" is further weakened by what is said of him in ch. 6. Like the Babylonian king in ch. 4, Darius also utters a beautiful prayer that reflects purely Jewish thought and devotion:

97 That it is reasonable to argue on the basis of solid evidence that in the original form of the tradition sedimented in the present narrative the mad king was not Nebuchadnezzar but Nabonidus (cf. COMMENT: DETAILED on ch. 4) is beside the point being made here, viz. it is unreasonable to accept this story as a historical event occurring in the life of the real Nebuchadnezzar.

He is the living God, enduring forever;
his kingdom is never destroyed,
and his dominion is without end.
He is a savior and deliverer,
performing wondrous miracles in heaven and on earth,
such as rescuing Daniel from the power of the lions (6:27–28).

But the humility and piety, the monotheism and praiseworthy sentiments attributed to Nebuchadnezzar, a Babylonian polytheist, and to Darius the Mede, whose very existence cannot be proved, are the stuff not of history[98] but of religious folklore and fiction. It is the same type of material we find in the Book of Jonah where as a result of the preaching of the Israelite prophet the eighth-century B.C. king of Nineveh, who significantly is unnamed, and all his "more than a hundred and twenty thousand" subjects (Jonah 3:11) come to believe in the God of Israel, and repent of their sins in sackcloth, call loudly to God in order to be forgiven, and then are indeed spared by God.

9. Ben Sira, who wrote his book in Hebrew ca. 180 B.C., has a long section (44:1 – 50:21) devoted to the "Praise of the Fathers." Among the worthies of Israel he lists the major prophets Isaiah (48:20), Jeremiah (49:6), and Ezekiel (49:7) by name and the twelve minor prophets as a group (49:10). Daniel receives no mention at all—a noteworthy omission. But I Maccabees, which was composed in Hebrew (now lost) ca. 100 B.C. and translated into the extant Greek shortly thereafter, does refer to Daniel in a brief passage similar to Ben Sira's "Praise of the Fathers":

Hananiah, Azariah and Mishael, for their faith,
were saved from the fire.
Daniel, for his innocence,
was delivered from the jaws of lions (I Macc 2:59–60).

The second of these verses refers to Daniel 6. The other verse is an unambiguous reference to Dan 3:*88* (now extant in the deuterocanonical Greek section of the chapter):

Hananiah, Azariah, Mishael, bless the Lord. . . .
He has freed us from the raging flame
and delivered us from the fire.

It is to be observed that the same order of names appears in I Macc 2:59 and Dan 3:*88*. But in the MT-part of the narrative in ch. 3, the three men are called only by their Babylonian names, Shadrach, Meshach, and

[98] The well-meaning attempt of Boutflower, *In and around the Book of Daniel*, pp. 92–104, 160–165, to establish the historical accuracy of these narratives concerning the monotheism and piety of Nebuchadnezzar and Darius the Mede will convince few, if any, readers today.

Abednego in that order. In Dan 1:6–7, the order of the names is this: Hananiah, Mishael, and Azariah, which correspond to Shadrach, Meshach, and Abednego, respectively. Ben Sira's omission of any reference to Daniel and the clear mention of two episodes from Daniel in I Maccabees suggest a second-century B.C. dating for the book.

These and other more or less obvious cases which are at variance with available ancient Near Eastern and biblical data regarding the situations described throughout the book provide decisive evidence that the inspired authors of Daniel did not live or write in the sixth century B.C. nor did they write historical accounts but rather edifying or midrashic stories and apocalyptic visions. The principal thrust of the book as a whole was threefold: (1) to remind the Jews that their monotheistic religion is a glorious heritage infinitely superior to paganism with its gross idol worship; (2) to encourage the Jews to remain loyal to that heritage like the outstanding protagonists of the book who were willing to risk their social, economic, and political status and even their lives by steadfastly refusing to compromise their faith; and (3) to show dramatically and imaginatively that the God of Israel comes to the rescue and delivers those who believe in him despite even the severest reverses, including death by martyrdom. The inerrancy of these narratives and apocalypses is not the truth of history but rather the infallible truth of stories similar to the parables of Jesus, which are fictional accounts regarding the Prodigal Son, the Good Samaritan, etc., but which teach a profound and absolutely true theological point. As in the parables of Jesus, the verification of apparently historical data was of no significant import for the inspired authors of Daniel. They utilized some of the erroneous traditions of the four kingdoms, which they had inherited, as merely the commonly accepted "historical" framework for the all-important religious message. It could also be suggested that the book was composed in this way so as to demonstrate that the sixth-century B.C. prophet Daniel and his companions faced and surmounted religious crises similar to the ones inflicted by Antiochus IV on the Jews of the second century B.C. The apparently historical framework could also have been employed in order to avoid censorship on the part of Antiochus' agents. If the book were to be charged with defamation of the Seleucid tyrant, one could always allege that it dealt with the long distant past and had no particular statement to make regarding the political situation in second-century B.C. Palestine.

Thus on the one hand, the so-called liberal has no right to sniff at the factual inaccuracies of the Book of Daniel, for it is unfair, not to say impious, to demand of ancient writers an awareness of the canons of nineteenth- and twentieth-century critical history in a book whose intent is essentially religious and not historical. But on the other hand, the so-called conservative also does the Word of God a huge disservice by insisting that the book does in fact deal with real persons and events of the seventh and sixth centuries B.C., as if the authors of Daniel intended to write history.

The position taken in the present commentary with respect to the literary genres in Daniel is a commonly shared conclusion of most contemporary scholars—Jewish, Roman Catholic, and Protestant. It is a reasonable position based on sound methodological principles that can be accepted by an intelligent reader of whatever religious persuasion. At the same time it should be emphasized that in no way at all does the argument presented above impugn or even call into question the sacredness, authority, and inerrancy of the Book of Daniel which are accepted here without question as truths of Christian faith. The Book of Daniel, then, contains two basic literary genres: midrash or edifying story (chs. 1–6 as well as the deuterocanonical Susanna, Bel, and the Dragon in the Greek forms of the book); and apocalypse (2:13–45 and chs. 7–12).

IX. THE ROMANCE OF THE SUCCESSFUL COURTIER

The specific type of midrash or edifying stories in the anonymous Part One of the book, chs. 1–6 (and in the three deuterocanonical tales of Susanna, Bel, and the Dragon in the two Greek forms of the book), is a Jewish adaptation of a literary genre found elsewhere in the Old Testament and in other ancient Near Eastern literature, viz. the religious romance or popular tale of the successful or wise courtier.[99] Examples of such tales are: several narratives of the Joseph cycle in Genesis; the account in the Book of Esther of Mordecai's victory over Haman; the deuterocanonical books of Tobit and Judith; the story of the three bodyguards of Darius in apocryphal I Esdras (also known as III Esdras) 3:1 – 4:63;[100] and the Story of Ahiqar.[101] Tobit, Judith, the final edition of Esther, and I Esdras are all to be dated in the second century B.C. and are thus roughly contemporaneous with the publication of the tales in Daniel 1–6. The Joseph stories in Genesis are of course much older, as is also the original version of the Story of Ahiqar.

1. *Ahiqar*

Fragments of the Story of Ahiqar were found among the Aramaic papyri from Elephantine, an island on the Nile near modern Aswan, where there was a Jewish colony in the fifth century B.C. This version of the story dates to ca. 500 B.C.[102] The Story of Ahiqar, however, is extant, with many variations, also in Syriac, Arabic, Armenian, Ethiopic, Old Turkish, Greek, and Slavonic, and is probably derived from an Assyrian original. The name in Assyrian means "The brother is precious." Ahiqar, a wise and trusted official in the court of King Sennacherib of Assyria, had no

[99] Cf. R. B. Y. Scott, "I Daniel, the Original Apocalypse," *AJSL* 47 (1931), 290–291; W. L. Humphreys, "The Motif of the Wise Courtier in the Old Testament"; J. J. Collins, "The Court-Tales in Daniel and the Development of Apocalyptic," *JBL* 94 (1975), 218–234.

[100] I Esdras is not considered canonical by any religious group, Roman Catholic Protestant, or Jewish.

[101] G. W. E. Nickelsburg, *Resurrection, Immortality, and Eternal Life in Intertestamental Judaism*, HTS 26, pp. 48–58, provides a slightly different analysis of Joseph and his brothers, the Story of Ahiqar, the Book of Esther, Daniel 3 and 6, and the story of Susanna. He views these narratives as examples of the story of the persecution and exaltation of the righteous man or woman.

[102] For a translation of the fragments, cf. *ANET*, pp. 427–430.

son and so adopted as heir his nephew Nadan or Nadin (Nadab in the Book of Tobit). An ungrateful wretch, Nadan falsely accuses his benefactor of treason. Ahiqar manages to flee from the royal wrath and goes into hiding. Eventually Nadan's shameless perfidy is discovered and punished, and Ahiqar is restored to a high place in the realm. This story must have been very popular among the Jews, for the author of the Book of Tobit not only Judaized Ahiqar but made him the pious, alms-giving nephew of Tobit himself (cf. Tobit 1:21–22; 2:10; 11:18; 14:10).

2. *Joseph*

The episodes in the Joseph narratives are so well-known that a brief summary here will do: Joseph, sold by his jealous brothers, becomes a member of the household of Potiphar, a courtier of Pharaoh (Gen 37:2–36). Joseph, now in charge of Potiphar's household, virtuously resists the seductive advances of Potiphar's wife who then seeks her revenge for being spurned by falsely accusing Joseph of attempted rape (39:1–23). Later in prison, Joseph correctly interprets the dreams of two fellow prisoners, the cupbearer and baker of Pharaoh (40:1–23). Joseph, summoned from the dungeon, interprets Pharaoh's dreams of the seven fat and seven lean years, and as a reward for his services and wise counsel is appointed vizier of Egypt (41:1–57).

There are unmistakable resemblances and relationships between details of these stories and Daniel 1–6. Joseph is described as "strikingly handsome in countenance and body" (Gen 39:6). Daniel and his companions are also "flawless and handsome young men, intelligent and clever, and quick to learn and understand" (1:4). In Gen 41:39, Pharaoh says to Joseph, "Since God has made all this known to you, no one can be as wise and discerning as you are." In Dan 1:20, we are told, "In any matter requiring wisdom and understanding on which the king consulted [Daniel and his companions] he found them ten times better than all the magicians and enchanters in his whole realm." Daniel stoutly refuses "to defile himself with the king's menu or with his wine" (1:8), just as Joseph manfully refuses to defile himself with his master's spouse (Gen 39:9). Joseph receives from God the ability to interpret dreams (Gen 40:8; 41:16). God also reveals to Daniel the content and interpretation of Nebuchadnezzar's dreams (2:18–19; 4:6,15) and the meaning of the handwriting on the wall during Belshazzar's banquet (5:11,14). Because of his God-given talents Joseph is installed as vizier over "the whole land of Egypt" (Gen 41:43). Similarly Nebuchadnezzar makes Daniel "a magnate" and "ruler over the whole province of Babylon and chief prefect over all the wise men of Babylon" (2:48); and Belshazzar proclaims Daniel "a triumvir in the government of the kingdom" (5:29).

3. *Esther*

The Book of Esther contains the story of Mordecai's victory over his pagan rival Haman the Agagite (3:1–8:2).[103] King Ahasuerus (Xerxes I) appoints Haman to high rank, "seating him above all his fellow officials" (3:1). All the king's servants are ordered to "kneel and bow down before Haman" (3:2). Mordecai, being a Jew, refuses; Haman becomes enraged (3:4–5). Because the Jews "do not obey the laws of the king" (3:8), Haman persuades Ahasuerus to kill all the Jews (3:9). To prevent this disaster, Mordecai enlists the aid of Queen Esther, his cousin and foster daughter (2:7). She succeeds in getting Haman hanged on the very gallows he had erected for the execution of Mordecai (7:9–10). Finally the king removes his signet ring from Haman and gives it into the keeping of Mordecai whom Esther then puts in charge of the house of Haman (8:2).

A similar motif can be seen in Daniel 3 and 6. Shadrach, Meshach, and Abednego, who are royal officials in Babylon thanks to their outstanding wisdom, refuse to serve the pagan gods or worship the golden image Nebuchadnezzar had set up (3:12). In a rage, the king orders the three to be cast into a furnace "to be heated seven times as much as it usually was" (3:19). Because the furnace was so overheated, the flames kill "the men who carried Shadrach, Meshach, and Abednego up into it" (3:22), but the three Jews remain unharmed. When the monarch discovers what has happened he releases the three, praises their God, and gives them a promotion. In Daniel 6, the chief ministers and satraps of Darius the Mede become jealous of Daniel and hatch a plot to do him in. They trick the king into issuing a decree that "for thirty days no one is to address a petition to any god or man except to you, O king; otherwise, he shall be cast into the lions' den" (6:8). Daniel, however, continues his practice of prayer three times a day (6:11). The plotters catch Daniel at prayer and report him to the king. Though grieved, the king is constrained to cast Daniel to the lions. The lions, however, do not hurt Daniel in the least. Pleased at this unexpected turn of events, Darius removes Daniel from the

[103] W. L. Humphreys, "A Life-Style for Diaspora: A Study of the Tales of Esther and Daniel," *JBL* 92 (1973), 211–223, argues that "One could, as a Jew, overcome adversity and find a life both rewarding and creative within the pagan setting and as a part of this foreign world; one need not cut himself [*sic*] off from that world or seek or hope for its destruction. . . . Judaism of the last centuries before the common era was a remarkably rich and varied composite of often competing and contrasting traditions and styles of life and thought. The tales of Esther and Daniel, freed from their present literary contexts, present one aspect of that rich tapestry, one which events in time seemed in large part to submerge, and which has therefore received little attention" (p. 223). Humphreys makes a good case for his thesis; but here our concern with the narratives is only as they appear in their present contexts in the Book of Daniel.

den and replaces him there with his accusers and their wives and children who are summarily dispatched by the voracious beasts (6:24–25). "Thereafter Daniel fared well in the reign of Darius and in the reign of Cyrus the Persian" (6:29). Besides being tales of the successful courtier, these two chapters also have a secondary motif which is found in a type of literature known as the martyr or witness story. The intent of this literary genre in Jewish writings is to teach that martyrdom is preferable to disloyalty to the faith and practices of the Fathers.

A splendid example of the martyr story and of its purpose is the Martyrdom of Eleazar in II Macc 6:18–31:

> Eleazar, one of the foremost scribes, a man of advanced age and noble appearance, was being forced to open his mouth to eat pork. But preferring a glorious death to a life of defilement, he spat out the meat, and went forward of his own accord to the instrument of torture, as men ought to do who have the courage to reject food which it is unlawful to taste even for love of life (II Macc 6:18–20).

Several friends try to persuade Eleazar to pretend to eat some of the forbidden meat so as to escape the death penalty. Eleazar courageously refuses, explaining,

> At our age it would be unbecoming to make such a pretense; many young men would think the ninety-year-old Eleazar had gone over to an alien religion. Should I thus dissimulate for the sake of a brief moment of life, they would be led astray by me, while I would bring shame and dishonor on my old age. Even if, for the time being, I avoid the punishment of men, I shall never, whether alive or dead, escape the hands of the Almighty. Therefore, by manfully giving up my life now, I will prove myself worthy of my old age, and I will leave to the young a noble example of how to die willingly and generously for the revered and holy laws (II Macc 6:24–28).

Another outstanding illustration is the well-known story of the Martyrdom of a Mother and Her Seven Sons in II Macc 7:1–41. After seeing six of her sons put to death in her own presence, she encourages the seventh son to remain steadfast and to refuse the blandishments of Antiochus IV who offers the lad wealth and status: "Do not be afraid of this executioner, but be worthy of your brothers and accept death, so that in the time of mercy I may receive you again with them" (II Macc 7:29). The youth makes a fine speech, praising the mysterious providence of God who will reward fidelity to the Law of Moses and punish the arrogance of the insolent. Then he is martyred, "undefiled, putting all his trust in the Lord. The mother was last to die, after her sons" (II Macc 7:40–41).

Although Daniel 3 and 6 have the secondary motif of the martyr story, there is a significant difference from the normal type; that is to say, the worthies in question are not in fact martyred but are rescued from death by a spectacular intervention of the God whom they serve so courageously.

4. *Tobit*

The Book of Tobit is a delightful romance or religious novel that can also be classified as a tale of the successful courtier. To be sure, only in ch. 1 is Tobit graced by the Most High with "favor and status with Shalmaneser, so that I became purchasing agent for all his needs" (1:13). Shalmaneser dies in 1:15, and under his successor Sennacherib, pious Tobit suffers great reverses and must go into hiding because of his religious practice of burying the Israelites slain by the king (1:18–21). Sennacherib is assassinated by two of his sons. His son Esarhaddon succeeds him as king and appoints Tobit's nephew Ahiqar "chief cupbearer, keeper of the seal, administrator, and treasurer" (1:22). Through Ahiqar's influence, Tobit can return to his home in Nineveh. But adversity strikes again. Tobit goes to sleep next to the wall of his courtyard, unaware that birds were perched above him, "till their warm droppings settled in [his] eyes, causing cataracts" (2:10). There follow the sub-plot of Sarah and her loss of seven husbands the night of each successive wedding; the journey of Tobit's son Tobiah and successful (and lasting) marriage to Sarah; and finally the cure of Tobit's blindness through the peculiar medicine prescribed by Raphael, an angel in disguise. Before dying at a ripe old age, Tobit predicts the destruction of Assyria and Nineveh and so urges his son Tobiah to flee with his family to Media. Before his death in Media, Tobiah hears of the destruction of Nineveh exactly as his father had foretold.

Interpreting Nebuchadnezzar's strange dream of the composite statue, Daniel predicts the destruction of the successive empires of Babylon, Media, Persia, and Greece (ch. 2). In place of these regimes, God "will set up a kingdom that will never be destroyed" (2:44). Thus the romance of the successful courtier often contained apparent predictions of future events. In actual fact, of course, these forecasts were merely examples of the literary convention known as *prophetia ex eventu,* which will be discussed below in Part X, "Apocalyptic."

5. *Judith*

The Book of Judith is a kind of proto-feminist romance in which the central figure is not a successful male courtier like Joseph, "strikingly handsome in countenance and body" (Gen 39:6), or Daniel, "flawless and handsome" (Dan 1:4), but a wise woman (Judith 8:29), "beautifully formed and lovely to behold" (8:7). Judith (the name means "a woman of Judah") uses her ravishing beauty (10:14,19,23) in the cause of the

Lord. She has her hair done, puts on the festive attire she wore while her husband Manasseh was still living, chooses sandals for her feet, and wears "anklets, bracelets, rings, earrings, and all her other jewelry. Thus she made herself very beautiful, to captivate the eyes of all the men who should see her" (10:3–4). Her ploy is successful; she gains access to the tent and heart of Holofernes, general-in-chief of King Nebuchadnezzar of Assyria (2:4). Holofernes, "in rapture over her" and "burning with the desire to possess her, for he had been biding his time to seduce her from the day he saw her" (12:16), invites the gorgeous and resplendent woman to a banquet. Charmed by Judith, Holofernes consumes "a great quantity of wine, more than he had ever drunk on one single day in his life" (12:20). He stretches out on his bed in a drunken stupor. Judith, after a quick prayer to the Lord, takes Holofernes' sword and hacks off his head. She puts the severed head into her food pouch, and with her maid she goes off to pray as usual, thus making good her escape from thc Assyrian camp (13:1–10). The Israelites attack the next day. When the Assyrians go in to wake up Holofernes, they discover his headless corpse. They are forced to admit that "A single Hebrew woman has brought disgrace on the house of King Nebuchadnezzar" (14:18). Dismay and confusion then grip the Assyrians as they flee from the rampaging Israelites (14:11 – 15:7).

6. *The Three Bodyguards of Darius*

The story of the three young bodyguards of King Darius in apocryphal I Esdras 3:1 – 4:63, is another good illustration of the romance of the successful courtier. The three youths had a contest to determine who could come up with the wisest answer to the question, "What is the strongest of all?" The first wrote, "Wine is the strongest"; the second, "The king is strongest"; the third, "Women are strongest, but truth conquers all" (3:10–12 *NEB*). Each contestant then makes a speech to defend his answer. Only the third youth is named, Zerubbabel the Jew. His speech begins: "Sirs, it is true the king is great, men are many, and wine is strong, but who rules over them? Who is the sovereign power? Women, surely!" (4:14 *NEB*). Then follows a long description of activities which prove that women are in control of men and events and hence are strongest (4:14–32). But even so, wise Zerubbabel goes on to demonstrate that truth is "great and stronger than all else. . . . Hers are strength and royalty, the authority and majesty of all ages. Praise be to the God of truth" (4:35,40 *NEB*). As could be expected in a Jewish romance, Zerubbabel is acclaimed the winner. The king says to him: "You have been proved the wisest; and you shall sit by me and be called my Kinsman" (4:42 *NEB*). The king also says he will grant Zerubbabel anything he requests. The Jew reminds the king of his promise to rebuild Jerusalem and the Temple and asks him to honor that promise. The king gladly agrees to do so, appointing Zerubbabel in charge of the rebuilding operation (4:43–63).

It is to be noted that there are several fixed literary conventions followed in these pious romances, including Daniel 1–6 and Susanna, Bel, and the Dragon in the Greek forms of the book. The geographical setting of most of the tales is outside the Holy Land: Ahiqar is in Assyria, Joseph in Egypt, Esther in Persia, Tobit in Nineveh, Zerubbabel in Persia, and Daniel in Babylon. Only Judith is in Palestine, in the impossible-to-identify town of Bethulia (Hebrew *bᵉtûlāh* means "virgin"), "which is on the way to Esdraelon, facing the plain near Dothan" (4:6). As regards their chronological setting, all the stories take place in the long distant past, a convention that may have arisen to avoid censorship on the part of the ruling political authorities. More likely, this convention was utilized to add authority and luster to the stories and their protagonists; everybody loves an *old* story, and dead heroes are easier to admire than live ones. Since these narratives are all essentially didactic, however, it would be a mistake to try to find in them precise historical or geographical information. In these ancient tales, a rough historical and geographical verisimilitude sufficed, as in the case of contemporary historical novels. In general, the principal theme of these religious romances is the serious problem that faced Israel as God's holy people living in a pagan environment; and the intention of the authors was to dramatize, often with great imagination and ingenuity, the truth that the almighty and omniscient God of the Fathers will protect and rescue the current Israel of faith from disaster and will raise up wise and stalwart men and women who will overwhelmingly confound the wisdom and might of the Gentiles.

X. APOCALYPTIC

Apocalyptic is the literary genre of 2:13–45 (the inner core of the second midrashic story) and chs. 7–12. Apocalyptic goes beyond the exhortation and encouragement which the six edifying narratives have as their essential purpose. It claims to know the inner plan of God who is Lord of history and Vindicator of his people Israel. Because of this knowledge, apocalyptic can assure believers that present distress will come to an end, and an age of bliss will follow in the reign of God.

When we characterize 2:13–45 and Part Two of the Book of Daniel (chs. 7–12) as apocalyptic, it should not be thought that we refer to a restricted or small body of literature. On the contrary, apocalyptic became an increasingly popular and widespread type of literature for almost three hundred years, say, from Maccabean times to the Second Jewish Revolt (A.D. 132–135). In the Bible the following books or portions have been classified as apocalyptic or proto-apocalyptic: Second Isaiah (chs. 40–55), Ezekiel, Isaiah 24–27, Deutero-Zechariah (chs. 9–14), Third Isaiah (chs. 56–66), Joel, Daniel, Revelation, and Mark 13 (and parallels, Matt 24:1–44; Luke 21:5–36). D. S. Russell[104] gives the following list of other apocalyptic writings with their approximate dates:

I Enoch 1–36, 37–71, 72–82, 83–90, 91–108 (from ca. 164 B.C. onwards)
The Book of Jubilees (ca. 150 B.C.)
The Sibylline Oracles, Book III (from ca. 150 B.C. onwards)
The Testaments of the Twelve Patriarchs (late second century B.C.)
The Psalms of Solomon (ca. 48 B.C.)
The Assumption of Moses (A.D. 6–30)
The Martyrdom of Isaiah (first century A.D.)
The Life of Adam and Eve (shortly before A.D. 70)
The Apocalypse of Abraham 9–32 (ca. A.D. 70–100)
The Testament of Abraham (first century A.D.)
II Enoch (first century A.D.)
The Sibylline Oracles, Book IV (ca. A.D. 80)
II Esdras (=IV Ezra) 3–14 (ca. A.D. 90)
II Baruch or The Apocalypse of Baruch (after A.D. 90)
III Baruch (second century A.D.)
The Sibylline Oracles, Book V (second century A.D.).

[104] *The Method and Message of Jewish Apocalyptic*, pp. 37–38.

Russell also provides[105] a list of Qumran works "whose outlook, in greater or less degree, has a close association with the apocalyptic books listed above, even though they may not share all their characteristic marks":

Commentaries on Isaiah, Hosea, Micah, Nahum, Habakkuk, Zephaniah, and Psalm 37
The Zadokite Document (or the Damascus Document)
The Manual of Discipline (or the Rule of the Community)
The Rule of the Congregation
A Scroll of Benedictions
The Testimonies Scroll (or a Messianic Anthology)
Hymns (or Psalms) of Thanksgiving
The War of the Sons of Light against the Sons of Darkness
The Book of Mysteries
A Midrash on the Last Days
A Description of the New Jerusalem
An Angelic Liturgy
The Prayer of Nabonidus and a Pseudo-Daniel Apocalypse
A Genesis Apocryphon.

The English word "apocalyptic" is derived from Greek *apokalypsis* (used in the title of the New Testament Book of Revelation, 1:1), which means "uncovering or disclosure, manifestation or revelation." But unlike the word "prophecy" which has a fairly precise meaning today as well as in antiquity, apocalyptic has come to mean many different things in contemporary literature and speech. The ancient writers who employed this literary genre can offer no help as to the exact definition of the term for they did not use the term themselves to describe their writing. Yet it is certain they knew they were writing a type of literature which we now classify as apocalyptic. Thus, despite the universal usage of the word "apocalyptic" today, there is no consensus among scholars as to its exact meaning or the extent of what can properly be classified as apocalyptic literature. Nevertheless, apocalyptic and apocalyptic literature remain useful and quite necessary expressions and categories.

One point about apocalyptic that can be taken for granted is that this genre was devised to meet a pressing religious need of the day. Although apocalypses were not homogeneous in every respect, they did contain many of the same general features or broad characteristics. J. Lindblom offers the following list: transcendentalism, mythology, cosmological orientation, pessimistic treatment of history, dualism, division of time into periods, doctrine of two ages, playing with numbers, pseudo-ecstasy, artificial claims to inspiration, pseudonymity, mysteriousness. H. H. Rowley, who cites this list from Lindblom, correctly remarks: "Some of these are rather

[105] Ibid., p. 39.

the accidents than the essence of apocalyptic, however."[106] Russell adds to Lindblom's list the following features: the idea of the unity of history and the conception of cosmic history which treats of earth and heaven; the notion of primordiality with revelations concerning creation and the fall of men and angels; the source of evil and the part played by angelic powers; the conflict between light and darkness, good and evil, God and Satan; the emergence of a transcendent "Son of Man"; the belief in life after death with various compartments of Hell, Gehenna, Paradise, and Heaven and the significance of the individual in the resurrection, judgment, and eternal bliss. Russell is quick to note, however: "These various 'marks' belong to apocalyptic not in the sense that they are essential to it or are to be found in every apocalyptic writing, but rather in the sense that, in whole or in part, they build up an *impression* of a distinct kind which conveys a particular *mood* of thought and belief."[107]

Indeed all such features or marks must be viewed only as formal elements of apocalyptic works in general, and in no way did they predetermine the theme of an individual author and the purpose of his literary enterprise. Since Dan 2:13–45 and chs. 7–12 are the only portions of the Old Testament that can be described as apocalyptic in the strict sense, it is methodologically more sound to derive a definition of the genre used by the authors of the book from a careful study of the work itself, rather than *a priori* to accept a definition of apocalyptic and then try to understand how Daniel fits into that genre. In this way we can avoid the confusion often accompanying a discussion of Daniel as an apocalyptic work. Thus we shall attempt to analyze three things: (1) religious situation of the day, or *Sitz im Leben;* (2) the intention and theme of the authors; and (3) the literary characteristics of the five apocalypses in Daniel 2 and 7–12.

1. *Religious Situation of the Day*

As explained in Parts VI and VII, "The Historical Background" and "The Ḥasidic Origin of the Book," a monumental religious crisis faced the Jews living during the reign of Antiochus IV Epiphanes (175–164 B.C.). This monarch engaged in a determined and well-planned campaign to establish in his realm the Greek way of life, including religion. No one was to be exempted from participation in the cultic practices of the state, and there would be no freedom of religion, not even in private. Anyone who refused to submit to the tyrant's directives would be liable to the death penalty. Weak in faith and unwilling to lose their wealth or their lives,

[106] H. H. Rowley, *The Relevance of Apocalyptic: A Study of Jewish and Christian Apocalypses from Daniel to the Revelation*, rev. ed., p. 25, n. 2.

[107] *Method and Message of Jewish Apocalyptic,* p. 105. Similar lists of characteristics of apocalyptic can be found in L. Morris's excellent little book, *Apocalyptic* (Grand Rapids: Eerdmans, 1972).

many Jews apostatized. Others came to terms with Hellenization, for they were convinced that accommodation was the only way possible to live their Jewish faith in those troublous times. The rest were sorely tempted to compromise. The crowning blow to Jewish sensitivities was the setting up of the statue of Olympian Zeus in the Jerusalem Temple itself in December 167 B.C. This disastrous state of affairs was the *Sitz im Leben* for the publication of the four apocalypses in Daniel 7–12 and of the re-edited apocalypse in ch. 2. These works were composed by men of faith and addressed to fellow believers who had no political or economic power but only an abiding trust and unshaken confidence in the God of Israel. These chapters also served as tracts dealing with the problem of evil and suffering which shook the foundations of Judaism in the second century B.C., as in recent times they were shaken by Hitler's murder of six million European Jews.

2. *The Intention and Theme of the Authors*

Faced with this calamitous situation which threatened to put an end to Judaism as a religion in the Holy Land, the authors and editors of the Daniel-apocalypses were raised up by God to console, strengthen, and exhort their coreligionists. The unflinching faith of these inspired men was firmly grounded in the divine power and will to rescue all who trusted in God and in his providence. And these men persevered in this conviction despite all appearances that God was silent and not at work. Their outlook and attitude could be neatly summarized in the words of Shadrach, Meshach, and Abednego: "If there is a God able to save us, such as our God whom we serve, he will save us from the white-hot furnace and from your hand, O king" (Dan 3:17). These words also represent a pristine form of non-violent resistance and pacifism for which one particular segment of Judaism, viz. the Ḥasidim (or at least some of them), was noted during the brutal persecution of Antiochus. The writer of the fifth apocalypse (Daniel 10–12) who together with the authors and editors of the other four apocalypses (chs. 2, 7, 8, and 9) lived during the evil days of Antiochus IV looked upon the violent and often cruel resistance of Mattathias and his son Judas Maccabee as "a little help" (Dan 11:34). What happened is described in I Macc 2:44–46: "They [the Jewish resistance force] gathered an army and struck down sinners in their anger and lawbreakers in their wrath, and the survivors fled to the Gentiles for safety. Mattathias and his friends went about and tore down the pagan altars; they also enforced circumcision for any uncircumcised boys whom they found in the territory of Israel" (cf. Josephus *Antiquities* xii 6, 2–4 [vol. 7, pp. 142–147, in the LCL edition]). The phrase "a little help" accurately describes the singularly unenthusiastic attitude which the sacred author had toward armed intervention and resistance.[108] "The people who are loyal to their God" (Dan 11:32) are the ones "who act wisely (and) make the multitude understand" (11:33). The practicing Jew will be tested with sword and flames, exile and plunder (11:33) "to refine, cleanse, and purify them" (11:35). Violence and bloodshed are not the answer to persecution. It is patience and perseverance alone that enable the believer in the God of Israel to overcome (12:12), for even death itself becomes for them a means of an ultimate and glorious victory: "Those who act wisely will shine brightly like the brilliance of the firmament; and those who lead the multitude to righteousness will shine like the stars forever and ever" (12:3). The author of the third apocalypse also clearly implied that non-violent resistance coupled with a dynamic faith in a saving and just God is the correct attitude for the loyal Jew to cultivate: "His [i.e. Antiochus'] cunning will be against the holy people, and his treacherous efforts will succeed. Proud of heart, he will suddenly destroy many. But when he rises up against the Prince of princes, he will be broken—but not by human hand" (8:25). Similar ideas are found also in the other three apocalypses. "In the days of those regimes the God of heaven will set up a kingdom that will never be destroyed, nor will this kingdom ever be delivered up to another people. It will crush and put an end to all those other kingdoms, while it itself will stand forever, just as you saw that a stone was cut out from the mountain, without a hand being put to it, and that it crushed the iron, the bronze, the terra cotta, the silver, and the gold [symbols of the four pagan kingdoms]" (2:44–45). "But when the court sits in judgment, its [i.e. Antiochus'] dominion will be taken away, by final and utter destruction. Then the kingship and dominion and the grandeur of all the kingdoms under the heavens will be given to the people of the holy ones of the Most High. Their royal rule will last forever, and all dominions will serve and obey it" (7:26–27). What is clearly implied in these statements from chs. 2 and 7 is made an explicit theological affirmation in the fourth midrashic narrative: "The Most High has dominion over man's kingdom, and . . . he gives it to whom he wishes" (4:22). "Seventy weeks are decreed for your people and your holy city, until crime is stopped, sins brought to full measure, guilt expiated, everlasting justice in-

[108] G. von Rad, *Old Testament Theology,* vol. 2 (tr. D. M. G. Stalker), p. 315, writes: "Without any doubt, the writer of Daniel sides with those who endure persecution rather than those who take up arms against it, and in so doing he is only being true to his own basic conviction that what must be will be. He is far removed from the Maccabees and their policy of active resistance; their large following is actually suspect in his eyes. There is something almost sublime about the way in which, as he tells the story, he sets down a whole series of their amazing victories simply as something relatively unimportant, 'a little help' which the oppressed receive at this time (Dan. xi.34). His gaze is imperturbably fixed on the goal which God has appointed for history, and this forbade him to glorify this mighty upsurge of human fortitude."

troduced, the prophetic vision confirmed, and the Holy of Holies anointed" (9:24). "For one week he [Antiochus] will make a strong alliance with many; for half a week he will abolish sacrifice and oblation; and upon their place will be an appalling abomination, until the decreed ruin is poured out upon the appaller" (9:27). All these mighty acts will take place not because of human activity or military might on Israel's part but because the Lord of history fulfills the great expectations and desire for deliverance of those who put their faith in him.

3. *The Literary Characteristics*

Under this heading we shall consider the following features that the reader will easily observe: (*a*) anonymous and pseudonymous authorship; (*b*) dreams and visions; (*c*) *prophetia ex eventu;* (*d*) symbolic language; (*e*) esoteric content.

a. Anonymous and pseudonymous authorship. As indicated above, the six midrashic narratives are, properly speaking, anonymous; only the hero's name is given, but not the name(s) of the author(s). Thus in ch. 2, the apocalypse which is the central element (vss. 13–45) of the edifying story is also anonymous unlike the other four apocalypses in chs. 7–12, which are pseudonymous, i.e. the unknown second-century B.C. authors identify themselves with the sixth-century B.C. Daniel of the first part of the book. Later writers of apocalyptic took up the device of pseudonymity probably in imitation of Daniel 7–12. But anonymity and pseudonymity must not be thought of as inventions of the authors of the Book of Daniel. Indeed most of the Old Testament is either anonymous or pseudonymous. Some obvious examples are: the Tetrateuch (Genesis, Exodus, Leviticus, Numbers), the Deuteronomistic History (Deuteronomy, Joshua, Judges, I–II Samuel, I–II Kings), Proverbs, Psalms, Job, Second and Third Isaiah, Jonah, Deutero-Zechariah (chs. 9–14), Ruth, Qoheleth, Esther, Judith, Tobit, Wisdom of Solomon. There is no reason to believe that the inspired writers of the Bible who used these literary devices had the intention of deceiving anyone. In fact, because anonymity and pseudonymity were such widespread phenomena in ancient literature, we may securely conclude that the biblical authors were merely employing standard, perfectly legitimate literary conventions even though the reasons why these were used are not easy for us to determine today.[109] In Part II, "Attribution to Daniel," we discussed the reasons why the name "Daniel" was attached to the book as a whole, including its deuterocanonical parts (Susanna, Bel, and the Dragon).

[109] For a good survey of many possible reasons why apocalyptic writers in general employed pseudonymity, cf. Russell, *Method and Message of Jewish Apocalyptic,* pp. 127–139.

b. Dreams and visions. In the apocalypses of chs. 2 and 7, which have great similarities to one another, dreams are the vehicles of divine revelation; in chs. 8, 9, and 10–12, visions perform that function. In both dreams and visions, however, the content of the revelation has to do with the future. The chronological setting of each apocalypse is the sixth century B.C., and the recipient of the dream or vision is granted by God information as to what will take place in the next three or four centuries. In the first three apocalypses (chs. 2, 7, and 8), the information is so cryptic that an interpreter is needed. In ch. 2, Daniel first tells King Nebuchadnezzar (who is the dreamer in the case) the content of his dream and then supplies the meaning of the esoteric symbols. In ch. 7, Daniel is the dreamer, and an angel is the interpreter. In ch. 8, Daniel receives a vision, the meaning of which completely escapes him; again the *angelus interpres* provides the necessary enlightenment. In the last two apocalypses (chs. 9 and 10–12), Daniel has a vision of the *angelus revelator* whose function is to describe, either in broad strokes (ch. 9) or in surprisingly accurate detail (chs. 11–12), the future course of events in Palestine and environs. Angels acting as interpreters of visions or revealers of mystery do not appear for the first time in the Book of Daniel. In Zechariah 1–6, for instance, angels perform both functions for the sixth-century B.C. prophet.[110] It is noteworthy that in ch. 2, the pagan King Nebuchadnezzar is the one who has the mysterious dream of what is to transpire in the following centuries. The God of Israel is Lord of all nations and peoples and times and is sovereignly free to choose whomever he wishes as an instrument of his revelation. The vision also plays a part in the midrashic story of ch. 4 which describes Nebuchadnezzar's dream of "a tree of great height in the center of the world" (4:7).

c. Prophetia ex eventu. The literary convention utilized for the content of these dreams and visions is the commonly employed device known as *prophetia* (or *vaticinium*) *ex eventu* (or *post eventum*), "prophecy from (or after) the event." The author of each of these apocalypses is actually writing in the third (ch. 2) or second century B.C. (chs. 7, 8, 9, and 10–12); but from his fictional time-frame of the sixth century B.C. he presents past history as if it were a prediction or forecast of the future. This is another literary device that had become standardized even in biblical literature, as for instance in the "Testament of Jacob" in Gen 49:1–27, and, as we saw, in Tobit 14:4–5. It can be safely assumed that the biblical writers used *prophetia ex eventu* not for purposes of deception but rather to give to their works greater authority by reason of antiquity and the nature of fulfilled prediction itself.[111]

110 The inaugural prophetic experience of Zechariah is dated in October/November 520 B.C.

111 On this question, cf. further E. Osswald, "Zum Problem der *vaticinia ex eventu*," *ZAW* 75 (1963), 27–44; and Hengel, *Judaism and Hellenism*, vol. 1, p. 184.

d. Symbolic language. The dreams in chs. 2 and 7 and the visions in chs. 8, 9, and 10–12 are described in language that is highly symbolic. The writers display a fertile and even extravagant imagination. In ch. 2, for example, the colossal statue of a man aptly symbolizes the powerful kingdoms of the world; and each of its principal component parts are depicted as materials symbolizing the successive world-empires: "The head of the statue was of pure gold [=Babylon], its chest and arms were of silver [=Media], its belly and hips of bronze [=Persia], its legs of iron [=Greek kingdom of Alexander], and its feet partly of iron and partly of terra cotta [=Alexander's divided empire]" (2:32–33). The symbolism in ch. 7, which is thematically related to ch. 2, strikes the modern reader as even more fantastic if not utterly bizarre. The spectacle is presented of four immense beasts: a lion with eagle wings and three tusks in its mouth (=Babylon); a bear with a man's heart (=Media); a leopard with bird wings and four heads (=Persia); an unclassified beast that was "dreadful, terrifying, and exceedingly strong, with great teeth of iron and claws of bronze" and ten horns (=the Greek kingdom), out of which "another horn, a small one, sprouted up among them" (7:7–8), symbol of Antiochus IV, the curse and scourge of the writer's day. Such imagery appears utterly outlandish to a modern audience who may be unfamiliar with ancient Near Eastern symbolism. The symbolism in Daniel and in much of the rest of the Old Testament (especially the Song of Songs) as well as in the Book of Revelation is not representational, and therefore it cannot be pictured realistically as if in a colored photograph. Rather the symbolism is suggestive; that is to say, images are projected in order to suggest (and not to depict) the realities the writer wishes to convey. An example will perhaps best illustrate this important point. In Rev 5:6, Jesus is described as a Lamb with seven horns and seven eyes. It would surely be freakish as well as repulsive to visualize realistically such an animal. What the author of the Book of Revelation intended by these symbols is that Jesus has universal dominion (seven horns) and knowledge of all things (seven eyes), the number seven signifying perfection or universality, the horn dominion or power, and the eye knowledge.

e. Esoteric content. What is portrayed in the five Daniel apocalypses is not the usual experience of normal people, even of those who have a deep faith in God. These works claim to reveal the future which God or his angel disclosed to a privileged character from antiquity named Daniel. In the third and fifth apocalypses Daniel is expressly commanded to keep the revelation a secret and to seal it up till the appropriate time in the far-off future, which as a matter of fact is the writer's own day in the early second century B.C. "As for you, keep the vision a secret, for it refers to the distant future" (8:26). "As for you, Daniel, keep the words secret and seal the book until the time of the final phase" (12:4). The same idea is unambiguously implied in the second apocalypse: "Here the account concluded. I, Daniel, was so greatly terrified by my thoughts that my face blanched. But I kept the matter to myself" (7:28). The authors of Daniel also relate the divine judgment of the wicked and the vindication of the righteous in a dramatic ushering in of the everlasting Kingdom of God. Stalwart believers, especially those who are martyred for their faith, will experience resurrection and will live forever, but the evildoers "will become everlasting objects of contempt and abhorrence" (12:2). The faithful who persevere during persecution will be rescued because their names are "written in the book" (12:1), presumably a ledger like "the book of the living" in Rev 3:5; 13:8; 17:8; 20:12,15; 21:27, and Philip 4:3 (cf. Luke 10:20). The authors and glossators of Daniel also provide approximate timetables for the duration of the desecration of the Jerusalem Temple by Antiochus—three and a half years in 7:25; 9:27; and 12:7; but 1,150 days (2,300 evenings and mornings) in 8:14, and 1,290 days in 12:11, whereas in 12:12 the time is 1,335 days. In addition, the author of Daniel 9 presents an interpretation of Jeremiah's prophecy of the seventy years that Babylon will dominate the Near East (Jer 25:11–12 and 29:10). The predicted period turns out to be seventy weeks of years (=490 years).[112] Numerology or mystical mathematics or, to use D. S. Russell's phrase, allegorical arithmetic[113] is also one of the interests of later apocalyptic writers. In the Book of Revelation, for example, the second wild beast receives "a number that stands for a certain man. The man's number is six hundred sixty-six" (13:18). Another exotic feature of Daniel is celestial warfare between Michael, angel-prince of Israel, and the unnamed angel-prince of the kingdom of Persia (10:13). The notion of angelic battles in heaven later becomes a commonplace in apocalyptic literature. In Rev 12:7–9, for instance, war breaks out in heaven; Michael and his angels wage war against the dragon and his angels. The huge dragon, also called the ancient serpent, is explicitly identified with the devil or Satan, "the seducer of the whole world" (12:9). In Jude 9; I Enoch 9:1; and 71:3, Michael is designated "archangel," a title which corresponds to the phrase "great prince" in Dan 12:1.

Definition of Apocalyptic

From what has been said above, we are now in a position to define apocalyptic in the Book of Daniel as a literary genre (1) that employs the devices of anonymous and pseudonymous authorship, dreams and visions as vehicles of revelation, historical panoramas in the form of *vaticinia ex*

[112] L. Hartman, "The Functions of Some So-Called Apocalyptic Timetables," *NTS* 22 (1975), 1–14, concludes his article by observing: "The timetables were aimed less at the brain than at the heart and hands."
[113] *Method and Message of Jewish Apocalyptic*, p. 195.

eventu, symbolic language understandable to the Jewish audience intended, and esoteric content; (2) that was devised as non-violent resistance literature having as its purpose to console, strengthen, and exhort the Jews persecuted by Antiochus IV Epiphanes in the present wicked age to remain faithful to their religious heritage; and (3) that promises as a reward for such fidelity eternal life by means of resurrection in the new age which will be the Kingdom of God.[114]

[114] For more information on apocalyptic, cf. J. Bloch, *On the Apocalyptic in Judaism,* JQRMS 2; J. J. Collins, "Jewish Apocalyptic against Its Hellenistic Near Eastern Environment," *BASOR* 220 (1975), 27–36; F. M. Cross, "New Directions in the Study of Apocalyptic," in *Apocalypticism* (ed. R. W. Funk), JTC 6, pp. 157–165; S. B. Frost, *Old Testament Apocalyptic: Its Origin and Growth;* P. D. Hanson, *The Dawn of Apocalyptic; idem,* "Jewish Apocalyptic against Its Near Eastern Environment," *RB* 78 (1971), 31–58; *idem,* "Old Testament Apocalyptic Reexamined," *Int* 25 (1971), 454–479; K. Koch, *The Rediscovery of Apocalyptic* (tr. M. Kohl), SBT 2/22; H.-P. Müller, "Märchen, Legende und Enderwartung: Zum Verständnis des Buches Daniel," *VT* 26 (1976), 338–350; J. M. Schmidt, *Die jüdische Apokalyptik: Die Geschichte ihrer Erforschung von den Anfängen bis zu den Textfunden von Qumran;* W. Schmithals, *The Apocalyptic Movement: Introduction and Interpretation* (tr. J. E. Steely).

XI. TEXTS AND VERSIONS

1. *The Qumran Manuscripts*

The oldest manuscript fragments of the Book of Daniel were recovered from Caves 1, 4, and 6 at Qumran. 1QDan[a] (1:10–17 and 2:2–6) and 1QDan[b] (3:22–30) were published by J. C. Trever.[115] 4QDan[a] (2:19–35 and part of the middle portion of the book), 4QDan[b] (the middle portion of Daniel), and 4QDan[c] will be published by F. M. Cross.[116] 6QDan (8:16–17?; 8:20–21?; 10:8–16; and 11:33–36,38) was published by M. Baillet and J. T. Milik.[117] Trever dates 1QDan[a] to the end of the Herodian period, and 1QDan[b] to the Herodian period, which he places as late perhaps as A.D. 60.[118] Cross describes the writing of 4QDan[b] as "a developed Herodian formal script (*ca* A.D. 20–50),"[119] and 4QDan[c] as "a semicursive script. . . . *Ca.* 100–50 B.C."[120] Baillet and Milik date 6QDan to ca. A.D. 50.[121] The meager fragments of 1QDan[a], 1QDan[b], and 6QDan were utilized in the present volume.[122] Unfortunately, the fairly substantial portions of Daniel preserved in 4QDan[a,b,c] are not yet available for general study, even though these manuscripts were discovered more than a quarter of a century ago.[123]

115 "Completion of the Publication of Some Fragments from Cave I," *RevQ* 19 (1965), 323–336; Daniel fragments are found on plates v and vi.

116 In "Editing the Manuscript Fragments from Qumran: Cave 4 of Qumran (4Q)," *BA* 19 (1956), 86, Cross gives this report: ". . . A sizeable proportion of the book of Daniel is extant in three relatively well preserved MSS." For a discussion of the fragments of Dan 11:32 and 12:10 in 4Q174 (4QFlor), cf. Part V, "Place in Canon."

117 *Les 'Petites Grottes' de Qumran,* DJD 3, pp. 114–116, and plate xxiii.

118 Trever, *RevQ* 19 (1965), 323–336.

119 Cross, "The Development of the Jewish Scripts," *The Bible and the Ancient Near East,* p. 139, *line 6.*

120 Ibid., p. 149, *line 2.*

121 Baillet and Milik, *Les 'Petites Grottes' de Qumran,* DJD 3, pp. 114–116.

122 Cf. A. Mertens, *Das Buch Daniel im Lichte der Texte vom Toten Meer,* SBM 12, pp. 29–31, for a convenient listing of the few readings of 1QDan[a], 1QDan[b], and 6QDan that vary from the MT. Mertens concludes (p. 31): "Die Daniel-Fragmente aus den Höhlen 1 und 6 von Qumran bieten im grossen ganzen den späteren masoretischen Text in einer guten, kaum veränderten Gestalt; sie sind somit ein wertvolles Zeugnis für die grosse Treue, mit der der heilige Text überliefert worden ist."

123 P. Benoit, "Editing the Manuscript Fragments from Qumran," *BA* 19 (1956), 76, writes that the scientific excavation of Cave 4, which produced the Daniel fragments entrusted to F. M. Cross's care for future publication, took place from 22 to 29 September 1952.

The most significant information 1QDan^a has provided is that the Aramaic section of the book begins at 2:4b, exactly the same place as in the MT; but instead of the MT gloss *'ărāmît,* "Aramaic," 1QDan^a leaves a space between the Hebrew and Aramaic text. 1QDan^b, in which not even a single line of text is preserved in full, is noteworthy because like the MT it also omits Dan 3:24–90, the interpolated materials found in the longer Greek, Syriac, and Latin forms of the book. Cross notes that the switch from Aramaic back to Hebrew is preserved in 4QDan^a and 4QDan^b and takes place in both at 8:1, exactly as in the MT.[124] 4QDan^c is the oldest of the manuscripts and potentially the most valuable for it is so close in time to the actual autograph of the book. Cross writes: "The text of Daniel in these scrolls conforms closely to later Massoretic tradition; there are to be found, however, some rare variants which side with the Alexandrian Greek against the MT and Theodotion."[125]

2. *The Hebrew Text*

As explained in Part III, "Unity of the Book and Date," the hypothesis behind the present translation of Daniel and commentary is that Aramaic was the original language of the entire twelve chapters now extant in the MT of the book. The Hebrew parts (1:1 – 2:4a and chs. 8–12) were later translated from this Aramaic original. Detailed evidence in support of this hypothesis will be provided in the critical notes on the Hebrew of the MT and in the NOTES on those texts in particular where the Hebrew translator either misunderstood the Aramaic *Vorlage* or else took the wrong sense out of an Aramaic expression that can have several possible meanings. In general, the Hebrew translator did his work competently, but on occasion he nodded. Thus, at times the Hebrew portions of Daniel are difficult to read. But if one retroverts the Hebrew of these troublesome sections back into their original Aramaic, then one finds the MT Hebrew a generally reliable, albeit indirect, witness to the original form of the book.

3. *The Aramaic Text*

The Aramaic of the Book of Daniel has been the subject of intensive study for many years. Here we need mention only a few of the principal scholars engaged in this enterprise: W. Baumgartner,[126] J. A. Montgomery,[127] F. Rosenthal,[128] and K. A. Kitchen.[129] There are also available today several excellent grammars of Biblical Aramaic by H. Bauer and

[124] Cross, *BA* 19 (1956), 86.
[125] Ibid.
[126] "Das Aramäische im Buche Daniel," *ZAW* 45 (1927), 81–133.
[127] *The Book of Daniel,* pp. 15–23.
[128] *Die aramäistische Forschung seit Th. Nöldeke's Veröffentlichungen.*
[129] "The Aramaic of Daniel," in *Notes on Some Problems in the Book of Daniel,* pp. 31–79.

P. Leander,[130] L. Palacios,[131] and F. Rosenthal,[132] among others. As regards lexicography, three dictionaries deserve special attention: F. Brown, S. R. Driver, and C. A. Briggs, *A Hebrew and English Lexicon of the Old Testament;*[133] L. Koehler and W. Baumgartner, *Lexicon in veteris testamenti libros;*[134] and E. Vogt, *Lexicon linguae aramaicae veteris testamenti.*[135] The dialect to which the Aramaic portions of Daniel belong is probably Official Aramaic, often called Imperial Aramaic or *Reichsaramäisch,* which is dated roughly from 700 to 200 B.C. It seems best to place Daniel here even though the final written form of the book is dated somewhat later than 200 B.C.[136] As will be pointed out in the NOTES on the text, the Aramaic of Daniel contains a number of words borrowed from Persian, Akkadian, and Greek. The presence of Persian words in the vocabulary of Daniel provides one more argument, among others suggested elsewhere, that the contents of Part One of the book (chs. 1–6) could go back at least in oral form to the Persian period.[137]

4. *The LXX and Theodotion-Daniel*

The somewhat involved history of the LXX and so-called Theodotion-Daniel as well as the editions thereof will be treated in Part XII, "The Greek Forms of Daniel." What needs to be said here is that both LXX and Theodotion-Daniel have been utilized critically in the translation, NOTES and COMMENT below. J. A. Montgomery's evaluation of the Greek evidence in the textual criticism of Daniel is still the most valuable to date.[138] His conclusions should be kept in mind when one grapples with the complexity of the MT and the two diverse forms of Daniel in Greek. The fact that LXX and Theodotion-Daniel, or the Syriac Peshiṭta and Theodotion-Daniel, agree with each other may mean nothing at all. But when these pairs disagree, one should take note. LXX readings against Theodotion-Daniel always deserve respect, as does the combination MT plus LXX or MT plus Theodotion-Daniel against the later versions. But the evidence of LXX plus Theodotion-Daniel against MT is precarious, since Theodotion-Daniel may depend on LXX. Thus, the possibility of in-

[130] *Grammatik des Biblisch-Aramäischen.*

[131] *Grammatica Aramaico-Biblica,* 2d ed.

[132] *A Grammar of Biblical Aramaic.*

[133] Oxford: Clarendon, 1907.

[134] Baumgartner was responsible for the Aramaic part of this dictionary; he did his work competently. The Hebrew part by Koehler is not so successful.

[135] Vogt's work is by far the best Biblical Aramaic dictionary published to date.

[136] Cf. J. A. Fitzmyer, *The Genesis Apocryphon of Qumran Cave I: A Commentary,* pp. 22–23, for a brief sketch of the classification of the Aramaic dialects; see also E. Y. Kutscher, "Aramaic," *Current Trends in Linguistics,* vol. 6: *Linguistics in South West Asia and North Africa* (ed. T. A. Sebeok), pp. 347–412; *idem,* "Aramaic," *EncJud* 3, cols. 263–266.

[137] Cf. also Delcor, p. 35.

[138] *The Book of Daniel,* pp. 24–29, 35–42, 46–55.

terlocking witnesses must not be overlooked: when Theodotion-Daniel depends on LXX, or the Peshiṭta and the Vulgate depend on Theodotion-Daniel, their combined evidence may count as only one unit.[139] Thanks to Cross's preliminary observations on his Cave 4 Daniel fragments, we should now add to Montgomery's conclusions that the combination of 4QDan[a,b, or c] plus LXX against MT and Theodotion-Daniel should be taken seriously. All of which is to say that in the textual criticism of the Book of Daniel there are no iron rules or golden rules. Rather the scholar must weigh the evidence of the MT, the Qumran fragments, and the ancient versions with great skill and discretion—no easy task even under the best of circumstances.

5. *The Syriac Peshiṭta*

The Syriac Peshiṭta[140] contains, as we saw in Part V, "Place in Canon," the longer form of the book found also in LXX and Theodotion-Daniel. There can be no question that the Peshiṭta of Daniel was a primary version from the Hebrew and Aramaic of the book.[141] But at times the Peshiṭta reflects Theodotion-Daniel.[142] It received, however, little or no influence from the LXX, and none at all from Origen and Lucian.[143] Of Christian provenance, the Peshiṭta of Daniel was translated in Edessa between A.D. 200 and 300, probably before 250.[144] Being translated directly from the Hebrew and Aramaic, the Peshiṭta has value for the textual criticism of Daniel, but because as already noted it is colored by Theodotion-Daniel one may not assume that in every case it reflects the original state of its *Vorlage*. Where the Peshiṭta agrees with Theodotion-Daniel, it may not be an independent witness but may simply reflect the latter.[145]

6. *The Latin Vulgate*

The Latin Vulgate of Daniel was one of the first books of the Old Testament that St. Jerome translated. He worked on Daniel between 389 and 392, translating directly from the Hebrew and Aramaic but occasionally with an eye on Theodotion-Daniel as well as other earlier versions.[146] Thus, evidence from the Vulgate, where it agrees with one of these versions, is suspect.[147]

139 Ibid., p. 57.

140 The Peshiṭta of Daniel appears in the following editions: Walton's London Polyglot (the text of which was taken over from the Paris Polyglot), Lee (1823), Urmia (1852), Mosul (1951), and the photolithographic facsimile of the sixth-century Ambrosian Codex published by A. Ceriani in 1876 (for a brief discussion of the Book of Daniel in this splendid edition see Part V, "Place in Canon").

141 Cf. M. J. Wyngarden, *The Syriac Version of the Book of Daniel.* This work was a Ph.D. dissertation written under the direction of J. A. Montgomery at the University of Pennsylvania.

142 Ibid., pp. 19–21. 143 Ibid., pp. 18–19, 21–23.

144 Ibid., p. 36. 145 Ibid., pp. 39–40.

146 Cf. G. Rinaldi, pp. 17–18.

147 Montgomery, p. 56.

XII. THE GREEK FORMS OF DANIEL

Discoveries of biblical texts at Qumran and elsewhere have occasioned a better understanding of the Greek forms of the Old Testament. D. Barthélemy, for instance, has demonstrated that the text-form in the Greek fragments of the Twelve Minor Prophets from Wadi Khabra (Naḥal Ḥeber), south of Wadi Murabba'at in the Judean Desert, represents a recension of the pre-Christian Old Greek, also known as the Septuagint (LXX). This recension was produced on the basis of Hebrew texts circulating in Palestine during the first century B.C. and the early part of the first Christian century.[148] It is this recension which St. Justin Martyr (died ca. A.D. 165) cited in his *Dialogue with Trypho* about the middle of the second century. The translation technique of this recension is the same as the one employed in so-called "Theodotion," which has generally been assigned by scholars to the second century A.D. Hence, Barthélemy and others call this recension Proto-Theodotion. It is also called the *kaige* recension because *kaige* is invariably the expression adopted as a translation of Hebrew *w^egām*. Barthélemy identified Proto-Theodotion with a certain Jew named Jonathan ben 'Uzziel, disciple of the famous Rabbi Hillel, and accordingly goes on to argue that the work was produced in Palestine between A.D. 30 and 50.[149] Other scholars disagree with such a late dating, preferring instead a first-century B.C. date.[150] The careful studies of Barthélemy and others on the *kaige* recension have prompted a new look at some old problems concerning the Greek forms of the Book of Daniel and at some further problems that have exercised students of Daniel.

1. *LXX-Daniel and Theodotion-Daniel*

The assumption that a single, more or less stable Hebrew text-type formed the basis of the Old Greek (LXX) and its later recensions has now been called into serious question. On the basis of recent data from the Qumran caves and elsewhere, F. M. Cross has attempted to prove that complex Hebrew textual traditions paralleled the development of the vari-

[148] D. Barthélemy, *Les devanciers d'Aquila,* VTSup 10.

[149] Ibid., p. 148.

[150] Cf., for example, S. Jellicoe, "Some Reflections on the *KAIGE* Recension," *VT* 23 (1973), 23–24.

ous Greek recensions.[151] Each sequence in one had its correspondent in the other. Cross has argued for the existence of three Hebrew textual traditions: the Egyptian, the Palestinian, and the Babylonian. Each of these has its reflex in the Greek recensions: the Egyptian tradition is transmitted in the Old Greek (LXX); the Palestinian in the Proto-Lucianic recension; and the Babylonian, which had moved back to Palestine during the Hasmonean or Herodian period, in the Proto-Theodotionic or *kaige* recension.

Whatever the merits of the case presented by Cross with regard to the older books of the Hebrew Bible that may have had such a complex textual history, his theory of local texts would not apply to the Book of Daniel. The reason is that, as Cross himself writes, "distinct textual families take centuries to develop,"[152] and the MT-form of Daniel is simply not old enough to develop into three textual traditions. The two fully extant Greek forms of Daniel—the LXX and so-called Theodotion-Daniel—need therefore to be explained on a basis other than the one suggested by Cross.

The complete text of the LXX-form of Daniel is now found in only two witnesses: the Chisian MS, called 87 in the edition of H. B. Swete,[153] but 88 in the editions of A. Rahlfs[154] and J. Ziegler;[155] and the Syrohexaplar. Codex 88, which unfortunately is marred by numerous corruptions, is dated variously from the ninth to eleventh centuries.[156] The Syrohexaplar,

[151] F. M. Cross, "The History of the Biblical Text in the Light of Discoveries in the Judean Desert," *HTR* 57 (1964), 281–299; "The Contribution of the Qumrân Discoveries to the Study of the Biblical Text," *IEJ* 16 (1966), 81–95; and "The Evolution of a Theory of Local Texts," in *1972 Proceedings: IOSCS and Pseudepigrapha Seminar* (ed. R. A. Kraft), Septuagint and Cognate Studies 2, pp. 108–126.

[152] Cross, "The Evolution of a Theory of Local Texts," p. 111.

[153] H. B. Swete, *The Old Testament in Greek,* vol. 3, 4th ed., pp. 498–593. In his edition of the LXX, which is printed on the left-hand page, Swete provides the text of Codex 87 (88) and variants from the Syrohexaplar. For Theodotion-Daniel, which appears on the right-hand page, Swete prints the text of Codex Vaticanus (B) and variants from three other uncials: Alexandrinus (A), Marchalianus (Q), and the fragmentary Cryptoferratensis (Γ).

[154] A. Rahlfs, *Septuaginta,* vol. 2: *Libri poetici et prophetici,* pp. 864–941. The LXX in an eclectic text—Codex 88 and Syrohexaplar—appears at the top of the page, and at the bottom Theodotion-Daniel again in an eclectic text based primarily on the uncials B, A, and Q, and three cursives, 22, 48, and 51.

[155] J. Ziegler, *Susanna, Daniel, Bel et Draco,* Septuaginta, Vetus Testamentum Graecum, Auctoritate Societatis Litterarum Gottingensis editum 16/2. Ziegler gives the LXX with apparatus at the foot of the page, and Theodotion-Daniel with variants on the rest of the page. For the LXX Ziegler employs Codex 88, Syrohexaplar, and the Chester Beatty fragments of the early third-century A.D. Papyrus 967; cf. his pp. 7–8, 19–21. For Theodotion-Daniel Ziegler uses seven uncials and forty cursives; S. Jellicoe, *The Septuagint and Modern Study,* p. 302, wrongly says there are thirty-one cursives, apparently failing to notice the nine other cursives listed on p. 3 of Ziegler's Introduction. For both LXX and Theodotion-Daniel, Ziegler gives evidence from the daughter versions as well as the Fathers. Thus, in all respects, Ziegler's superb edition now supersedes Swete's and Rahlfs' hand editions.

[156] Cf. Swete, *The Old Testament in Greek,* vol. 3, 4th ed., p. xii.

a meticulously literal and accurate Syriac translation of the LXX made from the fifth column of Origen's Hexapla by Bishop Paul of Tella in Mesopotamia, dates to the years 615–617.[157] Most of LXX-Daniel is also extant in the early third-century A.D. Chester Beatty-Cologne Papyrus 967.[158] This papyrus possesses singular importance because it contains a text that is pre-hexaplaric[159] whereas the hexaplaric text is found in Codex 88 and the Syrohexaplar.

Some phrases of LXX-Daniel appear in the Greek text of I Maccabees. I Macc 1:9, *eplēthynan kaka en tę̄ gę̄,* corresponds to Dan 12:4; I Macc 1:18, *kai epesan traumatiai polloi,* to Dan 11:26; I Macc 4:41,43, *katharizein ta hagia,* to Dan 8:14; and I Macc 1:54, *bdelygma erēmōseōs,* to Dan 11:31. From this evidence it can rightly be assumed that LXX-Daniel goes back to at least the date of the Greek text of I Maccabees. As I Maccabees, originally composed in Hebrew, was translated into Greek no earlier than 100 B.C., we may safely conclude that LXX-Daniel originated at about that time.[160] It is generally agreed that LXX-Daniel was prepared in Egypt, presumably at Alexandria.[161]

The reason for the extreme scarcity of witnesses to LXX-Daniel is that very early in her history the Christian Church abandoned LXX-Daniel and replaced it with Theodotion-Daniel in the LXX MSS. R. H. Pfeiffer states that Theodotion-Daniel triumphed over LXX-Daniel between 150 and 200 in the Greek Church and between 230 and 250 in the Latin Church.[162] S. Jellicoe places the transition approximately in the second half of the third century, and writes that "if a name is desiderated it

[157] About half the Syrohexaplar is preserved in the magnificent ninth-century Codex Ambrosianus, and was published in a splendid facsimile edition by A. M. Ceriani, *Codex syro-hexaplaris Ambrosianus photolithographice editus,* Monumenta sacra et profana 7. The first volume of this MS disappeared during the sixteenth century. The extant volume contains Psalms, Job, Proverbs, Ecclesiastes, Song of Songs, Wisdom of Solomon, Sirach, the Minor Prophets, Jeremiah, Baruch, Lamentations, Epistle of Jeremiah, Daniel 1–12 (including 3:24–90), Susanna, Bel, and the Dragon, Ezekiel, and Isaiah. The Book of Daniel, Susanna, Bel, and the Dragon are found on folios 143a–151b.

[158] Ziegler's critical edition (see fn. 155 above) gives variants from only the Chester Beatty fragments of Papyrus 967. Unfortunately, Ziegler did not have available at the time the Cologne fragments of 967 which were published by A. Geissen, *Der Septuaginta-Text des Buches Daniel, Kap. 5–12, zusammen mit Susanna, Bel et Draco, nach dem Kölner Teil des Papyrus 967,* Papyrologische Texte und Abhandlungen 5; W. Hamm, *Der Septuaginta-Text des Buches Daniel, Kap. 1–2, nach dem Kölner Teil des Papyrus 967,* Papyrologische Texte und Abhandlungen 10; and *idem, Der Septuaginta-Text des Buches Daniel, Kap. 3–4, nach dem Kölner Teil des Papyrus 967,* Papyrologische Texte und Abhandlungen 21. Geissen, *Der Septuaginta,* p. 11, mentions that there is also one further leaf of the papyrus (pp. 181–182) that remains unpublished in Barcelona.

[159] Cf. Ziegler, *Susanna, Daniel, Bel et Draco,* p. 19.

[160] For further details, cf. Montgomery, p. 38.

[161] Cf. Pfeiffer, *History of New Testament Times,* p. 440.

[162] Ibid., pp. 443–444.

would be that of Origen himself."[163] The reason for the replacement escaped even such a worthy as St. Jerome (d. 420), who wrote in the preface to his translation of Daniel: "The Churches of the Lord Savior do not read the prophet Daniel according to the Seventy Interpreters, but use the edition of Theodotion; why this happened I do not know. . . . But this much I can affirm: [the LXX] differs a great deal from the truth [*veritas hebraica,* the Aramaic and Hebrew MT] and for good reason was rejected."[164] In his commentary on the Book of Daniel, Jerome complains that the LXX omits the text of Dan 4:6, and then he writes: "Therefore, in the judgment of the Church's leaders, the [LXX] edition of this book has been rejected; and in public is read the edition of Theodotion, which agrees both with the Hebrew and with other translators."[165]

Most modern critics have been hardly less severe in their evaluation of LXX-Daniel, accusing it of all sorts of translational infelicities or even downright infidelities.[166] A few scholars, however, have come to the defense of LXX-Daniel. A. Bludau, for instance, calls it "an astounding achievement."[167] And after a minute analysis of this Greek version J. A. Montgomery concludes

> that the translator worked faithfully word by word, especially in the obscure passages, and that the present muddled condition is largely due to the shuffling into the text of true glosses or doublets which once stood in the marg[in]. . . . Literarily the translator was worthy of such a task, for he was a writer of skill in Greek and of ingenious spirit.[168]

The place and date of Theodotion-Daniel are not as certain as in the case of LXX-Daniel. But as regards so-called "Theodotion" in other parts of the Old Testament, some bits of information are at hand. Irenaeus (d. ca. A.D. 202) refers to the man Theodotion as an Ephesian, and his own use of the recension "Theodotion" clearly contradicts Epiphanius' statement (*De mensuris et ponderibus* 17, written in A.D. 392) which places the translator in Commodus' reign ca. 180. Irenaeus also implies

[163] Jellicoe, *Septuagint and Modern Study,* pp. 86–87.

[164] *PL* 28, col. 1357: "Danielem prophetam juxta Septuaginta Interpretes Domini Salvatoris Ecclesiae non legunt, utentes Theodotionis editione, et hoc cur acciderit, nescio. . . . Hoc unum affirmare possum, quod multum a veritate discordet, et recto iudicio repudiatus sit."

[165] *PL* 25, col. 514: "Unde iudicio magistrorum Ecclesiae, editio eorum [LXX] in hoc volumine repudiata est; et Theodotionis vulgo legitur, quae et Hebraeo, et caeteris translatoribus congruit."

[166] Cf. the remarks of Montgomery, pp. 35–37; Pfeiffer, *History of New Testament Times,* p. 439; and Delcor, pp. 20–21.

[167] "Eine staunenswerthe Leistung"—A. Bludau, *Die alexandrinische Übersetzung des Buches Daniel und ihr Verhältniss zum massorethischen Text,* BibS 2/2-3, p. 87. This work provides the fullest comparison of LXX-Daniel with the MT.

[168] Montgomery, pp. 36–37.

that "Theodotion" is prior to Aquila (another person whose name is attached to an ancient form of the Greek Old Testament[169]) when he argues for the use of Greek *parthenos* in Isa 7:14 and states that *neanis* is not correct, "as Theodotion the Ephesian has interpreted [the word], and Aquila the Pontian, both being Jewish proselytes."[170] Barthélemy calls attention to the fact that "Theodotion" must be prior to Aquila for the simple reason that Aquila as well as Symmachus (whose name represents still another Greek form of the Old Testament) did not revise or correct the LXX translation, as had been previously supposed by scholars, but rather revised Proto-Theodotion (*kaige*) or "Theodotion." Barthélemy's conclusions have been roundly confirmed by K. G. O'Connell who has demonstrated that "Theodotion" was the basis of Aquila's work on the Book of Exodus.[171]

Montgomery dates the age of the translator Theodotion to the early second century A.D., noting at the same time that such a late date cannot account for the citation by the New Testament, especially Hebrews and Revelation, of many phrases from Theodotion-Daniel.[172] Montgomery lists six Revelation and Theodotion-Daniel correspondences: Rev 9:20 and Dan 5:23; Rev 10:5–6 and Dan 12:7; Rev 11:7 and Dan 7:21; Rev 12:7 and Dan 10:20; Rev 16:18 and Dan 12:1; and Rev 19:6 and Dan 10:6.[173] He calls particular attention to Heb 11:33 which bears a very close resemblance to Theodotion-Daniel 6:22(23). R. H. Charles adds six more cases: Rev 1:7a and Dan 7:13; Rev 1:19 and Dan 2:29,45; Rev 10:4 and Dan 8:26; Rev 11:13 and Dan 2:18,19,37; Rev 20:4 and Dan 7:22; and Rev 20:11 and Dan 2:35.[174] Three more examples could be added: Rev 1:18 and Dan 4:31; Rev 12:8 and Dan 2:35; and Rev 13:8 and Dan 12:1.[175] To resolve the chronological difficulty that phrases from Theodotion-Daniel are found in the New Testament, Montgomery[176] and others[177] postulated an Ur-Theodotion, perhaps as a Hellenistic oral targum. This Ur-Theodotion must not be confused with Proto-Theodotion (*kaige*) for the existence of which around the turn of the Christian era there is now firm evidence, as was indicated above.

J. Gwynn's old but still valuable article on "Theodotion"[178] has been the

[169] As regards Aquila, cf. Jellicoe, *Septuagint and Modern Study*, pp. 76–83.

[170] Irenaeus *Adversus haereses* iii 21, 1 (*PG* 7, col. 946).

[171] K. G. O'Connell, *The Theodotionic Revision of the Book of Exodus*, HSM 3.

[172] Montgomery, p. 47.

[173] Ibid., p. 49.

[174] R. H. Charles, p. liv.

[175] Cf. P. Grelot, "Les versions grecques de Daniel," *Bib* 47 (1966), 390.

[176] Montgomery, pp. 46–50.

[177] For example, J. W. Wevers, "Theodotion," *IDB* 4, pp. 618–619; and Jellicoe, *Septuagint and Modern Study*, pp. 83–94.

[178] J. Gwynn, "Theodotion," *Dictionary of Christian Biography*, vol. 4, pp. 970–979.

most imaginative and in general most accurate with regard to an Ur-Theodotion behind the second-century A.D. "Theodotion." He has argued that side by side with LXX-Daniel there was current among the Jews from pre-Christian times another Greek form of the book. It was this form that was known: (1) to the Greek translator of the apocryphal or deuterocanonical Book of Baruch, many phrases of which correspond to Theodotion-Daniel (Bar 1:15 and Dan 9:7; Bar 1:16 and Dan 9:8; Bar 1:18 and Dan 9:10; Bar 2:2 and Dan 9:12–13; Bar 2:7 and Dan 9:13; Bar 2:11 and Dan 9:15; Bar 2:14 and Dan 9:17; and Bar 2:16 and Dan 9:18); (2) to the New Testament authors noted above; and (3) to the Apostolic Fathers Clement (late first century A.D.) and Hermas (ca. 140) who were also familiar with Theodotion-Daniel. Gwynn then concludes that this second pre-Christian Greek form of Daniel supplied the foundation for the work of the assumed historical Theodotion.

J. Ziegler, however, in the Introduction to his splendid critical edition of Daniel in Greek, notes in passing that Theodotion-Daniel may have nothing in common with "Theodotion."[179] Pursuing this lead, one of Ziegler's students, A. Schmitt, published an important monograph[180] in which he proves after a minute and elaborately detailed comparison that Theodotion-Daniel is not in the same textual tradition as Proto-Theodotion (*kaige*)/"Theodotion" existing in the other books of the Old Testament. Thus, the identification of Theodotion-Daniel with Proto-Theodotion (*kaige*) that has been made by Barthélemy,[181] P. Grelot,[182] M. Delcor,[183] and others should no longer be maintained.

Rather I should like to propose a fresh approach to the question of Theodotion-Daniel. According to an opinion commonly held by scholars, the Old Greek (LXX) is not a homogeneous or uniformly felicitous Alexandrian translation but often differs from book to book in the quality and style of its results. In somewhat the same manner, Proto-Theodotion (*kaige*) is best considered as only one form of Greek literary activity in the first century B.C.; Proto-Lucian is another. Theodotion-Daniel is the outcome of still another type of translation enterprise in Palestine or Asia Minor during pre-Christian times, a date required by the fact that the New Testament, as noted above, quotes or alludes to this form of Greek Daniel. Indeed the widespread use of Greek in Palestine during pre-Christian times can no longer be seriously doubted. The Greek fragments recovered from Qumran Caves 4 and 7 and from Wadi Khabra, among other data,

179 Ziegler, *Susanna, Daniel, Bel et Draco,* p. 61.

180 A. Schmitt, *Stammt der sogenannte "Θ"-Text bei Daniel wirklich von Theodotion?* Mitteilungen des Septuaginta-Unternehmens 9.

181 Barthélemy, *Les devanciers d'Aquila,* pp. 46–47.

182 Grelot, *Bib* 47 (1966), 392.

183 Delcor, p. 22.

provide sufficient evidence that the Greek Old Testament was copied and read also by Palestinian Jews, and not just by Diaspora Jews in Egypt.[184] It has likewise been well established that during this same period there were sizable communities of Greek-speaking Jews in Asia Minor.[185] Moreover, the library at Pergamum was reputed to hold two hundred thousand volumes—surely an indication of intense literary activity and interest in learning. It is not unreasonable to assume, therefore, that Theodotion-Daniel was produced in a Jewish community of Palestine or even Asia Minor by a scholar who was disturbed by the fact that the Alexandrian Old Greek (LXX) of Daniel was at times less than accurate in relation to the Hebrew and Aramaic of the book. On the basis of a careful study of the list of officers in Dan 3:2—somewhat meager evidence at best—K. Koch has proposed that the most likely place for the origin of Theodotion-Daniel is Syria-Mesopotamia.[186]

It is best to consider Theodotion-Daniel a fresh translation of the Hebrew and Aramaic form of the book with an eye on LXX-Daniel rather than a recension in the usual sense of that word.

Thus, the expression "Theodotion-Daniel" is a misnomer. But in order to avoid even further confusion it seems advisable to keep this title, but as a hyphenated word. (To conserve space in our notes and commentary we simply use the expression "Theodotion," abbreviated "Theod.") Moreover, there are no adequate grounds for questioning that Theodotion-Daniel as it is now extant in nearly all the Greek MSS is essentially what existed in the first pre-Christian century. It is this Theodotion-Daniel that appears in Greek Baruch, the New Testament citations, and the Apostolic Fathers mentioned above. The hypothesis I have presented here is considerably different from Gwynn's theory which was outlined above. Gwynn concludes that a pre-Christian Greek text of Daniel (an Ur-Theodotion) became the point of departure for a real historical Theodotion in the second century A.D., whereas what I am arguing for here, from evidence supplied in part by Gwynn himself and in part by A. Schmitt, is that Theodotion-Daniel essentially in its present state is a first-century B.C. production which was never reworked by the recensionist Theodotion.

Finally, it should be noted that the New Testament cites or alludes to

184 Cf. J. N. Sevenster, *Do You Know Greek? How Much Greek Could the First Jewish Christians Have Known?* NovTSup 19; and J. A. Fitzmyer, "The Languages of Palestine in the First Century A.D.," *CBQ* 32 (1970), 507–518, with ample bibliography.

185 Detailed evidence for the presence of Jews in almost every quarter of Asia Minor is provided by E. Schürer, "Diaspora," *Dictionary of the Bible,* vol. 5 (ed. J. Hastings), pp. 93–95.

186 K. Koch, "Die Herkunft der Proto-Theodotion-Übersetzung des Danielbuches," *VT* 23 (1973), 362–365.

not only Theodotion-Daniel but also LXX-Daniel and at least one other Greek translation no longer extant or even otherwise known.[187] In some seven instances, Revelation corresponds to LXX-Daniel: Rev 1:14a and Dan 7:9; Rev 1:14c and Dan 10:6; Rev 4:1 and Dan 7:6; Rev 10:1 and Dan 10:6; Rev 10:5–6 and Dan 12:7; Rev 20:15 and Dan 12:1; and Rev 20:12 and Dan 7:10.[188] Furthermore, Dan 7:13 is quoted from the LXX in Matt 24:30 and 26:64 and in Rev 14:14–16 (the Son of Man "on," Greek *epi,* the clouds of heaven), but from Theodotion-Daniel in Mark 14:62 and Rev 1:7 ("with," Greek *meta,* the clouds of heaven).[189] The original Aramaic preposition here is *'im* which means "with," as Theodotion-Daniel rightly has it. To complicate the picture, Mark 13:26 and Luke 21:27 speak of the Son of Man "in," Greek *en,* the clouds of heaven; no extant Greek MS of Dan 7:13 contains that preposition or Greek *epanō,* "over, above, on," cited by St. Justin Martyr (*Dialogue with Trypho* 14, 8; 120, 4; and *Apology* 51, 9). It appears plausible to conclude, therefore, that the New Testament writers and the early Christian community employed more than two different Greek forms of the Book of Daniel, or at least of Dan 7:13.[190]

2. *The "Additions to Daniel"*

It has generally been held that the Greek versions which contain the deuterocanonical or apocryphal "Additions to Daniel"—Greek 3:24–90 and the narratives of Susanna, Bel, and the Dragon—represent only the Old Testament list of sacred books accepted by Jews in Egypt where the LXX was translated. But since, as already shown above, Theodotion-Daniel was produced in Asia Minor or Palestine (or possibly Syria-Mesopotamia) in pre-Christian times, and since both the LXX and Theodotion-Daniel contained the "Additions"—there is no cogent evidence to the contrary[191]—then the canonical status of the longer Greek form of the book among Jews should be re-examined and re-evaluated. Indeed, it would appear less than accurate to speak of the "Additions" as being sacred only in Egyptian Jewish circles while in fact the fourteen-chapter Theodotion-Daniel was published and undoubtedly received as a holy book also by many Jews in Palestine or Asia Minor during the first century B.C. Thus, for the period before the fixing of the Jewish Canon by the rabbis of Pharisaic Judaism near the end of the first Christian century, it is altogether appropriate to speak of at least one Jewish collection of sa-

[187] On this question cf. Montgomery, p. 49.
[188] Cf. Grelot, *Bib* 47 (1966), 390.
[189] Although Codex Q of Theodotion-Daniel reads *epi,* as does LXX.
[190] For a detailed account of all the Greek forms of Daniel, including the Lucianic, cf. Montgomery, pp. 35–50; and Ziegler, *Susanna, Daniel, Bel et Draco,* pp. 7–76.
[191] Cf. Pfeiffer, *History of New Testament Times,* pp. 441–442.

cred books in Palestine or Asia Minor that included the "Additions to Daniel."[192]

As was pointed out in Part V, "Place in Canon," Roman Catholics believe the "Additions" to be sacred and inspired by God; hence the term "deuterocanonical." Jews and Protestants view the "Additions" as apocryphal.

[192] For a recent study of these additions in LXX and Theodotion-Daniel, cf. J. Schüpphaus, "Das Verhältnis von LXX- und Theodotion-Text in den apokryphen Zusätzen zum Danielbuch," *ZAW* 83 (1971), 49–72.

XIII. "THE SON OF MAN" IN DANIEL 7

1. *Introduction*

There seems to be no end in view to the arguments for or against the unity of Daniel 7. But regardless of one's opinion as to the unity of the chapter, a strong case can be made that the meaning of the expression "the holy ones (of the Most High)" remains the same throughout the apocalypse. It is our thesis that this expression refers to only one group of individuals even if, as many scholars seriously contend, one or more later glosses containing the phrase have been added by another hand (cf. COMMENT: DETAILED on 7:20b–22,24b–25). Since there is sufficient consensus that *k^ebar 'ĕnāš,* "one in human likeness" (7:13), is a symbol of *qaddîšê 'elyônîn,* "the holy ones of the Most High," the understanding of this much disputed person will not be influenced in any appreciable way by one's hypothesis that there may be two hands at work in the chapter.

2. *Analysis of* bar 'ĕnāš *and* ben 'ādām

In order to understand adequately the meaning of *bar 'ĕnāš* in Dan 7:13, which is the only place in the Old Testament where the phrase occurs in Aramaic, and about which a vast amount of commentary has been produced over the centuries (particularly the present one), it is necessary to examine in some detail the linguistic evidence for the expression. In the MT, *ben 'ādām,* literally, "son of man(kind)," the Hebrew equivalent of the Aramaic *bar 'ĕnāš/'ĕnôš,*[193] occurs 108 times. In the Book of Ezekiel, it is the expression used by God ninety-three times when he addresses the prophet. It is employed fifteen times[194] in other books where it is a lofty designation for "man" in poetic and solemn contexts: Num 23:19; Isa 51:12; 56:2; Jer 49:18,33; 50:40; 51:43; Pss 8:5; 80:18; 146:3; Job 16:21; 25:6; 35:8; Dan 8:17; 10:16.[195] In the Hebrew fragments of the Book of Sirach, the singular form *ben 'ādām* does not occur, but the plural *b^enê 'ādām* is found in 3:24a; 16:16b,17d; 34:32b; 36:28b; 38:8c

[193] The orthography *'ĕnôš* is a Hebraism in Aramaic; cf. J. A. Fitzmyer, *The Genesis Apocryphon,* p. 151.

[194] C. Colpe, *"ho huios tou anthrōpou," TDNT* 8, p. 402, says there are only fourteen occurrences outside Ezekiel; he failed to count Dan 10:16 where the preferred reading is *ben 'ādām.* Cf. fn. 198 below.

[195] F. Maass, *"'ādām," TDOT* 1, pp. 75–87, gives a brief survey of the 562 occurrences of *'ādām* in the MT.

(MS B^{text}; margin *aliter*); 40:1b.[196] Daniel is called *ben 'ādām* in 8:17, the only place outside Ezekiel where a prophet is so addressed.[197] In Dan 10:16, *ben 'ādām*[198] simply means "a man, or human being." The word *'ādām* alone appears in Dan 8:16 and 10:18; since the word occurs after a construct in both cases, the meaning is "human"—"human voice" and "human appearance," respectively.

In Aramaic the oldest occurrence of *br 'nš/'nwš* is found in Sefire Stele III (mid-eighth century B.C.), line 16: *bkl mh zy ymwt br 'nš,* "in whatever way a man shall die."[199] Before the third century A.D. the only other occurrence of the expression outside Dan 7:13 is in 1QapGen 21:13 (first century B.C.): *dy l' yškḥ kwl br 'nwš lmmnyh,* "which no man [or no one] can number."[200] In both the Sefire and Qumran passages, *br 'n(w)š* has a generic sense, "a human being, someone." The plural form *b[ny] 'nwš* is found in 1QapGen 19:15 and means "some men, or men."[201] In the Aramaic parts of Daniel the plural form *bᵉnê 'ănāšâ* (literally, "sons of man") occurs in 2:38 and 5:21 and is to be translated simply as "men" or "human beings." The determinate or emphatic form alone, *'ănāšâ,* has the generic meaning "human" in 2:43; 4:13; and 7:8. The same form has a collective sense in 4:14 (twice[202]),22 (twice),29 (twice),30; and 5:21; and it means "man" or "men." The indeterminate or absolute form *'ĕnāš* means an individual person or human being in 2:10; 5:5; 6:8,13; and 7:4 (twice). The same form has a collective sense in Ezra 4:11. In Dan 3:10; 5:7; and 6:13 as well as in Ezra 6:11, the phrase *kol-'ĕnāš dî* (literally, "every man who") has a pronominal sense, "whoever" or "anyone who."[203] Finally, it should be noted that in Dan 7:4 there is an occurrence of the preposition *kᵉ* with *'ĕnāš* that is quite similar to the phrase *kᵉbar 'ĕnāš* in 7:13. In 7:4, *ke'ĕnāš* follows *'al-raglayin,* and the words can be translated "on two feet like a man [or human being]."

In view of the manifold occurrences of Aramaic *'ĕnāš/'ănāšâ* and Hebrew *ben 'ādām* (twice) and *'ādām* (twice) in Daniel and its more or less

196 Cf. D. Barthélemy and O. Rickenbacher, *Konkordanz zum hebräischen Sirach,* pp. 4–5, 57–58.

197 W. Eichrodt, *Ezekiel* (tr. C. Quinn), p. 61, writes that Dan 8:17 is derived from Ezek 2:1, a passage in which the title "son of man" expresses "the weakness of the creature to whom the mighty Lord shows such condescension."

198 The preferred reading with one Kenicott MS, "Theodotion," and Vulgate. MT has *bᵉnê 'ādām.*

199 J. A. Fitzmyer, *The Aramaic Inscriptions from Sefîre,* BibOr 19, pp. 98–99, 115. Cf. also F. Vattioni, "La prima menzione aramaica di 'figlio dell' uomo,'" *Biblos-Press* 6/1 (1965), 6–7.

200 Fitzmyer, *The Genesis Apocryphon,* pp. 68–69, 151; *CBQ* 30 (1968), 426.

201 Fitzmyer, *The Genesis Apocryphon,* pp. 58–59.

202 MT has *'ănāsîm* in the second occurrence, but that is a Hebrew plural; *'ănāšâ* should be read. Cf. the lexicons.

203 Colpe, *"ho huios,"* p. 402; F. Maass, "*'ĕnôš,*" *TDOT* 1, p. 347.

stable meaning, it appears surprising that so much has been made of the expression *k^e^bar 'ĕnāš* in 7:13. The avid interest may of course derive from the fact that the New Testament often has Jesus calling himself "the son of man," *ho huios tou anthrōpou.* In Dan 7:13, however, the expression simply means "one in human likeness," or "one like a human being," or "what looked like a human being" (*TEV*); these translations are to be preferred since they allow the possibility of woman being included in the symbol.[204] The Aramaic phrase should not be translated "one like a son of man" (*RSV, JB, NAB*) or "one like the Son of man" (*KJV*), as if the expression were a proper designation or title of a specific historical or mythological or supernatural person of the male sex. Just as the four horrifying and vile beasts (7:3–7) are not real animals but symbols, pure and simple, of the pagan kingdoms of the Babylonians, Medes, Persians, and Greeks, so too the "one in human likeness" is not a real individual, celestial or terrestrial, but is only a symbol of "the holy ones of the Most High," a title given, as we shall see, to the faithful Jews—men, women, and children—who courageously withstood the persecution of Antiochus IV Epiphanes. Hence, there seems to be no mystery as to the meaning and background of the "one in human likeness."

3. *The Alleged Background of* bar 'ĕnāš *in Daniel*

The search, however, for the background of *bar 'ĕnāš* continues. Perhaps it may appear harsh, if indeed not totally unjustified, to describe the quest for an assumed prehistory of this expression as an unusually intricate and often frustrating enterprise which is nevertheless pursued with vigor by an increasing number of like-minded researchers. But it does seem fair to say that the search is an achingly tedious and not overly productive exercise in literary imagination and scholarly ingenuity. And the results have never been convincing for the simple and disconcerting reason that there has hardly been any significant consensus as to where precisely to look for a satisfying solution. E. W. Heaton has appositely remarked that "Daniel has suffered the misfortune of being classed with his second-rate imitators."[205] It seems almost as if the author should be denied any creative talent in composing this apocalypse as something uniquely his own. To be sure, he found some of the images and vocabulary in his biblical sources (e.g. the chaotic sea, the clouds, the "one in human likeness"), but his true genius lay in combining traditional elements with his own ideas into a colorful and imaginative drama of compelling interest.

It is even more regrettable that some have engaged in intensive study of

[204] It should be observed that in 8:15 the angel Gabriel is described as *k^e^mar'ēh-gāber* which clearly refers to a male, and in 9:21 he is called *hā'îš gabrî'ēl,* "the *man* Gabriel."

[205] *The Book of Daniel,* p. 37.

the use of the term "son of man" in the apocalyptic literature after Daniel and then worked out a series of conclusions as to what the expression should mean in Daniel 7. F. Dexinger, for instance, traces the development of "one like a son of man" in Daniel into a Messianic expression particularly in the Parables of Enoch (46:1,3; 47:3; 48:2–6), and in IV Ezra (=II Esdras) 13:1–3,25–26. He admits quite frankly that the term does not refer clearly to a Messianic figure in Daniel. Nevertheless he argues that the writer of Daniel 7 must have held in some way the Messianic views later to be found in Enoch and IV Ezra.[206] Such a methodology is questionable, for it leads to "eisegesis," or reading into a text ideas that arose only at a much later date. In this regard the polite admonition of A. C. Welch should be kept in mind: "It may be wiser to interpret Daniel from his predecessors than from his successors."[207]

But even examining Daniel's predecessors, except the older biblical books, has its pitfalls. For scholars have come up with many possible sources for the phrase "son of man." These are some of the alleged backgrounds: the enthronement festival which then was eschatologized by the author of Daniel 7 (A. Bentzen); the myth of the solar heavenly Man (H. Gressmann); the Iranian rites of enthronement (E. Herzfeld); something similar to the Babylonian enthronement of Marduk (C. H. Kraeling); an ancient solar ritual related to one acted out in Tyre (J. Morgenstern); a royal enthronement festival, patterned on a Canaanite model, in which "the son of man" plays a role that once was Yahweh's (J. A. Emerton).[208] C. Colpe argues vigorously that an Israelite genealogy for the expression is impossible and then proceeds to demolish untenable hypotheses regarding the non-Israelite background of the concept. Thus he eliminates the Middle Persian Gayōmart and Yama-Yima myths as well as the Babylonian Adapa and Ea-Oannes myths. The Egyptian sun god Re, the Jewish Adam Qadmônî (or hā-Rîšôn) and related *anthrōpos ouranios,* and finally

[206] F. Dexinger, *Das Buch Daniel und seine Probleme,* SBS 36, pp. 55–67. Enoch 46, 47, and 48, three chapters of the book's second section (chs. 37–71) called the Parables or Similitudes of Enoch, are to be dated either to the years 94–79 or to 70–64 B.C., according to R. H. Charles, "Book of Enoch," *APOT* 2, p. 171. O. Eissfeldt, *The Old Testament,* p. 619, dates the Parables in the period of Alexander Jannaeus (103–76 B.C.), and on p. 626, dates IV Ezra in the reign of Domitian (A.D. 81–96) or soon after his death. Recently, J. T. Milik, "Problèmes de la littérature hénochique à la lumière des fragments araméens de Qumrân," *HTR* 64 (1971), 373–378, makes a good case that the Parables are a Christian composition in Greek; he dates the work to about the year A.D. 270 or a little later. P. W. Skehan, "Henoch Literature," *NCE, Supplement 1967–1974,* pp. 205–206, who apparently is in sympathy with the Christian provenience of the Parables, nevertheless notes that Milik's "evaluation will no doubt be controverted."

[207] *Visions of the End,* p. 129.

[208] For details and bibliography, cf. F. H. Borsch, *The Son of Man in Myth and History,* pp. 139–143.

Gnosticism's *Urmensch*-redeemer myths are also ruled out.[209] Colpe then defends the Canaanite hypothesis which he modestly labels as possible. First, he provides with scholarly dispassion numerous objections to the hypothesis. A careful scrutiny of the Ugaritic legends, however, has convinced him of

> . . . the mythographical similarity between the relation of the Ancient of Days and Son of Man on the one side and that of El and Baal on the other, which fits into the broader conclusion that older material lives on in the tradition of Israel and Judah. . . . The transfer of dominion from the Ancient of Days to the Son of Man would seem to go back to the wresting of power from an old god by a young one as this was handed down in Canaanite mythology.[210]

Thus far the alleged religio-historical background of the expression in Canaan and elsewhere.

4. *The Interpretation of* bar 'ĕnāš *and* qaddîšê 'elyônîn

The meaning of *kᵉbar 'ĕnāš* is altogether another problem. Colpe speaks of two stages of interpretation. In the first stage, the "one in human likeness" changes from a symbol of eschatological dominion to a representative of "the holy ones of the Most High," an expression which refers to the angelic host; their role in the end time will extend also to earthly empires. In the second stage, "the holy ones of the Most High" become the faithful Jews who were persecuted by Antiochus IV, and the "one in human likeness" is to be taken as a symbol of the Israel of faith which will replace the pagan empires. In both stages of interpretation the "one in human likeness" is a collective person with a saving eschatological function, though he is not directly Messiah or Redeemer.[211]

Taking a position similar to Colpe's first stage of interpretation, J. Coppens argues that in Daniel 7, as it now stands, the "one in human likeness" and "the holy ones of the Most High" refer to angels.[212] This view is not something recent, for others before Coppens have also held it, and it has become one of the common understandings today.[213] A variant of Colpe's

[209] Colpe, *"ho huios,"* pp. 406–415.

[210] Ibid., pp. 415–419.

[211] Ibid., pp. 422–423. On pp. 423–477, Colpe gives a fine survey of the usage and interpretation of the expression "son of man" in Jewish apocalyptic literature and in the New Testament.

[212] "Le Fils d'homme daniélique et les relectures de Dan., vii, 13, dans les apocryphes et les écrits du Nouveau Testament," *ETL* 37 (1961), 5–19; "La vision daniélique du Fils d'homme," *VT* 19 (1969), 171–182.

[213] For example, O. Procksch, "Der Menschensohn als Gottessohn," *Christentum und Wissenschaft* 3 (1927), 429; L. Dequeker, "Daniel vii et les Saints du Très-Haut," *ETL* 36 (1960), 353–392; M. Noth, "The Holy Ones of the Most High," in *The Laws in the Pentateuch and Other Essays* (tr. D. R. Ap-Thomas), pp. 215–228;

two stages of interpretation has been proposed by Z. Zevit who favors the opinion that the "one in human likeness" is the angel Gabriel who represents "the holy ones of the Most High," i.e. the Jewish people in the kingdom of the future.[214] U. B. Müller, however, maintains that the "one in human likeness" symbolizes Michael, who is the guardian angel of Israel (Dan 10:13,21; 12:1). Since the guardian angel represents the nation, the "one in human likeness" comes to symbolize further eschatological Israel.[215] Along somewhat similar lines, J. J. Collins writes in the conclusion of his study of the question:

> We have argued that the "one like a son of man" in Daniel 7 symbolizes primarily the angelic host and its leader [Michael] but also the faithful Jews in so far as they are associated with the heavenly host in the eschatological era. This cannot be established conclusively from the usage of the term "holy ones" in Jewish writings but emerges from the parallelism between the various sections of the Book of Daniel itself. The view that the "son of man" and the holy ones are primarily angelic beings in Daniel corresponds with the expectation of a heavenly savior, accompanied by his host elsewhere in intertestamental and NT works.[216]

Indeed one may not argue from the use of "the holy ones" meaning angels elsewhere in the Old Testament that the term must refer to angels in Daniel 7. True, in most cases *qᵉdôšîm* in the MT and *hagioi* in the deuterocanonical books of the Old Testament are angels.[217] But in Ps 34:10, which is earlier than Daniel, the *qᵉdôšîm* are certainly men as are the *hagioi* in Tobit 12:15 (Codex B tradition only), Wis 18:9, and I Macc 1:46, all three of which are some years later than Daniel. "The holy ones" also appear in the Pseudepigrapha and Qumran literature, and the expression refers to men as well as angels.[218] Thus while it is antecedently possible that "the holy ones of the Most High" in Daniel 7 are angels, only a careful study of the context, rhetoric, and intent of the whole chapter will enable one to determine whether or not angels are in fact

---

L. Dequeker, "The 'Saints of the Most High' in Qumran and Daniel," *OTS* 18 (1973), 108–187; and B. Lindars, "Re-Enter the Apocalyptic Son of Man," *NTS* 22 (1975), 55–56.

[214] Z. Zevit, "The Structure and Individual Elements of Daniel 7," *ZAW* 80 (1968), 385–396.

[215] U. B. Müller, *Messias und Menschensohn in jüdischen Apokalypsen und in der Offenbarung des Johannes,* SNT 6, pp. 19–60. Cf. also W. Wifall, "Son of Man—A Pre-Davidic Social Class?" *CBQ* 37 (1975), 339.

[216] "The Son of Man and the Saints of the Most High in the Book of Daniel," *JBL* 93 (1974), 66.

[217] C. H. W. Brekelmans, "The Saints of the Most High and Their Kingdom," *OTS* 14 (1965), 307–310, lists and examines all the occurrences of "the holy ones" in the Old Testament.

[218] Cf. ibid., pp. 310–325, for lists of occurrences and comments; see also G. F. Hasel, "The Identity of 'The Saints of the Most High' in Daniel 7," *Bib* 56 (1975), 176–185.

meant. It is precisely an investigation of this type that argues strongly against the meaning of angels in the disputed texts.

The first major difficulty with the opinion that "the holy ones of the Most High" are angels or Michael together with the heavenly host and not primarily the people of Israel is that Daniel 7 would then have virtually no meaning or relevance for the addressees of the book, viz. the disenfranchised Jews who were being hounded by Antiochus IV, "the small horn . . . that sprouted up" (vss. 8,11,20–21,24). This basic consideration appears noticeably absent in the studies consulted which plead for such a view. Yet this consideration is crucial if one is to assume, as one should, that this apocalypse was composed and circulated in order to console and encourage the suffering Jews to remain steadfast and faithful. Thus, if we substitute "the angels" wherever "the holy ones (of the Most High)" appear, we shall see that there would be small comfort for the persecuted community to be promised that "[the angels] will receive the kingdom and possess it forever" (vs. 18); and that "dominion was given to [the angels]. Thus the time came when [the angels] took possession of the kingdom" (vs. 22). "The kingship and the dominion and the grandeur of all the kingdoms under the heavens will be given to [the people of the angels, or angelic people]. Their royal rule will last forever, and all dominions will serve and obey it" (vs. 27). Moreover, the Jews on hearing or reading the apocalypse would surely have been baffled by vss. 21–22, "that horn [= Antiochus IV] waged war against [the angels] and was prevailing against them until the Ancient One arrived"; and by vs. 25, "He [Antiochus] will utter words against the Most High, and [the angels] he will devastate, planning to change the feast days and the law; they will be handed over to him for a year, two years, and half a year."

The second objection to the theory that the "one in human likeness" symbolizes Michael and the angels, i.e. the holy ones of the Most High, as well as the loyal Jews, is that the final redactor, and the author before him, must then be judged guilty of unusually careless rhetoric and of a deplorable use of symbolism. Since, as is generally agreed, the four hideous beasts in 7:3–7 symbolize only the four pagan empires, "the little horn" symbolizes Antiochus IV, and the "Ancient One" (vss. 9,13,22) symbolizes the God of Israel, then we must assume that those responsible for this apocalypse meant each of these symbols to have a one-to-one relationship with the respective reality being symbolized. Thus, to coin two new (but, I think, patently descriptive) terms, unireferential symbols were employed in this chapter, and not multireferential symbols which can have more than a one-to-one relationship.[219] Since the four ferocious beasts, the little

[219] I avoid P. Wheelwright's terms, "steno-symbol" and "tensive symbol," which he discusses in *Metaphor and Reality,* p. 94, because these expressions, legitimate though they may be in the author's literary theory, have given rise to some dispute as

horn, and the Ancient One are unireferential symbols with referents that are easily recognizable, then the "one in human likeness," symbol of "the holy ones of the Most High," should also bear, for reasons of rhetorical consistency, a one-to-one relationship to its referent which would also be readily identifiable by the original audience for whom the apocalypse was composed. If this analysis is correct, the "one in human likeness" cannot at the same time symbolize Michael, who in turn symbolizes his heavenly cohorts, i.e. "the holy ones of the Most High," and then the historical Jews as well. Rather the "one in human likeness" must be a unireferential symbol of only "the holy ones of the Most High," i.e. the historically recognizable Jews who suffered and died rather than apostatize.

There remains to be discussed the suggested parallel between the angel imagery in the apocalypse found in section 4 of I Enoch 83–90, often called the Book of Dreams, and the contested symbolism of Daniel 7. But first a brief account of scholarly opinions regarding the date of this portion of I Enoch. If R. H. Charles[220] is correct in dating the section before the death of Judas Maccabaeus (160 B.C.), the work is contemporary with the Book of Daniel. O Eissfeldt,[221] however, calls attention to the differing opinions as to whether the lambs and goat-kids with horns in 90:9–16 refer only to Judas and John Hyrcanus (134–103 B.C.), or also to Alexander Jannaeus (103–76 B.C.). If the former be true, the work is to be dated under Hyrcanus; if the latter, under Jannaeus. More recently, J. T. Milik[222] has argued that the work was composed a few weeks or months after the battle of Beth-zur (II Macc 11:1–12), which took place at the beginning of 164 B.C. This date would coincide with the commonly accepted dating of the publication of Daniel. For the purposes of our discussion we will accept the dating of Charles and Milik, a dating which makes the Book of Dreams a potentially important source for determining the meaning of the symbolism in Daniel 7.

In the second dream-vision (Enoch 85–90), the Israelites are symbolized by "good" animals, i.e. the patriarchs by bulls (e.g. Noah in 89:1) and the faithful of later times by sheep (e.g. 89:68); the Gentiles are symbolized by wild beasts and birds of prey, e.g. the ancient Egyptians by wolves (89:13) and the Egyptians under the Ptolemies by vultures and kites (90:2–4). Fallen angels are symbolized by stars (86:1–6); angels

---

to their precise meaning and applicability in the exegesis of biblical texts. Cf., for example, the articles by N. Perrin, "Eschatology and Hermeneutics: Reflections on Method in the Interpretation of the New Testament," *JBL* 93 (1974), 3–14; and J. J. Collins, "The Symbolism of Transcendence in Jewish Apocalyptic," *BR* 19 (1974), 5–22, especially pp. 15–17.

220 Charles, "Book of Enoch," *APOT* 2, p. 171. All my references to and translations of I Enoch 83–90 are from Charles, *APOT* 2, pp. 248–260.

221 Eissfeldt, *The Old Testament,* p. 619.

222 Milik, *HTR* 64 (1971), 358–359.

who proved faithless in the discharge of their God-given trust, by shepherds (89:59–65); and the good angels, by men (87:2–3). This symbolism of men for angels has been brought forth as support for the view that the "one in human likeness" in Daniel 7 represents an angel, presumably Michael, who then symbolizes the angelic host who are "the holy ones of the Most High."[223]

A closer look at the Book of Dreams, however, reveals a confusing use of symbolism. In fact, R. H. Charles writes in his introduction to chs. 85–90: "The symbolism is . . . sometimes dropped, and the same symbol may vary in meaning."[224] Here are some examples. In 86:6, men are not referred to as animals but are simply called "the children of the earth"; and here men do not symbolize angels as elsewhere in the work. In 89:1, we read of Noah: "He was born a bull and became a man, and built for himself a great vessel and dwelt thereon." Presumably when the text says Noah became a man, it does not intend to suggest that he became an angel. In 89:6, the result of the Deluge was that "all the oxen and elephants and camels and asses [=sinners of all stripes] sank to the bottom with all the animals." It is obvious in this context that the expression "all the animals" does not symbolize people but simply means beasts of the field. In 89:66, "the wild boars" are the Edomites; but in 89:72, "the wild boars" are Samaritans. In 90:2, the vultures and kites symbolize the Egyptians; but the same birds have a different symbolism in vs. 13 of that chapter. Charles writes: "The symbolism becomes looser here, and the 'vultures' and 'kites' are no longer restricted to the Graeco-Egyptians as in *v.* 2. . . . Perhaps here the vultures and kites are Ammon and Moab."[225] The confused and confusing symbolism of the Book of Dreams must be classified as multireferential symbolism of a rather pedestrian sort. The author of Daniel 7 has none of that confusion in his vision or in his rhetoric which employs consistent and straightforward unireferential symbols whose referents are clearly recognizable. It seems most implausible, therefore, that the "one in human likeness" can be interpreted as an angel on the basis of parallelism with the human beings that appear as angels in the Book of Dreams.

Nor does it appear convincing to argue for angels in Dan 7:13 on the basis of Dan 8:15 where an angel is called "a manlike figure" (*kᵉmar'ēh-gāber*).[226] Since in the very next verse, the figure is explicitly identified as Gabriel, the author of ch. 8 is using a clear-cut unireferential symbol about which there can be no ambiguity. The same is true of Dan 9:21 which speaks of "the man(like) Gabriel" (*hā'îš gabrî'ēl*). In 10:5, Daniel sees "a man clothed in linen" (*'îš-'eḥād lābûš baddîm*); a similar expression

223 Cf. Collins, *JBL* 93 (1974), 61–62.
224 Charles, "Book of Enoch," *APOT* 2, p. 250.
225 Ibid., p. 258.
226 Collins, *JBL* 93 (1974), 61, argues in this fashion.

occurs in 12:6–7 (*lā/hā'îš lᵉbûš habbaddîm*), clearly a reference to the same figure as in 10:5. The author borrowed this description from Ezek 9:2,3,11, and 10:2,6,7, where the figure so clothed is patently an angel. Moreover, the person in Dan 10:5–6 is described as wearing "a belt of pure gold around his waist. His body was like beryl, his face shone like lightning, his eyes were like flaming torches, his arms and feet had the gleam of burnished bronze, and his voice sounded like the roar of a multitude." Although the men who were with Daniel did not see this dazzling sight, "they were overwhelmed with great fear, so that they fled and hid themselves" (10:7). And Daniel himself says: "On seeing this great sight, no strength remained in me, and I turned deathly pale" (10:8). Thus there is no mistaking the man in linen for anyone other than an angel. The beginning of the man's speech makes it even more certain that an angelic figure is being portrayed: "I *have* now *been sent* with news for you. . . . From the first day you made up your mind to gain understanding by afflicting yourself before God, *your prayer was heard;* and that is why *I started out*" (10:11–12). It is noteworthy that the angels in chs. 8, 9, and 10–12 are easily recognized as such. In ch. 7, however, the "one in human likeness" and "the holy ones of the Most High" are in no way recognizable as angels from what is said about them.

Yet, interestingly enough, angels do appear in the heavenly scenario of judgment in Daniel 7. "The Ancient One" is served by "thousands of thousands" and attended by "myriads of myriads" (7:10). Without the slightest doubt, the figures here are angels. Then in 7:11–12, the beasts (=the *earthly* kingdoms of the pagans) are deprived of their dominion. Next the "one in human likeness" appears on the scene "with the clouds of the heavens" (7:13). Now unlike the numberless angelic attendants who in 7:10 *are already present* at God's throne, the "one in human likeness" *arrives* where the Ancient One is enthroned and *is brought* into the divine presence (7:13). The text continues:

> Then to him was given dominion—glory and kingship.
> Every nation, tribe, and tongue must serve him;
> His dominion is to be everlasting, never passing away;
> his kingship never to be destroyed (7:14).

Daniel is duly troubled by what he has witnessed, and so he writes: "I went up to one of those who were standing by, and I asked him what all this really meant" (7:16). "One of those standing by" is obviously a reference to one of the angels in attendance at God's throne (7:10), for he is privy to the divine plan which is about to unfold. The angel explains: "These great beasts, four in number, mean that four kingdoms will rise up on the earth. But then the holy ones of the Most High will receive the kingdom and possess it forever. . . ." These verses prove that the "one in human likeness" is a symbol of "the holy ones of the Most High." Then Daniel adds:

> But I wished to make certain about the fourth beast . . . and about the ten horns on its head, and the other that sprouted up, . . . the horn with eyes in it and a mouth speaking arrogantly [=Antiochus IV), which was seen surpassing its fellows. As I watched, that horn waged war against the holy ones and was prevailing over them until the Ancient One arrived. Then the court sat in judgment, and dominion was given to the holy ones of the Most High. Thus the time came when the holy ones took possession of the kingdom (7:19–22).

Among other things the angel explains that "He [=Antiochus] will utter words against the Most High, and the holy ones of the Most High he will devastate, planning to change the feast days and the law; they will be handed over to him for a year, two years, and half a year" (7:25). If "the holy ones (of the Most High)" were to be understood as angels, then Antiochus is being said to fight against the angels, and to change the feast days and the law of the angels, and to have control over the angels for three and a half years. It hardly seems plausible that the author of Daniel 7 meant to imply that Antiochus was capable of such activities, not to mention the curiosity that angels would have feast days that could be changed by a mere mortal. But Antiochus did fight against the Jews because of their adherence to the Mosaic Law, and he did abolish the celebration of the Jewish feast days, and the Jews were in his control for some three years (I Macc 1:41–63; 4:26–55). Thus "the holy ones of the Most High" must refer to the faithful men, women, and children who were being persecuted by the Seleucid tyrant.

Corroboration for this exegesis comes from what is said in Dan 7:27: "Then the kingship and the dominion and the grandeur of all the kingdoms under the heavens will be given to the people of the holy ones of the Most High." The Aramaic expression *'am qaddîšê 'elyônîn* is normally understood as an epexegetical or appositional construct chain—"the people, i.e. the holy ones of the Most High," a meaning that is commonly accepted by scholars. The Hexaplaric witnesses to Theodotion-Daniel, 61′ (= 62–147), have *tǭ laǭ hagiois hypsistou* (all other MSS omit *tǭ laǭ*). This being the case, the angelic interpretation of "the holy ones" is further weakened. The same is true if one translates the expression as a hendiadys, "the holy people of the Most High," as in the Peshiṭta, *'ammâ qaddîšâ dam^{e}raymâ,* and in the LXX, *laǭ hagiǭ hypsistou.* A parallel can be seen in 8:24 where the Hebrew phrase *'am q^{e}dôšîm* can also be translated as a hendiadys, "the holy people." An analogous case of hendiadys (but of a later date) that would support our exegesis is Ps 149:9 in the Qumran Psalter, in which there is an interpolation after *ḥăsîdāyw* of *lbny yśr'l 'm qwdšw,*[227] "to the children of Israel, his holy people" (literally, "the people of his holiness"). Grammatically, of course, it is possible to construe the Aramaic expression as a possessive construct chain, in which case the meaning would be "the people of [i.e. belonging to] the holy ones of the Most High."[228] But that meaning is not at all probable in view of the fact that "the holy ones" in 7:18 and 22 (twice) receive the kingdom and dominion exactly as do "the people of the holy ones of the Most High" in vs. 27. Hence, it seems fair to conclude that "the holy ones" and "the people of the holy ones" are the same individuals.

One final objection to our interpretation needs to be considered. In a lengthy section of his commentary on Heb 2:6, G. W. Buchanan has argued that Judas the Maccabee was the "one in human likeness" in Daniel 7.[229] He writes of Judas:

> To him was given the dominion and glory and a kingdom (Dan 7:14). His was the rule that followed the rule of Antiochus IV Epiphanes, the last remnant of the fourth beast, over the saints of the Most High after the temple had been cleansed and sacrifice restored (Dan 7:23–27). Although he was not officially a king, he was "*like* a son of man," which may have meant that he was *like* a king.[230]

Buchanan, who dates the Book of Daniel *after* the rededication of the Temple and the restoration of worship in Jerusalem, is of the opinion that the whole book is centered around the Maccabean victory over the Syrians. The first objection to this theory is that the book was written *before,* and not after, the rededication. The argument for this date of composition is as follows: (*a*) the author of ch. 9 predicted that the "abomination of desolation" (9:27; 11:31; 12:11; cf. 8:13) would remain in the Temple three and a half years (9:27; cf. 7:25 and 12:7); (*b*) as a matter of fact, the Temple was cleansed only three years and eight days after the

[227] Published by J. A. Sanders, *The Psalms Scroll of Qumrân Cave 11 (11QPs*[a]*)*, DJD 4, p. 47. Sanders, p. 9, assigns the writing of the scroll to the first half of the first century A.D.

[228] Such is the view of, among others, Dequeker, *OTS* 18 (1973), 179–187; and Collins, *JBL* 93 (1974), 62. V. S. Poythress, "The Holy Ones of the Most High in Daniel vii," *VT* 26 (1976), 210–213, who agrees with our interpretation, offers some good arguments against the views of Dequeker and Collins.

[229] *To the Hebrews,* AB 36, pp. 42–48. H. Sahlin, "Antiochus IV. Epiphanes und Judas Mackabäus: Einige Gesichtspunkte zum Verständnis des Danielbuches," *ST* 23 (1969), 41–68—not mentioned by Buchanan—also holds Judas to be the "son of man." Because of a misunderstanding of what Jerome wrote in his Commentary on Daniel (*PL* 25, col. 533) it has often been said, erroneously, that Porphyry considered Judas to be the "son of man." Actually, Porphyry maintained that the "son of man" was merely a symbol of "the holy ones of the Most High" who were the Maccabees in general; cf. P. M. Casey, "Porphyry and the Origin of the Book of Daniel," *JTS* N.S. 27 (1976), 20–23, for a fine discussion of this issue.

[230] *To the Hebrews,* p. 48.

profanation; (*c*) since the book did not give the exact timetable, it seems an inescapable conclusion that it was written before the reconsecration. The second objection to Buchanan's hypothesis is that the Book of Daniel is considered to be a pacifistic manifesto of primitive Ḥasidism.[231] As such, it would hardly glorify Judas or his military successes, which it calls "a little help" (11:34), a phrase that accurately conveys the singularly unenthusiastic attitude of the sacred author toward armed intervention and military prowess. The book has no sympathy at all for the violent and often cruel resistance of Mattathias and his son Judas Maccabee. The activities of these leaders are described in I Macc 2:44–46:

> They [the Jewish resistance force] gathered an army and struck down sinners in their anger and lawbreakers in their wrath, and the survivors fled to the Gentiles for safety. Mattathias and his friends went about and tore down the pagan altars; they also forcibly circumcised any uncircumcised boys whom they found in the territory of Israel.[232]

G. von Rad correctly observes:

> Without any doubt, the writer of Daniel sides with those who endure persecution rather than those who take up arms against it, and in so doing he is far removed from the Maccabees and their policy of active resistance; their large following is actually suspect in his eyes.[233]
> only being true to his own basic conviction that what must be will be. He is

Thus we may conclude that the expression *kᵉbar 'ĕnāš,* "one in human likeness," does not in itself point to an angel or to a mysterious figure of the past or present or to a figure to appear in the distant eschatological future. Rather the expression is nothing more or less than a symbol of "the holy ones of the Most High," who are, as we have seen and as many commentators agree,[234] the faithful Israelites to be rewarded for their

[231] True, there were some Ḥasidim who did take up arms and join the Maccabean forces (I Macc 2:42); Judas is even called their leader in II Macc 14:6. But the Ḥasidim responsible for the Book of Daniel belonged, in the words of Montgomery, p. 87, to "the principled pacifistic wing of the party." Cf. also Pfeiffer, *Introduction to the Old Testament,* pp. 772–781; Delcor, pp. 15–19; and Hengel, *Judaism and Hellenism* (tr. J. Bowden), vol. 1, pp. 175–180 with notes in vol. 2, pp. 116–120.

[232] Cf. also Josephus *Antiquities* xii 6, 2–4 (vol. 7, pp. 142–147, in the LCL edition).

[233] *Old Testament Theology* (tr. D. M. G. Stalker), vol. 2, p. 315.

[234] For example, Driver, pp. 102–108; Montgomery, pp. 317–324; F. Nötscher, *Daniel,* Echter-Bibel 6, pp. 39–41; Heaton, pp. 182–186; S. Mowinckel, *He That Cometh* (tr. G. W. Anderson), pp. 349–350; S. B. Frost, "Daniel," *IDB* 1, p. 762; G. Rinaldi, pp. 106–113; D. S. Russell, *Method and Message of Jewish Apocalyptic,* pp. 326–327; Brekelmans, *OTS* 14 (1965), 305–329; R. Hanhart, "'Die Heiligen des Höchsten' (Dan 7, 21.25)," VTSup 16 (1967), 90–101; Delcor, pp. 39, 153–167; H. L. Ginsberg, "Daniel, Book of," *EncJud,* vol. 5, col. 1280; A.-M. Dubarle, "Prophètes d'Israël: Daniel," *DBSup,* vol. 6, pp. 743–747; A. Lenglet, "La structure littéraire de Daniel 2–7," *Bib* 53 (1972), 175–179; Hasel, *Bib* 56 (1975), 173–192; and Poythress, *VT* 26 (1976), 208–213.

steadfastness in the face of persecution and martyrdom. There is nothing strange or unusual in using this expression as a symbol of Israel. Indeed the Semitic mentality was fond of personifying the people or a portion thereof, as H. W. Robinson has amply demonstrated in his well-known studies, "The Hebrew Conception of Corporate Personality" (1935), and "The Group and the Individual in Israel" (1937).[235] Among examples of personification are the so-called "I-Psalms" (e.g. Ps 44, especially vss. 5–7), the Servant Songs (Isa 42:1–4; 49:1–6; 50:4–9; 52:13–53:12), and the Testament of Jacob in Gen 49:1–27 where each tribal head represents the respective tribe and not the individual person named.

In Psalm 8, the Hebrew term *ben 'ādām* also has a collective sense:

> What is man that you should be mindful of him;
>   or the son of man that you should care for him?
> You have made him little less than the angels,
>   and crowned him with glory and honor.
> You have given him rule over the works of your hands,
>   putting all things under his feet (vss. 5–7).

It will be observed at once that in vs. 5 "the son of man," or more exactly "a human being," is in synonymous parallelism with "man" (*'ĕnôš*) and therefore simply means man as a group or men and women in general in their lowliness. It is also noteworthy that "the son of man" is contrasted with the angels. It is quite possible that the writer of Dan 7:13 was conscious of the phrase "the son of man" in Psalm 8, for in this psalm and in Genesis 1 the status of man and woman in God's design is represented. If this be so, then we may conclude in the words of E. W. Heaton that the

> vision of the subjection of the beasts to the man-like figure with the clouds, that is, of the subjection of the kingdoms of the world to the true Israel, represented for [the author] nothing less than a new creation, the final redemption of God's People and the accomplishment of his aboriginal purpose.[236]

The author of Daniel 7 also had at hand Ps 80:18–20 which describes the plea of oppressed Israel for deliverance and restoration:

> May your help be with the man of your right hand,
>   with the son of man whom you yourself made strong.
> Then we will no more withdraw from you;
>   give us new life, and we will call upon your name.
> O LORD of hosts, restore us;
>   if your face shine upon us, then we shall be safe.

[235] Both essays are reprinted in *Corporate Personality in Ancient Israel,* FBBS 11.
[236] Heaton, p. 186.

It is probable that Dan 7:13 was composed in the light of Psalm 80 because the distress of Israel in the psalm is similar to the plight of the Jews in Daniel. Indeed, as C. H. Dodd appropriately remarks, "There is a clear analogy with the 'Son of Man' of Ps. lxxx and Dan. vii, which speak of Israel, under the similitude of a human figure, humiliated into insignificance until visited by God and raised to glory."[237]

Another passage the author of Daniel 7 probably had in mind is Job 25:4–6:

> How can a man (*'ĕnôš*) be just in God's sight,
> or how can any woman's child (*yᵉlûd 'iššâ*) be innocent?
> Behold, even the moon is not bright
> and the stars are not clear in his sight.
> How much less man (*'ĕnôš*), who is but a maggot,
> the son of man (*ben 'ādām*), who is only a worm?

The relationship between this text and Daniel 7 suggests that the "one in human likeness," symbol of "the holy ones," will be granted an eternal kingdom despite his lowly estate and past sins. This interpretation is bolstered by the sentiments expressed in the interpolated prayer in ch. 9:

> We have sinned, acted wickedly, and done evil; we have rebelled and turned aside from your commandments and your laws (vs. 5). . . . All Israel, not listening to your voice, transgressed your law and went astray; so the sworn malediction written in the Torah of God's servant Moses has been poured out upon us, because we sinned against you (vs. 11). . . . Incline your ear, O my God, and listen; open your eyes and see our devastated city, which bears your name; for not on our own merits but on your great compassion do we rely in presenting our petition before you. O Lord, hear; O Lord, pardon; O Lord, be attentive and act! For your own sake, O my God, do not delay; for your city and your people bear your name (vss. 18–19).

A text parallel to Job 25:4–6 is Job 15:14–16:

> What is man (*'ĕnôš*) that he should be blameless,
> one born of woman (*yᵉlûd 'iššâ*) that he should be righteous?
> If in his holy ones God places no confidence,
> and if the heavens are not clean in his sight,
> How much less so is the abominable, the corrupt:
> man (*'îš*), who drinks in iniquity like water!

If the author of Daniel 7 had in mind Job 15:14–16 as well as Job 25:4–6, then more support is given to our exegesis that the "one in human likeness" symbolizes the faithful Jews, and not an angel (Gabriel or

[237] *According to the Scriptures*, p. 117.

Michael) who then symbolizes the rest of the angels who in turn symbolize the nation Israel. For in Job 15:15, "his holy ones" (*qᵉdôšāw*), who in this context certainly are angels, are placed in sharp contrast with man who is prone to sin and evil.

Reinforcement for our interpretation comes also from a study of Daniel 2 and 7, which (like chs. 3 and 6, and chs. 4 and 5) are generally recognized as being related. In chs. 2 and 7, mention is made, in symbol, of the four successive pagan empires, the last of which will be succeeded by the everlasting kingdom of God. It seems plausible, therefore, that the author who wrote about the "one in human likeness," symbolizing "the holy ones of the Most High," who will receive "the kingdom and the dominion and the grandeur of all the kingdoms under heaven," and whose "royal rule will last forever" (7:27), had in mind the same ones (i.e. the loyal Jews) who are symbolized by "the stone that struck the statue and became a great mountain and filled all the earth" (2:34–35). Now just as the statue symbolizes the four pagan kingdoms (2:37–43), so the stone symbolizes the kingdom "that will never be destroyed. . . . It will crush and put an end to all those other kingdoms, while it itself will stand forever, just as . . . [the] stone . . . cut from the mountain" (2:44–45). It is to be noted that the statue and the stone are both unireferential symbols, with a one-to-one relationship to their respective referents. Since this is so, the case for interpreting the "one in human likeness" and "the holy ones of the Most High" as multireferential symbols both of the angels (or Michael and the angelic host) and of the people of God as well, is further weakened. For there is no indication in ch. 2 that the eternal kingdom spoken of has anything to do with angels or with their leader.

The resurrection passage in Daniel 12 also argues against interpreting the "one in human likeness" and "the holy ones" as angels:

> At that time your people will be rescued, every one of them who is found written in the book. Many of those who sleep in the dirt of the earth will awake; some will live forever, while others will become everlasting objects of contempt and abhorrence. But those who act wisely [*hammaśkîlîm*] will shine brightly like the brilliance of the firmament; and those who lead the multitude to righteousness [*maṣdîqê hārabbîm*] will shine like the stars forever and ever (vss. 1c–3).

Regardless of the extent of the good and the wicked to receive retribution —a question that is hotly disputed (see COMMENT: DETAILED on 12:1–3)—there is no doubt that the author affirmed that the loyal faithful of his day would experience resurrection and eternal life (vs. 2). Presumably these individuals are the same group, "the holy ones," who in ch. 7 will receive kingship and dominion. Now in 12:3 a specified number of the faithful are singled out for special glory in the resurrection. Although it is possible that the verse refers to two different classes of heroes (i.e. *hammaśkîlîm* and *maṣdîqê hārabbîm*[238]), it seems more probable in view of 11:33,35 and the present context that only one specific class of people is being described under two different titles.[239] These outstanding persons will have a greater degree of glory and will even share in the splendor of the angels, if, as one may concede, the stars here symbolize the angelic host. But of the faithful in general, vs. 2 simply states that they "will awake . . . and live forever." Nothing at all is affirmed of their elevation to the angelic ranks.[240] This being the case, it appears quite implausible that angels are meant in ch. 7 which also speaks of the group, viz. "the holy ones," who are to receive the kingdom. Put differently, ch. 7 speaks of the faithful only as a group; ch. 12 speaks of them as a group in vs. 2, but of special persons within the group in vs. 3. Only the latter, who do not appear as such in ch. 7, are said to be associated with the angels.

5. *Conclusion*

It should be stated that the interpretation proposed here of the "one in human likeness" and "the holy ones of the Most High" is the most natural and obvious one, and seems to do greatest justice to the genius of the author of Daniel 7 who, though quite at home in the Old Testament, displayed great originality and ability in his selection and use of traditional materials.[241] Indeed, since he chose four horrifying and monstrous *beasts* as symbols of the four world-empires, doubtless he thought it most appropriate to symbolize the members of the kingdom of God by the figure of "one in *human* likeness." In so doing, he created a striking and deliberate contrast between the four immense beasts which emerge from the great *sea* (7:2–3), symbol of chaos and nothingness in the *Urzeit* (cf. Gen 1:1–2), and the "one in human likeness" who in the *Endzeit* comes "with the *clouds* of heaven," clouds being one of the usual accompaniments of a theophany (e.g. Exod 13:21; 19:16; 20:21; Deut 5:22; I Kings 8:10; Sir 45:5). As Moses, "whom the LORD knew face to face" (Deut 34:10), "passed into the midst of the cloud" (Exod 24:18), so too the "one in human likeness," the Israel of faith, comes "with the clouds of the

[238] This view is favored by Charles, p. 330; and by Jeffery, p. 543.

[239] This view is favored by Montgomery, p. 471; Heaton, p. 248; Plöger, p. 171; and Delcor, pp. 255–256.

[240] To support the interpretation that "the holy ones of the Most High" are angels in Daniel 7, Collins, *JBL* 93 (1974), 57–58, lumps together the faithful in general of 12:2 with the special class of the faithful in 12:3. It is only the latter who can be said to have a share in the special glory of the angels, if indeed the stars here do symbolize the angels.

[241] Montgomery, pp. 323–324, aptly observes: "We must allow [the chapter] its own originality and do justice to the simply but finely limned features of the drama without thinking that every detail is a painful borrowing on the part of a second-hand *littérateur*."

heavens" and arrives at the throne of the Ancient One. Then the "one in human likeness" is brought into the presence of the Ancient One (7:13d–e). The Aramaic words here, *q^{e}dāmôhî haqr^{e}bûhî,* "he was brought into his presence,"[242] are the same ones used in the Aramaic Story of Ahiqar, col. 4, line 50, *qrbtk qdm snḥ'ryb mlk',*[243] "I brought you into the presence of King Sennacherib." As J. A. Montgomery points out, "The idea is that of a royal audience."[244] Thus the "one in human likeness" did not *descend* or *come from* God as if he had been an angel in the divine presence, but rather he *ascended* or *came to* God and *was brought* into his presence.[245] In effect, the author is saying that "the holy ones of the Most High," faithful Israel responsive to the demands of the reign of God even in the face of their present humiliation and suffering, will come into the divine presence in order to receive everlasting dominion in holiness, nobility, and grandeur, and so will replace the depraved, brutal, and vile kingdoms of the pagan world which were opposed to the reign of God and to his holy people.

[242] The verb *haqr^{e}bû* is third person plural perfect active, but the passive is the correct translation of the Aramaic idiom. Other examples of this idiom occur in Dan 2:13,18,30; 3:4; 4:4,13,22,28; 7:5,12.

[243] A. Cowley, *Aramaic Papyri of the Fifth Century B.C.*, p. 213.

[244] Montgomery, p. 304.

[245] Along the same lines, cf. M. Delcor, "Les sources du chapitre vii de Daniel," *VT* 18 (1968), 305.

XIV. THE BOOK OF DANIEL TODAY

The bulk of the present Introduction and indeed of the rest of this volume is concerned with such questions as authorship and date of the Book of Daniel, literary genres, historical background, textual criticism, life-setting, and the like. An understanding of these questions is important, not to say vital, for if we wish to have some idea of what the book can mean for us today we must first learn what its authors intended to convey to its original audience in the historical context of the second century B.C. But knowing the contents of the book and the when, where, how, why, and for whom it was composed does not necessarily give much of a clue as to what the book can mean for readers today even when they are disposed to accept that God's word in the Bible has relevance for believers of every age and place.

In fact, several of the stories in the first part of the Book of Daniel (chs. 1–6) appear mildly incredible or even childish—something along the lines of a glorified fairy tale which ends with the *de rigueur* righting of all wrongs and for the virtuous the inevitable "they lived happily ever after." But there is one notable difference. Nebuchadnezzar, Belshazzar, and Darius the Mede, the pagan antagonists of these narratives, and Hananiah, Mishael, and Azariah, three of the Jewish heroes, do not even have the merit of widespread notoriety enjoyed by, say, Snow White and the Seven Dwarfs, or Little Red Riding Hood and the Big Bad Wolf. Yet one sees almost at once that the stories in Daniel and the exotic and often bizarre apocalypses (chs. 7–12) convey something more significant than any of Grimm's Fairy Tales.

In reading the Book of Daniel one senses that the work was composed in response to some of the pressing questions men and women have always asked themselves, especially in moments of adversity: What is the meaning of the human enterprise? What sense can evil and suffering possibly have? If God is all just and all powerful, why does he remain silent and inactive when men, women, and children suffer unjustly? What lies in store for people after death? If there is retribution for a person's moral decisions, when and where will it take place? Is there more to human existence than tending to one's needs and attaining a place in the world? If God has spoken to men and women in Israel's history, what does that truth imply for the believer today? In view of the chaotic forces at large in human history, can one seriously affirm that God exists, or, perhaps more pointedly, that God really cares about what happens to people?

That the Book of Daniel was published as resistance literature for a persecuted religious minority of the second century B.C. is beyond dispute. What seems equally clear is that the book provided for those afflicted Jews consoling and encouraging answers to many of the above questions. All of which brings us to ask some further questions: Does the Book of Daniel have any relevance for an aimless and practically non-religious majority of today who are looking for something more out of life than the satisfaction of material, psychological, and emotional needs? Does authenticity as a human being require at times the price of substantial risk as in Daniel 1, or of mortal peril as in Daniel 2, 3, and 6? Is it not a bit much to expect one to lose one's most precious possessions, including personal freedom and even life itself, in order to gain oneself as a person at the deepest level of one's reality and being? In answer to these questions it may be suggested that the situation which prompted the publication of the Book of Daniel in the second century B.C. may be viewed as a kind of universal paradigm of the basic crisis facing men and women of goodwill in every age and place. Each person has the radical choice of accepting or rejecting the demands of God as constitutive of a truly human and humane existence. Benign neutrality is impossible. The refusal to make a decision is itself a decision—the worst possible. The man or woman who in faith lives by God's declared will when other options are available and perhaps more immediately satisfying already has a clear idea as to how to answer these questions. Such a person becomes, like Daniel, a signal and symbol of transcendence for many who in quiet desperation concern themselves chiefly, if not exclusively, with the needs and cares of a this-worldly existence that hopes for nothing beyond the grave.

The six edifying stories in the first part of the Book of Daniel are all concerned with some kind of ordeal that is occasioned by the pagans and that Daniel and his faithful companions become involved in. In each case, the Jewish heroes win out at the climactic moment, thanks to the spectacular intervention of God. To which a person today could respond that it would be easy and indeed pragmatic to live by the demands of God if only everything turned out well in the end. But the authors and readers of the Book of Daniel were not naïve. They were painfully aware that fidelity to the Covenant did not always assure personal well-being or deliverance from unjust suffering and untimely death. As a matter of fact, many Jews of that time were exemplary in the observance of their religious practices, "preferring a glorious death to a life of defilement" (II Macc 6:19), but for them there were no dramatic rescues by God. Two Jewish women, for example, who in keeping with the Law of Moses had their children circumcised were paraded through the streets with their babies hanging at their breasts and were "thrown down from the top of the city wall" (II Macc 6:10). Other pious Jews who had gathered together in caves to observe the Sabbath in secret were swiftly punished by being burned to death (II Macc 6:11). Real fire really burns. And the authors of the Book of Daniel and the original readers knew that fact of life. Yet in Daniel 3, Shadrach, Meshach, and Abednego, who had defied King Nebuchadnezzar's order to worship the golden statue he set up, were preserved unharmed from the raging flames of the furnace. "The fire had not had any power over the bodies of these men; the hair of their head was not singed, and their clothes were not affected; not even a smell of fire came from them" (3:27[*94*]).

The affirmation of faith the three stalwart Jews made in response to the pagan king's sneering question, "What god is there who is able to save you from my hand?" (3:15), is the key to understanding this narrative as well as the five others: "There is no need for us to give you an answer to that question. If there is a God able to save us, such as our God whom we serve, he will save us from the white-hot furnace and from your hand, O king. But even if there were not, you can be sure, O king, that we would not serve your gods or worship the golden image you have set up" (3:16–18). The implication of that last sentence, of which the Aramaic original is admittedly difficult, is quite clear: The problem of God which every thinking man and woman must confront is difficult enough to resolve when one believes in the living and true God who revealed himself to Israel; but the problem becomes impossible to resolve when one accepts pagan polytheism and idol worship. This passage also suggests that faith in divine intervention does not necessarily mean that God will suspend nature's laws but rather that God will enable the believer to transcend nature's capabilities by choosing suffering and death rather than the convenience of apostasy. Put differently, authentic faith in the true God who sustains all believers enables them, against odds of every sort, to remain constant even when that same God chooses to remain silent.

Accordingly, the point of the six narratives in the first part of the Book of Daniel was not to make the living God of Israel a *deus ex machina* or a life-saving device, but to dramatize that obedience and loyalty to God are more important on a deep personal level than even the prolongation of life at the expense of devastating compromise. The details and somewhat simplistic plots of these stories may not appear very appealing to contemporary tastes, but for the Jew who had to suffer economic, social, and political losses and face death itself during the persecution of Antiochus IV Epiphanes, these stories as well as the apocalypses provided the encouragement and comfort needed to remain steadfast like the heroes of the book.

Believers today—particularly in countries ruled by totalitarian regimes in Eastern Europe, Asia, South America, and Africa—may also be faced with the military might and the civil and economic sanctions of the state. Yet despite a gnawing feeling of powerlessness and helplessness they can still maintain personal integrity and moral rectitude as well as a lively religious faith that can supply meaning and direction to an otherwise dismal and chaotic existence. To persons who are forced to choose between the demands of the state and the demands of God, all may appear lost in terms of life, liberty, and the pursuit of happiness. But they are firm in their belief that only the ephemeral is lost whereas what is gained is the everlasting kingdom of God (Daniel 2 and 7).

Consequently, human power even at its greatest and most intrusive into personal affairs cannot thwart the will and plan of God. Like the four earthly kingdoms of Daniel 2 and 7, political societies come and go and can never achieve true permanence. Only men and women who accept in faith and trust God's charter of human life will form the eternal Kingdom where personal fulfillment becomes attainable because the will of God for mankind is perfectly realized. Purpose and meaning in life cannot be achieved by political acumen or technological gadgets but, paradoxically, only by submission to the will of a loving God who as Creator can alone reveal to men and women what it means to be authentically human.

To be sure, the problem of unmerited evil and innocent suffering receives in the Book of Daniel no theoretical solution but a practical one. The kings and kingdoms of this world are unjust and make life for the believer miserable and often impossible. But for some mysterious reason God, who is Lord of history and King of all nations, permits these dreadful episodes to take place. God is, however, also the merciful and just Judge of all men and women; he punishes the wicked and rewards the upright (Dan 12:1–3). The absolute conviction that God in his time will right all wrongs does not necessarily remove or alleviate the believer's distress in day-to-day living and coping with suffering and sudden death in an oppressive society. In fact, historical realism makes the believer keenly aware that matters are not always set straight in the present age. The Book of Daniel challenges men and women, therefore, to accept in faith the revealed notion of retribution in the afterlife (2:44; 7:14,18,22,27; 12:1–3). Seen in this light, the problem of evil does not cease to be a problem nor does it become less irksome; but it does become a mystery one can learn to live with and accept when one has a lively and abiding faith in an all-wise and almighty God who can and will save. Accordingly, the end and goal of human history are in God's hand, not man's. For the believer the inauguration of the Kingdom of God is unquestionably certain; the timetable, however, is not (compare 7:25; 9:27; 12:7 with 8:14; 12:11; 12:12). For this reason the believer can experience in the present moment of crisis and decision a well-grounded hope in the power of God who cannot and will not remain indifferent to human sin but will redress all evils and restore balance to an otherwise topsy-turvy and often unjust world.

The Kingdom of God which replaces the kingdoms of the godless cannot be inaugurated by military means or purely human resources. The Maccabean victories in the field are quietly put down by the author of the last apocalypse of the Book of Daniel as "a little help" (11:34). The Kingdom of God is God's achievement, not man's. Yet, paradoxically, men and women of faith are called upon to work mightily for the Kingdom and to respond with conviction and energy to the demands of the Kingdom. Those demands include obedience and constancy to the will of God (Dan 1:8; 3:16–18; 6:11), acknowledgment of God as Source of all life and ultimate meaning (Dan 2:20–23; 3:28[*95*]–33[*100*]; 4:31–34; 6:27–28), willingness to suffer and even die to preserve one's faith intact (Dan 3:12; 6:11–12), enthusiasm in sharing with others the good news of God's Kingdom (Dan 11:33; 12:3). Living up to these demands and challenges is a sign that a person is destined for God's everlasting Kingdom (Dan 7:13–14,18,22,27). Responsibility with accountability for one's life and conduct as well as loyal service of God and neighbor are the hallmarks of membership in the Kingdom. Callous disregard of others and the quest for power and prestige at any cost have no place in God's Kingdom. Sin of this kind is not only the enemy of the unseen God but also the enemy of real men and women, its victims.

The high and the mighty have no intrinsic superiority over the lowly and the weak. What one is is more important than what one has or what one does. In our book, Daniel and his companions at the beginning of their careers have little more than their faith in God to sustain them, but their personalities are far more authentic and human than those of the pagan rulers and courtiers who have considerable power, wealth, and status but nothing else.

The first man and woman (original mankind, Hebrew *'ādām*) were created in the divine image and likeness (Gen 1:26–27) and were commissioned by God to have dominion over the fish of the sea, the birds of the air, and all living creatures that move on the earth (Gen 1:28). In somewhat the same manner, "the one in human likeness"—symbol of "the holy ones of the Most High," i.e. the men, women, and children who remain true and faithful to the Covenant—receives everlasting dominion, glory, and kingship (Dan 7:13–14,18,22,27). Thus, the Israel of faith is called to become what the Creator intended the human being to be, viz. the image and likeness of God, a person in the fullest and best sense of the term, one who is responsive and responsible to God and neighbor; one who with divinely endowed wisdom discerns the truth and falsity of historical contingencies (Dan 1:17–20; 2:11,21–23,28,47; 4:27–29,34; 5:11–

16,18–22); one who opposes oppression and perversity of any form (Dan 6:11–17), particularly pride which arrogates to itself what belongs by nature to God alone (Dan 5:18–23); one who promotes God's Kingdom of peace and justice for all in an unsettled and unjust world. Seen from this viewpoint, eschatology becomes protology, i.e. the end of mankind becomes what the Creator had commissioned man and woman to be in the beginning.

In the pre-scientific, or mythological, mind-set of ancient Israel, creation was considered as the activity of God over the chaotic waters of the abyss (Gen 1:1–3; 7:11; 8:2; 49:25; Job 9:13; 26:12–13). But God is always in unquestioned control; never is his creative power or dominion in jeopardy. In like manner, the kingdoms of Babylon, Media, Persia, and Greece, symbolized by the four immense beasts that arise from the great sea or abyss, also come under the sovereign sway of history's Lord (Dan 7:2–8). God alone can give sovereignty and kingship even to pagan rulers. Daniel's words to the arrogant and insolent King Nebuchadnezzar are particularly instructive: "You, O king, [are] king of kings, to whom the God of heaven has given sovereignty and power, strength and glory, and to whom he has handed over the men, the wild animals, and the birds of the air in the whole inhabited world, making you ruler of them all" (2:37–38). Immediately obvious is the striking similarity of this passage to the words God addressed to the first man and woman: "Have dominion over the fish of the sea, the birds of the air, and all the living things that move on the earth" (Gen 1:28).

The Book of Daniel teaches unambiguously that the God of Israel is Lord of history and King of all peoples and nations. "The Most High has dominion over man's kingdom, and . . . he gives it to whom he wishes" (4:22). Everything in time and place forms part of the divine plan, mysterious though it may appear even to the convinced believer. Nothing merely happens. In Dan 1:2, it is the Lord who handed King Jehoiakim of Judah over to King Nebuchadnezzar of Babylon. The latter's military might and prowess were simply the instruments God used for his own purposes. Even the arch-villain Antiochus IV Epiphanes ruled over and suppressed the Chosen People only by tacit divine permission (Dan 8:23–26; 9:26–27). Simplistic as these assertions may appear to the sophisticated reader today, they nevertheless convey a calm and serene assurance that history is not an often cruel and haphazard succession of fundamentally meaningless events in which the weak and the poor turn out to be the inevitable victims, but is rather a mysterious unfolding of a plan in which the will of a concerned and loving God will ultimately prevail regardless of the obstinacy and pride of sinful men and women.

It should also be observed that high position in society or in government and possession of power need not of themselves exclude a person from becoming a member of God's Kingdom. After all, Daniel and his companions, who as Jewish exiles had started out with essentially no political power or social status, did eventually achieve considerable prestige and exercise significant influence in the Babylonian court, thanks to the God-given wisdom that earned them frequent promotions over their peers (Daniel 1–6). But in the inspired perspective of the Book of Daniel, what makes these Jews notable and admirable for generations of believers is not their exalted office and their extraordinary success in a pagan court but their loyalty to God which remained constant even when they could well have lost everything including their lives. Today's reader of the Book of Daniel may experience little, if any, of the social, economic, or religious misfortunes of the Jewish heroes who first received the book in the second century B.C. Yet the profound message of the book remains valid and timely also for contemporary men and women living in an affluent, comfort-conscious, and politically free society. If one is to be true to the God-given vocation of becoming fully human and of realizing one's potential as a person, fidelity to the living creative God is just as necessary for the citizens of the First World today as it is for the suffering and persecuted citizens of the Second and Third Worlds who may more readily identify with the oppressed Jews originally addressed by the Book of Daniel.

It is significant that even the wealthy and powerful pagan kings Nebuchadnezzar of Babylon (Daniel 1–4) and Darius the Mede (Daniel 6), who were responsible for the adversity that Daniel and his companions suffered, ultimately experienced conversion and came to believe in the true God of Israel. Thus, the Book of Daniel makes it clear that there is hope even for the rich and influential. It is a hope that can lead to repentance, conversion, and faith.

Faith in a God who cares and who wills the liberation of men and women and children from the manifold slaveries that keep them from becoming what they can and should be will prompt and urge the believer today to resist oppression in all its ugly forms, personal and communal, secular and religious, economic and social, political and civil. The man or woman of today who takes to heart the inspired message of the Book of Daniel by seeking to do the will of God, come what may, will never use political or religious structures and language to validate middle-class standards and values that are opposed to the coming of God's Kingdom of justice and peace, of equity and opportunity for people of every state and race everywhere in the world. Like Nebuchadnezzar and Darius, people today who have aided and abetted social or political systems that keep others in subjection, can be assured that the God of mercy offers them the chance to change. Like Daniel and his companions, the sensitive and mature believer will expose injustice wherever it is found even when doing so may entail great personal loss. This kind of faith-life may not in every case bring dazzling success as in the charming stories of Daniel 1–6, but it will give the believer a deep and abiding sense of what it means to be a person fashioned in the image and likeness of God who is involved in human history and misery and who has given men and women a share in his dominion over the world.

SELECTED BIBLIOGRAPHY

Abel, F.-M. *Histoire de la Palestine depuis la conquête d'Alexandre jusqu'à l'invasion arabe.* Tome 1: *De la conquête d'Alexandre jusqu'à la guerre juive.* EBib. Paris: Gabalda, 1952. *Cited as* Abel.

——— and J. Starcky. *Les livres des Maccabées. SBJ,* 3d ed. Paris: Cerf, 1961.

Alfrink, B. J. "L'idée de résurrection d'après Dan., XII, 1.2," *Bib* 40 (1959), 355–371.

Allegro, J. M. *Qumrân Cave 4:1 (4Q158–4Q186).* DJD 5. Oxford: Clarendon, 1968.

Alonso Schökel, L., M. I. Gonzalez, and J. Mateos. *Daniel.* Los Libros Sagrados 18. Madrid: Ediciones Cristiandad, 1976. Pages 9–121.

Augé, R. *Daniel.* La Biblia de Montserrat 15/2. Montserrat: Monastery of Montserrat, 1954.

Baillet, M. "Un recueil liturgique de Qumrân, Grotte 4: 'Les Paroles des Luminaires,'" *RB* 68 (1961), 195–250.

——— and J. T. Milik. *Les 'Petites Grottes' de Qumran.* DJD 3. Oxford: Clarendon, 1962.

Baron, S. W. *A Social and Religious History of the Jews.* 8 vols. and Index Vol. 2d ed. Columbia University Press, 1952–60.

Barr, J. "Daniel," *Peake's Commentary on the Bible,* eds. M. Black and H. H. Rowley. London: Nelson, 1963. Pages 591–602.

Barth, C. *Diesseits und Jenseits im Glauben des späten Israel.* SBS 72. Stuttgart: Katholisches Bibelwerk, 1974.

Barthélemy, D. *Les devanciers d'Aquila.* VTSup 10. Leiden: Brill, 1963.

——— and O. Rickenbacher. *Konkordanz zum hebräischen Sirach.* Göttingen: Vandenhoeck & Ruprecht, 1973.

Bauer, H., and P. Leander. *Grammatik des Biblisch-Aramäischen.* Halle-Saale: M. Niemeyer, 1927.

Baumgartner, W. "Das Aramäische im Buche Daniel," *ZAW* 45 (1927), 81–133.

——— *Das Buch Daniel.* Giessen: Töpelmann, 1926.

——— "Ein Vierteljahrhundert Danielforschung," *TRu* 11 (1939), 59–83, 125–144, 201–228.

Behrmann, G. *Das Buch Daniel.* HKAT 3/3,2. Göttingen: Vandenhoeck & Ruprecht, 1894.

Bentzen, A. *Daniel.* HAT 1/19, 2d ed. Tübingen: Mohr, 1952. *Cited as* Bentzen.

Bevan, A. A. *A Short Commentary on the Book of Daniel.* Cambridge University Press, 1892. *Cited as* Bevan.

Bevan, E. R. *The House of Seleucus.* 2 vols. London: E. Arnold, 1902; reprinted New York: Barnes & Noble, 1966.

Bloch, J. *On the Apocalyptic in Judaism.* JQRMS 2. Philadelphia: Dropsie College, 1952.

Bludau, A. *Die alexandrinische Übersetzung des Buches Daniel und ihr Verhältniss zum massorethischen Text.* BibS 2/2-3. Freiburg i. B.: Herder'sche Verlagshandlung, 1897.

Bogaert, P. *L'Apocalypse syriaque de Baruch: Introduction, traduction du syriaque et commentaire.* 2 vols. Sources Chrétiennes 144, 145. Paris: Cerf, 1969.

Borgongini-Duca, F. *Le LXX Settimane di Daniele e le date messianiche.* Padua: Pontificia Basilica del Santo, 1951.

Borsch, F. H. *The Christian and Gnostic Son of Man.* SBT 2/14. Naperville, Ill.: Allenson, 1970.

——— *The Son of Man in Myth and History.* Philadelphia: Westminster, 1967.

Boutflower, C. *In and around the Book of Daniel.* London, 1923; reprinted Grand Rapids: Zondervan, 1963, 1964.

Braaten, C. E. "The Significance of Apocalypticism for Systematic Theology," *Int* 25 (1971), 480–499.

Braude, W. G., tr. *The Midrash on Psalms,* vol. 1. Yale Judaica Series 13. Yale University Press, 1959.

Brekelmans, C., ed. *Questions disputées de l'Ancien Testament.* Louvain: Duculot-Louvain University Press, 1974.

Brekelmans, C. H. W. "The Saints of the Most High and Their Kingdom," *OTS* 14 (1965), 305–329.

Bright, J. *A History of Israel,* 2d ed. Philadelphia: Westminster, 1972.

——— *Jeremiah.* AB 21. Garden City, N.Y.: Doubleday, 1965.

Brown, F., S. R. Driver, and C. A. Briggs. *A Hebrew and English Lexicon of the Old Testament.* Oxford: Clarendon, 1907.

Brown, R. E. *The Book of Daniel.* Pamphlet Bible Series 34. New York: Paulist Press, 1962.

——— "The Pre-Christian Semitic Concept of Mystery," *CBQ* 20 (1958), 417–443.

Bruce, F. F. "The Book of Daniel and the Qumran Community," in *Neotestamentica et Semitica: Studies in Honour of Matthew Black,* eds. E. E. Ellis and M. Wilcox. Edinburgh: T. & T. Clark, 1969. Pages 221–235.

——— "Josephus and Daniel," *ASTI* 4 (1965), 148–152.

Buchanan, G. W. *To the Hebrews.* AB 36. Garden City, N.Y.: Doubleday, 1972.

Caquot, A. "Sur les quatre bêtes de *Daniel* VII," *Sem* 5 (1955), 5–13.

——— "Les quatre bêtes et le 'Fils d'homme' (Daniel 7)," *Sem* 18 (1968), 37–71.

Casey, M. "The Corporate Interpretation of 'One like a Son of Man' (Dan. VII 13) at the Time of Jesus," *NovT* 18 (1976), 167–180.

Casey, P. M. "Porphyry and the Origin of the Book of Daniel," *JTS* N.S. 27 (1976), 15–33.

Ceriani, A. M. *Codex syro-hexaplaris Ambrosianus photolithographice editus.* Monumenta sacra et profana 7. Milan: Pogliani, 1874.

——— *Translatio Syra Pescitto veteris testamenti ex codice Ambrosiano sec. fere VI photolithographice edita.* Milan: Pogliani, 1876.

Charles, R. H., ed. *The Apocrypha and Pseudepigrapha of the Old Testament in English.* 2 vols. Oxford: Clarendon, 1913; reprinted 1963, 1964. Cited as *APOT.*

——— *A Critical and Exegetical Commentary on the Book of Daniel.* Oxford: Clarendon, 1929. *Cited as* Charles.

——— *Eschatology: The Doctrine of a Future Life in Israel, Judaism and Christianity.* Introduction by G. W. Buchanan. Reprint of 2d ed., 1913. New York: Schocken, 1963.

Childs, B. S. *Biblical Theology in Crisis.* Philadelphia: Westminster, 1970.

Clifford, R. J. "History and Myth in Daniel 10–12," *BASOR* 220 (1975), 23–26.

Collins, J. J. "Apocalyptic Eschatology as the Transcendence of Death," *CBQ* 36 (1974), 21–43.

——— "The Court-Tales in Daniel and the Development of Apocalyptic," *JBL* 94 (1975), 218–234.

——— "Jewish Apocalyptic against Its Hellenistic Near Eastern Environment," *BASOR* 220 (1975), 27–36.

——— "The Mythology of Holy War in Daniel and the Qumran War Scroll: A Point of Transition in Jewish Apocalyptic," *VT* 25 (1975), 596–612.

——— "The Son of Man and the Saints of the Most High in the Book of Daniel," *JBL* 93 (1974), 50–66.

——— "The Symbolism of Transcendence in Jewish Apocalyptic," *BR* 19 (1974), 5–22.

Colpe, C. *"ho huios tou anthrōpou," TDNT* 8. Grand Rapids: Eerdmans, 1972. Pages 400–477.

Coppens, J. "Le Fils d'homme danielique et les relectures de Dan., vii, 13, dans les apocryphes et les écrits du Nouveau Testament," *ETL* 37 (1961), 5–51.

——— *Le messianisme royal: Ses origines. Son développment. Son accomplissement.* LD 54. Paris: Cerf, 1968.

——— "La vision danielique du Fils d'homme," *VT* 19 (1969), 171–182.

——— and L. Dequeker. *Le Fils d'homme et les Saints du Très-Haut en Daniel, vii, dans les Apocryphes et dans le Nouveau Testament.* ALBO 3/23, 2d ed. Bruges-Paris: Desclée de Brouwer, 1961.

Cortés, J. B., and F. M. Gatti. "The Son of Man or The Son of Adam," *Bib* 49 (1968), 457–502.

Cowley, A. *Aramaic Papyri of the Fifth Century B.C.* Oxford: Clarendon, 1923.

Coxon, P. W. "Daniel III 17: A Linguistic and Theological Problem," *VT* 26 (1976), 400–409.

Cross, F. M. *The Ancient Library of Qumran and Modern Biblical Studies.* Rev. ed. Anchor Books. Garden City, N.Y.: Doubleday, 1961.

Cross, F. M. "The Contribution of the Qumrân Discoveries to the Study of the Biblical Text," *IEJ* 16 (1966), 81–95.

——— "The Development of the Jewish Scripts," in *The Bible and the Ancient Near East,* ed. G. E. Wright. Garden City, N.Y.: Doubleday, 1961. Pages 133–202.

——— "Editing the Manuscript Fragments from Qumran: Cave 4 of Qumran (4Q)," *BA* 19 (1956), 83–86.

——— "The Evolution of a Theory of Local Texts," in *1972 Proceedings: IOSCS and Pseudepigrapha Seminar,* ed. R. A. Kraft. Septuagint and Cognate Studies 2. Missoula, Mont.: Society of Biblical Literature, 1972. Pages 108–126.

——— "The History of the Biblical Text in the Light of Discoveries in the Judean Desert," *HTR* 57 (1964), 281–299.

——— "New Directions in the Study of Apocalyptic," in *Apocalypticism,* ed. R. W. Funk. JTC 6. New York: Herder & Herder, 1969. Pages 157–165.

——— "A Reconstruction of the Judean Restoration," *JBL* 94 (1975), 4–18, 279.

Dahood, M. *Psalms I: 1–50.* AB 16. Garden City, N.Y.: Doubleday, 1966.

Delcor, M. "Un cas de traduction 'targoumique' de la LXX, à propos de la statue en or de Dan. III," *Textus* 7 (1969), 30–35.

——— *Le livre de Daniel.* SB. Paris: Gabalda, 1971. *Cited as* Delcor.

——— "Les sources du chapitre vii de Daniel," *VT* 18 (1968), 290–312.

Dennefeld, L. *Les grands prophètes: Daniel. La Sainte Bible,* vol. 7, eds. L. Pirot and A. Clamer. Paris: Letouzey et Ané, 1946. Pages 631–714.

Dequeker, L. "Daniel vii et les Saints du Très-Haut," *ETL* 36 (1960), 353–392.

——— "The 'Saints of the Most High' in Qumran and Daniel," *OTS* 18 (1973), 108–187.

De Vries, S. J. "Calendar." *IDB* 1. Nashville: Abingdon, 1962. Pages 483–488.

Dexinger, F. *Das Buch Daniel und seine Probleme.* SBS 36. Stuttgart: Katholisches Bibelwerk, 1969.

Di Lella, A. A. "Conservative and Progressive Theology: Sirach and Wisdom," *CBQ* 28 (1966), 139–154.

——— "Daniel." *IDBSup.* Nashville: Abingdon, 1976. Pages 205–207.

——— "The Problem of Retribution in the Wisdom Literature," in *Rediscovery of Scripture: Biblical Theology Today.* Burlington, Wis.: Franciscan Educational Conference, 1967. Pages 109–127.

Dodd, C. H. *According to the Scriptures.* London: Nisbet, 1952.

Dommerschausen, W. *Nabonid im Buche Daniel.* Mainz: Grunewald, 1964.

Dougherty, R. P. *Nabonidus and Belshazzar: A Study of the Closing Events of the Neo-Babylonian Empire.* Yale Oriental Series Researches 15. Yale University Press, 1929.

Driver, G. R. "The Aramaic of the Book of Daniel," *JBL* 45 (1926), 110–119.

Driver, S. R. *The Book of Daniel.* The Cambridge Bible for Schools and Colleges. Cambridge University Press, 1900. *Cited as* Driver.

Driver, S. R. *An Introduction to the Literature of the Old Testament.* Reprint of the 7th ed., 1898. Cleveland: World Publishing Co., 1956. *Cited as* Driver, *Introduction.*

Dubarle, A.-M. "Prophètes d'Israël: Daniel." *DBSup,* vol. 6. Paris: Letouzey et Ané, 1972. Cols. 736–758.

Eichrodt, W. *Ezekiel,* tr. C. Quinn. Philadelphia: Westminster, 1970.

——— *Theology of the Old Testament,* 2 vols., tr. J. A. Baker. Philadelphia: Westminster, 1961–67.

Eissfeldt, O. "Die Menetekel Inschrift und ihre Bedeutung," *ZAW* 63 (1951), 105–114.

——— *The Old Testament: An Introduction,* tr. P. R. Ackroyd. Oxford: Blackwell, and New York: Harper & Row, 1965.

Ellenbogen, M. *Foreign Words in the Old Testament: Their Origin and Etymology.* London: Luzac, 1962.

Emerton, J. A. "The Origin of the Son of Man Imagery," *JTS* 9 (1958), 225–242.

Feuillet, A. "Le Fils de l'homme de Daniel et la tradition biblique," *RB* 60 (1953), 170–202, 321–346.

Fitzmyer, J. A. *The Aramaic Inscriptions from Sefîre.* BibOr 19. Rome: Pontifical Biblical Institute, 1967.

——— "The Contribution of Qumran Aramaic to the Study of the New Testament," *NTS* 20 (1973–74), 382–407.

——— *The Dead Sea Scrolls: Major Publications and Tools for Study.* Sources for Biblical Study 8. Missoula, Mont.: Society of Biblical Literature and Scholars Press, 1977.

——— *The Genesis Apocryphon of Qumran Cave I: A Commentary,* 2d rev. ed. BibOr 18A. Rome: Pontifical Biblical Institute, 1971.

——— "The Languages of Palestine in the First Century A.D.," *CBQ* 32 (1970), 501–531.

Flusser, D. "The Four Empires in the Fourth Sibyl and in the Book of Daniel," *Israel Oriental Studies* 2 (1972), 148–175.

Ford, J. M. *Revelation.* AB 38. Garden City, N.Y.: Doubleday, 1975.

Forestell, J. T. "Christian Revelation and the Resurrection of the Wicked," *CBQ* 19 (1957), 165–189.

Freedman, D. N. "The Flowering of Apocalyptic," in *Apocalypticism,* ed. R. W. Funk. JTC 6. New York: Herder & Herder, 1969. Pages 166–174.

——— "The Prayer of Nabonidus," *BASOR* 145 (1957), 31–32.

Frost, S. B. "Daniel," *IDB* 1. Nashville: Abingdon, 1962. Pages 761–768.

——— *Old Testament Apocalyptic: Its Origin and Growth.* London: Epworth, 1952.

Gammie, J. G. "The Classification, Stages of Growth, and Changing Intentions in the Book of Daniel," *JBL* 95 (1976), 191–204.

——— "Spatial and Ethical Dualism in Jewish Wisdom and Apocalyptic Literature," *JBL* 93 (1974), 356–385.

Gaster, T. H. *Myth, Legend, and Custom in the Old Testament: A Comparative Study with Chapters from Sir James G. Frazer's Folklore in the Old Testament.* New York: Harper & Row, 1969.

Geissen, A. *Der Septuaginta-Text des Buches Daniel, Kap. 5–12, zusammen mit Susanna, Bel et Draco, nach dem Kölner Teil des Papyrus 967*. Papyrologische Texte und Abhandlungen 5. Bonn: R. Habelt, 1968.

Gelb, I. J. et al., eds. *The Assyrian Dictionary*. Chicago: Oriental Institute 1956– . Cited as *CAD*.

Gilbert, M. "La prière de Daniel, Dn 9,4–19," *RTL* 3 (1972), 284–310.

Ginsberg, H. L. "The Composition of the Book of Daniel," *VT* 4 (1954), 246–275.

——— "Daniel, Book of." *EncJud*, vol. 5. New York: Macmillan, 1971. Cols. 1277–1289.

——— " 'King of kings' and 'lord of kingdoms,' " *AJSL* 57 (1940), 71–74.

——— "The Oldest Interpretation of the Suffering Servant," *VT* 3 (1953), 400–404.

——— *Studies in Daniel.* Texts and Studies of the Jewish Theological Seminary of America 14. New York: Jewish Theological Seminary, 1948. *Cited as* Ginsberg.

Ginzberg, L. "Daniel." *The Jewish Encyclopedia,* vol. 4. New York: Funk & Wagnalls, 1903. Pages 426–428.

——— *The Legends of the Jews,* 7 vols. Philadelphia: Jewish Publication Society, 1909–38.

Glasson, T. F. "The Son of Man Imagery: Enoch xiv and Daniel vii," *NTS* 23 (1976), 82–90.

Goettsberger, J. *Das Buch Daniel.* Die Heilige Schrift des Alten Testamentes 8/2. Bonn: Peter Hanstein, 1928.

Goldstein, J. A. *I Maccabees*. AB 41. Garden City, N.Y.: Doubleday, 1976.

Grelot, P. "La Septante de Daniel IV et son substrat sémitique," *RB* 81 (1974), 5–23.

——— "Soixante-dix semaines d'années," *Bib* 50 (1969), 169–186.

——— "Les versions grecques de Daniel," *Bib* 47 (1966), 381–402.

Gruenthaner, M. J. "The Four Empires of Daniel," *CBQ* 8 (1946), 72–82, 201–212.

Gwynn, J. "Theodotion." *Dictionary of Christian Biography,* vol. 4. London: J. Murray, 1887. Pages 970–979.

Hallo, W. W. "Akkadian Apocalypses," *IEJ* 16 (1966), 231–242.

Hamerton-Kelly, R. G. "The Temple and the Origins of Jewish Apocalyptic," *VT* 20 (1970), 1–15.

Hamm, W. *Der Septuaginta-Text des Buches Daniel, Kap. 1–2, nach dem Kölner Teil des Papyrus 967*. Papyrologische Texte und Abhandlungen 10. Bonn: R. Habelt, 1969.

——— *Der Septuaginta-Text des Buches Daniel, Kap. 3–4, nach dem Kölner Teil des Papyrus 967*. Papyrologische Texte und Abhandlungen 21. Bonn: R. Habelt, 1977.

Hammer, R. *The Book of Daniel.* The Cambridge Bible Commentary, *NEB*. Cambridge University Press, 1976.

Hanhart, R. " 'Die Heiligen des Höchsten' (Dan 7,21.25)," VTSup 16 (1967), 90–101.

Hanson, P. D. *The Dawn of Apocalyptic*. Philadelphia: Fortress, 1975.

——— "Jewish Apocalyptic against Its Near Eastern Environment," *RB* 78 (1971), 31–58.

——— "Old Testament Apocalyptic Reexamined," *Int* 25 (1971), 454–479.

Harnish, W. *Verhängnis und Verheissung der Geschichte: Untersuchungen zum Zeit- und Geschichtsverständnis im 4. Buch Esra und in der syr. Baruch-apokalypse*. FRLANT 97. Göttingen: Vandenhoeck & Ruprecht, 1969.

Hartman, L. "The Functions of Some So-Called Apocalyptic Timetables," *NTS* 22 (1975), 1–14.

——— *Prophecy Interpreted: The Formation of Some Jewish Apocalyptic Texts and of the Eschatological Discourse, Mark 13 Par,* tr. N. Tomkinson with the assistance of J. Gray. ConB, N.T. Series 1. Lund: Gleerup, 1966.

Hartman, L. F. "Daniel." *The Jerome Biblical Commentary,* ed. R. E. Brown et al. Englewood Cliffs, N.J.: Prentice-Hall, 1968. Pages 446–460.

——— "The Great Tree and Nabuchodonosor's Madness," in *The Bible in Current Catholic Thought,* ed. J. L. McKenzie. New York: Herder & Herder, 1962. Pages 75–82.

Hasel, G. F. "The Identity of 'The Saints of the Most High' in Daniel 7," *Bib* 56 (1975), 173–192.

Heaton, E. W. *The Book of Daniel.* Torch Bible Commentaries. London: SCM Press, 1956. *Cited as* Heaton.

Hengel, M. *Judaism and Hellenism: Studies in Their Encounter in Palestine during the Early Hellenistic Period,* tr. J. Bowden. 2 vols. Philadelphia: Fortress, 1974.

Hölscher, G. "Die Entstehung des Buches Daniel," *TSK* 92 (1919), 113–138.

Humphreys, W. L. "A Life-Style for Diaspora: A Study of the Tales of Esther and Daniel," *JBL* 92 (1973), 211–223.

——— "The Motif of the Wise Courtier in the Old Testament." New York: Union Theological Seminary dissertation, 1970.

Hurwitz, A. "The Chronological Significance of 'Aramaisms' in Biblical Hebrew," *IEJ* 18 (1968), 234–240.

Jeffery, A. "The Book of Daniel." *IB* 6. Nashville: Abingdon, 1956. Pages 339–549. *Cited as* Jeffery.

Jellicoe, S. *The Septuagint and Modern Study*. Oxford: Clarendon, 1968.

——— "Some Reflections on the *KAIGE* Recension," *VT* 23 (1973), 15–24.

Jepsen, A. "Bemerkungen zum Danielbuch," *VT* 11 (1961), 386–391.

Jones, B. W. "The Prayer in Daniel IX," *VT* 18 (1968), 488–493.

Josephus. *Jewish Antiquities* ix–xi and xii–xiv. LCL, *Josephus,* vols. 6 and 7, tr. R. Marcus. Harvard University Press, 1958 and 1961.

——— *The Life • Against Apion*. LCL, *Josephus,* vol. 1, tr. H. St. J. Thackeray. Harvard University Press, 1966.

Käsemann, E. "On the Subject of Primitive Christian Apocalyptic," in *New Testament Questions of Today*. Philadelphia: Fortress, 1969. Pages 108–137.

Keil, C. F. *The Book of the Prophet Daniel,* tr. M. G. Easton. Edinburgh: T. & T. Clark, 1884. *Cited as* Keil.

Kepler, T. S. *Dreams of the Future: Daniel and Revelation.* Bible Guides 22. Nashville: Abingdon, 1963.

Kitchen, K. A. *Notes on Some Problems in the Book of Daniel.* London: Tyndale, 1965.

Koch, K. "Die Herkunft der Proto-Theodotion-Übersetzung des Danielbuches," *VT* 23 (1973), 362–365.

——— *The Rediscovery of Apocalyptic,* tr. M. Kohl. SBT 2/22. Naperville, Ill.: Allenson, 1972.

Koehler, L., and W. Baumgartner. *Lexicon in veteris testamenti libros.* Leiden: Brill, 1958.

Kraeling, E. G. "The Handwriting on the Wall," *JBL* 63 (1944), 11–18.

Kruse, H. "Compositio Libri Danielis et idea Filii Hominis," *Verbum Domini* 37 (1959), 147–161, 193–211.

Kutscher, E. Y. "Aramaic," in *Current Trends in Linguistics.* Vol. 6: *Linguistics in South West Asia and North Africa,* ed. T. A. Sebeok. The Hague: Mouton, 1970. Pages 347–412.

——— "Aramaic." *EncJud,* vol. 3. New York: Macmillan, 1971. Cols. 259–287.

Lacocque, A. *Le livre de Daniel.* CAT 15b. Neuchâtel: Delachaux et Niestlé, 1976. *Cited as* Lacocque.

Lattey, C. *The Book of Daniel.* Dublin: Browne & Nolan, 1948. *Cited as* Lattey.

Lebram, J. C. H. "König Antiochus im Buch Daniel," *VT* 25 (1975), 737–772.

Lenglet, A. "La structure littéraire de Daniel 2–7," *Bib* 53 (1972), 169–190.

Lindars, B. "Re-Enter the Apocalyptic Son of Man," *NTS* 22 (1975), 52–72.

Linder, J. *Commentarius in Librum Daniel.* Cursus Scripturae Sacrae 23. Paris: Lethielleux, 1939. *Cited as* Linder.

Maass, F. "*'ādām,*" *TDOT* 1. Tr. J. T. Willis. Grand Rapids: Eerdmans, 1974. Pages 75–87.

——— "*'ĕnôš,*" *TDOT* 1. Tr. J. T. Willis. Grand Rapids: Eerdmans, 1974. Pages 345–348.

McCullough, W. S. *The History and Literature of the Palestinian Jews from Cyrus to Herod: 550 BC to 4 BC.* University of Toronto Press, 1975.

——— "Israel's Eschatology from Amos to Daniel," in *Studies in the Ancient Palestinian World,* eds. J. W. Wevers and D. B. Redford. University of Toronto Press, 1972. Pages 86–100.

McHardy, W. D. "The Peshitta Text of Daniel XI 4," *JTS* 49 (1948), 56–57.

McNamara, M. "Daniel." *A New Catholic Commentary on Holy Scripture,* ed. R. C. Fuller et al. London: Nelson, 1969. Pages 650–675.

——— "Nabonidus and the Book of Daniel," *ITQ* 37 (1970), 131–149.

Maier, J., and J. Schreiner, eds. *Literatur und Religion des Frühjudentums.* Würzburg: Echter, 1973.

Manson, T. W. "The Son of Man in Daniel, Enoch and the Gospels," *BJRL* 32 (1949–50), 171–193.

Marlow, R. "The *Son of Man* in Recent Journal Literature," *CBQ* 28 (1966), 20–30.

Marti, K. *Das Buch Daniel.* Kurzer Hand-Commentar zum Alten Testament 18. Tübingen: Mohr, 1901.

Mastin, B. A. "Daniel 2:46 and the Hellenistic World," *ZAW* 85 (1973), 80–93.

de Menasce, P. J. *Daniel,* 2d ed. *SJB.* Paris: Cerf, 1958.

Mertens, A. *Das Buch Daniel im Lichte der Texte vom Toten Meer.* SBM 12. Stuttgart: Katholisches Bibelwerk, 1971.

Milik, J. T. " 'Prière de Nabonide' et autres écrits d'un cycle de Daniel," *RB* 63 (1956), 407–415.

———"Problèmes de la littérature hénochique à la lumière des fragments araméens de Qumrân," *HTR* 64 (1971), 333–378.

Momigliano, A. *Alien Wisdom: The Limits of Hellenization.* New York: Cambridge University Press, 1976.

Montgomery, J. A. *The Book of Daniel.* ICC. New York: C. Scribner's Sons, 1927. *Cited as* Montgomery.

Moore, C. A. "Toward the Dating of the Book of Baruch," *CBQ* 36 (1974), 312–320.

Morgenstern, J. "The 'Son of Man' of Daniel 7,13f.: A New Interpretation," *JBL* 80 (1961), 65–77.

Morris, L. *Apocalyptic.* Grand Rapids: Eerdmans, 1972.

Mowinckel, S. *He That Cometh,* tr. G. W. Anderson. Nashville: Abingdon, 1956.

Muilenburg, J. "The Son of Man in Daniel and the Ethiopic Apocalypse of Enoch," *JBL* 79 (1960), 197–209.

Müller, H.-P. "Magisch-mantische Weisheit und die Gestalt Daniels," *UF* 1 (1969), 79–94.

——— "Mantische Weisheit und Apokalyptik," in *Congress Volume, Uppsala 1971.* VTSup 22. Leiden: Brill, 1972. Pages 268–293.

——— "Märchen, Legende und Enderwartung: Zum Verständnis des Buches Daniel," *VT* 26 (1976), 338–350.

Müller, U. B. *Messias und Menschensohn in jüdischen Apokalypsen und in der Offenbarung des Johannes.* SNT 6. Gütersloh: Mohn, 1972.

Muraoka, T. "Notes on the Syntax of Biblical Aramaic," *JSS* 11 (1966), 151–167.

Murray, R. *Symbols of Church and Kingdom: A Study in Early Syriac Tradition.* Cambridge University Press, 1975.

Myers, J. M. *Ezra • Nehemiah.* AB 14. Garden City, N.Y.: Doubleday, 1965.

Nickelsburg, G. W. E. *Resurrection, Immortality, and Eternal Life in Intertestamental Judaism.* HTS 26. Harvard University Press, 1972.

Noth, M. *The History of Israel,* 2d ed. rev., tr. P. R. Ackroyd. London: A. & C. Black, 1960.

——— "The Holy Ones of the Most High," in *The Laws in the Pentateuch and Other Essays,* tr. D. R. Ap-Thomas. Philadelphia: Fortress, 1967. Pages 215–228.

——— "The Understanding of History in Old Testament Apocalyptic," in *The Laws in the Pentateuch and Other Essays,* tr. D. R. Ap-Thomas. Philadelphia: Fortress, 1967. Pages 194–214.

——— "Zur Komposition des Buches Daniel," *TSK* 98–99 (1926), 143–163.

Nötscher, F. *Daniel.* Echter-Bibel 6. Würzburg: Echter, 1948.

O'Connell, K. G. *The Theodotionic Revision of the Book of Exodus.* HSM 3. Harvard University Press, 1972.

Oppenheim, A. L. *Ancient Mesopotamia: Portrait of a Dead Civilization.* University of Chicago Press, 1964.

Osswald, E. "Zum Problem der *vaticinia ex eventu,*" *ZAW* 75 (1963), 27–44.

Overholt, T. W. "King Nebuchadnezzar in the Jeremiah Tradition," *CBQ* 30 (1968), 39–48.

Palacios, L. *Grammatica Aramaico-Biblica,* 2d ed. Rome-Paris: Desclée, 1953.

Parisot, I. *Patrologia syriaca,* vol. 1, ed. R. Graffin. Paris: Firmin-Didot, 1894.

Perrin, N. "The Son of Man in Ancient Judaism and Primitive Christianity: A Suggestion," *BR* 11 (1966), 17–28.

Peters, F. E. *The Harvest of Hellenism.* New York: Simon & Schuster, 1970.

Pettinato, G. "The Royal Archives of Tell Mardikh-Ebla," *BA* 39 (1976), 44–52.

Pfeiffer, R. H. *History of New Testament Times, with an Introduction to the Apocrypha.* London: A. & C. Black, 1949.

——— *Introduction to the Old Testament,* rev. ed. London: A. & C. Black, 1952.

van der Ploeg, J. "Eschatology in the Old Testament," *OTS* 17 (1972), 89–99.

Plöger, O. *Das Buch Daniel.* KAT 18. Gütersloh: G. Mohn, 1965. *Cited as* Plöger.

——— *Theocracy and Eschatology,* tr. S. Rudman. Richmond: John Knox, 1968.

——— "Zusätze zu Daniel," in *Jüdische Schriften aus hellenistisch-römischer Zeit 1/1: Historische und legendarische Erzählungen,* ed. W. G. Kümmel. Gütersloh: Mohn, 1973. Pages 63–86.

Polybius, *The Histories.* LCL, 6 vols., tr. W. R. Paton. New York: G. P. Putnam's Sons, 1922–27.

Pope, M. H. "Number, Numbering, Numbers." *IDB* 3. Nashville: Abingdon, 1962. Pages 561–567.

Porteous, N. W. *Daniel.* Philadelphia: Westminster, 1965. *Cited as* Porteous.

Poythress, V. S. "The Holy Ones of the Most High in Daniel vii," *VT* 26 (1976), 208–213.

Pritchard, J. B., ed. *Ancient Near Eastern Texts Relating to the Old Testament,* 2d ed. Princeton University Press, 1955. Cited as *ANET.*

von Rad, G. *Old Testament Theology,* tr. D. M. G. Stalker. 2 vols. New York: Harper & Row, 1962, 1965.

Rahlfs, A. *Septuaginta,* vol. 2: *Libri poetici et prophetici.* Stuttgart: Privilegierte Württembergische Bibelanstalt, 1935.

Redford, D. B. *A Study of the Biblical Story of Joseph* (*Genesis 37–50*). VTSup 20. Leiden: Brill, 1970.

Rhodes, A. R. "The Kingdoms of Men and the Kingdom of God: A Study of Daniel 7:1–14," *Int* 15 (1961), 411–430.

Rinaldi, G. *Daniele,* 4th rev. ed. La Sacra Bibbia. Turin: Marietti, 1962. *Cited as* Rinaldi.

Robinson, H. W. *Corporate Personality in Ancient Israel.* Reprint of "The Hebrew Conception of Corporate Personality" (1935) and "The Group and the Individual in Israel" (1937), FBBS 11. Philadelphia: Fortress, 1964.

Rosén, H. B. "On the Use of the Tenses in the Aramaic of Daniel," *JSS* 6 (1961), 183–203.

Rosenthal, F., ed. *An Aramaic Handbook.* 2 vols. Porta linguarum orientalium, N.S. 10. Wiesbaden: O. Harrassowitz, 1967. *Cited as* Rosenthal, *Handbook.*

——— *Die aramäistische Forschung seit Th. Nöldeke's Veröffentlichungen.* Leiden: Brill, 1939.

——— *A Grammar of Biblical Aramaic.* Wiesbaden: O. Harrassowitz, 1961. *Cited as* Rosenthal, *Grammar.*

Rowley, H. H. "The Belshazzar of Daniel and of History," *Expositor* 9/2 (Sept.–Oct. 1924), 182–195, 255–272.

——— *Darius the Mede and the Four World Empires in the Book of Daniel: A Historical Study of Contemporary Theories.* 2d ed. Cardiff: University of Wales Press, 1959.

——— "The Meaning of Daniel for Today: A Study of Leading Themes," *Int* 15 (1961), 387–397.

——— *The Relevance of Apocalyptic: A Study of Jewish and Christian Apocalypses from Daniel to the Revelation,* rev. ed. New York: Association Press, 1963.

——— "The Unity of the Book of Daniel," in *The Servant of the Lord and Other Essays on the Old Testament.* 2d ed. rev. Oxford: Blackwell, 1965. Pages 249–280.

Russell, D. S. *The Jews from Alexander to Herod.* New Clarendon Bible 5. London: Oxford University Press, 1967.

——— *The Method and Message of Jewish Apocalyptic, 200 B.C.–A.D. 100.* Philadelphia: Westminster, 1964.

Sahlin, H. "Antiochus IV. Epiphanes und Judas Mackabäus: Einige Gesichtspunkte zum Verständnis des Danielbuches," *ST* 23 (1969), 41–68.

Sanders, J. A. *The Psalms Scroll of Qumrân Cave 11 (11QPs^{a}).* DJD 4. Oxford: Clarendon, 1965.

Sarna, N. M. "Bible: Canon." *EncJud,* vol. 4. New York: Macmillan, 1971. Cols. 814–836.

Schalit, A., ed. *The World History of the Jewish People. First Series: Ancient Times,* vol. 6: *The Hellenistic Age.* Rutgers University Press, 1972.

Schedl, C. *History of the Old Testament,* vol. 5. Staten Island, N.Y.: Alba House, 1973.

——— "Mystische Arithmetik oder geschichtliche Zahlen (Dan., 8, 14; 12, 11–13)," *BZ* 8 (1964), 101–105

Schmidt, J. M. *Die jüdische Apokalyptik: Die Geschichte ihrer Erforschung von den Anfängen bis zu den Textfunden von Qumran.* Neukirchen-Vluyn: Neukirchener Verlag, 1969.

Schmithals, W. *The Apocalyptic Movement: Introduction and Interpretation,* tr. J. E. Steely. Nashville: Abingdon, 1975.

Schmitt, A. *Stammt der sogenannte "Θ"-Text bei Daniel wirklich von Theodotion?* Mitteilungen des Septuaginta-Unternehmens 9. Göttingen: Vandenhoeck & Ruprecht, 1966.

Schneider, H. *Das Buch Daniel.* Herders Bibelkommentar 9/2. Freiburg: Herder, 1954.

Schüpphaus, J. "Das Verhältnis von LXX- und Theodotion-Text in den apokryphen Zusätzen zum Danielbuch," *ZAW* 83 (1971), 49–72.

Schürer, E. "Diaspora." *Dictionary of the Bible,* vol. 5, ed. J. Hastings. New York: C. Scribner's Sons, 1904. Pages 91–109.

——— *The History of the Jewish People in the Age of Jesus Christ (175 B.C.–A.D. 135),* vol. 1 revised and edited by G. Vermes and F. Millar. Edinburgh: T. & T. Clark, 1973. *Cited as* Schürer.

Scott, R. B. Y. "I Daniel, the Original Apocalypse," *AJSL* 47 (1931), 289–296.

Sevenster, J. N. *Do You Know Greek? How Much Greek Could the First Jewish Christians Have Known?* NovTSup 19. Leiden: Brill, 1968.

Siegman, E. F. "The Stone Hewn from the Mountain (Daniel 2)," *CBQ* 18 (1956), 364–379.

Silberman, L. H. "The Human Deed in a Time of Despair: The Ethics of Apocalyptic," in *Essays in Old Testament Ethics (J. Philip Hyatt, In Memoriam),* eds. J. L. Crenshaw and J. T. Willis. New York: Ktav, 1974. Pages 191–202.

Skehan, P. W. "Henoch Literature." *NCE, Supplement 1967–1974.* New York: McGraw-Hill, 1974.

von Soden, W. *Grundriss der akkadischen Grammatik.* AnOr 33. Rome: Pontificium Institutum Biblicum, 1952.

Sokoloff, M. "*'ămar nĕqē',* 'Lamb's Wool' (Dan 7:9)," *JBL* 95 (1976), 277–279.

Speiser, E. A. *Genesis.* AB 1. Garden City, N.Y.: Doubleday, 1964.

Spiegel, S. "Noah, Daniel, and Job," in *Louis Ginzberg Jubilee Volume.* New York: Jewish Theological Seminary, 1945. Pages 305–355.

Steinmann, J. *Daniel.* Paris: Cerf, 1950.

——— *Daniel: Texte français, introduction et commentaires.* Connaître la Bible. Bruges: Desclée de Brouwer, 1961. *Cited as* Steinmann.

Strugnell, J. "Notes en marge du volume V des 'Discoveries in the Judaean Desert of Jordan,'" *RevQ* 7/2 (1970), 163–276.

Sullivan, K. *The Book of Daniel, The Book of Jonah.* Old Testament Reading Guide 28. Collegeville, Minn.: Liturgical Press, 1975.

Sundberg, A. C., Jr. "The Bible Canon and the Christian Doctrine of Inspiration," *Int* 29 (1975), 352–371.

——— "The Protestant Old Testament Canon: Should It Be Re-examined?" *CBQ* 28 (1966), 194–203.

Swain, J. W. "The Theory of the Four Monarchies: Opposition History under the Roman Empire," *Classical Philology* 35 (1940), 1–21.

Swete, H. B. *The Old Testament in Greek,* vol. 3, 4th ed. Cambridge University Press, 1912.

Szörényi, A. "Das Buch Daniel, ein kanonisierter Pesher?" in *Volume du Congrès Genève*. VTSup 15. Leiden: Brill, 1966. Pages 278–294.

Tcherikover, V. *Hellenistic Civilization and the Jews,* tr. S. Applebaum. Philadelphia: Jewish Publication Society of America, 1961. *Cited as* Tcherikover.

Torrey, C. C. "Notes on the Aramaic Part of Daniel," *Connecticut Academy of Arts and Sciences Transactions* 15 (1909), 241–282.

Towner, W. S. "The Poetic Passages of Daniel 1-6," *CBQ* 31 (1969), 317–326.

Trever, J. C. "Completion of the Publication of Some Fragments from Cave I," *RevQ* 19 (1965), 323–344; Daniel fragments on plates v and vi.

Tsevat, M. "God and the Gods in Assembly: An Interpretation of Psalm 82," *HUCA* 40–41 (1969–70), 123–137.

Van Zeller, H. *Daniel: Man of Desires.* Westminster, Md.: Newman, 1951.

Vawter, B. "Apocalyptic: Its Relation to Prophecy," *CBQ* 22 (1960), 33–46.

Vermes, G. "The Use of *br nš/br nš'* in Jewish Aramaic." Appendix to M. Black, *An Aramaic Approach to the Gospels and Acts,* 3d ed. Oxford: Clarendon, 1967. Pages 310–328.

Vogt, E. *Lexicon linguae aramaicae veteris testamenti.* Rome: Pontifical Biblical Institute, 1971.

——— " 'Mysteria' in textibus Qumran," *Bib* 37 (1956), 247–257.

Wagner, M. *Die lexikalischen und grammatikalischen Aramaismen im alttestamentlichen Hebräisch.* BZAW 96. Berlin: Töpelmann, 1966.

Walters, P. (formerly Katz). *The Text of the Septuagint: Its Corruptions and Their Emendation,* ed. D. W. Gooding. Cambridge University Press, 1973.

Welch, A. C. *Visions of the End: A Study of Daniel and Revelation.* London: J. Clark, 1922; reprint 1958.

Wevers, J. W. "Theodotion." *IDB* 4. Nashville: Abingdon, 1962. Pages 618–619.

Wheelwright, P. *Metaphor and Reality.* Indiana University Press, 1962; Midland Book ed., 1968.

Whitcomb, J. C. *Darius the Mede: A Study in Historical Identification.* Grand Rapids: Eerdmans, 1959.

Wifall, W. "Son of Man—A Pre-Davidic Social Class?" *CBQ* 37 (1975), 331–340.

Wilder, A. N. "The Rhetoric of Ancient and Modern Apocalyptic," *Int* 25 (1971), 436–453.

Willi-Plein, I. "Das Geheimnis der Apokalyptik," *VT* 27 (1977), 62–81.

Wilson, R. D. "The Book of Daniel and the Canon," *Princeton Theological Review* 13 (1915), 352–408.

——— "The Title 'King of Persia' in the Scriptures," *Princeton Theological Review* 15 (1917), 90–145.

Winston, D. "The Iranian Component in the Bible, Apocrypha, and Qumran: A Review of the Evidence," *HR* 5 (1965–66), 183–216.

Wisemann, D. J. *Notes on Some Problems in the Book of Daniel.* London: Tyndale Press, 1965.

Wolf, C. U. "Daniel and the Lord's Prayer: A Synthesis of the Theology of the Book of Daniel," *Int* 15 (1961), 398–410.

Wood, L. *Commentary on Daniel*. Grand Rapids: Zondervan, 1973.

——— *Daniel: A Study Guide*. Grand Rapids: Zondervan, 1975.

Wyngarden, M. J. *The Syriac Version of the Book of Daniel*. Leipzig: W. Drugulin, 1923.

Zevit, Z. "The Structure and Individual Elements of Daniel 7," *ZAW* 80 (1968), 385–396.

Ziegler, J. *Susanna, Daniel, Bel et Draco*. Septuaginta, Vetus Testamentum Graecum, Auctoritate Societatis Litterarum Gottingensis editum 16/2. Göttingen: Vandenhoeck & Ruprecht, 1954.

Zimmermann, F. *Biblical Books Translated from the Aramaic*. New York: Ktav, 1975.

TRANSLATION
Notes and Comments

I. DANIEL AND HIS COMPANIONS AT THE COURT OF NEBUCHADNEZZAR (1:1–21)

1 1 In the third year of the reign of Jehoiakim king of Judah
Nebuchadnezzar king of Babylon came and besieged Jerusalem.
2 [a]The Lord[a] handed over to him Jehoiakim king of Judah together
with some of the articles of God's house. These he brought to the land
of Shinar[b] and deposited them in the treasure house of his god.
3 The king later told Ashpenaz, chief of his palace servants, to
bring in some of the Israelites of royal blood or of the aristocracy
4 [c]and have them taught the language and literature of the Chaldeans[c]. They were to be flawless and handsome young men, intelligent and clever, and quick to learn and understand—such as would
have the ability to take their place in the royal palace; 5 [c]at the end of
three years of training they would serve at the royal court[c]. The king
assigned them a daily allotment of the royal menu and of the wine
that he drank. 6 Among these men of Judah were Daniel, Hananiah,
Mishael, and Azariah; 7 but the chief of the palace servants gave them
new names: Daniel he called Belteshazzar, Hananiah he called Shadrach, Mishael he called Meshach, and Azariah he called Abednego.
8 Daniel, however, had made up his mind not to defile himself with
the king's menu or with his wine; so he asked the chief of the palace
servants to spare him this defilement. 9 Though the chief of the palace
servants was moved by God to be kind and sympathetic towards
Daniel, 10 he said to him, "I'm afraid of my lord the king; it is he who
assigned your food and drink. If he sees you looking less healthy than
the other young men of your group, you will bring the king's judgment on my head." 11 But Daniel said to the steward in whose charge
he as well as Hananiah, Mishael, and Azariah, had been placed by the
chief of the palace servants, 12 "Please test your servants for ten days

[a–a] Many Hebrew MSS have "Yahweh."

[b] So LXX; MT adds, by dittography from the end of the verse, "to the house of his god"; cf. LXX^{967}.

[c–c] MT has these phrases at the end of vss. 4 and 5.

by giving us only vegetables to eat and water to drink; 13 then compare our appearance with that of the young men who partake of the king's menu, and deal with your servants on the basis of what you see." 14 The steward agreed to their proposal and tested them for ten days. 15 At the end of the ten days they looked healthier and better fed than any of the young men who partook of the king's menu. 16 So the steward continued to take away the royal menu and wine that they were to receive and gave them instead only vegetables.

17 God, on his part, gave these four young men knowledge and skill in all literature and science, and Daniel was also endowed with the understanding of every kind of vision and dream. 18 At the end of the period that the king had assigned for their training, the chief of the palace servants brought them to Nebuchadnezzar's court. 19 When the king interviewed them, not one of all the other young men was found to be the equal of Daniel, Hananiah, Mishael, and Azariah.

Thus they entered the king's service. 20 In any matter requiring [d]wisdom and understanding[d] on which the king consulted them he found them ten times better than all the magicians and[e] enchanters in his whole realm. 21 Daniel was there until the first year of King Cyrus.

[d–d] So LXX, Theod., and Syr.; MT has "wisdom of understanding."
[e] So LXX and Theod.; MT omits.

Notes

1:1. *the third year of . . . Jehoiakim.* The year 606 B.C., since Jehoiakim began to reign in 609. But in 606 Nebuchadnezzar was still in northern Syria; it was only in the following year that he won his decisive victory over the Egyptians at Carchemish, and it was not until 598 that he first appeared before the walls of Jerusalem, as correctly stated in II Kings 24:10–12 and as is now known from the Babylonian Chronicle (see *BASOR* 143 [1956], 28–33; *BA* 19 [1956], 50–60). Apart from the strange date, Dan 1:1–2 is evidently dependent on II Chron 36:5–7: "Jehoiakim . . . reigned eleven years at Jerusalem. . . . Nebuchadnezzar, the king of Babylon, came up against him and bound him with chains to take him to Babylon. Nebuchadnezzar also brought some of the articles of the house of Yahweh to Babylon and put them in his palace at Babylon." However the "third" year here in Dan 1:1 is hard to account for. One might suppose that in the original text there were some words now lost that referred to some event of that year about which we otherwise know nothing. But there is not the slightest textual evidence to support such a supposition. It seems simpler to think that our author merely followed an earlier folk legend without being concerned about the accuracy of the date. The legend may have gotten the "third" year (literally, "in the year [of] three" in the Hebrew of Dan 1:1) from II Kings 24:1 ("In his [Jehoiakim's] days Nebuchadnezzar king of Babylon came up, and Jehoiakim became his servant three years; then he turned and rebelled against him"), even though this really refers to events that happened some time after the battle of Carchemish (605 B.C.).

2. *Shinar.* An archaizing use of the ancient name of Babylonia (Gen 10:10; Isa 11:11; Zech 5:11). The "articles of God's house" are mentioned in this introductory chapter because they will play a part in the story of ch. 5.

3. *Ashpenaz.* Almost the same consonants (*'spnz*) occur as a personal name on an Aramaic incantation bowl of ca. A.D. 600 from Nippur (D. W. Myhrman, "An Aramaic Incantation Text," in *Hilprecht Anniversary Volume* [Leipzig: J. C. Hinrichs, 1909], p. 345, line 1). The name is apparently Persian (cf. the Pahlavi word, *aspanj,* "guest") and thus reflects the Persian setting of the original legend. LXX$^{88\text{-Syh.}}$ substitutes a good Hebrew name, Abi-ezer (cf. Judg 8:32; Josh 17:2; II Sam 23:27; etc.). LXX^{967} merely transliterates into Greek letters—*Aspanes.*

palace servants. In Hebrew, *sārîsîm,* a word borrowed from the Assyrian term, *sa rêsi* (*sarri*), corresponding to the Babylonian, *ša rêši* (*šarri*), literally, "he of the head (of the king)," denoting originally a "confidant" of the king, but later used of any "palace servant." The Hebrew word is often rendered in English as "Eunuch," but even in the Persian period the *sārîsîm* were not necessarily castrated. In any case, the text does not imply that the Israelite youths in the care of Ashpenaz were made eunuchs.

aristocracy. In Hebrew, *partᵉmîm,* "nobles," a word borrowed from the Persian. In the Bible it is used only here and in Esther 1:3; 6:9—an indication that this passage could hardly antedate the Persian period. Our author presupposes that his readers know of the deportation of the Jewish nobility at the time of Nebuchadnezzar's first siege of Jerusalem as recounted in II Kings 24:12.

4. *language and literature.* Literally, "book and tongue."

Chaldeans. This term designated originally an Aramaic-speaking people who infiltrated into Babylonia in the first half of the first millennium B.C. and gradually gained the ascendancy there. But in Hellenistic times, when itinerant astrologers and fortune-tellers from Babylonia were well-known throughout the Mediterranean world, the term "Chaldean" was often used, not in its original, political sense (as in Dan 5:30; Ezra 5:12), but in the derived sense of "astrologer, fortune-teller" (as certainly in Dan 2:2–5,10; 4:4; 5:7,11, and probably also in 3:8). Here, therefore, "the language and literature of the Chaldeans" does not mean Babylonian (Akkadian) cuneiform literature as such, but rather the omen lore for which the Babylonians were famous. It is part of our author's satire on paganism to have his Jewish heroes beat their pagan colleagues at their own game.

flawless. Literally, "in whom there was no blemish." The same Hebrew expression is used in Lev 21:17–23 to describe one of the requisites for an Israelite priest to perform his functions in the sanctuary, and in Lev 22:18–25 to describe one of the conditions necessary in an animal that is fit for sacrifice.

4–5. *to take their place in the royal palace . . . serve at the royal court.* Perhaps our author has in mind the prophecy of Isaiah to King Hezekiah: "Some of your descendants will be taken and made palace servants [*sārîsîm*] at the court of the king of Babylon" (Isa 39:7).

5. *three years of training.* This is more in keeping with Persian than with Babylonian education. A triennium of education is prescribed in the Avesta: "How long a time of a year's length shall a student go to a master of spiritual learning? For a period of three springtides [years] he shall gird himself with the holy education" (*Sacred Books of the East,* 2d ed., 4:311*ff,* cited by Montgomery, p. 122).

a daily allotment of the royal menu. Literally, "a daily amount from the *pat-bag* of the king." The Hebrew term *pat-bag* (with artificial division, as if it contained the Hebrew word, *pat,* "morsel") is derived from the Old Persian word, *patibaga,* a technical term designating a government-supplied "portion, ration" of food. Although the terminology in Daniel is influenced by Persian usage, the custom that is referred to reflects correctly the Neo-Babylonian period. It seems likely that our author here depends on the account given in II Kings 25:30; Jer 52:34 concerning the daily allotment of food granted by the king of Babylon to the exiled King Jehoiachin, for he uses the same rather strange Hebrew expression for "daily amount" (*dᵉbar-yôm bᵉyômô*) that is used in these passages. A cuneiform text has been found that records the daily portion of food allotted to King Jehoiachin and his sons while they were exiled in Babylon (*BA* 5 [1942], 49–55). The common rendering of the Hebrew word *pat-bag* as "dainties" or "delicacies" is merely a free translation according to the context.

7. *Belteshazzar.* In Hebrew, *bēlṭᵉša'ṣṣar,* which contains a faulty vocalization of the Babylonian name, *Balāṭšu-uṣur,* "Guard his life!"; this, however, is a shortened form of a name that would have begun with the invocation of a god, such as, *Marduk-balaṭšu-uṣur* or *Bēl-balāṭšu-uṣur.* The vocalization of the name in the MT seems to assume that even in its shortened form it contains the name of the god Bel (cf. 4:5). The meaning of the names Shadrach and Meshach is uncertain. The name Abednego (MT *'ăbēd-nᵉgô*) is a distortion, perhaps caused by accidental dissimilation rather than by deliberate intent, of the Hebrew name Abednebo, corresponding to the Babylonian name *Arad-Nabu,* "servant of [the god] Nabu."

11. *steward.* In Hebrew, *melṣar,* a word borrowed, probably through Aramaic, from the Babylonian word *maṣṣaru* (originally, *manṣaru*), "guardian." Probably the dissimilation of *ṣṣ* into *lṣ* had already taken place in Late Babylonian (cf. W. von Soden, *Grundriss der akkadischen Grammatik,* AnOr 33, §30, f–g).

12. *ten days.* A relatively short time. The period of ten days for a spiritual trial is a common motif in the literature of the time (cf. Rev 2:10; Jubilees 19:8; Testament of the Twelve Patriarchs, Joseph 2:7; Pirke Abot 5:4).

15. The idea that fasting improves a person's health and beauty is found also in the more or less contemporaneous Book of Judith (8:6–7) and in the slightly later Test. Twelve Patriarchs (Joseph 3:4).

17. In the ancient Near East, ritual and ascetical purification was always regarded as a necessary preparation for contact with the deity and as a prereq-

uisite for receiving mystical revelations. But even stronger emphasis was laid on this idea in the Hellenistic age, as evidenced by the practices of the Therapeutae, the Essenes, and the Qumran sectaries. Thus, our heroes too obtain their deeper knowledge and wisdom by fasting and apparently, since no reference is made anywhere in the book to wives or children of these men, also by celibacy. Our author, however, is careful to note that the superior knowledge and wisdom of these men came, not as a direct result of their asceticism, but as a gift from God.

20. *magicians.* In Hebrew, *ḥarṭummîm,* a word of Egyptian derivation that, apart from this book, occurs only in reference to the soothsayers of Egypt in the accounts of Joseph in Egypt (Gen 41:8,24) and of Moses and Aaron at the court of Pharaoh (Exod 7:11,22; etc.)—an indication, among others (see COMMENT on Daniel 2), of our author's dependence on the story of Joseph.

enchanters. In Hebrew, *'aššāpîm* (only here and in 2:2), a much more appropriate term, since it is derived from the Akkadian word, *āšipu,* "incantation priest" (apparently through the Aramaic; cf. the *'āšepîn* in the Aramaic sections of Daniel [2:10,27, etc.] and thus better reflects the Babylonian background of the story. The author correctly reflects the immense development of diplomatic divination and the tremendous influence of omen literature in the court life of ancient Mesopotamia. (See A. L. Oppenheim, *Ancient Mesopotamia: Portrait of a Dead Civilization,* "The Arts of the Diviner," pp. 206–227.)

21. *the first year of King Cyrus.* The year 538 B.C. The period of Daniel's activity in Babylon is considerable (from 606 to 538) but not absolutely impossible. The author was probably not concerned here with the fact that this period amounts to almost seventy years, the length of time, as foretold by Jeremiah, for the Babylonian exile, that Daniel 9 will be concerned with. For a more likely reason why this chronological remark is made here, see COMMENT.

COMMENT

The first chapter of the book serves primarily as an introduction; it sets the scene for the other stories and the visions (chs. 7–12) that make up the rest of the book. The author here brings together various strands that appear as separate units in the other chapters of the book.

This can be seen, first of all, in the way our author, who edited the five older stories of chs. 2–6, introduces all of the four heroes of these stories in ch. 1 practically on a par, although a certain prominence is already given to Daniel. In the older stories Daniel alone is the hero of chs. 4–6, as well as in the original form of ch. 2, where the mention of his companions (2:17*f*,49) seems to be a later addition (see COMMENT on ch. 2). On the other hand, the only heroes of ch. 3 are solely the three companions of Daniel.

Moreover, the double set of names would seem to show that the older stories about the three men once existed in two distinct forms, one calling them by "foreign" names and the other calling them by Hebrew names. In ch. 3 (and also in 2:49) they are spoken of only by their foreign names. On the contrary, in 2:17 (and also in the fragment of the longer Greek version [3:*24–90*], where Azariah is their spokesman) they are mentioned only by their Hebrew names. The author of the first chapter, in editing the two variant forms of the stories, offers an explanation of how they happened to have two sets of names: at the Babylonian court their Hebrew names were changed into "Babylonian" names. It could, of course, have been possible that many Jews in the Babylonian exile took Babylonian names in addition to their Hebrew names, just as in New Testament times many had Greek, as well as Hebrew or Aramaic, names.

The various older stories that our author compiled are presented as taking place under the kings Nebuchadnezzar (2:1; 3:1; 4:1), Belshazzar (5:1; 7:1; 8:1), Darius (6:1; 9:1), and Cyrus (6:29; 10:1)—in that order. Therefore, the author of the first chapter summarizes Daniel's career at the imperial court by saying that he was there from the reign of Nebuchadnezzar to the reign of Cyrus (1:21). [It should be recalled that "the first year of King Cyrus" (1:21), or 538 B.C., is not the end of Daniel's career but simply the end of his service in the Babylonian court. Daniel experiences his final vision "in the third year of King Cyrus" (10:1), i.e. in 536 B.C. Cf. COMMENT: DETAILED on 10:1.]

Since Daniel is to show forth his God-given wisdom by interpreting dreams and visions in chs. 2, 4, and 5, the author of ch. 1 is careful to prepare the reader for this by stating here (1:17) that God gave him and his companions great knowledge and wisdom and endowed Daniel in particular with the understanding of every kind of vision and dream. The superiority over the Babylonian wise men that Daniel shows in chs. 2, 4, and 5 is likewise foreshadowed in ch. 1 (vs. 20).

In ch. 3, Daniel's three companions are put to a test (the fiery furnace) to prove their fidelity to the Lord, and the Lord rescues them miraculously. In ch. 6, Daniel is put to a test (the lions' den) for the same purpose and with the same result. Therefore, in ch. 1, all four men are introduced as proving their fidelity to the Lord by abstaining from forbidden food, and the Lord shows his power by miraculously rewarding them with perfect health.

Inasmuch as the sacred vessels that the Babylonians had taken from the Temple of Jerusalem play a part in the story of ch. 5 (5:2*f*,23), our author does not fail to note in 1:2 how these articles as well as his heroes were taken to Babylon.

Since, therefore, ch. 1 was written to serve as an introduction to the older stories of chs. 2–6, it may be essentially an *ad hoc* composition and not in itself an older story. If this be so, one may assume that the author-compiler of the book wrote the first chapter in Hebrew, while he left the older stories of the following chapters (except for the transitional verses of 2:1–4a) in their original Aramaic.

It is, however, more probable that the author used an older Aramaic story for the account of the "food test" in ch. 1. [Cf. Introduction, Part III, "Unity of the Book and Date," regarding the hypothesis of an Aramaic original of the whole book.] In any case, this part of the chapter can hardly be used as an argument to prove that the chapter was written during Epiphanes' persecution of the Jews on the ground that in this persecution the eating or non-eating of pork was used as a test to show whether a Jew preferred Hellenism or Judaism (I Macc 1:14–64; II Macc 6–7). No doubt, the final editor, who surely compiled the Book of Daniel during this persecution, included this story of the food test for the purpose of encouraging his persecuted compatriots to be faithful to the dietary laws of their religion. But these laws themselves were much older than the third or second century B.C. Various taboos against "unclean" food must have gone back to the very oldest period of Israelite history, even though in the form in which they are now found in the Pentateuch (in the so-called Priestly Document) they may have been codified only in the Babylonian exile. It was the observance of these laws during and after the exile that helped to preserve the Jews as a distinct people. Therefore, the Book of Daniel does not fail historical verisimilitude in portraying its heroes as being as conscientious about these laws in the sixth century B.C. as the Jews were in the third and second centuries B.C.

Since Daniel and his companions believed that with good conscience they could eat only vegetables (literally, "seed-bearing plants"), it seems that they feared that any meat or fish they received as royal rations might include forbidden species or might have been prepared in an "unclean" way. It is not as easy, however, to say why they abstained also from wine, since wine as such was not forbidden by any Jewish law. Perhaps they acted as Nazirites, who abstained from all alcoholic beverages, or perhaps they thought that part of the wine had been poured out in libation to pagan gods and thus became ritually unclean for Jews.

II. NEBUCHADNEZZAR'S DREAM OF THE COMPOSITE STATUE (2:1–49)

2 1 In the second year of the reign of Nebuchadnezzar, the king
had dreams that left his mind no peace and [a]deprived him of sleep[a].
2 So he had the magicians, enchanters, sorcerers, and Chaldeans summoned, that they might tell him what he had dreamed. When they
came and presented themselves before the king, 3 he said to them, "I
had a dream that will leave my mind no peace until I know what it is."
4 The Chaldeans answered the king (Aramaic), "O king, live forever!
Tell your servants the dream, and then we shall give its meaning."
5 The king replied to the Chaldeans, "This is the decree that I proclaim[b]: if you do not let me know both the dream and its meaning, you
shall be torn limb from limb and your homes reduced to ruins. 6 But if
you show me what the dream is and what it means, you shall receive
from me gifts and presents and great honors. Tell me, therefore, the
dream and its meaning."

7 Again they answered, "If the king will please tell his servants
what the dream is, we shall give its meaning." 8 But in reply the king
said, "Now I know for certain that you are merely bargaining for
time, because you realize I have proclaimed the decree 9 that, if you
do not let me know the dream, there can be only one fate for you.
You have agreed on presenting me with some vile lie until the situation becomes different. Therefore, tell me the dream, that I may be
sure that you can also give its interpretation." 10 The Chaldeans answered the king, "There is not a man on earth who is able to make the
revelation that the king demands. In fact, no king, however great and
powerful, has ever asked such a thing of any magician, enchanter, or
Chaldean. 11 What the king is asking is so difficult that no one but divine beings can reveal it to him, and their abode is not among mortal

[a–a] *nād^{e}dāh,* conjecture, literally, "sleep fled from him"; see NOTES. MT has, "sleep became upon him."

[b] A Qumran fragment of Daniel (1QDan^{a}) inserts *dî,* "that," here, a reading that corresponds to LXX; cf. vss. 8–9.

men." 12 With that, the king became very angry, and in his rage
he ordered all the wise men of Babylon to be executed.

/ 13 When the decree was issued that the wise men were to be put
to death, Daniel and his companions were sought out also, that they
too should be slain. 14 But Daniel prudently took counsel with
Arioch, the chief of the royal police, who had set out to kill the wise
men of Babylon. 15 "Why is the order that the king issued so peremptory?" he asked Arioch, the king's officer. When Arioch explained the
matter to him, 16 Daniel went and requested the king to grant him
time, and he would give the king the interpretation. 17 Daniel then
went home and made the matter known to his companions, Hananiah, Mishael, and Azariah. 18 He asked them to implore the mercy of
the God of heaven in regard to this mystery, that he and his companions might not perish with the rest of the wise men of Babylon. 19 At
night the mystery was revealed to Daniel in a vision, and blessing the
God of heaven, 20 he said:

"May the name of God be blessed
from all eternity and forever,
for wisdom and power are his.
21 He brings about the changes in the times and the eras;
he deposes kings and sets up kings.
Wisdom he gives to the wise,
and knowledge to those who have understanding.
22 He reveals deep and hidden things
and he knows what is in the darkness,
for light abides in him.
23 To you, O God of my fathers,
I render thanks and praise
for you have given me wisdom and power.
Now you have shown me what we asked of you
and have made known to us what concerns the king."/

24 Accordingly, Daniel went[c] to Arioch, whom the king had ap-
pointed to destroy the wise men of Babylon, and he said to him,
"Don't destroy the wise men of Babylon. Bring me in to the king, and
I will tell him the meaning of the dream." 25 Rushing excitedly,
Arioch brought Daniel in to the king and said to the king, "I have
found a man among the exiles of Judah who can interpret the king's

[c] The standard MT accidentally repeats the word *'al*, "to", which in the context could also mean "entered"; but in the same phrase (though not according to the Masoretic cantillation marks) there is the verb *'ăzal*, "went."

dream." 26 The king asked Daniel, whose name was Belteshazzar, "Are you really able to tell me the dream that I had and show me its meaning?" 27 Daniel answered the king: "The mystery about which the king is inquiring no wise man, enchanter, magician, or diviner can explain to him. 28 But there is a God in heaven who reveals mysteries, and he has let King Nebuchadnezzar know what is to happen in the last days. Your dream, the vision that came to your mind as you were lying on your bed, is this:

/ 29 "To you, O king, as you were lying on your bed, thoughts came about what would happen hereafter; and the Revealer of mysteries has shown you what will happen. 30 To me, however, this mystery has been revealed, not because my own wisdom is more than that of other living persons, but in order that its meaning may be shown to you, and thus you may understand the thought that came to your heart. /

31 "In your vision, O king, you beheld standing before you a statue that was very large and extraordinary in appearance. The sight of it was terrifying. 32 The head of the statue was of pure gold, its chest and arms were of silver, its belly and hips of bronze, 33 its legs of iron, and its feet partly of iron and partly of terra cotta. 34 As you looked on, a stone was cut out[d], without a hand being put to it, and striking the statue on its feet of iron and terra cotta, it crushed them. 35 With that, the iron, the terra cotta, the bronze, the silver, and the gold were all crushed together, fine as the chaff on the threshing floor in summer; and the wind blew them away, so that no trace of them could be found. But the stone that struck the statue became a great mountain and filled all the earth. 36 This was the dream.

"Its meaning we will now tell the king. 37 You, O king—king of kings, to whom the God of heaven has given sovereignty and power, strength and glory, 38 and to whom he has handed over the men, the wild animals, and the birds of the air in the whole inhabited world, making you ruler of them all—you are the head of gold. 39 But your place will be taken by another kingdom, inferior to yours, and then by still another, a third kingdom, one of bronze, which will rule over all the earth. 40 Then there will be a fourth kingdom, as strong as iron; just as iron crushes and smashes everything / (and like iron that breaks things to pieces) /, it will crush and break all these others. 41 Inasmuch as you saw the feet // and the toes // partly of potter's terra cotta and partly of iron, it will be a divided kingdom, with some elements of iron in it.

[d] LXX and Theod. add "from a mountain"; cf. vs. 45.

/ "Just as you saw the iron mixed with terra cotta of clay // 42 and the toes of the feet partly of iron and partly of terra cotta, in part the kingdom will be strong, and in part it will be brittle. // 43 Just as you saw the iron mixed with terra cotta of clay, they will be mingled by intermarriage, but they will not hold together, just as iron does not unite with terra cotta. /

44 "In the days of those regimes the God of heaven will set up a kingdom that will never be destroyed, nor will this kingdom ever be delivered up to another people. It will crush and put an end to all those other kingdoms, while it itself will stand forever, 45 just as you saw that a stone was cut out / from the mountain /, without a hand being put to it, and that it crushed [e]the iron, the bronze, the terra cotta[e], the silver, and the gold. The great God has let the king know what will happen hereafter. This is certainly the dream, and its interpretation is trustworthy."

46 King Nebuchadnezzar thereupon prostrated himself in worship before Daniel, and he ordered that sacrifice and incense should be offered up to him. 47 "Your God," the king said to Daniel, "is truly the God of gods and the Lord of kings; he is the revealer of mysteries, for you have been able to reveal this mystery." 48 Then the king made Daniel a magnate and gave him many generous gifts; he made him ruler over the whole province of Babylon and chief prefect over all the wise men in Babylon. / 49 At Daniel's request the king appointed Shadrach, Meshach, and Abednego administrators of the province of Babylon, while Daniel himself functioned at the royal chancellery. /

[e–e] LXX[88-Syh.] and Theod. have: "the terra cotta, the iron, the bronze"; although this is the logical order of the items, it probably represents a deliberate correction of the careless order of the original.

NOTES

2:1. *In the second year of the reign of Nebuchadnezzar.* In 603 B.C. This is consistent with the date given in 1:1, "the third year of the reign of King Jehoiakim of Judah," i.e. 606 B.C., inasmuch as it allows for Daniel's three years of training at the Babylonian court. But the date here in 2:1 is inconsistent with ch. 1 inasmuch as it does not allow for these three years between the time King Nebuchadnezzar deported Daniel to Babylon and the second year of this king's reign. The date may have already been in the older story that our author incorporated as ch. 2 of his book, and he was not concerned about his historical accuracy. [LXX[967] reads here "In the twelfth year. . . ."] In any case, the date seems just as artificial as the dates in 7:1, 8:1, 9:1, and 10:1. A Jewish writer of the late postexilic period who put a reign of "Darius the Mede" between the last Babylonian king and the first Persian one would hardly have known enough of Babylonian chronology to correlate it correctly with biblical chronology. In the older form of the story the Babylonian king may have been Nabonidus (see COMMENT: DETAILED on 2:1–12).

deprived him of sleep. On the assumption that the Hebrew of vss. 1–4a has been translated from the Aramaic (see NOTE on vs. 4), the *ûšenātô nihyetāh ʻālāyw* of the MT represents *wešintēh naddat ʻĕlôhî,* the phrase that occurs in 6:19. Either the *nihyetāh* may be explained as meaning "fulfilled, completed, finished," (cf. Prov 13:19: *ta'ăwāh nihyāh,* "fulfilled desire"), or it may be corrected to *nādedāh,* "fled."

2. *sorcerers.* In Hebrew, *mekaššepîm,* practitioners of black magic who are condemned in the Old Testament (Deut 18:10; Mal 3:5; etc.). The term is connected with, though not necessarily derived from, the Babylonian verb *kašāpu,* "to bewitch, practice sorcery." On the "magicians, enchanters, and Chaldeans," see NOTES on 1:20 and 1:4. All these words, as well as the word "diviners" (Aramaic *gāzerîn,* literally, "deciders": 2:27; 4:4; 5:7,11), are used in Daniel, not as technical terms, but merely as various synonyms for "soothsayers." Since the term "Chaldeans" can occur in the midst of the other terms (4:4; 5:7,11) as well as at their end (2:2,10), it is evident that in this context it does not have its original ethnic meaning. In this chapter this is probably the case also when the term occurs alone, as summing up the other synonyms (2:4*f*,10).

4. *Aramaic.* This word is a gloss, inserted here in the text to show that from here on to the end of ch. 7 the language of the text is not Hebrew but Aramaic. In 1QDan[a] there is a space (not the gloss) before the beginning of the Aramaic. According to the hypothesis proposed in the Introduction, Part III, the writer who translated into Hebrew the Aramaic original of the book found this point in vs. 4 a convenient and "logical" place to stop his work of translation, since it seemed only natural to let the "Chaldeans" speak in their own language. The translator resumed his work at the beginning of ch. 8 and rendered the remainder of the book into Hebrew.

5. *This is the decree that I proclaim.* Literally, "The matter is publicly known (is decided) as far as I am concerned." The term *'azdâ,* "public knowledge, publicly known," is an Old Persian word.

torn limb from limb. Literally, "made [into] limbs." The word *haddāmîn,* "limbs," is derived from the Persian word **handāma.* For the sense, cf. II Macc 1:16.

ruins. Or perhaps, "a dump, a dunghill." For this sense, though not with a word of the same root, cf. II Kings 10:27. The Aramaic word *newālî,* "ruins," is of uncertain derivation.

6. *presents.* In Aramaic, *nebizbāh,* of uncertain derivation and meaning.

11. *divine beings.* In Aramaic-Daniel, "god" or "God" (=Yahweh) is regularly expressed by the singular *'ĕlāh, 'ĕlāhâ* (2:18*f*,23,28,37,44,47;

3:15,26,28,32; 5:3,18,21; 6:8,13,21,27). The plural *'ĕlāhîn* generally means "(pagan) gods" (3:12; 5:4,23), though sometimes "God" (=Yahweh: 6:17,21). But here, *'ĕlāhîn* seems to be used in a broad sense, to include all superhuman beings. The LXX$^{88\text{-}Syh.}$ takes it in the sense of "angel" (in the singular!); LXX^{967} has "angels"; cf. *bar 'ĕlāhîn,* "angel," in 3:25.

13–23. This passage seems to be a secondary intrusion into the main story of ch. 2. Besides several minor differences in style and vocabulary, it shows the following inconsistencies with the main story. (1) Here Arioch goes to Daniel (vs. 14), whereas in vs. 24 Daniel goes to Arioch. (2) Here Daniel visits the king quite freely, as if already known to the king, who readily grants him sufficient time to learn in a dream the nature of the king's dream and its interpretation (vss. 16–19), whereas in vss. 24–28 Arioch must first introduce Daniel to the king, who therefore had not known him before this; and Daniel can at once tell the king his dream and its interpretation. (3) Here the companions of Daniel play a role in the account (vss. 13,17*f*), whereas in the rest of the story, apart from vs. 49 (which is also a secondary addition), no reference is made to Daniel's companions. Other secondary elements occur in vss. 29*f*, 40–43. One may therefore assume that the story once circulated in at least two variant accounts, which have been combined, not very smoothly, in the account as now given in ch. 2. The present conflation, however, was probably made before the whole Book of Daniel was compiled in the first half of the second century B.C.

14. *Daniel prudently took counsel with Arioch.* Literally, "Daniel returned counsel and prudence to Arioch"; the free translation takes "counsel and prudence" as a hendiadys. The name "Arioch," of uncertain derivation, first appears as the name of a king of Ellasar in Gen 14:1,9. In the historical hodgepodge of the Book of Judith (1:6) it is the name of a king of Elam. Postexilic Jewish literature, borrowing the name from Genesis 14, apparently regarded it was a fitting name for any important Oriental.

chief of the . . . police. The Aramaic term used here, *rab-ṭabbāḥayyâ,* corresponding to the Hebrew term *rab-ṭabbāḥîm* (II Kings 25:8–20, where it is the title of a high-ranking officer in Nebuchadnezzar's army), meant originally "chief of the slaughterers," i. e. Lord High Executioner.

18. *the God of heaven.* A common term for Yahweh in postexilic times, which, however, fell into disfavor among the Jews in post-Maccabean times because of its similarity with the pagan term, "lord of heaven (*ba'al šemayin, Zeus Ouranios;* see NOTE on 9:27).

mystery. Or, "secret." The Aramaic term, *rāz,* which occurs also in 2:19, 27–30,47; 4:6, is a loanword from the Persian. The concept behind it goes back to the Hebrew term, *sôd,* which designates both a "council" and the "secret decisions" rendered in the council. In preexilic Israelite literature, *sôd* is used several times of God's council in heaven and of the decisions and decrees made there. These secret decrees that concern man God reveals to his prophets (e.g. Amos 3:7; Jer 23:18,22). In postexilic Jewish literature, both canonical and extracanonical, there is an extensive development of this concept of the divine mysteries or secrets (designated by *sôd* or *rāz* in Hebrew, and by *mystērion* in Greek) concerning a large variety of things which God reveals to men, often in symbolic language. Thus, in the Qumran literature there are "mysteries" of divine providence, cosmic "mysteries," and even "evil mysteries." Similarly, Paul speaks of "the mystery of Christ" (Col 4:3) as the divine plan for man's salvation in Jesus Christ, which God had kept secret in times past but which he has now revealed to Christians. On the use of the term *rāz* in the Jewish literature of the period, see E. Vogt, "'Mysteria' in textibus Qumran," *Bib* 37 (1956), 247–257; R. E. Brown, "The Pre-Christian Semitic Concept of Mystery," *CBQ* 20 (1958), 417–443; J. A. Fitzmyer, *The Genesis Apocryphon,* 2d rev. ed., BibOr 18A, p. 78.

with the rest of the wise men of Babylon. For the sake of bringing this verse in harmony with vs. 24, where Daniel is presented as wishing to save all the wise men, some would render the phrase here as "that he and his companions, together with the other wise men of Babylon, might not perish." But if the assumption is correct that there were originally two variant accounts of the story, there is no need for such harmonization.

19. *At night . . . in a vision.* Literally, "in a vision of the night"; cf. Job 4:13. The God-given revelation is distinguished from a mere dream.

22. *he knows what is in the darkness, for light abides in him.* The natural contrast beween light and darkness forms a common motif in Semitic literature. In the Old Testament, light is used symbolically for various concepts, such as sight, knowledge, truth, goodness, happiness, and even life itself; darkness is symbolic of the lack of these. In the present context, "light" is God's knowledge of "deep and hidden things," which for others are in "darkness." Both in the Qumran literature and in the New Testament, especially in the Johannine writings, the contrast is strongly pronounced: light and darkness stand for truth and error, goodness and wickedness, life and death; cf. "the sons of light and the sons of darkness" in the so-called War Scroll of Qumran and in I Thess 5:5; Eph 5:8; John 3:21; 8:12; 12:36; I John 1:7; 2:9*f.*

23. *wisdom and power.* Daniel shares in the wisdom and power that belong to God (vs. 20); hence the expression is probably not to be understood as a hendiadys for "mighty wisdom."

I . . . me . . . we . . . us. In shifting from the first person singular to the first person plural, Daniel wishes to include his companions, who had helped him by their prayers to obtain the revelation (vss. 17*f*).

28. *in the last days.* The Aramaic expression, *b*ᵉ*'aḥărît yômayyâ,* corresponding to the common Hebrew expression, *b*ᵉ*'aḥărît hayyāmîm* (Hosea 3:5; Isa 2:2; Dan 10:14, etc.), literally, "in the end of the days," is a typically eschatological term. It is stronger than the term, *'aḥărê d*ᵉ*nāh* ("hereafter"), which is used in the following secondary insertion.

29*f.* Instead of making certain deletions and transpositions in the text for the sake of obtaining a more smoothly flowing reading, as suggested by some scholars, it seems simpler to leave the text as it stands and to regard these two verses as a secondary addition coming from the same account of the story that is used in vss. 13–23, which tells how the mystery was revealed to Daniel.

33. *its legs . . . and its feet.* The terms are somewhat ambiguous; Aramaic *šāq* (Hebrew *šôq*) ordinarily designates only the upper leg. If it is so understood here, then *regel* (ordinarily, "foot") would designate the lower leg as well as

the foot, as in I Sam 17:6. However, it seems probable that *raglôhî* here means "his feet" (in the strict sense); in that case, *šāqôhî* here means "his legs"—both upper and lower legs.

terra cotta. In the context, the word *ḥăsap* means, not native "clay," but baked clay, terra cotta. "This is a clay which is plastic enough to model and yet also gives a dense smooth surface when burned—a surface that resists weather well. If the picture be taken literally, then it presents terra cotta inlays which were built into the iron feet of the great image, giving something like a pattern of cloisonné" (J. L. Kelso, "The Ceramic Vocabulary of the Old Testament," BASOR Supplementary Studies, Nos. 5–6 [1948], p. 7). A different picture is presented in Bel and the Dragon (Dan 14:7), where the whole statue of Bel is made of "clay inside and bronze outside."

38. According to the Masoretic punctuation marks, the passage would be literally: "And wherever men dwell, the wild animals and the bird he has handed over to you . . ." (cf. *KJV*), which is the interpretation of Theod. also. But since Daniel no doubt wished to stress Nebuchadnezzar's dominion over men more than over other creatures, the LXX understood the opening Aramaic phrase, *ûbᵉkol-dî dāyᵉrîn,* "and wherever they dwell," correctly as *en pasę tę oikoumenę,* "in all the inhabited world," and thus kept "men" as the first of the three objects of the verb "handed over."

40. The phrase in parentheses, "(and like iron that breaks things to pieces)," disturbs the syntax of the sentence and is not found in LXX, Theod., Syr., or Vulg. It is probably a later gloss.

41. *and the toes.* Not in LXX^{967}. Since there was no mention of "toes" in the description of the statue (vss. 33*f*), this is probably a later addition, coming from the same writer who added vs. 42 (see below).

41b–43. This whole paragraph is apparently a later addition, which contains within itself a still later addition (vs. 42). The original interpretation of the statue's feet as being partly of iron and partly of clay is given in vs. 41a as signifying "a divided kingdom" (for the historical allusion, see COMMENT). A later interpretation of the vision is given in vs. 43, where the mixture of iron and clay is understood of unsuccessful interdynastic marriages (for the historical allusion, see COMMENT). Finally, a still later glossator repeated the opening words of vs. 43 (now as vs. 41b) in order to introduce a new item in the image of the statue as now having only its toes partly of iron and partly of clay, for the sake of alluding to the relative strength of each of the two kingdoms.

44. *regimes.* Ginsberg, pp. 1,7, would vocalize the Aramaic *mlky'* (given in MT as *malkayyâ,* "kings") as *molkayyâ,* "kingdoms"; so also in 2:47; 7:17. In any case, the meaning "kingdoms" (so six Theod. MSS and Vulgate) rather than "kings" is required here.

45. *from the mountain.* This item is not given in the description of the vision, and so it may be a later addition here, perhaps suggested by the description of the stone itself becoming a great mountain in vs. 35.

47. *the Lord of kings.* According to H. L. Ginsberg ("'King of kings' and 'lord of kingdoms,'" *AJSL* 57 [1940], 71–74, the phrase, *mr' mlkyn,* is an Aramaic translation of the Greek *kyrios basileiōn,* "lord of kingships," a title of the Lagid kings of Egypt, and it should therefore be vocalized in Aramaic as

mārē' molkîn or mārē' mulkîn. But cf. Deut 10:17 ("God of gods and Lord of lords"); I Tim 6:15 ("King of kings [*basileuontōn*] and Lord of Lords"); Rev 17:14 ("Lord of lords and King of kings [*basileōn*]").

49. This verse gives the appearance of being an afterthought tacked on the end of the story. Probably it comes from the variant form of the story from which vss. 12–23 were taken.

royal chancellery. Literally, "the gate of the king." The word "gate" was a common Oriental term for "business office, court" (cf. Esther 3:2).

COMMENT: GENERAL

This second one of the older, once independent stories that the compiler of the Book of Daniel prefixed to his apocalyptic visions is made up of a theme within a theme. The latter (vss. 1–28,46–49), which forms the framework in which the former (vss. 29–45) is set, tells how the wisdom of the Jewish sage Daniel surpassed that of the pagan wise men, and it stresses the fact that such knowledge which is able to foretell four centuries of history can come only from the God of Israel (vss. 18–23,27*f*,47). There are several points of resemblance between this story and that told in Genesis 40–41 of Joseph's ability to interpret dreams in Egypt. But Daniel performs a feat greater than Joseph's: he not only interprets the ruler's dream; he even divines what the dream itself was. The story's dependence on Genesis, however, should not be overstressed. As stated in the Introduction, Part IX, this story, like the others in the first half of the Book of Daniel, is basically a Jewish adaptation of a type of tale that was widespread in the ancient Near East, the tale of the successful courtier. Moreover, the motif of the enigmatic dream and its interpretation was common in antiquity.

The core of the story is the account of Nebuchadnezzar's dream about a colossal statue, made of various materials, that was destroyed and displaced by a mysterious rock, together with the account of Daniel's interpretation of this dream as signifying the coming of the everlasting kingdom of God to supplant the earthly kingdoms of the Babylonians, the Medes, the Persians, and the Greeks. On the origin of the pre-Christian Jewish theory of these successive world-empires, see the Introduction, Part VI. Nebuchadnezzar's apocalyptic dream in this story is similar to but older than Daniel's apocalyptic vision of the four beasts that symbolize the same four world-empires in ch. 7.

In regard to the original date of composition of ch. 2, before it was incorporated into the Book of Daniel, one can, first of all, place the *terminus post quem* at least several generations after the establishment of the Persian empire by Cyrus in 539 B.C., as is evident from the nature of the Aramaic in which the story is written, containing as it does several loan words from Persian. As the *terminus ante quem* one can place the beginning of the second century B.C., for there is nothing in the chapter to suggest that its author knew anything of the troubles that Antiochus IV Epiphanes brought on the Jews. The Nebuchadnezzar of the story, who acknowledges that Daniel's God "is truly the God of gods and the Lord of kings," is certainly not intended as a symbol of Epiphanes. For an attempt at a more exact dating of the chapter, which ascribes the story as such to some time between 292 and 261 B.C and its later elements to some time between 246 and 220 B.C., see below.

Although the composition of the chapter thus antedates the time of Epiphanes' persecution of the Jews in the first half of the second century B.C., the compiler of the Book of Daniel, who published his work during this persecution, could well offer this story to his suffering compatriots in order to encourage them to remain faithful to their ancestral religion, for it both taught them the lesson that their God-given religion was far superior to the man-made philosophy and pagan religion of the Greeks and gave them the assurance that their God would destroy the world-empires of men and establish his own everlasting kingdom throughout the world.

COMMENT: DETAILED

Predicament of the Babylonian Wise Men (2:1–12)

As stated in the NOTES, the date given to this story as having happened in the second year of Nebuchadnezzar's reign (i.e. 603 B.C.) has no historical value. In fact, there may have been an older form of the story that made the king who had the strange dream not Nebuchadnezzar but Nabonidus; on the one hand, it is now known from the Qumran documents that at least the Daniel story of ch. 4 (see COMMENT there) once circulated in a form according to which the king of the story was Nabonidus, and on the other hand, the story of ch. 2 seems to echo both Nabonidus' conflict with the clergy of Babylon (see *ANET,* pp. 312b–315a) and his interest in dreams and their interpretation (see ibid., pp. 309b–310a). Although belief in dream omens was common throughout the history of ancient Mesopotamia (see A. L. Oppenheim, *Ancient Mesopotamia,* p. 222), Nabonidus' "preference for mentioning and, at times, reporting his own dreams represents another novum" (ibid., p. 150). At the same time, in Israel dreams were also commonly believed to be sent by God for the purpose of revealing important matters (*passim* in the Bible from Gen 20:6 to Matt 27:19), so that it is really not necessary to have recourse to Babylonian sources for the dream motifs of the Daniel stories (see also Daniel 4).

This story presents the king as greatly disturbed by his dream, as if he already had some inkling of its portentous importance. That he demands his soothsayers to tell him the dream itself should not be taken to mean that he had forgotten it; rather, he uses this as a test in order to have assurance that they can give him a reliable interpretation of it (vs. 9). The storyteller implies that, if the Chaldeans were given sufficient time to consult their dream books, they would naturally come up with a false interpretation; compare the ridicule heaped on the Babylonian astrologers in Isa 40:12–15. He also very cleverly puts in the mouths of the Chaldeans themselves the admission that the revelation of the dream and its meaning, which Daniel is about to give, can come only with God's help. The value that the Daniel stories attaches to dreams is not contrary to Sirach's strong condemnation of belief in dreams (34:1–8), since Sirach too admits that a dream may really be a vision sent by the Most High, which should then be carefully attended to (34:6).

Daniel's Intervention (2:13–28)

As pointed out in the NOTES on vss. 13–23, the present account of Daniel's intervention with the king to save the wise men of Babylon has apparently been conflated from two originally separate and somewhat divergent accounts.

In the account as given in vss. 13–23, Daniel and his three companions are regarded as belonging to the group of courtiers who assist the king with their wisdom. The royal decree that all these sages should be put to death affects the Jewish ones too. But Daniel has sufficient influence with Arioch, the Lord High Executioner, to withhold temporarily the execution of the royal decree. Thereupon he boldly comes before the royal throne and, rather surprisingly, is granted the very request (vs. 16) that had been refused to the Babylonian sages (vss. 8*f*)—sufficient time to find the answer to the king's problem. (Is this another indication that vss. 13–23 are secondary? In vs. 16 the omission of "entered and" in certain Theod. MSS and Syr., which thereby implies that Arioch acted as an intermediary for Daniel, is probably due to an attempt to harmonize this account with vss. 24*f* of the primary account.) Like the wise scribe of Sir 39:1–11 (especially vs. 6), Daniel and his companions pray for divine light to solve the king's mystery, so that, even though the rest of the wise men of Babylon are put to death, their own lives may be saved. God then reveals the mystery to Daniel in a nocturnal vision—a legitimate type of dream, but the reader is temporarily left in dramatic suspense concerning the nature of the mystery. In response, Daniel praises God in a typical Old Testament hymn of thanksgiving, cast in true poetic form and not without literary merit. Although some of the ideas and even phrases are borrowed from older Old Testament compositions (compare, e.g. vs. 20 with Ps 41:14; Neh 9:5; Job 12:13; and vs. 22 with Ps 36:10), this is an original composition, which not only fits the occasion but which also, in its praise of God as the one who "brings about changes in the times and the eras" and who "deposes kings and sets up kings," strikes the keynote of the whole Book of Daniel, that Yahweh is truly the Lord and Master of human history.

In the second account of Daniel's intervention, as given in vss. 24–28, the Jewish exile is evidently not regarded as having been one of the king's official sages. Although he himself, therefore, is in no danger of being put to death for not solving the king's problem, he intercepts Arioch, as the latter is about to carry out the royal decree to kill the wise men of Babylon, and he volunteers to tell the king his dream and its meaning for the sake of saving the lives of these men (vs. 24). The fact that Arioch, who is happy at this turn of events, must introduce Daniel to the king (vss. 25*f*) shows that this account does not consider the Jewish sage as having been among the wise men to whom the king had presented his problem. Therefore, apparently this account originally followed immediately after vss. 1–12. No mention is made in this account of Daniel's three companions. Even more strongly than the other account (in vss. 18–23) this one stresses the fact that the king's dream is really a vision sent by God (vs. 28) and that, consequently, it lies beyond the merely human wisdom of the Babylonian sages to understand it (vs. 27).

Daniel's Description of the King's Dream (2:29–36a)

The text seems to get off to a bad start in narrating Daniel's description of the king's dream. It would run much more smoothly if vss. 29*f* were deleted and vs. 31 were made to follow directly after vs. 28. Essentially vs. 29 is a duplicate of vs. 28, while vs. 30 says in a positive way (Daniel's ability to reveal and explain the dream) what vs. 27 says in a negative way (the inability of the Babylonian sages to do this). One may suppose that vss. 29*f* came from the secondary source used in vss. 13–23 (although nothing is preserved from this source concerning Daniel's return to the king) and that whoever made the conflation of the two sources thought it worthwhile to preserve from the secondary source Daniel's strong disclaimer of any personal merit in his God-given wisdom; the revelation came from God primarily for the benefit of the king (vs. 30). The resemblance of this passage to Gen 41:15*f* is striking: "Pharaoh said to Joseph, 'I had dreams that nobody can explain. But I heard it said of you that you can interpret a dream the instant you hear it.' 'Not I,' Joseph replied to Pharaoh, 'but God will give Pharaoh the right answer.'" In our book, however, there is this remarkable difference: before describing the dream and giving its interpretation, Daniel tells Nebuchadnezzar God's purpose in giving the king this vision. It is that Nebuchadnezzar may know "what is to happen in the last days" (vs. 28), i.e. at the end of the present era. The vision is eschatological, to reveal the ultimate destiny of the world.

In Daniel's description of the dream, the first thing to note is that the king is said to have seen a strange, colossal statue that showed the various parts of a human body (head, chest, arms, belly, hips, legs, and feet) and therefore clearly represented a gigantic man. As distinct from ch. 3 where the colossal golden statue is worshipped, nothing is said or even implied here to lead the reader to regard the statue as an idol. Rather, the statue, inasmuch as it represents a man, offers good symbolism for the human kingdoms of the world as distinct from the kingdom of God (the stone that destroys these kingdoms: vss. 34*f*,44). Scholars have tried, without much success, to find historical or literary sources for this image. It is, of course, possible, but by no means certain, that the author of the story knew of the gigantic statues of Egypt or of the celebrated Colossus of Rhodes. Somewhat more probable is the opinion that he was acquainted with the rather widespread concept in antiquity according to which the world was imagined to have the form of a gigantic man (for the references, see Bentzen, pp. 27–29). But why seek to deprive our author of all originality? His picture of the gigantic statue made up of various materials, which is "extraordinary" and "terrifying" (vs. 31), is original with him, insofar as he combines the concept of a manlike statue with another ancient concept that represented the successive ages of the world under the symbolism of various metals. Modern exegetes have pointed out the similarity between Daniel's four metals (gold, silver, bronze, and iron) and the four ages of mankind, symbolized by the same four metals in the same order, as mentioned by Hesiod (*Works and Days,* lines 109–180) and Ovid (*Metamorphoses* i 89–414). Even more striking are the Parsee texts in which the last age is "mixed with iron" or "clay-mixed" (for the references, see Montgomery, pp. 188*f*; Siegman, *CBQ* 18 [1956], 366*f*), but these are almost certainly later than Daniel. Since the motif was apparently widespread in antiquity, no direct dependence need be postulated for our author. Of the stuff that dreams are made of, although of importance in the interpretation of the dream, are such items as the rock detaching itself from the unmentioned background and then growing into an immense mountain, as well as the crumbling of the metal statue to dust and its complete disappearance.

Daniel's Interpretation of the Dream (2:36b–45)

The first person plural ("we") in vs. 36b is somewhat puzzling. It is probably to be explained as a sort of editorial "we" rather than as an inclusion of Daniel's three companions, as in the secondary insertion (vs. 23); the assumption made above is that the original story as told in this chapter made no mention of these companions.

The phrase within the dashes in vss. 37*f* is Daniel's flattery of the king as required by court etiquette. However, it can also be understood as giving the reason why Daniel interprets the statue's head of gold as symbolizing Nebuchadnezzar: inasmuch as the latter is described as the greatest of monarchs, he is fittingly symbolized by gold, the most precious of metals. In saying that Nebuchadnezzar's place will be taken by another "kingdom," our author shows that in certain contexts he uses the word "king" as synonymous with "kingdom," so that Ginsberg's revised vocalization of *mlky'* (see NOTE on vs. 44) is really not necessary; every postexilic Jew who knew his Bible knew that Nebuchadnezzar was not the last Babylonian king—unless the story of the dream was told originally of Nabonidus. In any case, since the three other metals represent kingdoms, the first metal must represent a kingdom also, which, in the context, is clearly that of Babylon. The title that Daniel gives Nebuchadnezzar, "king of kings," although used by earlier rulers of Mesopotamia (Akkadian *šar šarrāni*), is more typical of the Persian monarchs. The idea that God gave Nebuchadnezzar dominion even over the wild animals (vs. 38) goes back to Jer 27:6; 28:14, but hardly to Gen 1:28 or Ps 8:7*ff* (Nebuchadnezzar is not "mankind"). Daniel's enlargement of the king's dominion to include the birds of the air is found also in Judith 11:7; cf. Baruch 3:16.

As explained in the Introduction, Part VI, the second, third, and fourth kingdoms of ch. 2 are those of the Medes, the Persians, and the Greeks (or Macedonians), respectively.

In the ancient symbolism of the four metals as representing four ages of mankind the descending scale in the value of the metals portrays a constant deterioration of mankind from an ideal golden age to the debased state of the contemporary world. In adapting this symbolism to four successive kingdoms, does our author also wish to represent his four kingdoms in some sort of descending scale? Ginsberg (pp. 10–11) is no doubt correct in saying that nothing in the context implies a judgment on the relative morality of the four kingdoms. But he is hardly correct in insisting that "in physical power he [Daniel] clearly regards the second, third, and fourth monarchies as an *ascending* series (2:39–40)." For on the one hand, our author sees symbolic meaning in the hardness of the iron (vs. 40) and the weakness of the terra cotta (vs. 41) and perhaps also in the high value of gold (vs. 39; see above), while on the other hand, the expression used of the kingdom of the Medes in relation to Nebuchadnezzar in vs. 39, *'ăra' minnāk,* which we have translated as "inferior to you" (with *RSV* and *NAB*), signifies some kind of descending scale, most likely in political power, since Media never attained to true world-empire, as did the other three kingdoms. Morally inferior could hardly be meant; no postexilic Jew would have regarded Media, which was the conqueror of wicked Babylon (according to the history of this book), as morally worse than Babylon, which devastated Jerusalem. In itself, to be sure, the phrase *'ăra' minnāk* could be translated as "lower than you" and understood in a local sense. But the comparison here is not between the head and the chest of the statue, but between Nebuchadnezzar (or the Babylonian empire) and the kingdom of the Medes. Moreover, it should be noted that the "silver" is the only one of the four metals that is not explicitly mentioned in the interpretation of the dream. Is it perhaps implicitly contained in the word "inferior"?

There is no apparent reason why the third kingdom, i.e. that of the Persians, should be represented by bronze; this is a case where the older symbolism for the four ages of man was merely accommodated to the new symbolism for the four kingdoms. But the statement that this kingdom would "rule over all the earth," i.e. over the whole civilized world as it was then known to the people of the Near East, fits the Persian empire very well; at the height of their power under Darius I, Xerxes, and Artaxerxes I, the Persians ruled over a larger territory than had any monarch before their time.

The symbolism and its interpretation for the fourth kingdom, i.e. that of the Greeks, is more complicated. To begin with, even in the description of the statue a distinction is made between the iron legs and the iron and terra cotta feet (vs. 33). The complication is increased by the fact that on this imagery several variant interpretations are superimposed in vss. 40–43. As explained above in the NOTES on vss. 40–43, only vss. 40 and 41a (except for the gloss in each verse) belong to the original story. Here there is a double symbolism: the imagery of the iron legs is interpreted as referring to the Greek kingdom of Alexander the Great, who conquered all the lands once held by the preceding kingdoms (vs. 40), and the imagery of the partly iron and partly terra cotta feet is interpreted as referring to the division of Alexander's empire among his generals ("a divided kingdom"). Although his empire was eventually divided into four independent kingdoms, our author is naturally interested only in the two kingdoms that directly affected Palestine, the kingdom of the Ptolemies and that of the Seleucids; the term *malkû pᵉlîgāh,* "a divided kingdom," means more exactly "a kingdom split (in two)." It is not certain what is meant when it is said that this divided kingdom has "some elements of iron in it." Perhaps all that the original author meant was that the successors of Alexander would retain some but not all of his military and political power. The language and culture remain essentially the same, contrary to the previous changes.

In vss. 41b–42, however, a later glossator reinterpreted the imagery of the partly iron and partly terra cotta feet. He now puts the mixture of iron and terra cotta, not in the feet as such, but in "the toes of the feet," and therefore he inserts the words "and the toes" in vs. 41a. Apparently he means that some of the toes are of iron and some are of terra cotta. If he lays any stress on the number of the toes, ten in all, he may have in mind the "ten horns" and the "ten kings" of 7:7,24. In that case, "the kingdom" of vs. 42 would not be the (divided) kingdom of Alexander, but the kingdom of the Seleucids alone, some of whose kings were strong and some weak. But this reconstruction of the glossator's mind is uncertain, and it is difficult to say what he meant. However, it seems improbable (*pace* Ginsberg, pp. 8–9) that the glossator who deliberately brought in the element of the toes understood his "kingdom" of vs. 42 to refer to Alexander's divided kingdom, with the Ptolemaic part of it as strong and the Seleucid part as weak (see discussion below on the possible date of the glossator).

Another glossator (earlier than the one who wrote vss. 41b–42, if our analysis of the text as given above in the NOTES is correct) offered, in vs. 43, a different interpretation to the partly iron and partly terra cotta feet. Arguing from the premise that ordinarily "iron does not unite with terra cotta," he applied the imagery to the marriage(s) between the Seleucids and the Ptolemies that failed to achieve lasting peace between these two rival houses. It is not certain whether he refers to the marriage (ca. 250 B.C.) between the Seleucid Antiochus II and Berenice, the daughter of Ptolemy II (for its tragic outcome, see COMMENT: DETAILED on 11:6) or to the marriage (ca. 193 B.C.) between Ptolemy V and Cleopatra, the daughter of Antiochus III (see COMMENT: DETAILED on 11:17) or to both dynastic marriages.

In vss. 44*f*, Daniel reaches the climax of his interpretation of the king's dream. Just as the mysterious stone that smashed the tile feet of the statue caused the whole statue to tumble down and be reduced to dust, which the wind carried away, while the stone itself grew into a mountain that filled the whole earth, so the God of Israel will annihilate the kingdoms of men and in their place establish his own universal kingdom. Whereas the pagan kingdoms of the world are man-made affairs and thus, like all the works of man, pass away, the new eschatological kingdom is the work of God—no human hand carves out the mysterious stone—and therefore it "will stand forever." That this is done by "the God of heaven" (on this term, see NOTES on vs. 18) does not mean that the new kingdom will be in heaven; rather, it is a kingdom on earth and indeed coextensive with the earth: the stone grew "and filled all the earth" (vs. 35; cf. Isa 11:9: "The earth shall be filled with the knowledge of Yahweh"). For the concept of "the great mountain" that the stone became, cf. Isa 2:2 (=Micah 4:1): "In days to come the mountain of Yahweh's house shall be established as the highest mountain." Although the image of the stone is eschatological here, it is not strictly speaking messianic, at least not in a personal sense. At most it can be considered, with some scholars (e.g. Siegman, *CBQ* 18 [1956], 364–371; Steinmann, p. 53), messianic in a certain broad sense, because some New Testament writers applied the concept of "stone" to Jesus Christ (Ps 118:22*f* is thus applied in Mark 12:10*f* [=Matt 21:42; Luke 20:17] and I Peter 2:6*ff*; and Isa 8:14 and 28:16 in Rom 9:32*f* and I Peter 2:6*ff*); the only possible allusion to the stone of Daniel 2 is in Luke 20:18.

Nebuchadnezzar's Reaction (2:46–49)

Without hesitation the king accepts Daniel's account of the dream and its interpretation. Not only does he bestow great honors on Daniel; he is even converted to the Jewish faith inasmuch as he believes that Yahweh, who can reveal such great mysteries, is "truly the God of gods." Apparently the Jews of the last pre-Christian centuries came to believe that Nebuchadnezzar had become a quasi-convert to Judaism. The belief may well have originated in the words of Jer 25:9; 27:6; 43:10, where Yahweh calls Nebuchadnezzar "my servant." Even though the prophet had meant this, no doubt, merely in the sense that Yahweh had chosen Nebuchadnezzar to be his instrument in punishing the sins of Judah (cf. T. W. Overholt, "King Nebuchadnezzar in the Jeremiah Tradition," *CBQ* 30 [1968], 39–48), popular notions may have extended this to make Nebuchadnezzar a conscious, willing "servant" of Yahweh.

Another difficulty is to see any plausibility in Daniel's acceptance of the divine worship that the king offers him; no pious Jew would do such a thing. One cannot evade the difficulty by supposing that the "worship" (*s^e^gid*) was merely civic homage; the words "sacrifice" (*minḥāh*) and "incense" (*nîḥōḥîn,* literally, "pleasant-smelling offerings") are strictly religious terms, borrowed in fact from the Hebrew ritual vocabulary—*minḥāh* and *rêaḥ nîḥōaḥ*. In answering Porphyry's objection that it was absurd to imagine Nebuchadnezzar worshipping Daniel, St. Jerome gave a good explanation why Daniel could accept the worship. Jerome interprets vs. 46 in the light of vs. 47 and says, "*Ergo non tam Danielem, quam in Daniele adorat Deum, qui mysteria revelat*—Therefore, he worshipped, not so much Daniel, as in Daniel the God who reveals mysteries." In this connection, Jerome refers to the story told by Josephus (*Antiquities* xi 8, 5 [vol. 6, pp. 474–477, in the LCL edition]) that Alexander justified the homage he gave the high priest of Jerusalem by saying, "I did not adore him, but the God who honored him with the high priesthood." (There is another striking parallel between the Alexander legend and the Daniel story: Alexander recognized the high priest as the one who had appeared to him while he was still in Macedonia and revealed to him that he would conquer Asia—another case of a pagan acknowledging the God of Israel as a revealer of mysteries.) Therefore, just as the Jewish high priest could legitimately accept Alexander's worship, Daniel could well accept Nebuchadnezzar's worship, not for himself, but for the God who used him as his instrument to reveal his mysteries. [For a somewhat different view of this question, cf. B. A. Mastin, "Daniel 2:46 and the Hellenistic World," *ZAW* 85 (1973), 80–93.]

The last verses of the chapter contain the motif that is common to all Oriental tales about the successful courtier: besides giving Daniel religious homage, Nebuchadnezzar makes him the superior of all the counselors at the Babylonian court. The political authority that the king bestows on Daniel is reminiscent of the high office in Egypt that Pharaoh gave Joseph because he had successfully interpreted the ruler's dreams. Daniel's three companions are again brought into the story, probably, as said above in the NOTES on vs. 49, from the variant form of the story. The compiler of the book may have thought that this reference to the three companions would make a good nexus between this story and the next one, in ch. 3, which is concerned only with these three men.

Date of Composition of Chapter 2

In dating ch. 2, a distinction must be made between (1) the primary story as we now have it in written form, (2) older material, either oral or written, that formed a *Vorlage* of the story, and (3) later additions that were inserted into the story.

1) The purpose of the story, viz. to encourage the Jews to remain faithful to the God of their fathers, who is shown here to be the Lord of human history, and to keep up their hope in the establishment of his kingdom on earth in the near future, would fit any part of the postexilic period, when the Jews had lost their national independence and were in danger of being lured away from him by the materially superior culture of the pagan world in which they lived. However, as stated above (see COMMENT: GENERAL), the account must have been written before the time of Antiochus IV Epiphanes (175–164 B.C.); nothing in the story even hints at this king's persecution of the Jews, and the Babylonian king of the story, who becomes a quasi-convert to Judaism, is in no way a symbol of Epiphanes. On the other hand, the item of the partly iron and partly terra cotta feet of the statue (vs. 33) and its interpretation as symbolizing the kingdom of the Greeks "divided" into the dynasty of the Ptolemies and that of the Seleucids belong to the primary stratum of the story, so that the account must have been written some time after the death of Alexander the Great (323 B.C.) and the subsequent division of his empire among his generals (312 B.C. for the Seleucid dynasty). Therefore, the written composition of the primary story should probably be dated toward the end of the fourth century B.C. or in the first quarter of the third century B.C.

Ginsberg endeavors to limit this period to the time between 292 and

261 B.C. He argues that the crumbling of the whole statue at one time (vs. 35) and the statement that this will happen "in the days of those regimes" (vs. 44) point to a time when all four kingdoms were still in existence. This, he says, would be in the three decades between 292 and 261, when the Seleucid kings of Antioch (the "Greek" kingdom) shared their royal title with their sons who ruled over the eastern provinces of the kingdom (the "Babylonian" kingdom of Daniel); at the same time there were rump kingdoms of the Medes in Atropatene (modern Azerbaijan in northwestern Iran) and of the Persians in Persis (modern Fars in southwestern Iran).

But this pinpointing of the date seems rather dubious, as A. Jepsen, "Bemerkungen zum Danielbuch," *VT* 11 (1961), 388–390, rightly notes. The collapse of the whole statue at one time may merely symbolize the annihilation of all the pagan kingdoms of the world as a prerequisite for the establishment of God's kingdom on earth. The kingdom directly destroyed in the story, the Greek one (the feet of the statue hit by the stone), inherited all the wickedness of the preceding kingdoms, and so they can be pictured as being destroyed together with it. Besides, Daniel's statement that the second kingdom will take the place of the first one (vs. 39: literally, "and after you there will arise another kingdom") at least implies that the Babylonian kingdom is no longer in existence at the time of the Median kingdom. Finally, the phrase "in the days of those regimes" (when God establishes his kingdom: vs. 44) can just as well be understood as referring to the time of the kings of the divided Greek kingdom, since the MT is literally "in the days of those kings" and the divided kingdom is mentioned in the immediately preceding verse of the original story.

2) There are certain details in the story that seem to point to an earlier date than that just given as the date of composition of the story. The description of the royal court, with its group of dream-interpreting counselors, indicates a knowledge of Babylon as it was before the Hellenistic period. One may therefore suspect that the basis of the story, or at least of the framework in which the apocalyptic vision and its interpretation are set, originated among Mesopotamian rather than Palestinian Jews. Moreover, as mentioned above in the COMMENT: DETAILED on vss. 1–12, the king of the story in an older form may originally have been Nabonidus, and this would also account for the fact that in the story Nebuchadnezzar is apparently made the last king of Babylon (vs. 39). Another possibility is that a form of the story existed in the time of Alexander the Great, i.e. before his empire was divided among his generals. In that form of the story the statue would have been pictured as having its whole legs, including the feet, made simply of iron; the present account of the statue, with its feet partly of iron and partly of terra cotta, would then be a later elaboration of an original four-metal symbolism. Finally, the variant account of

the story that brings Daniel's three companions into it may be older than the account in which Daniel alone is the hero.

3) The two glosses (one on vss. 41b–42 and the other on vs. 43) are definitely later than the basic story, but the date of their insertion is either uncertain or at most gives only a *terminus post quem.*

The glossator who inserted the "toes" into the picture (vs. 41) and interpreted the iron parts as referring to a strong kingdom and the terra cotta parts as referring to a weak kingdom (vss. 41b–42) surely had in mind the Ptolemaic and the Seleucid kingdoms. But it is not at all clear which one he regarded as strong and which one as weak. Under Ptolemy II Philadelphus (285–246 B.C.) Egypt was much stronger than the Seleucid kingdom. But Antiochus III the Great (223–187 B.C.) made the Seleucid kingdom much stronger than the Ptolemaic one. Seleucid supremacy may be implied if the assumption made above is correct, that this gloss is later than the other one. However, nothing in the text implies that the period referred to was that of the glossator. If any weight is to be attached to the number ten in regard to the toes (which is, of course, quite uncertain), the glossator may have inserted his gloss with Dan 7:7,24 in mind and thus have been acquainted with ch. 7 of the book, or at least he may have written his gloss at the time of Antiochus IV Epiphanes (175–164 B.C.) with the same count of ten Seleucid kings up to that time.

The glossator, who thought that the iron and terra cotta of the feet would not hold together and therefore interpreted this item of the image as referring to the failure of interdynastic marriage to bring lasting peace between the Ptolemaic and the Seleucid kingdoms, may have had in mind the marriage of ca. 250 B.C., with its disastrous results, rather than the one of ca. 193 B.C. (see above). But again, nothing in the text implies that this was a recent event; the date of the marriage gives merely a *terminus post quem.*

In conclusion, then, we can say the story of the Babylonian king's dream of the composite statue originated in the fourth century B.C., in an oral (?) form in which the king was perhaps Nabonidus rather than Nebuchadnezzar; that at the end of the fourth or the beginning of the third century B.C. at least two variant written forms of the story were in circulation; that later in the third century B.C. the present story, with its conflation of two variant forms, was composed; and that the present glosses were added to this composition some time before the author-compiler of the Book of Daniel, during Epiphanes' persecution of the Jews in the second quarter of the second century B.C., joined this story to the others that form the first half of his work.

III. WORSHIP OF THE GOLDEN IMAGE
(3:1–30)

3 1 King Nebuchadnezzar made a golden image, sixty cubits high
and six cubits wide, and he set it up on the plain of Dura in the province of Babylon. 2 He[a] then ordered an assembly of the satraps, prefects, and governors, [b]as well as[b] the counselors, treasurers, judges,
police magistrates, and all the other officials of the province, that they
should be present at the dedication of the statue he[a] had set up. 3 So
the satraps, prefects, and governors, [b]as well as[b] the counselors, treasurers, judges, police magistrates, and all the other officials of the
province assembled for [c]the dedication[c] and stood before the image
that Nebuchadnezzar had set up. 4 A herald then made the loud proc-
lamation: "To you of every nation, tribe, and tongue this command is
given. 5 When you hear the sound of the horn, the pipe, the lyre, the
trigon, the harp, the bagpipe, and all the other musical instruments,
you shall fall down and worship the golden image that King Nebuchadnezzar has set up. 6 Whoever does not fall down and worship it
shall be thrown at once into a white-hot furnace." 7 Therefore, as
soon as they heard the sound of the horn, the pipe, the lyre, the
trigon, the harp, [d]the bagpipe[d], and all the other musical instruments,
all the people of every nation, tribe, and tongue fell down and
worshipped the golden image that King Nebuchadnezzar had set up.
8 [e]At that point, certain Chaldeans came forward and denounced
the Jews. 9 They said to King Nebuchadnezzar, "O king, live forever!
10 You issued a decree, O king, that everyone who hears the sound of
the horn, the pipe, the lyre, the trigon, the harp, the bagpipe, and all
the other musical instruments shall fall down and worship the golden
image; 11 and whoever does not fall down and worship it shall be

[a] Literally, "King Nebuchadnezzar."
[b–b] Added in English for the sake of the sense; see NOTES.
[c–c] Literally, "the dedication of the image that King Nebuchadnezzar had set up."
[d–d] Many Hebrew MSS omit; but others and Theod. have the instrument; cf. vss. 5, 10,15.
[e] MT prefixes "Therefore"; omitted by Theod.; probably a dittography from vs. 7.

thrown into a white-hot furnace. 12 There are certain Jews—Shadrach, Meshach, and Abednego—whom you have appointed administrators of the province of Babylon. These men pay no attention to
you, O king; they do not serve your gods or worship the golden image
you have set up."

13 Thereupon King Nebuchadnezzar flew into a rage and ordered
Shadrach, Meshach, and Abednego to be brought in. When these men
were brought before the king, 14 Nebuchadnezzar said to them, "Is it
true, Shadrach, Meshach, and Abednego, that you do not serve my
gods or worship the golden image that I have set up? 15 I hope that
now, when you hear the sound of the horn, the pipe, the lyre, the
trigon, the harp, the bagpipe, and all the other musical instruments,
you will fall down and worship the image I have made. But if you do
not worship it, you will be thrown at once into a white-hot furnace.
And what god is there who is able to save you from my hand[f]?"
16 Shadrach, Meshach, and Abednego [g]answered King Nebuchadnezzar[g]: "There is no need for us to give you an answer to that question.
17 If there is a God able to save us, such as our God whom we serve, he
will save us from the white-hot furnace and from your hand, O king.
18 But even if there were not, you can be sure, O king, that we would
not serve your gods or worship the golden image you have set up."

19 At these words Nebuchadnezzar was filled with anger, and his
look was changed toward Shadrach, Meshach, and Abednego. He ordered the furnace to be heated seven times as much as it usually was,
20 and he commanded some strong men of his army to bind Shadrach,
Meshach, and Abednego and throw them into the white-hot furnace.
21 The latter were then bound, with their trousers, shirts, hats, and
other clothes still on, and thrown into the white-hot furnace. 22 Because the king's command was so peremptory and the furnace so
overheated, the raging flames killed the men who carried Shadrach,
Meshach, and Abednego up into it. 23 Yet these three men, Shadrach,
Meshach, and Abednego, bound in fetters, fell down into the white-
hot furnace.

24 *(91)* Then King Nebuchadnezzar was perturbed. He rose in haste
and asked his companions, "Didn't we throw three men, bound in fetters, into the fire?" "Certainly, O king," they answered him.
25 *(92)* "But look," he replied, "I see four men, completely unharmed,

[f] Read y^{e}*dî*, as in some MSS and versions; cf. vs. 17. MT has y^{e}*dāy*, "my hands."
[g–g] MT punctuation calls for "answered the king: 'O Nebuchadnezzar, . . .' "

[h]walking about[h] freely in the fire, and the fourth one looks like a divine
being."
26 (93) Nebuchadnezzar then went near the opening of the white-hot
furnace and said, "Shadrach, Meshach, and Abednego, servants of
the Most High God, come out here." Thereupon Shadrach, Meshach,
and Abednego came ouf of the fire. 27 (94) When the satraps, prefects,
and governors, as well as the companions of the king assembled, they
saw that the fire had not had any power over the bodies of these men;
the hair of their head was not singed, and their clothes were not
affected; not even a smell of fire came from them.
28 (95) Nebuchadnezzar said, "Blessed be the God of Shadrach,
Meshach, and Abednego, because he sent his angel and rescued his
servants who trusted in him; disregarding the king's orders, they
yielded up their bodies rather than serve or worship any god but their
own. 29 (96) For every nation, tribe, and tongue I therefore make this
decree: whoever utters a blasphemy[i] against the God of Shadrach,
Meshach, and Abednego will be torn limb from limb, and his house
will be laid in ruins, because there is no other god who can effect such
a rescue." 30 (97) Then the king promoted Shadrach, Meshach, and
Abednego in the province of Babylon.

[h–h] Probably read, with some MSS, *mᵉhallᵉkîn;* cf. the pa'el in 4:26. For the root *hlk,* "to walk," the haph'el would normally be causative in meaning, "to cause to walk, to lead," as in Hebrew the hip'il of *hlk* always is; yet cf. 4:34.

[i] Read *šillāh,* with the *kᵉtîb.* The *qᵉrē* of the MT, *šālû,* "neglect," hardly makes sense here.

NOTES

3:2. In this list of seven different officials, which is repeated in the next verse, the conjunction *û-*, "and," is used only before the third term. This seems to indicate that the first three kinds of officials form a group distinct from the last four. The first three were of higher rank: "the satraps" (Aramaic *'ăḥašdar-pᵉnayyâ,* a loanword from the Persian *ḫšatra-pāvan* through Akkadian *aḫ-šadrapanu* [see *CAD* 1, p. 195]) were in charge of the main divisions of the Persian empire (e.g. the satrapy of Abarnahara, the region west of the Euphrates), "the prefects" (Aramaic *signayyâ,* a loanword from Akkadian *šaknu*) were high civic officers directly responsible to the satraps, and "the governors" (Aramaic *paḥăwātâ,* a loanword from Akkadian *piḫātu, paḫātu*) were the heads of the divisions (e.g. Judea, Samaria, etc.) of the satrapies. The meaning of the terms designating the four classes of lesser officials is less certain, especially since the MT has not always transmitted the correct pronunciation of these terms, all of which are from the Old Persian. The Aramaic word for "the counselors," *'ădargāz^{e}rayyâ,* is thought to be from the Old Persian **handarza-kara;* the word for "the treasurers," *g^{e}dāb^{e}rayyâ,* given better as *gizbārayyâ* in Ezra 7:21, is presumed to be from the Persian *ganzabara;* the word for "the judges," *d^{e}tāb^{e}rayyâ,* which should have been vocalized as *dāt^{e}bārayyâ,* is from the Persian *dātabara* (literally, "law bearers"); and the word rendered here as "the police magistrates," *tiptāyê,* is perhaps from the Persian **tayu-pata.*

4. *A herald.* In Aramaic, *kārôzâ,* which is probably a loanword from the Old Persian **xrausa* rather than a borrowing from the Greek word for "herald," *kēryx.*

tongue. In the Persian empire, official recognition was made of the more important languages that were spoken throughout the realm; cf. the inscription of Darius I at Behistun in Persian, Akkadian, and Elamite, of which an Aramaic version has been partially preserved on papyrus.

5. Three of the names of the various musical instruments are loanwords from the Greek: the Aramaic word for "lyre," *qatrōs* (better in the *k^{e}tîb* as *qîtārôs*) is from the Greek *kitharis* (from which the English words "zither" and "guitar" are derived, although these terms designate somewhat different instruments); the Aramaic word for "harp," *p^{e}santērîn,* is from the Greek *psaltērion;* and the Aramaic word that is rendered here as "bagpipe," *sûmpōnyāh,* is from the Greek *symphōnia,* literally "accompanying sound." It is not certain, however, whether the bagpipe was known in early Hellenistic times, and the term *sûmpōnyāh* may here designate a sort of drum (cf. Isidore of Seville, *Etymologies* III xxii 14); after the first two terms for wind instruments and the next three terms for stringed instruments, one might expect the last term to designate a percussion instrument. The Greek term *symphōnia* in Luke 15:25 is usually understood as meaning "music" in general. The Aramaic word for "the trigon" (a triangular musical instrument with four strings), *śabb^{e}kâ/sabb^{e}kâ,* is probably of non-Semitic origin; it appears in Greek as *sambykē.*

6. *white-hot furnace.* Literally, "furnace of burning fire."

8. *Chaldeans.* The term is used here probably in its derived meaning of "astrologers, fortune-tellers"; see NOTES on 1:4.

13. *flew into a rage and ordered.* Literally, "in rage and anger ordered."

15. *I hope that now . . . you will fall down. . . .* In Aramaic the sentence is an incomplete conditional phrase, "If now . . . you will fall down . . . ," with an apodosis of something like "all well and good" understood.

16. *answered King Nebuchadnezzar.* The interpretation given to these words by the Masoretic punctuation marks, "answered the king: 'O Nebuchadnezzar,'" which is ancient (witnessed to by Jerome), seems less likely. Nowhere else in the book is the king addressed merely by his name, without his title, and there is no reason why the three Jews should here have had the discourtesy of failing to observe proper court etiquette.

17*f.* These verses are variously translated. *RSV,* following *KJV,* has "If it be so, our God . . . is able to deliver us . . . ; and he will deliver us. . . . But if not, be it known. . . ." However, it is doubtful whether *hēn 'îtay* can mean "If that be so" (the construction is not the same as in Ezra 5:17); and even if this is understood as meaning "If the king's sentence is carried out," the contrary in vs. 18, "But if not," makes no sense there with such a meaning. The first of the two variant translations given in the footnote of *RSV*, "Behold, our God . . . king," cannot be correct, for the *hēn* here must surely have the same meaning that it has in vs. 18. The second of these variant translations is, "If our God is able to deliver us, he will deliver us. . . . But if not, . . ." Similarly in *NAB:* "If our God . . . can save us, . . . may he save us! But even if he will not, . . ." The principal reason for not following either of the last two interpretations here is that they do not render the word *'îtay* correctly. According to Rosenthal, *Grammar*, §95, "*'îtay* indicates existence ('there is, exists'), or, with the negative, non-existence (*lā' 'îtay*, 'there does not exist'). . . . However, *'îtay* may take the place of the copula. . . . In this case, it takes the appropriate pronominal suffix." The present passage would be the only one in Daniel in which *'îtay* would be used without a pronominal suffix and yet take the place of the copula.

21. *trousers, shirts, hats.* All three Aramaic terms apparently designate parts of Persian dress: Aramaic *sarbāl* (in 1QDan[b] [3:27] the word begins with *ś* or *š*) is rendered as "trousers" in Sym. and Vulg., and it is no doubt connected with the Modern Persian word for "trousers," *šalvār;* Aramaic *paṭṭîš,* translated here as "shirt," is of uncertain derivation and of doubtful meaning; Aramaic *karb*[e]*lāh* is certainly related to the late Akkadian word *karballatu,* which designates some kind of headgear, but it is probably not of Persian or Akkadian origin.

24. *companions.* The Aramaic *haddābar* is a loanword from the Old Persian **hada-bāra* (cf. Middle Persian *hadbār*), "companion." Here it is used in the general sense of "official"; but in vs. 27, "the companions of the king," since they are mentioned after other classes of officials, seem to be a distinct group, bearing an honorific title like that of the Hellenistic "friends of the king" (I Macc 2:18; 3:38; etc.).

25. *a divine being.* Literally, "a son of God," rightly understood in vs. 28 as an angel; cf. also vs. 26.

26. *Most High.* The Aramaic term, *'illāyâ,* corresponding to the Hebrew term, *'elyôn.* Since the latter word occurs in the older Scriptures as used not only by Israelites, but also by pagans in speaking of the true God, e.g. by Melchizedek (Gen 14:18–20), Balaam (Num 24:16), and the king of Babylon in Isa 14:14, our author does not consider it inappropriate in the mouth of Nebuchadnezzar; cf. 4:31.

27. *came from them.* However, Rosenthal (*Handbook,* Part I/2, p. 33) suggests the rendering, "clung to them"; cf. Targumic *'adyâ, 'adîtâ,* "scab."

29. *torn limb from limb, and his house will be laid in ruins.* Almost exactly the same Aramaic words occur in 2:5; see NOTE there.

Comment: General

As stated in the Comment on ch. 1, the account of the three Jewish men who refused to worship the idolatrous statue that King Nebuchadnezzar had erected and whose loyalty to the God of their fathers was rewarded by a miracle that saved their lives was once an independent story that originally had no connection with the Daniel cycle of stories. Daniel, in fact, is not even mentioned in this chapter. The counterpart of this story in the original Daniel cycle is the account of Daniel in the lions' den of ch. 6 with its variant in the Greek versions (see Introduction, Part IV, "Other Daniel Stories"). The compiler of the book decided to incorporate the story of the Worship of the Golden Image in his work because it offered a good object lesson to his coreligionists who were being persecuted by Antiochus IV Epiphanes.

The three Jewish men (nowhere in the chapter are they called "youths" or "young men") are mentioned solely by their "Babylonian" names—Shadrach, Meshach, and Abednego, not only in the Aramaic text, but also in its Greek translations (the LXX and Theod.) However, in the apocryphal (or deuterocanonical) fragment of the variant story that is preserved in Greek they are given their Hebrew names—Hananiah, Azariah, and Mishael (vs. [*88*]—in a sequence that is not quite the same as in 1:7), and in this fragment Azariah acts as the leader of the group (vss. [*25*] and [*49*]). It seems, therefore, that the story once circulated in at least two different forms. Some inconsistencies between the two forms can be seen in the secondary fragment (vss. [*46*]–[*50*]).

Although a categorical denial cannot be given to the possibility that the kernel of this story may have been a historical event that happened in the time of Nebuchadnezzar, the story as we now have it was composed long after the time of that king. The rather frequent occurrence, in the Aramaic account, of words borrowed from the Persian language, especially the terms used for the high officials of the empire (see Notes on vss. 2,24), precludes a time of composition earlier than the Persian empire. The occurrence of three words borrowed from the Greek in the description of Nebuchadnezzar's "orchestra" (see Note on vs. 5) would seem to point to the Hellenistic period for the time of composition of the account. Yet this is not absolutely conclusive, for a large amount of Greek material culture had penetrated the Near East before the time of Alexander the Great.

The persecution of the three Jews because of their religious convictions, which plays such an important part in this story that was written to show that martyrdom is to be preferred to apostasy, cannot be used as a conclusive argument to prove that the story was composed in the days of Antiochus IV Epiphanes. There could have been some persecution of the Jews during the time of the Persian empire, and echoes of this may be heard in the story of Esther. In any case, the Nebuchadnezzar of this story, who eventually blesses the God of Israel and decrees the protection of the Jewish religion, is surely not a symbolic figure of Epiphanes.

The fragment of the variant form of the story that has been preserved in the Greek version of vss. (*46*)–(*50*) is probably as old as the main form. At least, the former does not depend on the latter, as can be seen from the elements in which it is different. However, the Prayer of Azariah (vss. [*25*]–[*45*]) and the Hymn of the Three Jews (vss. [*51*]–[*90*]) are no doubt later insertions into the story. The reference in the Prayer of Azariah to the "unjust king, the vilest in all the world" (vs. [*32*]) is evidently to Antiochus IV. See Appendix at the end of this section.

Essentially this composition belongs to the literary genre of the martyr story or witness literature (see Introduction, Part IX). But as Ginsberg (p. 28) points out, the religious element of the story has not completely obliterated the earlier motif of the Oriental tales about rival courtiers (vss. 8–12) that is common to all the stories in the first half of the book.

Comment: Detailed

The Golden Image (3:1–7)

The scene of the story is a place "on the plain of Dura." The name of the plain is not purely fictitious, even though the site cannot be identified with any certainty. It is derived from the Akkadian word *dūru,* "city wall, fortified place," which forms the first element in several Akkadian place names. The plain need not be imagined as extending over a vast area; not all the inhabitants of the empire were assembled there, but only the various officials as representatives of "every nation, tribe, and tongue" of the empire.

The remarkable thing about the statue that King Nebuchadnezzar is said to have erected there is its strange proportions—"sixty cubits high and six cubits wide" (note the allusion to the Babylonian sexagesimal system of numbers!), i.e. about ninety by nine feet. In appearance, therefore, the object resembled an obelisk. The story does not say that it was of solid gold. The plating of stone obelisks with precious metals was not unknown in ancient times. Yet the Aramaic word used to designate it, *ṣᵉlēm,* implies that it was an "image" or statue of some sort, and therefore apparently had human features in some way. In any case, since it was the object of religious worship (vss. 4,7,10, etc.), connected with the cult of Nebuchadnezzar's gods (vss. 12,14,18), it must have been a pagan idol of some kind.

The dedication of a newly erected or renovated temple, in the midst of joyous solemnities and with numerous high officials present, is mentioned in many of the inscriptions of the kings of ancient Mesopotamia. Assyrian reliefs also show musicians playing various kinds of harps or lyres (but not bagpipes!) on festive occasions.

Although the burning alive of criminals was not a common form of execution in the ancient Near East, it was practiced there to some extent. In fact, Jeremiah (29:21*f*) foresaw that Nebuchadnezzar would have the false prophets Ahab ben Kolaiah and Zedekiah ben Maaseiah "roasted in the fire," apparently for fostering sedition among the Jewish exiles in Babylonia. It is presumed, however, that in such executions the criminal was burned in a bonfire, whether tied to a stake or not (cf. Gen 38:24), and not thrown into a fiery furnace, as our heroes were. Yet in II Macc 13:4–6, it is related that Menelaus, the renegade Jewish high priest, was executed by Antiochus IV in 165 B.C. at Beroea (Aleppo) in Syria according to "the custom of that place," which consisted in pushing a criminal into an incinerator of sorts. The furnace of our story seems to have been more in the nature of a limekiln; the three men were carried up and thrown into the fire at the top of the furnace (vss. 20–22); and there must have been an opening at the lower part of the furnace, where the king could see them in the fire (vss. 24–26). It has been suggested (e.g. by Steinmann, p. 57) that the statue was set on top of the furnace, and the complex formed a fire altar of Moloch. But nothing in the text implies any connection between the statue and the furnace.

Denunciation of the Three Jews (3:8–12)

Since all the officials of the province of Babylon had to attend the solemn dedication of the statue (vs. 2), Shadrach, Meshach, and Abednego were naturally present for the occasion. Their refusal to worship the idol could thus be seen by their fellow officials. The term "Chaldeans," therefore, as used here to designate the men who brought the accusation against the three Jews, must be understood here, not in its original ethnic sense, but in its derived meaning of soothsayers. Their primary motive in making the accusation was professional jealousy, as implied in the way they speak to the king about the three Jews—"whom you have appointed administrators of the province of Babylon" (3:12).

If our assumption is correct that a cycle of stories about these three Jewish men once existed as an independent unit, distinct from the Daniel cycle of stories, we must also assume that some story in the cycle told how the three men arrived at their high position in the royal court of Babylon. However, all that we now have is the present book, in which their rise to political power is secondarily joined to that of Daniel. According to the theory proposed in our COMMENT on ch. 1, the author-editor of the Book of Daniel, who compiled the older stories of chs. 1–6, was able to explain in the introductory chapter how not only Daniel but also these three other Jews became officials in the service of Nebuchadnezzar (1:17–20). In 2:49, a secondary addition at the end of a story about Daniel, another explanation is given as to how the three men became "administrators of the province of Babylon" (the same Aramaic phrase as in 3:12!).

Interrogation (3:13–18)

In answer to the king's insolent question, "What god is there who is able to save you from my hand?" (3:15), one might have expected the devout men to say simply, "The God whom we serve is able to do so." However, the skillful storyteller has them first say dramatically that there is no need for them to discuss the matter; action will speak louder than words. Then they proceed to make a statement that, as explained in the NOTES on 3:17*f*, is not quite clear or certain, because of the difficulty in rendering the Aramaic text correctly. After saying that their God is able to save them, they might be expected to make the martyrs' proud boast that, even if God, for his own good reasons, should decide not to save them, they would still not worship the pagan idol. Yet the text apparently says, in direct response to the king's question, that even if there was not a God able to save them, they would still refuse to commit such a sin of idolatry—a hyperbolic statement that we have rendered as a condition contrary to fact, to preserve the martyrs' orthodoxy. [Cf. P. W. Coxon, "Daniel III 17: A Linguistic and Theological Problem," *VT* 26 (1976), 400–409.]

Condemnation and Execution (3:19–23)

The king had hoped that his threat to burn the three Jews alive would be effective. Therefore, when they obstinately refused to worship his idol, he ceased to regard them with friendly eyes. In his rage, he went to extremes. The ordinary fire of the furnace would not be sufficient; it must be made "seven times" hotter than ordinarily—an idiomatic way of saying "as hot as possible." This item and the other details—the need of muscular soldiers to tie up the three men, the deaths of the executioners from the flames that fly out of the furnace, and the helpless condition of the bound victims—are used by the storyteller both to ridicule the impotence of the pagan tyrant and to emphasize the miraculous nature of the martyrs' deliverance. Since the magnitude of the miracle demands that not even the victims' clothing be burned (vs. 27), the men were not stripped before their execution (contrary to the usual practice in ancient times), but were thrown fully clothed into the furnace. The itemized list of their varied attire, which was perhaps of a festive nature because of the solemn occasion, adds a touch of the bizarre to the narrative.

At this point, the Greek Bible has a much longer form of the text. This consists of three unequal parts: (1) a "Prayer of Azariah" in poetic form (vss. [*26*]–[*45*]), with a short prose introduction (vss. [*24*]–[*25*]); (2) a prose account of the fate of the three Jews in the fiery furnace (vss. [*46*]–[*50*]); and (3) a "Hymn of the Three Jews" while in the furnace (vss. [*52*]–[*90*]), introduced with a prose verse (vs. [*51*]). The first and the third of these three passages are undoubtedly later additions, enlarging an earlier form of the story. But the second passage may have formed part of the original story as it once circulated in variant forms. It is worth repeating here, even though it is given in the Appendix below.

> (*46*) Now the king's men who had thrown them in continued to stoke the furnace with brimstone, pitch, tow, and faggots. (*47*) The flames rose forty-nine cubits (*48*) above the furnace, and spread out, burning the Chaldeans nearby. (*49*) But the angel of the Lord went down into the furnace with Azariah and his companions, drove the fiery flames out of the furnace, (*50*) and made the inside of the furnace as though a dew-laden breeze were blowing through it. The fire in no way touched them or caused them pain or harm.

Some scholars argue that these verses formed an integral part of the story, since without them there would seem to be no apparent reason for the king's perturbation that is mentioned in 3:24. Others, on the contrary, claim that the additional verses spoil the dramatic effect of the shorter text: since only the king sees the fourth figure in the furnace, the reader is kept in suspense until the king says who the fourth one is (vs. 25). In any case, these verses could hardly have been added by anyone who knew the shorter form of the text. In the latter, the men who throw the martyrs into the furnace are at once killed by the flames that erupt from it (3:21), whereas in the longer form of the text these same executioners continue to stoke the fire after they have thrown the martyrs into it, and it is the nearby "Chaldeans" (the accusers of 3:8?) who get caught by the flames.

Conclusion (3:24–30)

Not only the king but also all his assembled officials are made witnesses to the miraculous deliverance of the Jewish martyrs from the fiery furnace. Nebuchadnezzar reacts to the miracle by praising the God of the three Jewish men, whom he calls "servants of the Most High God." On the use of this divine title by a pagan king, see NOTE on vs. 26.

Even though the decree that the story has Nebuchadnezzar make in favor of the Jews whereby Judaism is recognized as a legitimate and protected religion of the realm, is, no doubt, an *ad hoc* composition, it correctly reflects the situation of the Jews in the Persian period. At that time there were apparently various decrees and edicts in favor of the Jews, which in turn established a basis in custom, and probably also in law, for later Greek and Roman practice in regard to Judaism; cf. the various edicts and decrees of the Persian kings, recorded in the Book of Ezra, with regard to Jewish rights in Palestine and the rebuilding of the temple at Jerusalem, as well as the well-known "Passover Letter" of Elephantine, which demonstrates a strong governmental interest in the observance of Jewish religious laws on the part of the Jews throughout the Persian empire. There may well have been a sort of "Secretary for Jewish Affairs" in the Persian chancellery, and this in turn presupposes a body of statutes or edicts governing the work of such an office. The Book of Esther also reflects the same concern as the present chapter in the Book of Daniel for protective laws and actions on behalf of the Jews. Probably there were similar laws in the Greek period, which were abrogated by Antiochus IV when he persecuted the Jews. The restoration of these protective laws was something devoutly to be wished for when this older story was inserted into the Book of Daniel.

Appendix

Prayer of Azariah and Hymn of the Three Jews

3: 24 They walked about in the flames,
singing to God and blessing the Lord.
25 In the fire Azariah stood up and
prayed aloud:

26 "Blessed are you, and praiseworthy,
O Lord, the God of our fathers,
and glorious forever is your name.
27 For you are just in all you have
done;
all your deeds are faultless, all
your ways right,
and all your judgments proper.
28 You have executed proper judgments
in all that you have brought upon
us
and upon Jerusalem, the holy city
of our fathers.
By a proper judgment you have
done all this
because of our sins;
29 For we have sinned and transgressed
by departing from you,
and we have done every kind of
evil.
30 Your commandments we have not
heeded or observed,
nor have we done as you ordered
us for our good.
31 Therefore all you have brought
upon us,
all you have done to us,
you have done by a proper
judgment.
32 You have handed us over to our
enemies,

lawless and hateful rebels;
to an unjust king, the worst in all the world.
33 Now we cannot open our mouths;
we, your servants, who revere you,
have become a shame and a reproach.
34 For your name's sake, do not deliver us up forever,
or make void your covenant.
35 Do not take away your mercy from us,
for the sake of Abraham, your beloved,
Isaac your servant, and Israel your holy one,
36 To whom you promised to multiply their offspring
like the stars of heaven,
or the sand on the shore of the sea.
37 For we are reduced, O Lord, beyond any other nation,
brought low everywhere in the world this day
because of our sins.
38 We have in our day no prince, prophet, or leader,
no holocaust, sacrifice, oblation, or incense,
no place to offer first fruits, to find favor with you.
39 But with contrite heart and humble spirit
let us be received;
40 As though it were holocausts of rams and bullocks,
or thousands of fat lambs,
So let our sacrifice be in your presence today
as we follow you unreservedly;
for those who trust in you cannot be put to shame.
41 And now we follow you with our whole heart,
we fear you and we pray to you.
42 Do not let us be put to shame,
but deal with us in your kindness and great mercy.
43 Deliver us by your wonders,
and bring glory to your name, O Lord:
44 Let all those be routed
who inflict evils on your servants;
Let them be shamed and powerless,
and their strength broken;
45 Let them know that you alone are the Lord God,
glorious over the whole world."

46 Now the king's men who had
thrown them in continued to stoke the
furnace with brimstone, pitch, tow, and
faggots. 47 The flames rose forty-nine
cubits 48 above the furnace, and spread
out, burning the Chaldeans nearby.
49 But the angel of the Lord went
down into the furnace with Azariah
and his companions, drove the fiery
flames out of the furnace, 50 and made
the inside of the furnace as though a
dew-laden breeze were blowing through
it. The fire in no way touched them
or caused them pain or harm. 51 Then
these three in the furnace with one
voice sang, glorifying and blessing
God:

52 "Blessed are you, O Lord, the God of our fathers,
praiseworthy and exalted above all forever;
And blessed is your holy and glorious name,
praiseworthy and exalted above all for all ages.
53 Blessed are you in the temple of your holy glory,
praiseworthy and glorious above all forever.
54 Blessed are you on the throne of your kingdom,
praiseworthy and exalted above all forever.

55 Blessed are you who look into the depths
from your throne upon the cherubim,
praiseworthy and exalted above all forever.
56 Blessed are you in the firmament of heaven,
praiseworthy and glorious forever.
57 Bless the Lord, all you works of the Lord,
praise and exalt him above all forever.
58 Angels of the Lord, bless the Lord,
praise and exalt him above all forever.
59 You heavens, bless the Lord,
praise and exalt him above all forever.
60 All you waters above the heavens, bless the Lord,
praise and exalt him above all forever.
61 All you hosts of the Lord, bless the Lord;
praise and exalt him above all forever.
62 Sun and moon, bless the Lord;
praise and exalt him above all forever.
63 Stars of heaven, bless the Lord;
praise and exalt him above all forever.
64 Every shower and dew, bless the Lord;
praise and exalt him above all forever.
65 All you winds, bless the Lord;
praise and exalt him above all forever.
66 Fire and heat, bless the Lord;
praise and exalt him above all forever.
67 [Cold and chill, bless the Lord;
praise and exalt him above all forever.
68 Dew and rain, bless the Lord;
praise and exalt him above all forever.]
69 Frost and chill, bless the Lord;
praise and exalt him above all forever.
70 Ice and snow, bless the Lord;
praise and exalt him above all forever.
71 Nights and days, bless the Lord;
praise and exalt him above all forever.
72 Light and darkness, bless the Lord;
praise and exalt him above all forever.
73 Lightnings and clouds, bless the Lord;
praise and exalt him above all forever.
74 Let the earth bless the Lord,
praise and exalt him above all forever.
75 Mountains and hills, bless the Lord;
praise and exalt him above all forever.
76 Everything growing from the earth, bless the Lord;
praise and exalt him above all forever.
77 You springs, bless the Lord;
praise and exalt him above all forever.
78 Seas and rivers, bless the Lord;
praise and exalt him above all forever.
79 You dolphins and all water creatures, bless the Lord;
praise and exalt him above all forever.
80 All you birds of the air, bless the Lord;
praise and exalt him above all forever.
81 All you beasts, wild and tame, bless the Lord;
praise and exalt him above all forever.

82 You sons of men, bless the Lord;
praise and exalt him above all
forever.
83 O Israel, bless the Lord;
praise and exalt him above all
forever.
84 Priests of the Lord, bless the Lord;
praise and exalt him above all
forever.
85 Servants of the Lord, bless the Lord;
praise and exalt him above all
forever.
86 Spirits and souls of the just, bless
the Lord;
praise and exalt him above all
forever.
87 Holy men of humble heart, bless the
Lord;
praise and exalt him above all
forever.
88 Hananiah, Azariah, Mishael, bless
the Lord;
praise and exalt him above all
forever.
For he has delivered us from the
nether world,
and saved us from the power of
death;
He has freed us from the raging
flame
and delivered us from the fire.
89 Give thanks to the Lord, for he is
good,
for his mercy endures forever.
90 Bless the God of gods, all you who
fear the Lord;
praise him and give him thanks,
because his mercy endures
forever."

IV. NEBUCHADNEZZAR'S INSANITY (3:31–4:34)

3 31 (98) King Nebuchadnezzar to all the people of every nation,
tribe, and tongue, wherever they live on all the earth: "May you have
abundant peace! 32 (99) I am happy to make known the wonderful
miracles that the Most High God has performed in my regard.

33 (100) How great are his miracles,
how mighty his wonders!
His reign is an everlasting reign;
his dominion endures for ages and ages.

4 1 "I, Nebuchadnezzar, was at home in my palace, relaxed and
contented. 2 But as I was lying in bed, I had a frightening dream, and
the images of the vision that came to my mind terrified me. 3 So I issued an order to have all the wise men of Babylon brought before me,
that they might tell me the meaning of the dream. 4 When the magicians, enchanters, Chaldeans, and diviners had come in, I recounted
the dream to them. But none of them could tell me its meaning. 5 Finally there came before me Daniel, who was named Belteshazzar
after the name of my god, and who was endowed with a spirit of holy
Deity. I repeated the dream to him: 6 'Belteshazzar, chief of the magicians, since I know that you are endowed with a spirit of holy Deity
and that no mystery can baffle you, hear[a] the dream that I had and
tell me its meaning.

7 [b]" 'In the vision[b] that came to my mind as I was lying in bed, I saw
a tree of great height in the center of the world. 8 The tree grew large
and strong, so that its top reached the sky and it could be seen at the
ends of the whole world. 9 Its foliage was beautiful, and its fruit abundant, providing food for everyone. Under it the wild animals [c]sought
shelter,[c] and the birds of the air nested in its branches, while all living beings were nourished by it.

[a] Read *ḥăzî* for MT's *ḥezwê,* "the visions of," which has been influenced by the *ḥezwê* of the next verse.

[b–b] Read *beḥezwê;* cf. vs. 10. MT has "and the visions of."

[c–c] The *taṭlēl* of MT is probably to be vocalized as *tiṭṭallal* or *tiṭṭelēl;* see Rosenthal, *Handbook,* I/2, pp. 25–26.

10 " 'In the vision that came to my mind as I was lying in bed, I saw
a holy sentinel come down from heaven 11 and cry aloud:

"Chop down the tree and cut off its branches;
strip off its leaves and scatter its fruit.
Let the animals flee from beneath it,
and the birds from its branches.
12 But leave in the ground the stump at its roots,
with a band of iron and bronze, in the grass of the field.
With the dew of heaven let him be bathed;
with the beasts let his portion be the herbage of the earth.
13 Let his mind be changed from a man's,
and a beast's mind be given him,
until seven years pass over him.
14 By decree of the sentinels is this decision,
by command of the holy ones this sentence,
In order that all who live may learn
that the Most High has dominion over man's kingdom;
He gives it to whom he wishes,
and he sets over it the lowliest of men."

15 " 'This is the dream that I, King Nebuchadnezzar, had. Now it is
your turn, Belteshazzar, to tell me its meaning. Although none of the
wise men of Babylon could let me know its meaning, you can do so,
since you are endowed with a spirit of holy Deity.' "

16 Then Daniel, who was named Belteshazzar, was dismayed for a
moment, frightened by his thoughts. "Belteshazzar," the king said to
him, "don't let the dream and its meaning frighten you." "My lord,"
replied Belteshazzar, "may the dream be for your enemies, and its
meaning for your foes!

17 "The tree you saw which grew so large and strong that its top
reached the sky and thus could be seen throughout the world; 18 the
tree whose foliage was beautiful and whose fruit abundant, providing
food for everyone; the tree under which the wild animals stayed and
in whose branches the birds of the air nested—19 you, O king, are
that tree! You have grown great and powerful; your majesty has become so great as to reach to heaven, and your dominion to the ends of
the earth. 20 As for the king's vision of a holy sentinel coming down
from heaven and proclaiming, 'Chop down the tree and destroy it, but
leave in the ground the stump at its roots, with a band of iron and
bronze, in the grass of the field, while with the dew of heaven let him
be bathed and let his portion be with the beasts of the field until seven

years pass over him'—21 this, O king, is the meaning. The decree that
the Most High has passed on my lord the king is this: 22 you shall be
driven away from among men and live with the wild animals; like an
ox you shall be given grass to eat, and with the dew of heaven you
shall be bathed, until seven years pass over you and you learn that the
Most High has dominion over man's kingdom, and that he gives it to
whom he wishes. 23 The command that the tree's stump with its roots
should be left means that your kingdom will be saved for you, once
you have learned that it is Heaven that has supreme dominion.
24 Therefore, O king, take my advice: atone for your sins by good
deeds, and for your misdeeds by kindness to the poor; then you will
have lasting happiness."

25 All this happened to King Nebuchadnezzar. 26 Twelve months
later, as he was walking on the roof of the royal palace in Babylon,
27 the king exclaimed: "Ah, Babylon the great! Was it not I who built
it by my mighty power as a royal residence for my honor and glory?"
28 Scarcely had the king uttered these words when a voice spoke from
heaven: "This is decreed for you, King Nebuchadnezzar: your kingdom is taken from you! 29 You shall be driven away from among men
and live with wild animals; like an ox you shall be given grass to eat,
until seven years pass over you and you learn that the Most High has
dominion over man's kingdom, and that he gives it to whom he
wishes."

30 At that moment the word was fulfilled. Nebuchadnezzar was
driven away from among men; he ate grass like an ox, and his body
was bathed with the dew of heaven, while his hair grew like the
feathers of an eagle, and his nails like the claws of a bird.

31 "At the end of this period, I, Nebuchadnezzar, raised my eyes to
heaven: my reason was restored to me, and I blessed the Most High,
praising and glorifying him who lives forever.

His dominion is an everlasting dominion,
  and his kingdom endures throughout the ages.
32 All who live on the earth are accounted as nothing,
  and he does as he pleases with the army of heaven.[d]
There is no one who can stay his hand
  or say to him, 'What have you done?'

33 "At the same time when my reason was restored to me, my majesty and splendor returned to me for the glory of my kingdom. My

[d] MT adds, by dittography, "and those who live on the earth."

noblemen and magnates sought me out; [e]I was reinstated[e] in my kingdom, and I became much greater than before. 34 Now therefore, I, Nebuchadnezzar, praise and extol and glorify the King of heaven:

All his deeds are right,
and his ways are just;
[f]Those who walk[f] in pride
he is able to humble."

[e–e] Read with some MSS *hotqᵉnēt*. For the meaning of MT, see NOTES.
[f–f] Probably read, with some MSS, *mᵉhallᵉkîn;* see textual note [h–h] on 3:25.

NOTES

3:31. *all the earth.* Since Nebuchadnezzar reigned over most of the civilized world of his time, he could rightly imagine that he ruled over "all the earth."

32. *wonderful miracles.* Literally, "signs and wonders," understood in the translation as a hendiadys, although in the next verse the poetic parallelism requires the separation of the two terms. The expression, "signs and wonders," occurs frequently both in the Old Testament (Exod 7:3; Deut 6:22; 13:2; etc.) and in the New Testament (Mark 13:22; John 4:48; etc.).

4:1. *at home in my palace,* relaxed and contented. Literally, "relaxed in my house and prosperous in my palace." The adjective, *raʿnan* (perhaps borrowed into Aramaic from Hebrew), which is understood here as "prosperous" or "contented," elsewhere means "verdant," said of a tree (Deut 12:2; Isa 57:5; etc.); in Pss 37:35; 92:13*ff*, a verdant, flourishing tree is a symbol of a prosperous man.

2. Literally, "A dream I saw, and it frightened me, and thoughts upon my bed and the visions of my head terrified me." The plural, "visions," is understood in the translation as one "vision" embracing several "sights." So also in vss. 7 and 10.

4. *the magicians, enchanters, Chaldeans, and diviners.* See NOTES on 1:4,20.

5. *Daniel, who was named Belteshazzar after the name of my god.* The chief god of Babylon was Marduk, whose title was Bel ("lord"). But see NOTE on 1:7.

endowed with a spirit of holy Deity. The Aramaic *rûaḥ ʾĕlāhîn qaddîšîn bēh* is an echo of the Hebrew, *rûaḥ ʾĕlōhîm bô,* said of Joseph in Gen 41:38, which E. A. Speiser (*Genesis,* AB 1) renders well as "endowed with a divine spirit." By adding *qaddîšîn* here, the author probably wished to show that this divine spirit came from Yahweh, who is called *ʾĕlōhîm qᵉdōšîm* in Josh 24:19. The same expression occurs in Dan 4:6,15 (with *bēh* changed to *bāk*); cf. the simple "endowed with a divine spirit" in 5:14.

6. *hear the dream.* Thus understood freely with Theod. for the literal, "see the dream," based on a revised text (see textual note [a]).

8. *it could be seen at the ends of the whole world.* Literally, "its sight (was) to the end of the earth." Some emend *ḥăzôtēh* (or *ḥăzûtēh* of several MSS), "its sight," to *ḥăzôrēh,* "its circumference," i.e. the extent of its branches. Although this gives a good balance to the "height" of the tree, there is not sufficient reason for the emendation; it is not certain that Theod. (*kytos,* "hollow, vault") read *ḥăzôr,* and it is doubtful whether such an Aramaic word can mean "circumference." The same expression is used in vs. 17.

10. *sentinel.* Or, "watcher, watchman"; from the root *'îr* or *'ûr,* meaning "to be awake, to wake up" (intransitive). This is the earliest known use of the term *'îr* to designate an angel. In later apocryphal literature it is quite commonly used in this sense. The origin of the concept of the angels as "the vigilant ones" need not be sought outside Judaism, as if the word "holy" were added here to distinguish Yahweh's angels from pagan spirits; cf. Yahweh's *šōm^{e}rîm,* "watchmen," in Isa 62:6, who take no rest in reminding Yahweh to reestablish Jerusalem; or the many "eyes" of the cherubim chariot in Ezek 1:18, like the select stone's "eyes of Yahweh that range over the whole earth" in Zech 4:10. The term *'îr,* "sentinel," occurs also in vss. 14,20, but nowhere else in this book or any other book of the Old Testament.

11. *cry aloud.* The angelic sentinel addresses his companions (cf. vs. 14).

12. *the stump at its roots.* Or literally, "the stump of its roots." The tree is to be cut down at a short distance above the ground, so that a stump, supported by its roots in the earth, still remains standing.

in the grass of the field. That is where the stump, bound by metal clamps, remains standing. Some would delete *b^{e}dit'â dî bārâ,* "in the grass of the field," as a variant of *ba'ăśab 'ar'â,* "in the herbage of the earth" (at the end of the verse). Others, on the basis of vs. 29, would delete the latter phrase and supply a verb, such as *lēh y^{e}ṭa'ămû,* "let them give him to eat," with the former phrase. However, the text makes sufficiently good sense as it stands.

him. Since in the interpretation the tree represents Nebuchadnezzar (vss. 22*f*), the description of the tree changes here to a description of the king. In Aramaic, where the noun for tree (*'îlān*) is masculine, the transition from "it, its" to "he, his, him" is not noticeable.

13. *years.* Often translated as "times," since *'iddān* commonly means "time, period, season" (cf. 2:8*f*,12; 3:5,15; 7:12). But *'iddān* in this chapter (vss. 13, 20,22,29), as also in 7:25 and the Hebrew *mô'ēd* in 12:7 (and probably also in 9:29), evidently means "year," for in giving the explanation of the dream (vs. 29) Daniel would have used the unambiguous word for "years," *š^{e}nîn,* if *'iddānîn* did not also have this meaning. Ginsberg (pp. 1*f*) regards this usage of *'iddān* as a "translation loanword" from Greek *chronos,* which even in the classical period could mean "year" as well as "time."

14. *this sentence.* Literally, "the thing asked about" (*š^e'ēltâ*); cf. Akkadian *šītultu,* "counsel," *muštālu,* "counselor, decider."

16. *for a moment.* Although *šā'āh* was later used in the sense of an "hour," it originally designated any short period of time; cf. *bah ša'ătâ,* "at the same moment, at once" (3:6,15; 4:30; 5:5).

23. *Heaven.* In Judaism of the Hellenistic-Roman period, a surrogate for "God"; cf. I Macc 3:18*f;* 4:55; etc.; Matt 3:2; 4:17; etc. ("kingdom of heaven"="kingdom of God"); Luke 15:18,21.

24. *take my advice.* Literally, "may it be pleasing to you, may it seem good to you."

good deeds. Hebrew *ṣᵉdāqāh,* besides meaning "righteousness, justice," can also mean "an act of righteousness, a virtuous deed" (Isa 33:15; 64:5; etc.), "a meritorious deed" (Gen 15:6). In later Judaism, which laid great stress on charity to the poor (Tobit 4:7–11; 12:8*f;* Sir 3:29–4:10; 29:8–13), Hebrew *ṣᵉdāqāh* and the corresponding Aramaic *ṣidqāh* and Greek *dikaiosynē* frequently have the meaning of "almsgiving" (Matt 6:1; II Cor 9:9).

30. *his hair grew like the feathers of an eagle, and his nails like the claws of a bird.* The suggestion has been made to transpose "eagle" and "bird." This does indeed give a better picture, but unfortunately there is no textual evidence for emendation.

32. *the army of heaven.* The angels, as in Luke 2:13 (*stratia ouranios*). Aramaic *ḥêl šᵉmayyâ* corresponds to Hebrew *ṣᵉbā' haššamayîm,* which ordinarily refers to the stars or astral deities (Deut 17:3; Isa 34:4; Jer 8:2; 19:13; etc.), but may also refer to the angels of Yahweh's heavenly court (I Kings 22:19=II Chron 18:18).

33. *my majesty and splendor returned to me for the glory of my kingdom.* Literally, "for the glory of my kingdom, my majesty and my splendor returned to me." But the Aramaic text, which the Syriac does not reproduce, is uncertain. Some follow the reading of Theod., Vulg., and Rashi: "Into the glory of my kingdom I came back [for *hadrî,* reading *hadrēt*], and my splendor returned to me."

I was reinstated in my kingdom. The vocalization of the MT (*hotqᵉnat*) perhaps allows the variant reading of the LXX, "my kingdom was reestablished for me," or perhaps the vocalization of *htqnt* was accidentally influenced by the following verb, *hûspat.*

COMMENT: GENERAL

As in the case with the other folk tales that form the first half of the Book of Daniel, the story of Nebuchadnezzar's dream of the great tree and his subsequent insanity is an independent unit, which once circulated separately before being joined to the other stories by the author-compiler of the book. It resembles the story of Nebuchadnezzar's dream of the composite statue, as told in ch. 2, inasmuch as in both stories the same king (who in each case may have been originally Nabonidus instead of Nebuchadnezzar—see below) has a dream that none of the Babylonian soothsayers, but only Daniel, enlightened by Yahweh, can interpret. In both stories, too, the dream motif forms a framework for an inner theme: in ch. 2, the successive world empires; in ch. 4, the king's insanity and its cure.

The story in ch. 4, however, is unique in its literary form, inasmuch as it is cast in the style of an epistle, with standard epistolary introduction (3:31–33), the body of the letter that gives the account of the king's dream and its effects (4:1–33), and finally a conclusion (4:34) which reechoes the praises of God that were sounded in the introduction. As is proper to such epistolary style, the narrative, as a whole, is told in the first person by the writer of the epistle. But a short section, 4:25–30, is told of Nebuchadnezzar in the third person. There is a somewhat similar shift in the Book of Tobit, where, as the story begins, it is told by Tobit in the first person (1:3 – 3:6), and then, after an interlude that is not directly concerned with Tobit (3:7–17), the narrative is continued by speaking of Tobit in the third person (4:1 – 14:15). In Dan 4:25–30, however, the shift to the third person may be a certain literary device to show that the king himself was naturally unable to give an account of what happened to him while he was out of his mind.

It is difficult to say when the folk tale of Nebuchadnezzar's insanity originated. It may have begun in oral form at the end of the Neo-Babylonian period and found its literary expression in the Persian period, as indicated both by certain correct historical allusions and by the nature of the Aramaic in which it is written. In any case, it is certainly older than the time of the Maccabean revolt against Antiochus IV Epiphanes. The author-compiler of the book apparently took the story as he found it and made no attempt to change the character of the king, whom the story presents in the end as a worshipper of Yahweh, into a figure of the wicked Epiphanes. But at the time of this persecutor of the Jews the moral of the story—that Yahweh is truly the supreme Lord of the world (4:31*f*), who can humble proud rulers (4:34)—could well serve as encouragement for the afflicted Jews to remain faithful to their ancestral religion.

Like the other stories in the first half of the book, this one too has much of the repetitious language that is characteristic of folk tales. But here the repetitions are not as tedious for the modern reader as are, for instance, those in the story of the worship of the golden image (ch. 3). The present story is, in fact, composed in a pleasing lyrical strain, although the extent of true poetic structure in it is disputed. In the translation offered here only those parts that show more or less clear metrical form in the Aramaic and present genuine parallelism are printed in poetic lines (3:33; 4:11–14,31b–32,34b).

COMMENT: DETAILED

Epistolary Introduction (3:31*ff*)

The chapter division used in this translation is that of the MT, which in turn is that of the Vulgate, introduced into the text reputedly by Stephen Langton, ca. A.D. 1225. By it, the first three verses of the story were wrongly attached to the end of the preceding story. In the *KJV* and *RSV*, 3:31 of the MT is reckoned as 4:1.

The epistolary introduction, giving the name of the sender of the letter ("King Nebuchadnezzar"), the addressees ("all the people of every nation . . ."), and a greeting ("May you have abundant peace!"), is similar to the style used in the Akkadian letters of the Neo-Babylonian period, the Aramaic letters of the Persian period (e.g. among the Elephantine papyri), and the Greek letters of the Hellenistic period (e.g. I Macc 10:18,20; 14:20; 15:2,16; II Macc 1:1,10). This is followed, after a brief statement on the purpose of the letter, by a hymn of praise to God, as in certain New Testament Epistles (II Cor 1:3*ff*; Eph 1:3*ff*; I Peter 1:3*f*). The terms used to designate the addressees of the letter, *kol-'amᵉmayyâ 'ummayyâ wᵉliššānayyâ,* literally, "all the nations, peoples, and tongues," which occur also in 3:4,7; 5:19; 6:26; 7:14, is reminiscent of the many different ethnic and linguistic groups in the Persian empire, to whom proclamations in their own languages were sent by the Persian kings (cf. the Behistun Inscription, and Esther 1:22; 3:12; 8:9).

Nebuchadnezzar's Dream of the Great Tree (4:1–15)

As stated above (see COMMENT: GENERAL), the dream motif here is similar in several respects to the one in ch. 2: in both cases, the reader is first left in suspense concerning the content of the dream; in both, the pagan soothsayers fail utterly, whereas Daniel by special enlightenment from God (cf. his endowment "with a spirit of holy Deity" in 4:6 with his divinely infused knowledge of the king's dream in 2:17*ff*) is alone able to satisfy the king's request. But here the king is easier on his soothsayers; instead of demanding that they first tell him the content of the dream, as in ch. 2, here he himself describes the dream to them (4:4,7–14) and only asks them to interpret its meaning for him. The dream in ch. 2 merely prevented the king from falling back to sleep (2:1), but the present dream frightened him out of his wits (4:2), apparently because he had an inkling that the dire sentence pronounced in the dream (4:11–14) foreboded evil for himself. His happy condition at the time the dream came to him, when he was flourishing like a verdant tree (4:1), is expressly mentioned in order to stress the contrast with the abominable condition to which he would be reduced in punishment for his pride (4:30). Inasmuch as Daniel is here introduced as the king's "chief magician" (*rab hartūmayyâ:* 4:6), the reader is presumed to know from the other stories of the cycle how Daniel received this high office (cf. 2:48).

Although the motif of a "world tree" was rather widespread in antiquity, there is no need to look outside the Bible for the sources of this story's portrayal of the mighty king under the figure of a gigantic tree. First in consideration comes the allegory of the cypress of Lebanon in Ezekiel 31, where it is applied to the king of Egypt. As in Daniel 4, the great tree of Ezekiel 31 "was beautiful of branch, lofty of stature, and lifted its crest amid the clouds" (vs. 3); "in its boughs all the birds of the air nested, and under its branches all the beasts of the field gave birth" (vs. 6); but "because it became proud of heart at its height," God let it be cut down and its foliage and branches brought low (vss. 11*f*). Just as the paradise theme is connected with the tree of Ezekiel 31—"the cedars of the garden of God were not its equal . . . , no tree in the garden of God matched its beauty" (vs. 8); and it was "the envy of all Eden's trees in the garden of God" (vs. 9), so that all of Eden's trees, from which it had been stealing the life-giving water, rejoiced at its downfall (vs. 16)—so also in Daniel 4, the tree with its abundant fruit which provided nourishment for all (vs. 9) is similar to Eden's tree of life; Nebuchadnezzar in his pride would take the place of God, who alone sustains man's life.

The allegory of the transplanted shoot from the chopped-down tree in Ezek 22:22*ff*, which symbolizes the restoration of the Davidic dynasty, has also influenced Daniel 4; "it shall put forth branches and bear fruit, and become a majestic cedar; birds of every kind shall dwell beneath it, and every winged thing in the shade of its boughs." Here also the moral is similar; compare Ezek 22:24, "All the trees of the field shall know that I, Yahweh, bring low the high tree, lift high the lowly tree, wither up the green tree, and make the withered tree bloom," with Dan 4:14, ". . . The Most High has dominion over man's kingdom; he gives it to whom he wishes, and he sets over it the lowliest of men."

For the stump of the tree left in the ground (4:12), compare the "stump" of David's dynastic tree in Isa 11:1, and the "oak whose stump remains when its leaves have fallen" in Isa 4:13. There is no reason to think that the ancients actually clamped a metal band around the stump of a chopped-down tree, as if to keep it from splitting; here the image passes to the reality: the king is to be bound with metal fetters.

Daniel's Interpretation of the Dream (4:16–24)

Although Daniel understood at once the meaning of the dream, he hesitates for a moment, out of courtesy and humility, to explain its dire portent to his royal master. Encouraged by the king to speak up, Daniel first graciously expresses a wish that the sad fate decreed in the vision might befall the king's enemies, rather than the king himself.

Then, while repeating most of the king's description of the dream, Daniel explains its symbolic meaning. The king himself is symbolized by the tree whose magnificent growth is a figure of Nebuchadnezzar's vast empire. The fate decreed for Nebuchadnezzar is that for seven years he is to live like an animal. The meaning is not that the king would actually be changed into an animal. Rather, the sense is that Nebuchadnezzar would suffer a form of monomania known as zoanthropy, in which a man believes himself changed into an animal and acts like one.

However, as symbolized by the stump of the tree left in the ground, Nebuchadnezzar is not to be deprived of his kingdom forever. His affliction is to last only for seven years; at the end of this period he will be so humiliated that he will acknowledge God's supreme dominion over men. Then he will be cured of his affliction. But he must give proof of his sincere repentance by performing good deeds, particularly by practicing charity to the poor; otherwise he will have a relapse into his insanity and will not have "lasting happiness" (literally, "prolongation, extension" of happiness). The words in 4:24 about "atoning for sins" (literally, "breaking off, removing sins") by performing "good deeds" had once unfortunately been the source of needless polemics between Catholics and Protestants. Obviously, good deeds by themselves without faith in Christ are insufficient for salvation; but just as obvious is the praise of "good deeds" in the New Testament (Matt 6:1–4; Mark 10:21; Acts 9:36; 10:2).

The advice that Daniel gives in 4:24 is understood by some commentators to mean that, if Nebuchadnezzar performs good deeds during the respite given him, the fate that threatens him will be averted. But this seems less probable than the interpretation given above. The decree passed on him by the Most High (4:21) and proclaimed by the "holy sentinels" (4:14) appears to be an absolute sentence; justice demands that the king's pride be punished by the decreed humiliation.

Nebuchadnezzar's Insanity and Recovery (4:25–34)

That the dire prediction was not fulfilled until a year after it was made may be only a dramatic touch in the folk tale, to keep the reader in suspense. It seems unlikely that it was a God-given respite, to give the king a chance to repent. In any case, the blow fell just as the king was boasting about the great city of Babylon that he had built. There is a true historic touch here. Not only was Babylon one of the largest and most magnificent cities in the ancient world; it was to Nebuchadnezzar in particular that it owed most of its splendor, and several of his cuneiform inscriptions are preserved in which he boasts of the great buildings that he erected there.

In contrast to this genuinely historical detail in the story, the account of Nebuchadnezzar's seven-year insanity is, as such, entirely unhistorical. Enough is known of the forty-three-year reign of this great monarch to make it impossible to fit into it a seven-year period when he was deprived of his throne and lived among the wild animals like one of them.

After the publication of the "Nabonidus Chronicle" by T. G. Pinches in 1882 (for an English translation of it, see *ANET*, pp. 305–307), there was a growing suspicion that, in an earlier form of the present folk tale, the insane king was not Nebuchadnezzar II (605–562 B.C.), but his fourth successor, Nabunaid, or according to the Greco-Roman form of his name, Nabonidus (556–539 B.C.). According to this document, Nabonidus stayed, in several years of his reign for many months at a time, in Tema, an oasis town in Arabia, and he thus failed to carry out his religious functions in the New Year festivals at Babylon. Whatever his reasons for doing this may have been, the rumor could well have spread among his people that his prolonged stays in such a remote place indicated that something was wrong with him mentally.

The theory that people thought Nabonidus was out of his mind was confirmed by Sidney Smith's publication in 1924 of the "Verse Account of Nabonidus" (for an English translation of it, see *ANET*, pp. 312–315). This document, which is a biased account written by the priests of Babylon to justify the action of the gods in handing over Nabonidus' realm to the Persian King Cyrus, so vilifies the Babylonian king and accuses him of such ignorance and blasphemy that popular opinion could easily have regarded Nabonidus as a "mad king."

Further evidence to confirm the theory that the story told in Daniel 4 was originally concerned with Nabonidus is now available in a text found in Cave 4 at Qumran that was published by J. T. Milik, *RB* 63 (1956), 407–411. Although this fragmentary document, commonly called "The Prayer of Nabonidus," was written in the second half of the first century B.C., it is probably a copy of an older document; in any case it is no doubt based on a much older folk tale. Because of the importance of this text in connection with the story told in Daniel 4, it seems well to quote a translation of it here in full (with doubtful words in italics, and supplied words in brackets): "The words of the prayer that Nabonidus, the king of A[ssyria and Ba]bylon, the [great] king, prayed [when he was smitten] with a bad inflammation *by* the decree of the [*Most High God*] in [the city of] Tema. ['With a bad inflammation] I was smitten for seven years and *from* [*men*] *I was put away*. But when I *confessed my sins* and my faults,

He (God) allowed *me* (to have) a soothsayer. This was a Jewish [man *of the exiles in Babylon. He*] *explained* (*it*) and wrote (me) to render honor and *g*[*reat glor*]*y* to the name of the [Most High God. Thus he wrote: "When] you were smitten with a b[ad] inflammation in [the city of] Tema [by the decree of the Most High God] for seven years, [you we]re praying to gods of silver and gold, [of bronze,] iron, wood, stone, (and) clay . . . that *th*[*ese*] gods. . . .'"'"

There are certain striking similarities between this text and the story told in Daniel 4: in both accounts a Neo-Babylonian king, whose name begins with the name of the god Nabu, is afflicted by God for seven years, during which time he lives apart from ordinary social intercourse; a certain Jewish exile explains to him the meaning of his affliction and urges him to repent of his sins; when he does this, he is cured of his affliction and renders thanks to God; finally, each account is largely written in the first person.

Yet there are some equally striking differences between the two accounts. Although their names are similar, two different kings are involved in the stories, and one of them is smitten in Babylon, whereas the other is smitten in Tema (cf. Isa 21:14; Jer 25:23; Job 6:19). An even more important difference is the nature of the affliction of each king: the king of Daniel 4 is smitten with a form of monomania, whereas the king of the Qumran text is smitten with *šeḥîn* (literally, a "burning" or "inflammation"), a disease resembling leprosy (Lev 13:18*ff*,23), that causes the skin to break out in festering boils (Exod 9:9*ff*; Deut 28:27,35), which God sends to try men (Isa 38:12; Job 2:7).

Despite the occasional occurrence of the same terms in both documents (e.g. *pitgām*, "decree, decision": 4QPrayer of Nabonidus 2 and Dan 4:14; *gāzar*, "soothsayer, diviner": 4QPrayer of Nabonidus 4 and Dan 4:4), due to the similar content of each story, there is no literary dependence of one story on the other. Yet both probably go back to an early folk tale first transmitted in oral form. On the presumption that the early, orally told narrative arose from a historical fact, the story in the Qumran text appears to have preserved the early tale more faithfully than the one in Daniel 4; it is more plausible in having Nabonidus as the afflicted king, and it has correctly kept the historical fact of Nabonidus' long residence at Tema.

Although this Qumran text, as far as it is preserved, does not mention Daniel by name, a few other very fragmentary texts have been found in Cave 4 at Qumran that expressly mention a certain Daniel in contexts that do not duplicate anything in the Book of Daniel. Consequently, it seems certain that, besides the Daniel stories that are preserved in the Bible, there were several other such stories in circulation among the Jews of the last pre-Christian centuries, so that one can rightly speak of a "cycle" of Daniel stories; cf. Introduction, Part IV.

On these questions see: D. N. Freedman, "The Prayer of Nabonidus," *BASOR* 145 (1957), 31–32; L. F. Hartman, "The Great Tree and Nabuchodonosor's Madness," in *The Bible in Current Catholic Thought*, ed. J. L. McKenzie, pp. 75–82. [See also M. McNamara, "Nabonidus and the Book of Daniel," *ITQ* 37 (1970), 131–149, who argues that Daniel 2–5 contain a series of traditions in chronological order, originally connected with events from the life of Nabonidus. The figure of Nebuchadnezzar in these chapters represents Nabonidus, but some characteristics of the historical Nebuchadnezzar are also included (cf., for instance, 4:25–27, and Hartman's comment above).]

V. BELSHAZZAR'S FEAST
(5:1–6:1)

5 1 King Belshazzar made a great feast for his thousand grandees.
While he was drinking wine before them, 2 Belshazzar, under the
influence of the wine, gave orders to have the gold and silver vessels
that his father Nebuchadnezzar had taken from the Temple of Jerusalem brought in, so that he and his grandees, his wives and his concubines might drink from them. 3 When the gold [a]and silver[a] vessels
that [b]had been taken[b] from the house of God in Jerusalem [c]were
brought in[c], the king and his grandees, his wives and his concubines
drank from them. 4 As they drank the wine, they praised their gods of
gold and silver, bronze and iron, wood and stone.

5 Just then there appeared, next to the lamp, the fingers of a man's
hand that wrote on the plastered wall of the royal palace. When the
king saw the hand as it was writing, 6 his face blanched because of the
thoughts that frightened him; his legs gave way, and his knees
knocked. 7 Having called aloud for the enchanters, the Chaldeans,
and the diviners to be brought in, the king said to these wise men of
Babylon, "Whoever can read this writing and tell me what it means
shall wear the purple and have the golden torque on his neck and
shall be a triumvir in the government of the kingdom." 8 Yet, although all the king's wise men came in, they could not read the writing or tell the king what it meant. 9 King Belshazzar was therefore
greatly terrified, and his face turned ashen, while his grandees were
thrown into consternation.

10 When the queen heard of the discussion between the king and his
grandees, she entered the banquet hall and said, "O king, live forever!
Do not be so troubled in mind, or look so pale. 11 There is a man in
your kingdom who is endowed with a spirit of holy Deity; in your father's reign he was found to have brilliant insight and godlike wis-

[a–a] Added with Theod. and Vulg.; cf. vs. 2.

[b–b] Read *honpaqû* (passive). MT's vocalization, *hanpīqû* (active) would require *hnpyqw* at this period.

[c–c] Perhaps read, with LXX and Theod., *hêtayû* (passive) for MT's *haytîw* (active).

dom. In fact, your father King Nebuchadnezzar made him chief of
the magicians, enchanters, Chaldeans, and diviners,[d] 12 since such an
extraordinary mind and knowledge and understanding [e]to interpret[e]
dreams, explain enigmas, and solve[f] difficulties were found in this
Daniel, whom the king named Belteshazzar. Let Daniel, therefore, be
summoned, and he will tell you what this means."

13 So Daniel was brought into the presence of the king, and the
king asked him, "Are you the Daniel who is one of the Jewish exiles
my father brought here from Judah? 14 I have heard about you, that
you are endowed with a divine spirit and that you possess brilliant insight and extraordinary wisdom. 15 Now, the wise men and enchanters
were brought before me, that they might read this writing and tell me
its meaning; but they were unable to show me what the words mean.
16 However, I have heard about you, that you are able to interpret
dreams[g] and solve difficulties. If then you can read the writing and
tell me what it means, you will wear the purple and have the golden
torque on your neck, and you will be a triumvir in the government of
the kingdom."

17 Then Daniel answered the king, "You may keep your gifts, or
give your presents to someone else. But I will read the writing for the
king, and tell him what it means. 18 Hear, O king! The Most High
God gave your father Nebuchadnezzar a great kingdom and glorious
majesty; 19 and because he had bestowed on him such greatness, the
people of every nation, tribe, and tongue stood in fear and dread of
him; for he killed or spared whomever he wished, and he exalted or
humbled whomever he wished. 20 But when his heart became proud
and his spirit hardened into insolence, he was deposed from his royal
throne, deprived of his glory, 21 and cast out from among men. His
mind became like that of a beast, as he lived with the wild asses and
ate grass like an ox; and his body was bathed with the dew of heaven,
until he learned that the Most High God has dominion over man's
kingdom and appoints over it whom he wishes. 22 Yet you, his son
Belshazzar, have not humbled your heart, even though you knew all

[d] Either omit, with Theod. and Syr., MT's "your father the king" as a dittography, or take *ûmalkâ nᵉbūkadneṣṣar 'ăbûk* as a *casus pendens* which is resumed at the end by *'abûk malkâ.*

[e–e] Read *mipšar* (infinitive) with Vulg. MT vocalizes (*mᵉpaššar*) as pa'il participle, which does not fit in the structure of the sentence.

[f] Read *ûmišrê* (infinitive) with a few MSS and Vulg. MT vocalizes (*umᵉšārē'*) as pa'il participle, which does not fit in the structure of the sentence.

[g] Read *ḥelmîn* with one MS; cf. vs. 12. MT has "interpretations."

this. 23 Instead, you exalted yourself against the Lord of heaven; you
had the vessels of his house brought before you, so that you and your
grandees, your wives and your concubines might drink wine from
them. You praised your gods of silver and gold, of bronze and iron, of
wood and stone, who do not see or hear or know anything; but the
God in whose hand is your very breath and the whole course of your
life you did not glorify. 24 Therefore it was by him that the hand was
sent and this writing inscribed.

25 "This is the writing that was inscribed: MENE[h], TEQEL, PERES[i].
26 This is what the words mean:

MENE: God has numbered the days of your reign and brought it to an end.

27 TEQEL: you have been weighed on the scales and been found wanting;

28 PERES: your kingdom has been divided up and given to the Medes and the Persians."

29 Then Belshazzar gave orders to have Daniel clothed in purple, to
have a golden torque put on his neck, and to be proclaimed a triumvir
in the government of the kingdom.

30 That very night, the Chaldean King Belshazzar was slain;
6 1 and Darius the Mede succeeded to the kingdom at the age of
sixty-two.

[h] MT has *mᵉnēʾ* twice, apparently by dittography; omit one *mᵉnēʾ* with Josephus (*Antiquities* x 11, 3), LXX, Theod., Vulg.; cf. vs. 26.

[i] Read *pᵉrēs* with Josephus (loc. cit.), LXX, Theod., Vulg.; cf. vs. 28. See NOTES.

NOTES

5:1. *Belshazzar*. The Aramaic form of the name *belšaʾṣṣar* is a corruption of the Akkadian name *bēl-šarra-uṣur*, "O Bel, protect the king!"

a great feast. A state banquet. The word, *lᵉḥem*, translated here as "feast," meant originally "food" (in general), and hence here, "an eating"; ordinarily it means "bread" for agricultural people (Hebrew *leḥem*), or "meat" for pastoral people (Arabic *laḥm*). The more common word for "banquet" is *mištēʾ* (vs. 10; cf. Esther 1:2) from *šty*, "to drink."

2. *under the influence of the wine*. Literally, "under the taste of the wine" (the only occurrence in biblical Aramaic of *ṭʿm* in its original meaning of "taste"). Some, e.g. Montgomery (p. 251), render the phrase as "at the tasting

of the wine," and understand it to mean "when the wine began to be drunk" (at the end of the meal); but cf. Esther 1:10: "When the wine made the king feel merry."

5. *the lamp.* Or, less probably, "the lampstand." The Aramaic word thus translated, *nebraštâ,* is probably a loanword from the Persian.

the hand. Aramaic *pas yᵉdāh* (literally, "the palm of the hand") designates the hand from the wrist to the tips of the fingers, as distinct from simple *yᵉdāh,* which includes the forearm as well as the hand proper. The term, *pas yᵉdāh,* is used here to stress the fact that it was only a hand, with no other part of a human body appearing; so also in vs. 24.

6. *his face blanched.* Literally, "his radiance changed upon him"; for the concept, cf. Nahum 2:11.

his legs gave way. Literally, "the joints of his hips were loosened"; for the loosening of the loins or hip joints and the knocking of the knees as symptoms of panic, cf. Isa 21:3; Ezek 21:12; Nahum 2:11; Ps 69:24.

7. *the purple and . . . the golden torque.* The royal purple (really crimson) and the gold torque or collar (of solid metal, rather than in the form of a chain) were symbols of high nobility. The Aramaic word for "torque" (*hamyānkâ,* rather than MT *hamnîkâ*) is a loanword from Old Persian **hamyānaka;* in modern Persian, *hamyān* means "belt."

triumvir. Aramaic *taltâ* or *taltî* is a loan translation of Akkadian *šalšu,* "third," which as a title of a high official had, at this period, lost its original meaning. For the sense, cf. the "three chief ministers" in 6:3.

10. *When the queen heard . . . , she entered. . . .* Literally, "The queen, because of the words of the king and his grandees, entered. . . ."

the queen. The word *malkᵉtâ* probably means "queen mother" here, rather than "queen consort," for which the term *šēgal* would be expected (cf. Neh 2:6). The queen mother occupied a very influential position, not only in the kingdoms of Israel and Judah (Hebrew *gᵉbîrāh*), but also at the Assyrian, Babylonian, and Persian courts.

11. *endowed with a spirit of holy Deity.* See NOTE on 4:5.

brilliant insight (also in vs. 14). Literally, "brilliance and insight," taken here as a hendiadys.

12. Some commentators place a full stop at the end of vs. 11, and understand vs. 12 as "Since an extraordinary mind and knowledge . . . have been found in Daniel, . . . Belteshazzar, let Daniel now be summoned. . . ."

to interpret dreams, explain enigmas, and solve difficulties. These infinitives are really verbal nouns (literally, "the interpreting of dreams and the explaining of enigmas and the loosening of knots"); and all these words are parenthetical, explaining what Daniel's knowledge and understanding consisted of. The finite verb of the whole clause, *hištᵉkaḥat* (third person singular feminine) is made to agree with *rûaḥ yattîrāh,* "an extraordinary mind."

solve difficulties. Literally, "loosen knots," which some commentators take to mean "break magic spells." The expression may have such a meaning at times, but hardly in the present context.

Belteshazzar. On Daniel's Babylonian name, see NOTE on 1:7.

14. *a divine spirit.* See NOTE on 4:5.

18. *Hear, O king!* Literally, "You, O king." This is a *casus pendens* which is resumed at the beginning of vs. 22.

a great kingdom and glorious majesty. Literally, "the kingdom and the greatness and the glory and the majesty," taken here as a double hendiadys.

23. *silver and gold.* One MS, Theod., and Syr. have "gold and silver," as in vs. 4. But this is probably a later correction, to keep a decreasing value of the metals throughout; cf. the order of the metals in the Qumran Prayer of Nabonidus (see COMMENT: DETAILED on 4:25–34): "gods of silver and gold, of bronze, iron, stone, wood, and clay."

but the God in whose hand is your very breath and the whole course of your life you did not glorify. This translation takes the *lēh* as emphasizing *wᵉlēʾlāhâ:* "but the God in whose hand is . . . your life, him you did not glorify." However, the punctuation of the MT seems to call rather for the rendering: "but the God in whose hand is your life breath and to whom (*lēh*) belongs the whole course of your life you did not glorify."

24. *by him.* Literally, "from his presence."

25. *MENE, TEQEL, PERES.* In Aramaic, *mᵉnēʾ, tᵉqēl, pᵉrēs,* which mean, literally, "a mina, a shekel, a half mina." These were units of weight, used especially in weighing precious metals, the mina equaling fifty shekels. Instead of *pᵉrēs,* the MT has *ûparsîn,* "and half minas," which may be vocalized as *ûparsayin,* "and two half minas," in view of the double play on the word *pᵉrēs* in vs. 28.

26. *has numbered.* In Aramaic, *mᵉnāh,* a play on the word *mᵉnēʾ*.

27. *you have been weighed.* In Aramaic, *tᵉqîltāh,* a play on the word *tᵉqēl.*

28. *has been divided up.* In Aramaic, *pᵉrîsat,* a play on the word *pᵉrēs.*

the Persians. In Aramaic, *pārās,* another play on the word *pᵉrēs.*

6:1. By a faulty chapter division, this verse is made vs. 1 of ch. 6 in the Vulg. and MT. In *KJV* and *RSV* it is reckoned as 5:31.

COMMENT: GENERAL

The story of Belshazzar's feast, at which a mysterious hand appeared and wrote cryptic words that spelled the king's doom, is a mixture of folk legend and religious fiction. But it is not completely devoid of a historical basis. Apart from several minor details in the story that are in keeping with customs of the Neo-Babylonian and Persian periods, the chief item of historical truth in the story is the fact that it makes a genuine historical personage, Belshazzar, the last king of the Neo-Babylonian dynasty. In a broad sense, this is historically correct. Not that Belshazzar was ever king in the strict sense; he could not preside at the Babylonian New Year's Day celebration, for which the presence of the king was required. But in the third year of his father's seventeen-year reign he, as crown prince, was appointed coregent with his father; and during the many long periods when his father was absent from the capital, Belshazzar was, for all practical purposes, ruler of the Neo-Babylonian empire. It is also historically true that he had this position when the city of Babylon was captured by a foreign ruler in 539 B.C. But beyond that, the story told in ch. 5 is mostly legend and fiction. Thus, Belshazzar was not the son of Nebuchadnezzar, as the story depicts him to be; at best, he may have been a descendant of Nebuchadnezzar on his mother's side (cf. M. J. Gruenthaner, "The Last King of Babylon," *CBQ* 11 [1949], 406–427), although this is based on legendary, rather than historical evidence. Belshazzar's father was Nabonidus, who was not a descendant of Nebuchadnezzar but a usurper of the throne. However, as mentioned above in connection with the story of Nebuchadnezzar's insanity (ch. 4), the Daniel stories as preserved in the Book of Daniel have confused the two Babylonian kings whose names begin with the same element (Nabu-, Nebo-) and so apparently identified Nabonidus with Nebuchadnezzar. The same confusion is found in Bar 1:11*f*, perhaps influenced by Dan 5:11.

From a literary viewpoint, the present story is closely connected with the story of Nebuchadnezzar's insanity (ch. 4). Although it forms a narrative unit by itself, the present tale may have come from the same storyteller as the one who produced the tale in ch. 4; or if from a different storyteller, the present story at least shows acquaintance with the story told in ch. 4. Not only is reference made here to Nebuchadnezzar's insanity and subsequent cure; that story is partly retold here in almost the same words.

As in most of the stories in the first half of the Book of Daniel, one of the themes of the present story is the superiority of the God-given wisdom of the Jewish sage over the worldly wisdom of the Babylonian wise men. Daniel demonstrates this superiority by being the only one who can interpret the mysterious handwriting that appeared on the wall of Belshazzar's palace.

The main religious truth that the story conveys is God's justice in punishing the pagan king for his sacrilegious insolence against the Lord of heaven, who holds in his hand the destinies of men and nations.

Although this story is included in a book that was compiled during the persecution of the Jews under Antiochus IV Epiphanes in the first half of the second century B.C., there is nothing in the story to lead one to see in Belshazzar a persecutor of the Jews and thus a symbol of Epiphanes, even though the persecuted Jews of the second century B.C. could find religious comfort in the thought that, as God punished Belshazzar for desecrating the holy vessels of Jerusalem's Temple, so he would punish Epiphanes for plundering this temple. As such, the story is older than the second century

B.C. The most that can be said regarding its date of composition is that, from its acquaintance with Neo-Babylonian and Persian customs and from the nature of its Aramaic, which shows a fair sprinkling of Persian loanwords, one can conclude that the story first rose among the Jews of the eastern Diaspora sometime in the Persian period. Some parts of the story, such as the significance of the mysterious handwriting on the wall, probably once circulated in an earlier and different form, as is discussed below in the COMMENT: DETAILED on 5:13–29.

COMMENT: DETAILED

The Great Feast (5:1–4)

As in the Book of Esther, the story begins here with a description of a banquet. It is historically true that at the courts of the Assyrian, Babylonian, and Persian kings magnificent state banquets were held, and archeology has shown that in the palaces of these kings, particularly in the royal palace at Babylon, there were halls where a large crowd of people could assemble for a meal. In such a banquet hall the king would sit at one end, with his back to the wall and with his nobles facing him; hence, the present story has an accurate touch in depicting him as drinking wine "before" (in front of) his guests (cf. Jer 52:33: when King Jehoiachin dined at the table of King Evil-merodach, "he ate bread before him"—*weʾākal leḥem lepānāyw*).

There was a widespread legend in the ancient world that, when Babylon was captured in a surprise attack by the Medes and Persians, the Babylonian king and his nobles were carousing at a nocturnal banquet (Herodotus i 191; Xenophon *Cyropaedia* vii 5). Our Daniel story reflects the same legend. On the true account of the fall of Babylon, see below under *Belshazzar's Death* (5:30–6:1).

To prepare the reader for this scene in which the sacred vessels of Jerusalem's Temple were desecrated in the palace of the king of Babylon, the author-compiler of the Book of Daniel has been careful to note in his own introductory story how these vessels had been taken by Nebuchadnezzar from Jerusalem to a temple in Babylonia (1:2). Belshazzar now had the vessels brought from this temple to his palace, where he not only put them to profane use as mere drinking cups, but also added sacrilege to profanation by "praising" his pagan gods in a quasi-cultic act as the wine was drunk from the sacred vessels. This sacrilege called for immediate punishment from Yahweh.

The Handwriting on the Wall (5:5–9)

No sooner had the king committed this sacrilege than a hand appeared from nowhere—a hand alone, without the rest of a human body being visible—and wrote mysterious words on the white plaster of the wall of the banquet hall. Since the writing was done near a lamp, all those present could see it. Fearing that the strange writing boded no good for himself, Belshazzar was overcome with fright. Like Nebuchadnezzar, he called to his aid the professional soothsayers (cf. 2:2*ff;* 4:3*ff*). As in the manner of other Oriental tales, extravagant honors were promised to anyone who could read the writing; but none of the pagan soothsayers could do so. When the story says that the king's wise men "could not read the writing or tell the king what it meant," the meaning is probably, not that the writing was in an unknown script, but that it did not make sense. For the storyteller, the writing was apparently in regular Aramaic script, giving ordinary Aramaic words, but the message conveyed by the words was beyond the understanding of the pagan wise men; cf. the mysterious name of Isaiah's son, Maher-shalal-hash-baz, which the prophet inscribed "in ordinary writing" (*b*ᵉ*ḥereṭ 'ĕnôš*), but of which no one could grasp the significance until the prophet explained its meaning (Isa 8:1–4).

The Queen's Advice (5:10–12)

News of what had happened in the banquet hall soon reached the ears of the "queen." As mentioned in the NOTES on 5:10, by the term, "queen," is probably meant the queen mother, rather than the queen consort, even though in Esther 1:10*f* the "queen" (Vashti) who was not present at Ahasuerus's banquet was the queen consort. The present queen speaks to the king more like a mother than a wife, and her recollection of what Daniel had done in the reign of Belshazzar's "father" Nebuchadnezzar clearly implies that she is regarded as Belshazzar's mother rather than as his wife. Since the story mixes a certain amount of true history with mere legend, the lady may be thought of as the mother (or grandmother?) of Nabonidus whose basalt stele was discovered at Eski-Harran (see *ANET,* pp. 311*f*), or as the legendary Nitocris whom Herodotus (i 185*ff*) presents as the wife of Nebuchadnezzar. The classical example of a powerful queen mother in the history of ancient Mesopotamia is Naqia, who not only induced her husband Sennacherib to appoint their youngest son Esarhaddon as his successor, but was also influential in having Esarhaddon's younger son Ashurbanipal succeed him on the throne of Assyria.

Belshazzar's "queen" describes Daniel's God-given wisdom and success with such conviction (and in terms reminiscent of those used in 4:5*f* and 2:48!) that her advice to have Daniel summoned for solving the riddle of the mysterious handwriting on the wall is accepted by the king.

Daniel's Reading and Interpretation of the Writing (5:13–29)

Belshazzar greets Daniel courteously, and to make sure that the mysterious writing will be interpreted for him, he repeats the "queen's" glowing encomium of the Jewish sage and makes the same promise of rich rewards that he had made to his pagan soothsayers (5:13–16).

Disclaiming an interest in material rewards, Daniel affirms his intention to interpret the mysterious writing for the king—no doubt because he feels he must deliver God's message (5:17). Before coming to the handwriting on the wall and its meaning, Daniel delivers a stinging rebuke to the king in a short sermon, worthy of the ancient prophets (5:18–24). Its two halves are well balanced, each beginning in Aramaic with *'ant,* "you!" (5:18 and 22). In the first half he recounts, largely in the words of 4:29*ff,* the affliction and cure of Nebuchadnezzar—a much greater king, who nevertheless humbled himself in the end and acknowledged the supreme dominion of the Most High God. In the second half, the frivolous Belshazzar is contrasted with his "father" Nebuchadnezzar: instead of humbling himself before the God who holds in his hand the destinies of men, he insolently desecrated the Lord's sacred vessels, while praising his material idols. How much greater is his guilt because he knew what had happened to Nebuchadnezzar!

After this sermon, Daniel's reading and interpretation of the mysterious writing is brief and to the point. According to the MT, Daniel reads the writing as *m^e^nē' m^e^nē' t^e^qēl ûparsîn.* O. Eissfeldt ("Die Menetekel Inschrift und ihre Bedeutung," *ZAW* 63 [1951], 105–114), against the majority of modern scholars, defended this as the original text; since the Qumran *p^e^šārîm* ("interpretations" of Scripture, e.g. in the Habakkuk Scroll) show that an interpretation need not necessarily correspond exactly with the words that are being interpreted, one need not therefore correct the MT of Dan 5:25 to make it conform with Dan 5:26*ff.* Eissfeldt therefore renders the mysterious words of 5:25 as "gezähl: Mine, Schekel, Teilschekels." However, the majority of modern scholars, following Josephus and all the ancient versions, correct the MT of 5:25 to make it conform with the interpretation given in 5:26*ff* and thus make the handwriting on the wall consist of only the three words: *m^e^nē', t^e^qēl,* and *p^e^rēs.*

By using the roots of these words as verbs (see NOTES on 5:26*ff*), Daniel interprets them as meaning: the days of Belshazzar's reign are "numbered," i.e. they have come to an end; he has been "weighed" and found to be worthless (a spiritual "lightweight"); and his kingdom is now to be "divided" among the Medes and the "Persians."

It would be strange, however, if the three words had no meaning in themselves, other than the puns that Daniel sees in them. In 1886, C. Clermont-Ganneau (*Journal Asiatique,* 8th ser., 8, pp. 36–67) offered an explanation of the three Aramaic words which is now accepted by almost all scholars: *m^e^nē' t^e^qēl p^e^rēs* designate three weights or monetary units—the mina, the shekel (one fiftieth of a mina), and the half mina. In 1944, E. G. Kraeling ("The Handwriting on the Wall," *JBL* 63 [1944], 11–18) suggested that, because of the odd sequence in the value of the weights, there was an earlier form of the riddle than the quasi-"etymological" one given here in Daniel 5 in which the weights were symbols of successive kings; translating the MT of 5:25 as "a mina, a mina, a shekel, and two half minas," Kraeling proposed to understand these units as representing, respectively, the successors of Nebuchadnezzar: Evil-merodach (561–560 B.C.), Neriglissar (560–556), Labashi-Marduk (a few months in 556 and hence a mere "shekel"), and Nabonidus (556–539) with his crown prince Belshazzar (the two half shekels). His reasons, however, for his choice of these kings is not quite convincing. Ginsberg (pp. 24*ff*), considering the original text of 5:25 to contain only the three units, *m^e^nē' t^e^qēl p^e^rēs,* and arguing that the only Neo-Babylonian kings known to the Jews from about the time of Nehemiah on were Nebuchadnezzar, Evil-merodach (II Kings 25:27–30=Jer 52:31–34), and Belshazzar, saw these three kings as symbolized by the three weights; the Hebrew form (*'ĕwîl-m^e^rōdak*) of Evil-merodach's name (Akkadian *Amel-Marduk,* "Man of Marduk") made him look silly, since Hebrew *'ĕwîl* means "fool," and so he was worth only a shekel compared with Nebuchadnezzar and Belshazzar. D. N. Freedman ("The Prayer of Nabonidus," *BASOR* 145 [1957], 32) revises Ginsberg's theory by arguing on the basis of the Qumran "Prayer of Nabonidus" that the original king of Daniel 4 was Nabonidus (see COMMENT: DETAILED on 4:25–34) and that therefore in the earlier, Babylonian form of the story the three kings of Daniel 3, 4, and 5 were respectively Nebuchadnezzar, Nabonidus, and Belshazzar; and so he suggested that in the pre-Palestinian form of the story it was these three kings who were symbolized by the three weights. He might have added that, since Nabonidus was so greatly reviled by his compatriots, later tradition may have regarded him as not worth more than a mere shekel. Interesting as all these theories are, they still remain speculations that go beyond the *present* form of the Book of Daniel.

The nature of the folk tale that vindicates the God-given wisdom of the Jewish sage demands that he should receive the promised reward, though he had at first spurned it (5:17) and though the king could hardly feel grateful for the interpretation given to the mysterious writing. Like the victorious Mordecai (Esther 8:15), Daniel is given the insignia of nobility: the royal purple, the golden torque (a typically Persian ornament, not quite the same as the gold chain that Joseph received in Egypt: Gen 41:42), and the honorific title of a high government official.

Belshazzar's Death (5:30–6:1)

The story ends with dramatic brevity, if with less than historical accuracy: on the night of the banquet, Belshazzar is killed and his throne ceded to "Darius the Mede." The probable implication would seem to be that "Darius the Mede" made a surprise attack on the city, and Belshazzar lost his life in its fall. Here again there are echoes of the widespread legend about the Persians' surprise attack on Babylon, as told by Herodotus and Xenophon, although neither of these two Greek writers says anything about Belshazzar's death. The actual capture of the city by the army of Cyrus the Great, as now known from contemporary cuneiform inscriptions, was quite different. According to the so-called Nabonidus Chronicle (cf. *ANET*, pp. 305*ff*), "[In the seventeenth year (of Nabonidus)]. . . . In the month of Tishri, when Cyrus fought at Opis on the Tigris against the army of Akkad, the people of Akkad revolted. . . . On the fourteenth day, Sippar was captured without battle. Nabonidus fled. On the sixteenth day, Ugbaru (Greek, Gobryas), the governor of Gutium, and the troops of Cyrus entered Babylon without battle. Afterwards, when Nabonidus returned, he was arrested in Babylon. . . . In the month of Marchesvan, on the third day, Cyrus entered Babylon. . . ." Although the Barrel Inscription of Cyrus (cf. *ANET*, pp. 315*f*) is a piece of propaganda, written to show that it was Marduk's will that Babylon should be taken away from the wicked Nabonidus and given to the virtuous Cyrus, its description of the occupation of Babylon by the Persian king is sober history: ". . . Marduk called to Cyrus, the king of Anshan, and proclaimed him ruler of all the world. . . . He made him set out on the road to Babylon. . . . He made him enter his town Babylon without any battle, sparing Babylon any calamity. He delivered into his hands Nabonidus, the king who did not worship him. . . ." Nothing is known from the cuneiform inscriptions of Belshazzar's end. On the strange character whom the Book of Daniel calls "Darius the Mede," see Introduction, Part VI. Since the historical Books of Kings give the age of most of the kings of Judah when they began to reign (I Kings 14:21; 22:42; II Kings 7:26; 14:2; etc.), an age is given here to "Darius the Mede" when he began his reign over Babylon. Perhaps the age of sixty-two years is given him to suggest that he had a life expectancy of eight years at his accession (cf. Ps 90:10).

VI. DANIEL IN THE LIONS' DEN
(6:2–29)

6 2 Darius thought it well to set over his kingdom a hundred and
twenty satraps for all parts of his realm. 3 Over them were three chief
ministers, one of whom was Daniel, and to these ministers the satraps
had to give account, so that the king would not suffer any loss. 4 But
Daniel, because of the extraordinary spirit that was in him, so outshone the other chief ministers and the satraps, that the king was
inclined to set him over the whole kingdom.
5 The chief ministers and the satraps, therefore, tried to find grounds
for accusation against Daniel with regard to his administration. But
they could not find any grounds to accuse him of misconduct; since
he was trustworthy, no negligence or misconduct could be uncovered
against him. 6 Then these men said to themselves, "We shall never
find grounds for accusation against this Daniel except by way of his
religion."
7 So these chief ministers and these satraps went in collusion to the
king and said to him, "King Darius, live forever! 8 The kingdom's
chief ministers, prefects, satraps, councilors, and governors are all
agreed that by royal ordinance the following prohibition should be
put in force: for thirty days no one is to address a petition to any god
or man except to you, O king; otherwise he shall be cast into the
lions' den. 9 Therefore, O king, issue this written prohibition over
your signature, so that it will be as irrevocable as the other immutable
laws of the Medes and the Persians." 10 So King Darius signed the
written prohibition.
11 Even after Daniel learned that this document had been signed, he
continued his custom of going to his house, which had windows in the
upper chamber open toward Jerusalem, [a]to get down[a] on his knees [b]in
prayer[b] and offer grateful praise to his God three times a day. 12 Then
those men came in concert and discovered Daniel praying in supplica-

[a–a] Read *hăwā' bārēk* with several MSS for *hû' bārēk* of MT.
[b–b] Probably read *m^{e}ṣallē'* with some MSS for *m^{e}ṣallī'* of MT.

tion to his God. 13 So they approached the king and reminded him of the royal prohibition: "Did you not sign a decree forbidding everyone for thirty days to make a petition to any god or man except to you, O king, under pain of being cast into the lions' den?" "The decree is absolute," the king answered, "as immutable as the other laws of the Medes and Persians." 14 They then told the king, "Daniel, one of the Jewish exiles, pays no heed to you, O king, or to the prohibition you have signed; three times a day he says his prayers[c]."

15 When the king heard this, he was deeply grieved; he set his mind on saving Daniel and strove till sunset to rescue him. 16 But those men went in concert to the king and told him, "Bear in mind, O king, that there is a law of the Medes and Persians according to which every decreed prohibition that the king issues is irrevocable." 17 So the king gave orders to have Daniel brought in and cast into the lions' den. But to Daniel the king said, "Your God whom you serve so constantly will come to rescue you." 18 A stone was then brought and placed over the opening of the den, and the king sealed it with his own signet ring and with the signet rings of his grandees, so that the plans for Daniel might not be changed. 19 With that, the king went to his palace, where he spent the night fasting; he did not have supper brought to him, and sleep fled from him.

20 At dawn [at daybreak] the king rose and went in haste to the lions' den. 21 As he drew near the den, he called to Daniel with a cry of anguish. "O Daniel, servant of the living God," he said, "has your God whom you serve so constantly been able to rescue you from the lions?" 22 "O king, live forever!" replied Daniel. 23 "My God sent his angel, who closed the mouths of the lions, so that they have not hurt me. For I have been found innocent before him; and before you too, O king, I have done no harm." 24 At these words the king was very happy, and he gave orders to have Daniel taken up out of the den. When he was brought up from the den, he was found to be completely unhurt, because he had trusted in his God. 25 Then at the king's command, those men who had denounced Daniel, together with their wives and children, were brought in and cast into the lions' den; and before they reached the bottom, the lions overpowered them and tore their bodies to pieces.

26 Then King Darius wrote to all the people of every nation, tribe, and tongue, wherever they lived on the earth: "May you have abun-

[c] LXX and Theod. add "to his God," perhaps correctly.

dant peace! 27 I hereby decree that throughout my realm the God of Daniel shall be reverenced and feared.

"He is the living God, enduring forever;
his kingdom is never destroyed,
and his dominion is without end.
28 He is a savior and deliverer,
performing wondrous miracles in heaven and on earth,
such as rescuing Daniel from the power of the lions."

29 Thereafter Daniel fared well in the reign of Darius and in the reign of Cyrus the Persian.

NOTES

6:2. *Darius thought it well.* Literally, "It seemed pleasing to Darius"; cf. 3:32, where the same Aramaic expression is used, but with a somewhat different translation because of the context.

3. *chief ministers.* In Aramaic, *sārᵉkîn,* a word derived from the Old Persian **sāraka* (cf. Avestan *sāra,* "head").

satraps. See NOTE on 3:2.

4. *outshone.* Literally, "was distinguishing himself over."

inclined. In Aramaic, *'ăšît,* passive participle used in active sense or verbal adjective of the root *'št,* meaning "to give thought to something, to plan, intend," etc., which occurs as an Aramaism in the Hebrew of Jonah 1:6: *'ûlay yit'aššēt hā'ĕlōhîm lānû,* "perhaps God will show himself concerned about us."

5. *with regard to his administration.* Literally, "from the side of the kingdom."

6. *except by way of his religion.* Literally, "unless we find (it) against him in the law of his God." The expression, "the law [Aramaic *dāt,* a loanword from Old Persian *dāta*] of God," in the general sense of "the Jewish religion" (cf. Hebrew *tôrāh*), is used also in Ezra 7:12,14,25.

7. *went in collusion.* In Aramaic, *hargīšû.* Although this verb, which is used also in vss. 12 and 16, but nowhere else in Biblical Aramaic, has been variously translated as "assembled" (*KJV*), "came tumultuously" (margin of *KJV*), "came by agreement" (*RSV*), "came thronging" (margin of *RSV, NAB* in vs. 7), and "rushed in" (*NAB* in vs. 12), Montgomery (pp. 272*f*) is no doubt correct in arguing that it must mean "came in concert, came in collusion." In the Hebrew of Pss 2:1; 55:15; 64:3, the same root, *rgš* is used in close association with *sôd,* "secret council, secret counsel." M. Dahood, *Psalms I,* AB 16, p. 7, rightly concludes that this close association "is a safer guide to the meaning of *rgš* than the Syriac etymology which has served as the basis for traditional 'be in tumult, rage.'" Here in Daniel 6 the sense is "go together in secret agreement."

8. *prefects . . . and governors.* See NOTE on 3:2.

councilors. The Aramaic term, *haddābar,* should be translated literally as "friend" (see NOTE on 3:24); but in the present context it seems to designate a specific class of officials, freely rendered here as "councilors," a group distinct from the "counselors" of 3:2.

agreed . . . the lions' den. Literally, "have taken counsel with one another for the king to establish an ordinance and make strong a prohibition that anyone who would seek a request from any god or man for thirty days except from you, O king, should be cast into the lions' den."

9. *issue this written prohibition over your signature.* The literal rendering, "you shall establish the prohibition and sign the document," is taken here as containing a hendiadys. Some, however, understand *wᵉtiršum kᵉtābâ,* not as "sign the document," but as "write the document."

so that it will be as irrevocable as the other immutable laws of the Medes and Persians. Literally, "which is not to be changed, like the law of the Medes and Persians, which will not lapse." In the present context, as also in vs. 13, *dāt,* "law," is taken as a collective noun. The construction is different in vs. 16, where the reference is to a specific law of the Medes and Persians that renders all their laws irrevocable.

11. The verse is literally, "And Daniel, when he knew that the document was signed, went into his house, and there were windows to it open in its upper chamber facing Jerusalem, and three times a day he was getting down on his knees and praying and offering grateful praise before his God just as he used to do before this." The *lēh* in *'al lᵉbaytēh wᵉkawwîn lēh* apparently refers to *baytēh* (masculine), "his house," and not to Daniel (as in *RSV:* "where he had windows . . .").

12. *praying in supplication to his God.* Literally, "petitioning and imploring before his God" (hend.).

13. *they approached.* Like Hebrew *qārab* (e.g. in Isa 41:1; Mal 3:5), Aramaic *qᵉrîb* is used here in the specialized sense of starting a lawsuit, bringing a charge against someone, etc.

and reminded him of the royal prohibition. Literally, "and said before the king concerning the prohibition of the king." This is the sense demanded by the MT punctuation and especially by the construct state *'ĕsār.* The *RSV* translation, ". . . concerning the interdict, 'O king, . . . ,'" would require a textual emendation of *'ĕsār* to *'ĕsārâ* (cf. vs. 14). However, it seems more natural to regard *malkâ* as a vocative; hence some commentators delete *'al-'ĕsār* with LXX, Theod., and Syr.

16. *decreed prohibition.* Literally, "prohibition and decree" (hend.).

17. *will come to rescue you.* Some versions (e.g. *RSV, NAB*) take *yᵉšêzᵉbinnāk* as a jussive expressing a wish, "may he rescue you." But in Biblical Aramaic the personal suffix is attached directly to the jussive and imperative forms of the verb, without the connective -*(i)nn*- (see Rosenthal, *Grammar,* § 174); hence the verb here must be in the indicative. The use of *hû'* before the verb emphasizes the subject: "It is the God whom you serve so constantly who must come to your rescue."

19. *supper.* Based on Rosenthal (*Handbook,* Part I/2, p. 21), who defines *daḥăwān* as follows: "dining-board, portable table (cf. Hebrew plural *daḥăwānôt* in Tosephta Kelim, Baba Meṣi'a 5:3; Rashi and David Qimḥi, *Book of Roots,* end, *s.v.; *daḥăwāh* [plural *daḥăwān*] 'concubine' is unattested)."

20. A literal translation of this verse in the order of the Aramaic words would read: "Then the king at dawn arose at daybreak, and in haste to the den of the lions he went." The position of "at daybreak" (Aramaic *b^enāg^ehâ*) in the sentence seems to indicate that it is a marginal gloss on the rarer synonym "at dawn" (Aramaic *biš^eparpārâ*) that crept into the text in the wrong place. If both terms are original, they may perhaps be understood as strengthening each other: "at the crack of dawn."

23. *For I have been found innocent before him.* Literally, "for before him innocence has been found in me." The word used here for "innocence," *zākû,* is, like many other legal terms in Aramaic, probably a borrowing from Akkadian *zākûtu* (see *CAD* 21, pp. 23–33); since the proto-Semitic root is *ḏky,* the true Aramaic word would be *d^ekû.*

25. *their wives and children.* The Aramaic text has "their children and their wives," but the normal English order of the terms is followed in the translation. The similar reversal of the order of the terms in LXX, Syr., and Vulg. is no reason for correcting the Aramaic text.

tore their bodies to pieces. Literally, "pulverized their bones." But in the Semitic languages, "bones" (Hebrew *'ăṣāmîm, 'ăṣāmôt;* Aramaic *garmîn*) is often used, by synecdoche, for "body, corpse" (cf. Gen 50:25; Exod 13:19; Josh 24:33; Amos 6:10; etc.).

COMMENT: GENERAL

The story of Daniel's miraculous rescue from the lions' den, which forms the last of the folk tales that make up the first half of the Book of Daniel, has a close parallel in the story of the miraculous rescue of the three Jewish men from the fiery furnace, as told in ch. 3. Both stories belong to the literary genre of martyr stories or witness literature in which heroes are willing to suffer death rather than deny their faith. In both these stories, the heroes are saved from death by God's intervention, while their enemies suffer the dire fate that had been intended for the martyrs. Both stories also agree in having the pagan king profess, in the end, his faith in the God of Israel. Finally, the common motif of Oriental tales about rival courtiers (cf. the story of Ahiqar [*ANET,* pp. 427*f*] and the story of Mordechai [the Book of Esther]), which is present in Daniel 3 (cf. 3:12), is particularly prominent in the present story. See Introduction, Part IX.

On the other hand, there are certain clear differences between the two stories. Besides the obvious differences in the heroes (the three Jewish men in ch. 3, Daniel alone in ch. 6), in the pagan kings (Nebuchadnezzar in ch. 3, the more friendly figure of "Darius the Mede" in ch. 6), and in the nature of the threatened punishment (fire in ch. 3, lions in ch. 6), there is the difference in the religious test to which the martyrs are subjected. In ch. 3 this is of a negative character: the three Jewish men refuse to participate in idolatrous worship; in ch. 6 it is of a positive character: Daniel continues to practice his Jewish religion even after it is proscribed by the pagan king.

Although the present story was incorporated into the Book of Daniel by its author-compiler at the time of the persecution of the Jews by Antiochus IV Epiphanes, apparently because of its pertinent moral that God comes to the rescue of his faithful ones in times of persecution, nevertheless the story as such, like the other stories in the first half of the book, no doubt long antedates the time of Epiphanes. In view of the Persian loanwords in its Aramaic and of its knowledge of Persian law and customs, its origin is most likely to be placed in the eastern Diaspora of the Jews during the period of the Persian empire.

This story has a variant in the apocryphal (deuterocanonical) story of Daniel and the Dragon; see Introduction, Part IV.

Comment: Detailed

Daniel's Preferment (6:2–4)

The verse that is numbered as 6:1 in the MT, *JPS,* and *NAB,* but as 5:31 in *KJV* and *RSV,* serves as a connecting link between this story and the preceding one about the handwriting on the wall at Belshazzar's feast; Belshazzar is succeeded as king of Babylon by the strange character called "Darius the Mede" (see Introduction, Part VI). The genuinely historical figure Darius I the Great (king of Persia, 522–486), upon whom the figure of "Darius the Mede" is largely based, was in truth a famous reorganizer of his empire; he divided it into several large regions called satrapies, each of which was ruled over by an official called a satrap. The satrapies were in turn subdivided into numerous smaller provinces, ruled over by governors (Aramaic *paḥăwāt*). Thus, the satrapy of "Beyond the River" (the region west of the Euphrates) was divided into the provinces of Idumea, Judea, Ashdod, Samaria, Megiddo, Galilee, and various similar small districts in Transjordan and Syria.

Historically, the number of satrapies in the Persian empire varied at different times from twenty to about thirty. When Jewish tradition increased the number of satrapies by one hundred, as seen in the 120 satrapies mentioned here (6:2) and the 127 mentioned in Esther 1:1; 8:9; I Esd 3:2, it was apparently using the round number one hundred in reference to the minor provinces as included with the major regions under the term "satrapies" used in a broad sense.

Nothing is known historically of the "three chief ministers" who were set over the satraps (6:3). The number "three" may have come from the title *taltâ,* which had been rendered as "triumvir" in 5:7,16,29 (see NOTE on 5:7). In I Esd 3:9 mention is likewise made of "the three magnates" (*hoi treis megistantes*) who were the highest-ranking officials after the Persian king. The story does not say how Daniel happened to be one of these three chief ministers. Apparently the reader is presumed to know the other stories of the Daniel cycle, particularly the story of Daniel's success in reading the handwriting on the wall, for which feat Belshazzar made him a "triumvir" (5:29).

One of the main functions of the satraps and their subordinate governors was to see "that the king would not suffer any loss" (6:3) in the taxes collected throughout the empire; cf. Ezra 3:13–16. Despite the story's legendary features in other respects, it correctly reflects the bureaucratic organization of the Persian empire.

The Plot against Daniel (6:5–10)

When the other officials learned that the king was thinking of making Daniel head over all of them, they resolved to get him in trouble with the king. But because of Daniel's integrity, they could not bring a criminal or political charge against him. Their device, therefore, was to have the king issue a religious decree whereby he would unwittingly bring about the death of his Jewish friend.

The decree forbade everyone for thirty days to pray to any god or man except to the king under pain of being thrown to the lions. A decree of such a nature, which would make the king the only lawfully worshipped deity for a month, has no parallel in history, certainly not in the time of the tolerant rulers of the Persian empire. Even those Hellenistic kings who laid claim to divine honors, such as Antiochus IV Epiphanes, did not forbid the worship of any other god than themselves. But in the present story, Daniel is really a figure of the Jewish people; and the pagan king, therefore, is a symbol of paganism, which demands an exclusive worship of idols, as in the story of ch. 3.

On the "lions' den" and the "immutable laws of the Medes and the Persians," see below.

Daniel Cast into the Lions' Den (6:11–19)

Like all truly pious men, Daniel preferred to obey God rather than men (cf. Acts 5:29). Although he realized that he was endangering his life by disobeying the royal edict that forbade all worship except to the king, he continued his worship of the God of Israel. The account given in the story of how he prayed to his God presents a valuable picture of the manner in which Jews prayed in their postexilic Diaspora. The roof chamber of a house (cf. Judg 3:20; I Kings 17:19; II Kings 1:2; 4:10; Jer 22:14) provided the quiet and privacy conducive to undistracted prayer (cf. Judith 8:5; Matt 6:6; Acts 1:13*f;* 10:9). The Jewish custom of facing, while at prayer, toward the Temple of Jerusalem or its ruined site began during the Babylonian exile (cf. I Kings 8:44,48—in a passage written during the exile) and continued thereafter throughout the Diaspora (cf. I Esd 4:58). The first Muslims, following Jewish custom, faced Jerusalem in prayer; but the direction (*qiblah*) was soon changed toward the Kaaba in Mecca. When a Jew prayed in a room, he did so at an open window (cf. Tobit 3:11) facing Jerusalem. Daniel prayed three times a day, at dawn, at midday, and toward evening—a custom already referred to in Ps 60:18 and later prescribed in the Talmud (*Berakoth* iv 1). Daniel knelt down when he prayed. Although in public prayer, such as in a synagogue, people ordinarily prayed in a standing position, kneeling down for private prayer was no doubt common in Judaism of the Persian period (cf. Ezra 9:5), as it was in New Testament times (cf. Luke 22:41; Acts 9:46; 20:36).

Since Daniel prayed at an open window, his enemies were able to observe how he violated the royal decree, and so they accused him before the king. The latter did his best to save Daniel from being condemned to death; but he could not revoke his decree, because once a law was enacted among the Medes and Persians it could not be changed. This strange custom is attested to, not only in Esther 1:19; 8:8, but also in Diodorus Siculus xvii 30. Although there is scarcely any historical connection involved, it is interesting to note that the Code of Hammurabi (par. 5; *ANET*, p. 166) made it a crime for a judge to change a decision that he had once made.

After the king's efforts to rescue Daniel proved fruitless, Daniel was thrown into the lions' "den." The traditional term "den" has been retained, although the Aramaic word that it translates, *gōb* (emphatic *gubbâ*), really means "pit." The place where the lions were kept is therefore pictured here as a subterranean cave or room having a relatively small opening (Aramaic *pum,* "mouth") at the top, which could be closed by a large stone (vs. 18). Whereas the keeping of lions in captivity in ancient Mesopotamia is well attested in the inscriptions and stone reliefs of the Assyrian kings, who used to let the lions out of their cages to hunt them down, there is no ancient evidence for the keeping of lions in underground pits, apart from the present story and perhaps its variant in 14:28–42. Perhaps one might compare, for a later period, the hypogeum of the Roman Colosseum, where animals were kept before being brought up to the arena.

To prevent any unauthorized tampering with the stone that closed the top of the pit, the royal seal (cf. I Kings 21:8; Esther 3:12; 8:8,10) and the seals of the king's noblemen were impressed in wet clay at the juncture of the stone and the pit's opening. A parallel for this can be found in the sealing of the stone at the entrance to the tomb of Jesus (Matt 27:66).

Daniel's Rescue and the Fate of His Enemies (6:20–25)

The king seems to have trusted that Daniel's God would somehow rescue Daniel from the lions' den (cf. 6:17,21). Yet he spent a sleepless night worrying about the fate of his Jewish minister. As soon as the morning light allowed the king to see what had happened to Daniel, he hastened to the lions' den. To his happy surprise, he found Daniel unharmed. As in the story of the three Jewish men in the fiery furnace (3:28), it is not Yahweh himself, but his angel who effects the rescue; postexilic Judaism had developed a highly transcendental concept of God, which preferred not to represent Yahweh as intervening personally in human affairs, and thus made frequent use of the concept of "the angel of the Lord" that had ancient roots in Israelite thought.

Daniel explains to the king that his rescue was due to the justice of God, who would not permit the innocent to suffer unjustly. On the other hand, God's justice demanded that the wicked should suffer, and indeed in keeping with the command of the Torah in regard to a false witness: "You shall do to him as he planned to do to his fellow man" (Deut 19:19). So the men who falsely accused Daniel receive the punishment they had planned for him: they are thrown into the pit, and fall into the mouths of the hungry lions before they reach the bottom of the pit.

That the wives and children of these men had to share their gruesome fate seems repugnant to modern ideas of justice. But in Old Testament times the concept of family solidarity often caused a man's whole family to pay the penalty for his crime (cf. Num 16:27–33; II Sam 21:5–9; Esther 9:13*f*), even though the humane legislation of Deuteronomy (Deut 24:16; cf. II Kings 14:6) endeavored to check this barbarous custom.

[Aphraat the Persian sage (died ca. A.D. 345) wrote a lovely midrash on Daniel in the lions' den; see Introduction, Part IV.]

The Decree of Darius (6:26–29)

Like the story in ch. 3, this story also ends with the king issuing an edict in favor of the God of the Jews. But while the former story has Nebuchadnezzar forbidding everyone in his realm to speak evil of the God of Shadrach, Meshach, and Abednego (3:29), the present story goes further in having Darius publish a decree that positively orders all the people of his kingdom to revere the God of Daniel, and his decree ends in a typical Jewish hymn in praise of the God of Israel. On the benevolent attitude of the Persian kings toward Judaism, see COMMENT: DETAILED on 3:24[*91*]–30[*97*].

At the end of the story, the author-compiler of the Book of Daniel added a sentence (6:29) for the purpose of connecting these introductory folk tales, which form the first half of his work, with his account of Daniel's revelation of the Hellenistic wars, which is dated in the third year of King Cyrus of Persia (10:1); see COMMENT on ch. 1. The author clearly implies that, according to his chronology (see Introduction, Part VI), "Darius the Mede" was succeeded by Cyrus the Great.

VII. VISION OF THE FOUR BEASTS AND THE MAN (7:1–28)

7 1 In the first year of King Belshazzar of Babylon, Daniel had a
dream, and the vision that came to his mind as he lay in bed [a]terrified
him.[a] Then he wrote down his dream, thus beginning his account.[b]

2 In my vision at night I saw the four winds of the heavens stirring
up the great sea; 3 and four immense beasts, each different from the
others, came up out of the sea.

4 The first one was like a lion, but with eagle wings. [c]It had three
tusks in its mouth [between its teeth], and it was given the command:
"Up, devour much flesh!"[c] While I watched, its wings were plucked
off, and it was taken away from the earth.[d]

5 Then I saw another beast, a second one, that resembled a bear. It
raised one end upright, to stand on two feet like a man; and it was
given a man's heart.

6 After that, as I looked on, there was another one, which was like
a leopard, but with bird wings[e] on its back. This beast had four heads,
and it was given dominion.

7 After that, as I looked on in my vision at night, there was a fourth
beast, dreadful, terrifying, and exceedingly strong, with great teeth of
iron [f]and claws of bronze.[f] It devoured part of what it tore to pieces,
and the rest it trampled down with its feet. It differed in character
from the other beasts that preceded it. And it had ten horns.

/ 8 As I was gazing at the horns, another horn, a small one,

[a–a] Insert *y^{e}bahălunnēh;* cf. 4:2,16; 7:15.

[b] Omit, at the beginning of vs. 2, *'ānēh danîyē'l w^e'āmar* ("Daniel answered and said") with LXX, Theod.; gloss.

[c–c] Transpose *ût^{e}lāt 'il'în b^{e}pummah bên šinnayh w^{e}kēn 'ām^{e}rîn lah qûmî 'ăkūlî b^{e}śar śaggî'* from vs. 5, to follow *w^{e}gappîn dî-n^{e}šar lah;* see COMMENT: GENERAL.

[d] Transpose *w^e'al raglayin ke'ĕnāš hŏqāmat* (sic!) *ûl^{e}bab 'ĕnāš y^{e}hîb lah* to follow *w^{e}liśṭar-ḥad hăqîmat* (sic!) in vs. 5; see COMMENT: GENERAL.

[e] Omit *'arba';* dittography.

[f–f] Insert *w^{e}ṭiprayah dî-n^{e}ḥāš* with a few Greek MSS; cf. vs. 19.

[g]sprouted up[g] among them; and three of the previous horns were uprooted before it. In this horn there were eyes like the eyes of a man, and a mouth speaking arrogantly. /

9 As I looked on,
Thrones were set up,
and an Ancient One took his seat.
His clothing was as white as snow,
and the hair of his head was like clean fleece.
His throne was fiery flames,
with wheels of blazing fire.
10 A surging stream of fire
flowed forth from where he sat.
Thousands of thousands were serving him,
and myriads of myriads were attending him.
The court sat in judgment,
and the books were opened.

11 Then[h] / because of the arrogant words that the horn was
speaking, as I looked on / the beast was slain and its body destroyed, consigned to consuming fire. 12 As for the rest of the beasts,
their dominion had been taken away, but a prolongation of life had
been granted them for a limited time.

13 In my night vision I then saw
with the clouds of the heavens
there came one in human likeness.
When he arrived where the Ancient One was,
he was brought into his presence.
14 Then to him was given dominion—glory and kingship.
Every nation, tribe, and tongue must serve him;
His dominion is to be everlasting, never passing away;
his kingship never to be destroyed.

15 As for me, Daniel, my spirit was troubled in its sheath,[i] and the
vision that came to my mind frightened me. 16 So I went up to one of
those who were standing by, and I asked him what all this really
meant. To let me know the meaning of this thing, he said, 17 "These

[g–g] Read *silqat* with some MSS. The *silqāt* of the MT is a *lectio mixta*, allowing the word to be read as the participle, *sāl*^{e}*qāh*, as in vs. 2*f*.

[h] Omit *ḥăzēh hăwêt* ("as I looked on"); dittography.

[i] Read *n*^{e}*dānah;* see NOTES. The LXX (*en toutois*) apparently read *b*^{e}*gôn* (or *b*^{e}*gên*) *d*^{e}*nāh*, "on account of this."

great beasts, four in number, mean that four kingdoms[j] will rise up on
the earth. 18 But then the holy ones of the Most High will receive the
kingdom and possess it forever, yes, forever and ever."

19 But I wished to make certain about the fourth beast, different
from all the others and exceedingly dreadful, with teeth of iron and
claws of bronze, devouring part of what it tore to pieces, and trampling the rest down with its feet; 20 and about the ten horns on its
head, / and the other that sprouted up, before which three of the
previous horns had fallen—the horn with eyes in it and a mouth
speaking arrogantly, which was seen surpassing its fellows. (21 As I
watched, that horn waged war against the holy ones and was prevailing over them 22 until the Ancient One arrived. Then the court[k] sat in
judgment, and dominion was given to the holy ones of the Most High.
Thus the time came when the holy ones took possession of the
kingdom.) /

23 This is what he said: "The fourth beast means that there will be a
fourth kingdom on the earth, which will be different from all the
other kingdoms; it will devour the whole earth, trample it down, and
tear it to pieces. 24 And the ten horns mean that from that kingdom
ten kings will rise.

/ "But another king will rise after them. He will be different from
the previous ones, and he will lay low three kings. 25 He will utter
words against the Most High, and the holy ones of the Most High he
will devastate, planning to change the feast days and the law; they
will be handed over to him for a year, two years, and half a year. /

26 "But when the court sits in judgment, [l]its dominion[l] will be
taken away, by final and utter destruction. 27 Then the kingship and
the dominion and the grandeur of all the kingdoms under the heavens
will be given to the people of the holy ones of the Most High. Their
royal rule will last forever, and all dominions will serve and obey it."

28 Here the account concluded. I, Daniel, was so greatly terrified by
my thoughts that my face blanched. But I kept the matter to myself.

[j] Perhaps vocalize as *molkîn* in the meaning of "kingdoms"; MT's *malkîn* would ordinarily mean "kings."

[k] Insert *y*^{e}*tîb w*^{e}*šoltānâ;* MT omits by haplography because of the similarity of *y*^{e}*tîb* and *y*^{e}*hîb*. For *w*^{e}*dînâ y*^{e}*tîb,* cf. vss. 10,26; for *w*^{e}*šoltānâ y*^{e}*hîb,* cf. vss. 14,27.

[l–l] Read *šoltānah;* the vocalization of the MT, *šoltānēh,* "his dominion," was induced by the secondary insertion of vss. 24b–25.

NOTES

7:1. *vision.* Literally, "visions"; see NOTE on 4:2.

thus beginning his account. Literally, "head of words he said." Some understand this to mean, "and told the sum of the matter" (so *RSV*). But a comparison with vs. 28, *'ad-kāh sôpā dî-millᵉtā,* "Here the account concluded," shows that *rē'š,* "head," in vs. 2 signifies "beginning," not "summary."

2. *I saw the four winds.* Literally, "I saw, and behold the four winds." In the Semitic languages the object that one sees is often introduced by the interjection "behold" (Aramaic *'ărû, 'ălû;* Hebrew *hinnēh*), which is unnecessary in English.

4. *tusks.* Aramaic *'ăla'* (plural *'il'în*), like the cognate Arabic *ḍala',* Hebrew *ṣela',* and Akkadian *ṣēlu,* regularly means "rib." But the efforts of commentators to explain why "three ribs" (*tᵉlāt 'il'în*) should be in the mouth of a beast have proved futile. The commentary on Daniel attributed to Saadiah understands *'il'în* here to mean "incisors" or "fangs" (Hebrew *mᵉtallᵉ'ôt*). Ginsberg (p. 69, also in Rosenthal, *Handbook,* I/2, p. 34) emends *'il'în* to **tālᵉ'ān,* from a dubious root, *tl',* "to rend to pieces." R. Frank (*CBQ* 21 [1959], 505*f*) has shown that Arabic *ḍala',* "rib," is used at times metaphorically of a "tusk" or large tooth; the same metaphorical usage of Aramaic *'ăla'* may be postulated here without recourse to textual emendation. The gloss, "between its teeth," seems to indicate that an early glossator wished to show that *'il'în* here means "fangs, tusks."

it was taken away from the earth. It was destroyed, annihilated. On this meaning of Aramaic *nᵉṭîlat min-'ar'â,* see Ginsberg (p. 65, also in Rosenthal, *Handbook,* I/2, p. 31).

5. *It raised one end upright.* Literally, "it raised one side." It seems more natural to understand this of an animal standing only on its hind legs, a position which a bear often assumes, rather than to understand it of an animal raising its two right legs or its two left legs, a position which even a circus animal could not hold for any length of time. The verb, even in the vocalization of the MT (*hŏqīmat*), is active, and the *l* of *liśṭar-ḥad* serves to introduce a direct object quantitatively determined, the phrase equaling *lᵉḥad min śiṭrah;* hence the translation of *RSV* and *NAB,* "it was raised up on one side," is not correct.

6. *with bird wings on its back.* The "four" with "bird wings" of the MT is secondary, influenced by the "four" with "heads." The author merely wanted to say that in this respect the third beast resembled the first beast, which had only one pair of wings.

7. *and claws of bronze.* Although there is very little textual evidence for this phrase in the first description of the fourth beast, it is probably original here, not merely because it occurs in the second description (vs. 19), but even more

so because without it there would be no natural subject for the action of tearing the victim to pieces.

It devoured part of what it tore to pieces. Literally, "devouring and tearing to pieces"; but the following words show that the beast devoured only part of its prey.

tore to pieces. Although *maddᵉqāh* ordinarily means "crushing into fine pieces," said of stone or metal, such a meaning does not fit the present context. For the reason why this verb is used here, see COMMENT: GENERAL.

8. *a small one.* Naturally, the horn was small when it first sprouted, before it grew larger than the other horns (vs. 20). But its smallness is expressly mentioned in this secondary verse (see COMMENT: GENERAL) because this horn is the same as the "small horn" of 8:9, where it is small for a special reason (see NOTE on 8:9).

9. *an Ancient One.* Literally, "one advanced in days" (*'attîq yômîn*), i.e. an old man; the Hebrew equivalent is *bā' bayyāmîm* (Gen 24:1). Like Akkadian *etēqu,* the basic meaning of the root *'tq* in Aramaic is "to move forward, to advance"; however, the word *yômîn* could be dropped after *'attîq,* which then by itself came to mean "old."

clean fleece. Fleece that had never been soiled, which therefore retained its natural whiteness. According to the rabbis (Mishnah Nega'im i 1; Bab. Tal. Shabbat 54a), a sheep was at times made to wear a jacket up to the time of shearing, to keep its fleece unsoiled (see Ginsberg, p. 71). [M. Sokoloff (*JBL* 95 [1976], 277–279) makes a good case that the Aramaic phrase here, *'ămar nĕqē',* means "lamb's wool" and not "clean, or pure, wool, or fleece."]

10. *A surging stream of fire flowed forth from where he sat.* Literally, "A stream of fire was flowing and coming out from before him." The participles, "was flowing and coming out" (*nāgēd wᵉnāpēq*) could be taken as a hendiadys: "gushing forth" (so H. L. Ginsberg in Rosenthal, *Handbook,* I/2, p. 23); but the poetic structure is better preserved in the translation by keeping them as two separate verbs.

11. *because of the arrogant words.* Literally, "from the sound of the great words."

consuming fire. Literally, "the burning of the fire" (hend.).

12. *the rest of the beasts.* The second and the third beast; the first beast had already been "taken away from the earth" (vs. 4).

a limited time. Literally, "a time and a season" (hend.).

13. *with the clouds.* Not "on the clouds," which would ordinarily be said only of God; clouds accompany the human figure on its arrival.

one in human likeness. The Aramaic *bar 'ĕnāš,* like Hebrew *ben 'ādām,* "son of man," merely means an individual (*bar*) of the human race (*'ĕnāš*); cf. Introduction, Part XIII.

14. *must serve him.* In the Aramaic text, special emphasis is laid on the object pronoun by its position before the verb: "it is he whom all the nations . . . must serve."

15. *its sheath.* The Aramaic word for "sheath," *nᵉdān,* is derived from the Persian word, *nidāni,* "container"; cf. 1QapGen ii 10, *wnšmty lgw ndnh',* "and my breath within its sheath." The concept of the body as the container or

sheath of the soul, though known in rabbinical literature, is foreign to the older books of the Bible, and may have been influenced by Hellenistic philosophy; cf. the distinction between the material body and the spiritual soul in Eccles 12:7; Wisd Sol 8:19*f;* 9:15.

16. *I asked him what all this really meant.* Literally, "and certainty I asked of him concerning all this."

18. *the holy ones of the Most High.* The Aramaic term, *qaddîšîn,* "holy ones," in reference to the people of Israel is used only in this chapter (vss. 18,21,22,25,27); the Hebrew term, *qᵉdōšîm,* in the same sense only in 8:24; Pss 16:3; 34:10. (M. Dahood, in NOTE on Ps 16:3 [*Psalms I,* p. 87], understands *qᵉdōšîm* as referring to Canaanite deities, but not in Ps 34:10.) The concept was, no doubt, derived from Exod 19:6, where Israel is called *gôy qādôš,* "a holy people"; it was carried over into the early Christian Church, whose members called themselves *'oi 'agioi,* "the holy ones, the saints." The Aramaic term *'elyônîn,* "the Most High," which is used only in this chapter and here always in the combination *qaddîšê 'elyônîn* (vss. 18,22,25,27), has been influenced both by Hebrew *'elyôn,* "the Most High," and by Hebrew *'ĕlōhîm,* "God"; the genuine Aramaic word for "the Most High" is *'illāyâ* (3:26,32; 4:14,21*f;* etc.).

20. *which was seen surpassing its fellows.* Literally, "and its visibility was greater than that of its fellows." Possibly, its meaning is: "and its stoutness was surpassing that of its fellows" (cf. Ginsberg, p. 71).

25. *he will devastate.* Aramaic *yᵉballē'* is literally, "he will wear away," ordinarily said of wearing out clothing; but in I Chron 17:9, cognate Hebrew *blh* in the pi'el is used in the sense of oppressing people. The textual emendation proposed by some, to read *yᵉsallē',* "he will despise, reject," is uncalled for.

the feast days. Literally, "the times"; in the context, religious seasons or festivals are meant.

they. The holy ones of the Most High.

year. See NOTE on 4:13.

26. *its dominion.* The dominion of the fourth kingdom (vs. 24a). The original connection between vs. 24a and vs. 26 has been broken by the secondary insertion of vss. 24b–25 (see COMMENT: GENERAL).

by final and utter destruction. Literally, "by annihilating and destroying unto the end" (hend.).

27. *all the kingdoms under the heavens.* Literally, "the kingdoms under all the heavens."

Their royal rule. Literally, "its kingship"; the pronominal suffix of *malkûtēh* refers to *'am,* "people," of the preceding sentence.

28. *Here the account concluded.* Literally, "unto here the end of the matter" (*'ad-kāh sôpâ dî-millᵉtâ*), which is a fusion of the notion, "thus far the matter" (*'ad-kāh millᵉtâ*), and the notion, "here is the end of the matter" (*kāh sôpâ dî-millᵉtâ*).

to myself. Literally, "in my heart."

COMMENT: GENERAL

Chapter 7 is the core of the Book of Daniel, and not merely because it happens to lie approximately in the middle of the book. On the one hand, it is the first and (as will be shown later) the oldest of the four apocalypses that form the second half of the book. On the other hand, it connects these apocalypses with the folk tales of the first half of the book, not merely because linguistically it continues the Aramaic of the folk tales, as distinct from the Hebrew of the last three apocalypses, but especially because it is a deliberate revision and updating of the story of Nebuchadnezzar's dream of the composite statue as told in ch. 2.

In place of the four different metals in the statue of Nebuchadnezzar's dream (2:31*ff*), there are four different beasts in Daniel's dream (vss. 2–7)—in both cases symbolizing the four successive empires of the Babylonians, the Medes, the Persians, and the Greeks (see Introduction, Part VI). Corresponding to the stone that smashed the statue and became a mountain that filled all the earth (2:34*f*), there is here the manlike figure that receives universal dominion after the fourth beast is slain (vss. 11–14)—in both cases symbolizing the coming of God's kingdom on earth to supplant the pagan kingdoms of men.

Even on the supposition that the apocalypse of ch. 7 once circulated independently before it was appended to the stories of chs. 1–6, the author of this apocalypse surely knew the story of Nebuchadnezzar's dream as told in ch. 2, and modeled the account of his own dream on it. There may even be a sign of direct literary borrowing in his strange use of the verb "to crush to pieces" (haf'el of *dqq*) in vss. 7,19,23 in regard to an animal tearing its prey to pieces, since this verb occurs in 2:34,40,44*f* in its natural meaning of smashing metals and terra cotta into fine pieces; but cf. the use of this verb in 6:25.

However, despite the basic similarity between Nebuchadnezzar's and Daniel's dreams, there are striking differences between the two. In ch. 2 one could only deduce by inference that God's universal kingdom on earth (vs. 44) would be founded on God's people, Israel. In ch. 7, on the contrary, it is expressly stated that this kingdom of God will be given to "(the people of) the holy ones of the Most High" (vss. 18,27), i.e. the Jewish nation.

Moreover, in ch. 2 there is not the slightest reference to any persecution of the Jews, and as shown above (in the COMMENT on ch. 2), the story of ch. 2 was most likely written in the 3d century B.C., long before the time of Antiochus IV Epiphanes. But ch. 7, as will be shown below, was clearly written, even in its primary stratum, during the persecution of the Jews by Antiochus Epiphanes.

The translation and commentary offered here owe much to the valuable contribution made by Ginsberg (pp. 5–23, 63–75) to an understanding of this chapter. Ginsberg recognized: (1) that in the description of the first two beasts, the words which the MT uses in reference to the lion, "It raised one end upright, to stand on two feet like a man" (in vs. 4 of MT), really belong to the description of the bear; and the words that the MT uses in reference to the bear, "It had three tusks in its mouth [between its teeth], and it was given the command: 'Up, devour much flesh!'" (in vs. 5 of MT), really belong to the description of the lion; and (2) that all the passages that speak about the "small horn" (vss. 8,11a,20b,21,22,24b,25) constitute a later addition to the original apocalypse.

1) The mutual transference of the passages in the description of the first two beasts as mentioned above results in a picture of the animals that is much truer to their nature; it is not the omnivorous bear, but the carnivorous lion that "devours much flesh"; and even though rampant lions have been depicted since ancient times, one can speak much more properly of the plantigrade bear that it stands upright on its (hind) legs like a man.

But more important than this is the numerology involved in the description of the four beasts. The significance of the "ten horns" of the fourth beast (vs. 7) is explicitly given: they mean that "from that kingdom ten kings will rise" (vs. 24). It is natural, then, to suppose that the other numbers connected with the first three beasts have the same significance. But as the MT now stands, although the third beast has one number ("four heads"), the first beast has no symbolic number at all, and the second beast has two such numbers ("one side" and "three tusks"). With the proper transpositions made in vss. 4–5, the first beast, symbolizing the Babylonian empire, has "three tusks," i.e. the three Babylonian kings known to the author of this apocalypse; the second beast, symbolizing the Median empire, "raises one side," i.e. "Darius the Mede"; the third beast, symbolizing the Persian empire has "four heads," i.e. the four Persian kings known to the author; and the fourth beast, symbolizing the Greek empire, has "ten horns," i.e. the ten Greek kings up to and including Antiochus IV Epiphanes. (For the names of the individual kings in each case, see COMMENT: DETAILED below.)

Ginsberg supposes that the transposition of the phrases in vss. 4–5 as they now stand in the MT was intentionally made by the writer who added the secondary material about the small horn to the original apocalypse. But the reasons he offers why this transposition was made are far from convincing. It seems much more reasonable to suppose that the transposition was purely accidental on the part of some early copyist. Evidently, no one has yet pointed out that there is good, though indirect evidence to show that there was at least one ancient writer who was acquainted with a text of Daniel in which the accidental transposition had not yet been made, i.e. who read a text of 7:4–5 that agrees with the text as here emended, in which the striking thing about the lion is its mouth, and the striking thing about the bear its legs. This writer is the author of the Book of Revelation. All admit that the description of the beast from the sea in Revelation 13, symbolizing the Roman empire, combines characteristics taken from the description of all the four beasts of Daniel 7. Besides having ten horns like the fourth beast of Daniel, the beast that the seer of Revelation saw "was like a leopard, its feet were like a bear's, and its mouth was like the mouth of a lion" (Rev 13:1*f*). The author of these words surely read a text of Dan 7: 4*f* that was like the one emended here.

2) Following G. Hölscher ("Die Entstehung des Buches Daniel," *TSK* 92 [1919], 113–138) and E. Sellin (*Einleitung in das Alte Testament,* 5th ed. [1929], 153*f*), Ginsberg notes that Dan 7:8, where the first mention of the "small horn" appears, gives clear indications of being from a hand different from that of the author of ch. 7. This secondary insertion (vs. 8) uses *'ălû,* "behold," twice, whereas the primary account uses only the synonymous *'ărû* (vss. 2,5,6,7,13); it has two verbs in the perfect tense after its first *'ălû,* whereas the primary account has only participles after its *'ărû;* and it employs "man" as a symbol of arrogance, whereas in the primary account "man" is a symbol of holiness (on this last point, see COMMENT: DETAILED below).

Consequently, all subsequent references in this chapter to the "small" or eleventh horn (vss. 11a,20b,21,22,24b,25) are likewise secondary insertions. These are placed within slashes (slanted lines) in the translation. As will be shown in the COMMENT: DETAILED below, both the tenth horn of the fourth beast and the "small" (or eleventh) horn symbolize Antiochus IV Epiphanes.

Since the author of these secondary insertions in ch. 7 is concerned with prognosticating the length of the period of Epiphanes' persecution of the Jews—three and a half years (vs. 25)—it seems probable that he is the same man who composed the apocalypse of ch. 9, the main purpose of which is to predict that the persecution would not last longer than three and a half years—"half a week" of years (9:27).

On the date of composition of the basic apocalypse in ch. 7, see COMMENT: DETAILED on *The Fourth Beast,* below.

Comment: Detailed

The Four Beasts from the Sea (7:1–3,17)

Like the dream of Nebuchadnezzar that is narrated in ch. 2 and like the last three apocalypses of this book (chs. 8, 9, and 10–12), this apocalypse (ch. 7) is given a date. In each of these cases (but not in the stories of chs. 3, 4, 5, 6) prediction is made of future events that is to find its fulfillment in the reader's lifetime. According to Ginsberg (p. 64), these dates are given "obviously for the purpose of inspiring, by circumstantial detail, confidence in the genuineness of these long-term predictions." In any case, these dates have no historical value, although they are given in correct sequence according to the chronology of the book: the second year of Nebuchadnezzar (2:1), the first year of Belshazzar (7:1), the third year of Belshazzar (8:1), the first year of Darius the Mede (9:1), and the third year of Cyrus the Persian (10:1).

Whereas in the second apocalypse of the latter part of the book (ch. 8) Daniel receives merely a "vision" (Hebrew *ḥāzôn:* 8:1) and in the third (ch. 9) and fourth (chs. 10–12) apocalypses merely "revelations" from an angel, only in this first apocalypse (ch. 7) and in ch. 2 is the "vision" said to have come in a "dream"—another indication of the close connection between ch. 7 and ch. 2 (see Comment: General); for the phrase in 7:1, "the vision that came to his mind . . . terrified him," cf. 4:2.

In his dream-vision, Daniel sees "the four winds of the heavens stirring up the great sea" (7:2). The "four winds" come from "the four corners of the earth" (a common expression in Babylonian literature to designate the whole world), the north, east, south, and west. The vision is immediately given a cosmic aspect. Here "the great sea" (Aramaic *yammâ rabbâ*) is, of course, not the Mediterranean Sea (as Hebrew *hayyām haggādôl* is in Josh 1:4; 9:1; etc.), but the *tᵉhôm rabbāh,* the "great deep" or ocean of Gen 7:11; Isa 51:10; Amos 7:4. Our passage echoes Gen 1:2, where an awesome wind (*rûaḥ 'ĕlōhîm*) is said to sweep over the deep (*tᵉhôm*). The surging water of the ocean is here a fitting symbol of the turbulent nations of the world (cf. Isa 17:12; Jer 46:7*f*). From the chaotic waters there rise four monstrous beasts. This is not really in contradiction with vs. 17, where the beasts are said to rise from the earth; "sea" is, of course, on the "earth." The contrast is between the sea and the earth on the one hand, and "the heavens" on the other, where the one who is like a man appears (vs. 13).

There is, no doubt, a mythological element in the picture of the four monstrous beasts that emerge from the sea. But there is no need here to look for any direct borrowing from ancient mythological literature, such as the Babylonian epic *Enuma Elish*. Our author could easily have derived his idea of monsters coming up out of the sea from the Bible, which knows of such sea monsters of Canaanite mythology as Rahab (Ps 89:10*f;* Job 9:13; 26:12; Isa 51:9), Leviathan (Ps 74:13*f;* Isa 26:1), and the dragon *tannîn* (Isa 27:1; 51:9; Job 7:12). But essentially the four monstrous beasts of Dan 7:3–7 are *ad hoc* creations of the author, who gives them the characteristics that make them "each different from the others" for the purpose of symbolizing the four successive kingdoms of men; for, as he is told by the heavenly spirit who explains his dream-vision to him, these four beasts represent "four kingdoms" (vs. 17). The four kingdoms are the Babylonian, the Median, the Persian, and the Greek (see Introduction, Part VI).

The First Three Beasts (7:4–6,12)

The Babylonian Empire, which at least from the author's viewpoint was the first worldwide empire, is well represented by a lion, the king of beasts, with wings of an eagle, the king of birds. The lion is told to "devour much flesh." The ravenous appetite of Babylon, the devastator of the Kingdom of Judah, is strongly stressed in the prophets (Jer 5:15*ff;* Hab 2:5). The fangs of this lion are so long that our author calls them "tusks." It has three of them (instead of the usual two fangs) because the three fangs symbolize the three (and only three) Babylonian kings known to our author: Nebuchadnezzar, who is mentioned so often in the Bible and who plays a prominent part in the first half of the Book of Daniel; Evil-merodach, whom our author knew from II Kings 25:27; Jer 52:31; and Belshazzar, whom he knew from Daniel 5. But in 7:4 this lion's "wings were plucked off," i.e. it lost its dominion; and "it was taken away from the earth," i.e. at the time of our author not even a remnant of the Babylonian kingdom was left on earth.

The kingdom of the Medes is well compared to a bear. The relatively small Syrian bear (*Ursus syriacus*), which was fairly common in ancient Palestine, was much less dangerous than the lion and attacked men only when irritated, e.g. when a female bear was robbed of her cubs (II Sam 17:8; Hosea 13:8; Prov 17:12). For our author, the Medes, though pagans (represented by a "beast"), not only never harmed Israel; they even shared in a certain holiness, such as only men can have (the beast "was given a man's heart"), inasmuch as they were Yahweh's "consecrated" (*m^{e}quddāšāy:* Isa 12:3,17*ff; qadd^{e}šû:* Jer 51:28) warriors, summoned by him to take vengeance on wicked Babylon for her sacrilegious destruction of his temple (Jer 51:11). The "one" end that the bear raises, when it stands upright like a man on its hind legs, symbolizes the only Median king known to the author, "Darius the Mede." (In 9:1, Darius is indeed called "the son of Ahasuerus [=Xerxes]," but nothing is said there about this Ahasuerus being a ruler of the Median empire; moreover, ch. 9 was probably not written by the man who wrote ch. 7; see Introduction, Part III).

The third beast resembles a leopard, less strong than a lion ("What is stronger than a lion?": Judg 14:18), and it has smaller wings (of a mere "bird"—presumably an ordinary small bird) than the eagle wings of the lion. Again, a fitting image of the Persian empire, which resembled the Babylonian empire in the extent of its domain ("It was given dominion"), but which, at least from the Jewish viewpoint, was less destructive than the Babylonian empire. The "four heads" of the leopard symbolize the only four kings of the Persian empire known to our author from the Bible: Cyrus (Ezra 1:1*f*,7*f;* 3:7; etc.), Ahasuerus (Ezra 4:6), Artaxerxes (Ezra 4:7,11,23; 6:14; etc.), and "Darius the Persian," i.e. Darius II (Neh 12:22).

Whereas the lion, the Babylonian empire, "was taken away from the earth," the second and the third beast were granted "a prolongation of life for a limited period," even though "their dominion had been taken away" (vs. 12). This must mean that after the Medes and the Persians had lost their empires ("their dominion"), they still retained kingdoms of a sort for a while. Actually, throughout the Greek period both the Medes and the Persians still had small kingdoms, the more or less independent principalities of Media Atropatene (modern Azerbajan) and Persis (modern Fars), respectively (cf. Strabo *Geography* xi 5:6, 13:1; xv 3:24).

The Fourth Beast (7:7,11b,19–20a,23–24a,26)

The fourth beast of the dream-vision is so "dreadful, terrifying, and exceedingly strong" that our author can find no animal on earth with which to compare it. With its "great teeth of iron and claws of bronze," it is even more ferocious than the lion that symbolizes the Babylonian empire, and thus it is different from (i.e. worse than) all the other beasts that preceded it—a fitting description of the Greek kingdom of the Seleucids in our author's day. The most remarkable thing about this beast is that it has "ten horns," a feature that fits no beast of nature. The seer is later told that "the ten horns mean that from that kingdom ten kings will rise" (vs. 24a). Actually, the Greek kingdom of the Seleucids had many more than ten successive kings. But since the seer learns in his vision that this fourth "beast was . . . destroyed, consigned to consuming fire" (vs. 11b) and that therefore the Seleucid "dominion will be taken away, by final and utter destruction" (vs. 26), our author believed that the tenth Greek king would be the last ruler of the Greek kingdom—a prediction not borne out by events.

The tenth ruler of this kingdom that is like a monstrous beast in tearing its prey to pieces and trampling it down is surely the king who tried to Hellenize the Jews, Antiochus IV Epiphanes. But there is some difficulty in understanding how our author reckoned Epiphanes the tenth Greek king. Historically, if the list is begun with Alexander the Great, Epiphanes is the eleventh Greek king; if the list is begun with Seleucus I, the founder of the Seleucid dynasty, he is its eighth king. Probably our author thought that, after the death of Alexander the Great in 323 B.C., Philip Arrhidaeus, who really reigned as king from 323 to 316, was only acting as regent for the infant son of Alexander the Great, Alexander Aegus, who was reckoned as beginning his kingship alone in 316 B.C. In any case, Berosus [the third-century B.C. author of a history of Babylonia in Greek] reckoned Antiochus I, the son of Seleucus I, as the third king after Alexander the Great (cf. W. Baumgartner, "Ein Vierteljahrhundert Danielforschung," *TRu* 11 [1939], 204). Accordingly, the ten Greek kings of our author would be: (1) Alexander the Great, 336–323; (2) Alexander Aegus, 323–312; (3) Seleucus I, 312–280; (4) Antiochus I, 280–261; (5) Antiochus II, 261–246; (6) Seleucus II, 246–226; (7) Seleucus III, 226–223; (8) Antiochus III, 223–187; (9) Seleucus IV, 187–175; (10) Antiochus IV Epiphanes, 175–164.

The author of the basic stratum of ch. 7 stresses two things: (1) the Greek kingdom of the Seleucids was much worse than the three kingdoms that preceded it; and (2) just as the first three kingdoms ended with their third, first, and fourth kings respectively, so the fourth kingdom (the contemporaneous Greek one) would end with its present tenth king, Epiphanes. Our author is thus revising and updating the prediction contained in ch. 2. In that chapter, a writer of the third century B.C. foretold in a general way the end of the Greek kingdom, but without attempting to specify the time when this would take place. Building on the scheme of the four kingdoms found in ch. 2, our author, writing in the reign of Epiphanes (175–164 B.C.), states specifically that the Greek kingdom will come to its end with this wicked ruler: Epiphanes will be the last pagan ruler of the last pagan kingdom, and then Israel will receive the kingdom and possess it forever.

Evidently, our author wrote ch. 7 some time after Epiphanes had angered the Jews by his commercial exploitation of the high priesthood of the Jerusalem Temple (II Macc 4:7*f*) and his efforts at Hellenizing the Jews (I Macc 1:11–15), and probably after his plundering the Temple in 169 B.C. (I Macc 1:20–23). But since the author of the primary stratum of ch. 7 does not make even an obscure allusion to the king's desecration of the Temple and the beginning of his bloody persecution of the Jews in 167 B.C. (I Macc 1:54–61), he surely did not write ch. 7 after these latter events. Therefore, the primary stratum of ch. 7 can safely be dated between 169 and 167 B.C.

The Small Horn (7:8,11a,20b–22,24b–25)

As shown above in the COMMENT: GENERAL, all the passages in ch. 7 that refer to the "small horn" or are related to these passages are insertions made by some later writer (called here the "glossator") into the basic stratum of this chapter. On the whole, the insertions are skillfully interwoven into the basic text. But in vs. 24, where the glossator forgot to mention the small horn, he practically makes the interpreting angel say, "The ten horns are eleven kings." The glossator must have felt (1) that the author of ch. 7 was not specific enough in his description of Epiphanes, and (2) that a more definite date should be set for the termination of Epiphanes' persecution of the Jews.

1) First of all, it must be noted (cf. Hölscher, "Die Entstehung," *TSK* 92 [1919], 120) that, whereas the author of the primary stratum of ch. 7 contrasts the fourth *kingdom* as a whole with the three kingdoms that preceded it (7:7b,19,23), the glossator contrasts the *king* who is represented by the small horn with other kings (7:20b,24b). He apparently failed to recognize that the tenth horn represented Epiphanes, and so he added "another horn, a small one" (7:8) which he described in terms that would unmistakably identify it with Epiphanes. This Seleucid king, like King Sennacherib of Assyria as described in II Kings 19:22(=Isa 37:22), haughtily lifts up his eyes and arrogantly opens his mouth against the Most High. (Note that when the glossator says in 7:8 that the small horn has "eyes like the eyes of a man," he uses "man" [in contrast to God] as a symbol of arrogance, whereas in the primary stratum "man" is a symbol of holiness; see COMMENT: GENERAL above.) The king symbolized by the eleventh horn, in his persecution of the Jews, planned "to change the feast days and the law" (vs. 25), which is precisely what Epiphanes endeavored to do (cf. I Macc 1:44–50).

2) The glossator set a time limit for the end of the persecution: "The holy ones of the Most High . . . will be handed over to him for a year, two years, and a half year" (7:25)—not too cryptic a way of saying "three and a half years" or half a septennium. This passage is surely from the same hand that wrote the identical phrase in 12:7 (there in Hebrew), which is itself secondary in ch. 12. The same half of a septennium is given in 9:27 as "half a week" of years, and as a somewhat shorter period in 8:14 as "2,300 evenings and mornings," i.e., 1,150 days. (Three and a half lunar years would be about 1,260 days. The estimates of 1,290 days [12:11] and of 1,335 days [12:13] are still later additions to the text.) Half a septennium may be taken simply as a symbolic term for a period of evil, since it is merely half the "perfect" number "seven." If taken literally, these passages must be regarded as genuine, but unfulfilled predictions, and not as *prophetiae post eventum.* Actually, the persecution in the strict sense, which began with the desecration of the temple by Epiphanes

(I Macc 1:54) on Chislev 15, 145 S.E. (=6 December 167 B.C.) and ended with the reconquest and purification of the temple by Judas Maccabee (I Macc 4:52) on Chislev 25, 148 S.E. (=14 December 164 B.C.), lasted, at the most, three years and eight days, or 1,103 days. The glossator, therefore, probably made his insertions in ch. 7 some time in 167 B.C., when he could foresee the success of Judas's military operations, but not the speed with which it would be accomplished.

The glossator has the interpreting angel say of the king who is represented by the small horn that "he will lay low three kings" (vs. 24b). These three kings are no doubt the same as the three who are referred to in the vision of the small horn as "three of the previous horns were uprooted before it" (vs. 8) [*NAB*'s rendering as ". . . were torn away to make room for it" reads a wrong interpretation into the translation], or as "three of the previous horns had fallen" before it (vs. 20). Who are these three kings? Most of the exegetes have assumed that, since the author of the primary stratum of ch. 7 regarded the ten horns as representing ten successive kings of the Greek kingdom (vs. 24), the glossator (or whoever these exegetes consider the author of vss. 8,20,24b) must have regarded them in the same way; and therefore they have endeavored to find among the rulers of the Seleucid dynasty the three kings whom Epiphanes "laid low." But their efforts have been fruitless. The immediate predecessors of Epiphanes, Antiochus III and Seleucus IV, did indeed meet violent ends; but in neither case was Epiphanes responsible for their deaths. Demetrius I, the older son of Seleucus IV, cannot be one of the three; his exile was not the work of Epiphanes, and he was not king until three years after the death of Epiphanes. Heliodorus cannot be brought into the picture, since he was never king. The "young" Antiochus, the younger son of Seleucus IV, to whom Epiphanes gave a subordinate position as coregent during the first five years of his reign, was no doubt put to death at the instigation of Epiphanes; but he can hardly be reckoned as one of the three "kings" whom Epiphanes laid low.

Porphyry [the third-century A.D. Greek philosopher and chronicler] is quoted (and rejected on wrong grounds) by Jerome as identifying the three kings whom Epiphanes "laid low" or defeated in battle with King Artaxias of Armenia, Ptolemy VI Philometor, and Ptolemy VII Euergetes. It is historically true that Epiphanes defeated Ptolemy VI in 169 B.C. (cf. Polybius *History* xxxviii; Diodorus *History* xxx), Ptolemy VII in 168 B.C. (Polybius, loc. cit.; Diodorus, loc. cit.), and Artaxias of Armenia in 166 B.C. (cf. Diodorus xxxi 17a).

If these are indeed the three kings to whom the glossator of Daniel 7 refers as having been laid low by Epiphanes, and indeed such seems to be the case, then the glossator must have considered the ten horns of the fourth beast as representing, not ten consecutive rulers of the Greek kingdom, as the primary text does, but as ten more or less contemporaneous pagan rulers of his day. For him the fourth beast is not merely the Greek kingdom, but the totality of the pagan world in the Greek period. That he regards them as contemporaneous can be seen in his calling the ten horns the "fellows" (*ḥabrātah*) of the eleventh horn (vs. 20). However, because he is adding the eleventh horn to the ten that were already in the text, he speaks of the latter as the "previous" horns (vss. 8,20,24b), and of the king represented by the eleventh horn as rising "after" the other kings—terms which are to be understood, not in reference to a historical sequence, but in reference to the position in which the horns are mentioned in his expanded text.

It is idle to speculate who the seven contemporaneous kings were that were not laid low by Epiphanes. Probably the glossator himself never gave them a thought. But if he had been pressed to do so, he could have named almost a dozen more or less independent principalities of his day. Ginsberg (p. 22), who is essentially followed here, gives a list of seven such states, or even of nine of them, if one should want more; and to this list he could, of course, have added Rome.

The Divine Tribunal (7:9–10)

The description of the divine tribunal that passes judgment on the nations of the world (vss. 9*f*) is wholly the work of the author of the primary stratum in ch. 7; the glossator, who refers to it in a parenthetical statement (vss. 21*f*), which interrupts the question about the meaning of the fourth beast and its horns (vss. 19*f*), adds nothing new to the description of the celestial court.

As in the case of the description of the four beasts (see above), there is no need here to look for any direct borrowings from pagan mythology. All the ideas expressed here are either borrowings from the older books of the Bible, or they belong to the common stock of folk concepts that were widespread in the ancient Near East.

Ancient Israel had long envisaged Yahweh as the divine judge enthroned in the assembly of his angels; cf., for example, "God presides in the divine council, in the midst of the gods he judges" (Ps 82:1), or "I saw Yahweh sitting on his throne and all the hosts of the heavens standing beside him on his right and on his left" (I Kings 22:19). The "thrones" (plural!) are for the angelic associate judges who constitute the celestial "court [Aramaic *dînâ,* short for *bêt dînâ*] that sat in judgment" (vss. 10,26). The scene is not expressly said to be laid in heaven, but this is implied in vs. 13 ("the clouds of the heavens"). Nor is God explicitly mentioned by name, but every reader would at once recognize as God "the Ancient One" who presides at this celestial tribunal.

The term "the Ancient One" (see NOTES) as used of God, though not found in older biblical literature, is partly based on the biblical concept of God's eternal existence (cf. Pss 9:8; 29:10; 90:2), and partly on the popular notion of God as an old man (cf. the bearded Zeus). Not only does Yahweh have the white hair of an old man; his clothing is also "as white as snow," symbolizing unsullied majesty. This feature of celestial apparitions is new here in biblical literature, but it is carried on from here in the New Testament (Mark 9:2; Matt 27:3 [in the Greek quoting Theodotion-Daniel]; Rev 3:5; etc.) and in rabbinical literature. The concept of fire as surrounding the Deity goes back to general Old Testament sources (cf. Exod 3:2; Deut 4:24; 33:2; etc.), but the mention in 7:9 of the "wheels of blazing fire" shows that our author is indebted for his imagery here to Ezekiel's vision of Yahweh's chariot throne (Ezek 1:15–20; 10:9–17). The fire is pictured here as a "surging stream" (vs. 10), because this is the "consuming fire" (cf. Ps 50:3) that destroys the body of the fourth beast (vs. 11).

Innumerable celestial spirits (cf. Deut 33:2; Ps 67:18), like the courtiers of an earthly king, attend the divine throne. But it is probably the associate judges in the celestial court by whom "the books were opened." Although contemporaneous court procedure may have influenced the picture here, the concept of heavenly books is an ancient one in Israel. In the present context, these books would not be the biblical *seper haḥayyîm,* "the book of the living" or "the book of life," in which God keeps written down the names of all who live on earth (cf. Exod 32:32*f;* Ps 69:29), nor even the books of the divine decrees (cf. Dan 12:1; Ezek 2:9*f;* 3:1*ff;* Zech 5:1–4; Pss 40:8; 139:16), but the *seper zikkārôn,* the "record book" (Mal 3:16), in which men's good deeds (Neh 5:19; 13:14) and bad deeds (Isa 65:6; Pss 51:3; 109:14) are recorded. The pagan nations are condemned on account of their wicked deeds, whereas Israel is rewarded because of its fidelity to Yahweh.

The One in Human Likeness (7:13–14,18,27)

Just as the four successive pagan kingdoms are represented by four monstrous beasts (vss. 2–7), so the kingdom that the holy ones of the Most High are to receive is represented by a human being, the symbol of holiness (see above), as contrasted with the unholy beasts. The Aramaic term *bar 'ĕnāš,* literally, "a son of mankind," i.e., a member of the human race, Latin *homo,* as distinct from Aramaic *gᵉbar,* a male human being, Latin *vir,* may have been used here under the influence of the Book of Ezekiel, where the corresponding Hebrew term, *ben 'ādām,* is frequently used by God in addressing the prophet, a mere "mortal." There is a contrast here, not only between the four beasts and the man, but also between the Ancient One and the man. That the human figure is a symbol here for the holy ones of the Most High is evident from the interpretation of the vision; in the vision the "man" is "given dominion—glory and kingship," while in the interpretation it is "the holy ones of the Most High" who "will receive the kingdom" (vs. 18), and "the kingship and the dominion and the grandeur of all the kingdoms under the heavens will be given to the people of the holy ones of the Most High" (vs. 27). That the human figure is a mere symbol and no reality is clear from the use of *k* before *bar 'ĕnāš* (*k*ᵉ*bar 'ĕnāš,* literally, "in the likeness of a son of mankind"), just as *k* is used before *'aryēh* (*k*ᵉ*'aryēh,* "in the likeness of a lion") in vs. 4, and before *n*ᵉ*mar* (*kin*ᵉ*mar,* "in the likeness of a leopard") in vs. 6. Daniel does not see a real human being any more than he sees a real lion or a real leopard. (It should be noted that *k* is not used for obvious reasons before *'attîq yômîn,* "an Ancient One.") Scholars who have sought to find Daniel's "son of man" in a mythological *Urmensch* (primordial man) or in an astral god (Marduk or Nabu) have shown more ingenuity than common sense. That the figure in human likeness comes "with the clouds of the heavens" is said primarily to contrast it with the beasts that come from the chaotic ocean, and secondarily to point to the figure's heavenly holiness.

In Daniel 7 the symbolic manlike figure has no messianic meaning, except perhaps as connected with messianism in the broad sense, i.e. with God's plan of salvation for his Chosen People. But in later Jewish apocalyptic literature (the Parables of Enoch and II Esdras) the term "son of man" soon shifted from a mere personification to a real person, the Messiah. The question why Jesus used the term in regard to himself is solely a New Testament problem, treated in commentaries of the Gospels (cf. R. E. Brown, *The Gospel according to John i–xii,* AB 29 [Garden City, N.Y.: Doubleday, 1966], p. 84), and need not concern us here, except to note that Jesus borrowed the term from Dan 7:13, as is clear from Mark 14:62. [For a full discussion of the "son of man" in Daniel 7 see Introduction, Part XIII.]

The Explanation of the Dream (7:15–16,28)

The interpretation that the angel gives Daniel of his dream-vision has been explained above in connection with the various parts of the vision itself. It is sufficient here to note Daniel's reaction to his vision and its interpretation. Whereas in ch. 2 Nebuchadnezzar is terrified by his dream-vision, of which Daniel explains the meaning, in the present chapter it is Daniel who is terrified by his dream-vision (vss. 15,28), the interpretation of which is given him by "one of those who were standing by" in attendance at the heavenly court, i.e. by an angel (vs. 16). The conversation between Daniel and his interpreting angel takes place within the vision itself —a literary device already used by Ezekiel (Ezek 40:4,45; etc.) and

Zechariah (Zech 1:9*f;* 2:2*f;* etc.) and later to become a standard feature of apocalyptic literature.

There is no inconsistency in Daniel saying, "I kept the matter to myself" (7:28) and then recording it in writing in this chapter. This is merely a device of apocalyptic literature, in which a revelation of future events is presented as having been made and recorded in a secret document centuries before the events take place, so that the document may become known at the proper time when the final predictions in it are about to take place; cf. 12:4: "Keep the words secret and seal the book until the time of the final phase" (cf. also 8:26b). The revelation of future events—the number and nature of the kings in each of the four pagan empires—is presented in ch. 7 as having been given to Daniel in the first year of the reign of King Belshazzar of Babylon; but it is finally published in the days of Antiochus IV Epiphanes, almost four centuries later, so that the reader, seeing how the visionary had rightly predicted events that the God who rules history had actually brought to pass, might have faith in the genuine prediction contained in the book: the time is at hand when God will destroy the pagan kingdom that is persecuting his holy people and will bestow on them "the kingship and the dominion and the grandeur of all the kingdoms under the heavens" (vs. 27).

VIII. VISION OF THE RAM AND THE HE-GOAT (8:1–27)

8 1 In the third year of the reign of King Belshazzar, I, Daniel, was
granted a vision. This vision was after that first one. 2 In the vision I
saw myself in the fortress city of Susa in the province of Elam,[a] where
I was at the Ulai Gate.[b] 3 As I looked about, I saw a ram standing before the gate.[b] It had two long horns; one was longer than the other
and appeared after it. 4 I noticed that the ram was butting toward the
west, the north, and the south; and no beast could withstand it or be
rescued from its power. It did as it pleased and became mighty.
5 As I was looking on, I saw a he-goat come from the west, and
cross the whole earth without touching the ground; and a conspicuous
horn was on its forehead. 6 The he-goat came up to the two-horned
ram that I saw standing before the gate,[b] and rushed at it with savage
force. 7 I noticed that, when it reached the ram, it was enraged against
it, and gave it such a blow that it broke off its two horns; for the ram
had not the power to withstand it. The he-goat knocked the ram to
the ground and trampled it down; and there was no one to rescue the
ram from its power.
8 The he-goat then grew exceedingly. But at the height of its power,
its big horn broke off, and in its place four [c]conspicuous ones[c] came
up toward the four winds of the heavens. 9 From one of them there
came forth a small[d] horn, which grew mightily toward the south and
the east [and the Lovely One]. 10 It grew up to the host of the
heavens and hurled some of the host [[e]some of the stars[e]] to the earth,
where it trampled them down. 11 [f]Even over[f] the Prince of the host [g]it

[a] Omit, with LXX and Theod., *wā'ereh beḥāzôn* after *hammedînāh;* dittography, accidentally repeating the first words of the verse.

[b] Read *'ābûl* for *'ûbal;* see NOTE.

[c–c] Read *ḥazyôt* for *ḥāzût;* see NOTE.

[d] Read *ṣe'îrāh,* or possibly *miṣ'ārāh* (cf. Gen 19:20), for *miṣṣe'îrāh.*

[e–e] Omit *û* before *min-hakkôkābîm;* see NOTE.

[f–f] Read *we'al* for *we'ad;* dittography of preposition near the beginning of the verse.

[g–g] Read *tagdîl* for *higdîl.* Most likely the verbs in vss. 11 were originally in the feminine, as in vss. 8b–10,12; in vs. 11, a copyist may have lapsed by (rightly) identifying the feminine *qeren* ("horn") with Epiphanes (masculine). The verbs in vss. 11*f*

exalted itself[g]; [h]it removed[h] the daily sacrifice [i]from its stand[i] [j]and
defiled[j] [k]the sanctuary[k] [l]and the pious ones[l]; 12 and on the stand of
the daily sacrifice [m]it set up[m] [n]an offense[n]. It cast truth to the ground
and was successful in its undertaking.

/ 13 Then I overheard a holy one speaking, and another holy one
asked whichever one that spoke, "How long are the events of this vision to last: [o]the removing of[o] the daily sacrifice, the setting up of an
[appalling] offense, and the defiling of the sanctuary and the pious
ones?" 14 He answered him[p], "For two thousand and three hundred
evenings and mornings; then the sanctuary will be purified." /

15 While I, Daniel, was seeking to understand the vision I had seen,
I beheld a manlike figure standing in front of me.

/ 16 And at the gate[q] I heard a human voice cry out, "Gabriel, explain the revelation to this man." /

17 He then came near where I was standing, and as he came, I fell
prostrate in terror. But he said to me, "Understand, O man, that the
vision refers to the time of the end."

// 18 When he spoke with me, I dropped prostrate to the ground.
But he touched me and raised me to my feet. 19 "I will tell you," he
said, "what is to be at the last days of the time of wrath; for there will
be an end to [r]the period[r]. //

20 "The two-horned ram that you saw represents the kingdoms[s] of
the Medes and the Persians. 21 The he-goat represents the kingdoms[t]
of the Greeks, and the big horn on its forehead is the first kingdom[u].

---

are in *yiqṭōl* forms probably because of the Aramaic original. In Aramaic, *yiqṭul* forms are sometimes used after *q^{e}ṭal* forms with the force of historical presents or to express contemporaneity (cf. 4:2,31,33; 7:16,28; see also J. A. Fitzmyer, *The Genesis Apocryphon of Qumran Cave 1,* p. 202).

[h–h] Read *tārîm,* or perhaps better *tāsîr* (cf. 11:31; 12:11), for *hûram.*

[i–i] Read *mikkannô* or *mimm^{e}kônô* for *mimmennû.*

[j–j] Read *w^{e}tirmōs* (cf. vss. 7,10) for *w^{e}hušlak,* which is a corrupt dittography of *w^{e}tašlēk* of vs. 12; but see NOTE. Transpose *m^{e}kôn* to precede *hattāmîd* in vs. 12.

[k–k] Read *miqdāš* for *miqdāšô;* the *w* is a dittography of the following *w.*

[l–l] Join *w^{e}ṣābā'* to the end of vs. 11; but see NOTE.

[m–m] Read *w^{e}tintēn* for *tinnātēn.* The form *tintēn* is an Aramaism for *tittēn;* cf. *yintēn* (2:16).

[n–n] Read *happeša'* or *peša'* for *b^{e}peša';* cf. vs. 13.

[o–o] Insert, with LXX and Theod., *hārēm* or *hāsēr* after *hattāmîd;* cf. vs. 11.

[p] Read *'ēlā(y)w* for *'ēlay,* with LXX, Theod., Syr.

[q] Read *'ābûl* for *'ûlai;* cf. Theod.; see NOTE.

[r–r] Read *lammô'ēd* for *l^{e}mô'ēd;* cf. 11:27 (end),35 (end).

[s] Read *molkê* for *malkê.*

[t] Read *molkê* for *melek;* the final *y* was lost by haplography.

[u] Read *hammōlek* for *hammelek.*

22 That it broke off and four other ones rose in its place signifies that
four other kingdoms will rise [v]from its midst[v], but without its
strength.
23 "In the last days of their sovereignty, when crimes[w] reach their
full measure, there will rise a king, brazen-faced and skilled in trickery. 24 As his power grows mightily[x], [y]he will speak[y] arrogantly, succeed in his undertaking, and destroy mighty ones. 25 His cunning will
be against [z]the holy people[z], and his treacherous efforts will succeed.
Proud of heart, he will suddenly destroy many. But when he rises up
against the Prince of princes, he will be broken—but not by human
hand.
/ 26 "The revelation that was uttered about the evenings and mornings is true. /

"As for you, keep the vision a secret, for it refers to the distant future."

27 I, Daniel, was dazed and ill for some days; then I arose and took
care of the king's business.

/ But I was dismayed at the revelation, and I did not understand it. /

[v–v] Read *miggēwô* for *miggôy;* see NOTE.
[w] Read, with Syr. and Vulg. (cf. LXX and Theod.), *happ*^{e}*šā'îm* for *happōš*^{e}*'îm;* cf. 9:24.
[x] Omit *w*^{e}*lō' b*^{e}*kôḥô;* dittography of end of vs. 22.
[y–y] Read *y*^{e}*dabbēr* for *yašḥît;* see NOTE.
[z–z] Read *'am-q*^{e}*dôšîm* for *w*^{e}*'am q*^{e}*dôšîm,* and transpose the term from the end of vs. 24 to follow *w*^{e}*'al* at the beginning of vs. 25.

NOTES

8:1. Literally, "In the year of three to the reign of Belshazzar the king, a vision appeared to me, Daniel, after one that had appeared in the beginning." The Hebrew term, *batt*^{e}*ḥillāh,* literally, "in the beginning," is used idiomatically in the sense of "formerly, before" (cf. Gen 13:3; 41:24; etc.); it does not necessarily mean "in the beginning" of Belshazzar's reign, although this happens to be correct (cf. 7:1). The purpose of this verse is to connect ch. 8 with ch. 7.

2. Literally, "And I looked in the vision, and it came to pass, as I was looking, that I was in Susa, the fortress city, which is in Elam, the province, and I was at the Ulai Gate." The constructions, "Susa, the fortress city," and "Elam, the province," are Aramaisms.

the Ulai Gate. Since there was a river in Elam called the Ulai (classical

Eulaeus), the location of which is uncertain, MT's *'ûbal 'ûlāi* has commonly been translated as "the Ulai River"; *'ûbāl* is assumed to be related to Hebrew *yûbāl*, "stream, watercourse" (only in Jer 17:8), which is a variant of (or perhaps a scribal error for) *yābāl*, "stream, watercourse" (Isa 30:25; 44:4). But there is no satisfactory reason why *yûbāl* should here become *'ûbāl*. Most of the ancient versions (LXX, Syr., Vulg.) translated the word correctly as "gate"; they either read or understood *'wbl* as *'bwl*, which occurs (in slightly variant forms) in Mishnaic Hebrew, Targumic Aramaic, and Syriac as a loanword from Akkadian *abullu*, "city gate." The misplacing of the *w* in the MT form of the word in vs. 2 was probably caused by the place of the *w* in *'wly* that immediately follows. In vss. 3,6 the word is written ambiguously as *'bl;* see NOTE on vs. 16. The Ulai Gate at Susa was named after the river to which the road from this gate led. A city as large as Susa could, of course, have several gates, each with its own name; cf. *CAD* 1, Part I, p. 86, *abullu* "identified by proper names." If, as is commonly done, the Ulai is identified with the modern Disful Karun, several miles to the east of Susa, Daniel could not have been simultaneously both in Susa and at the Ulai River—even in spirit.

3. Literally, "It had two horns, and the horns were high, and one was higher than the other, and the higher one was coming up later."

4. *and no beast could withstand it or be rescued from its power*. Literally, "and all beasts could not stand before it, and there was not a rescuer from its hand." The masculine plural imperfect, *ya'amdû* ("they could stand") instead of the feminine plural imperfect (*ta'ămōdnāh*), is in keeping with Mishnaic Hebrew usage.

and became mighty. The force of the hiphil, *w^{e}higdîl*, here is rather "it became great" than "it acted greatly."

5. *As I was looking on*. The Hebrew *wa'ănî hāyîtî mēbîn* is a mistranslation of Aramaic *wa'ănāh hăwēt miśtakkal* (cf. 7:8); Aramaic *hithpa'al* of *śkl* means both "to comprehend" and "to consider, observe," but the translator confused it with Hebrew *hiśkîl*, which often means "to comprehend," but never "to consider, observe."

I saw. Literally, "and behold!" See NOTE on 7:2.

a he-goat. The word *ṣ^{e}pîr* (also in vss. 8,21) in Hebrew (cf. Ezra 8:35; II Chron 29:12) is a loanword from the Aramaic (cf. Ezra 6:17: *ṣ^{e}pîrê 'izzîn*). There is no need of a textual note deleting the article *ha-* before *'izzîn;* because Aramaic differs from Hebrew in its way of expressing determination, the translator is often at fault in his use or omission of the Hebrew article.

and cross the whole earth. Literally, "over the face of the whole earth."

without touching the ground. The Hebrew *w^e'ên nôgēa' bā'āreṣ* should mean, "with no one touching the ground," which would be nonsense here. To say, "without (his) touching the ground," good Hebrew would say, *w^e'ênennû nôgēa' bā'āreṣ*, literally, "and he was not touching the ground." Either *w^e'ên* of the MT should be considered a case of haplography for *w^e'ênennû* or, more likely, it is a blunder of the translator. In a Hebrew participial construction in which *lō'* is limited to certain specific cases, the particle *'ên* is regularly used to negate the subject, which, if definite, must be expressed by a noun or a pronoun, whereas in Aramaic, *lâ* negates the participle, and the subject need not be expressed. On the assumption that the underlying Aramaic was something like *wᵉlâ nāgaʿ bᵉʾarʿâ,* the translator would have used the correct Hebrew *ʾên* for Aramaic *lâ* in a participial construction, but without remembering that he should have expressed the subject with *ʾên.*

and a conspicuous horn was on its forehead. Literally, "and the he-goat—a horn of conspicuousness [?] (was) between its eyes." The phrase, *qeren ḥāzût,* "a horn of conspicuousness" [?], is difficult. Outside of Daniel, the Hebrew noun *ḥāzût* occurs only in Isa 20:2; 29:11, where it means "sight, vision." Perhaps the Aramaic original had a feminine passive participle here, *ḥazyāh,* "seen, visible," in the sense of "prominent, conspicuous," and the translator mistook the participle for a noun; but cf. *ḥăzôtēh,* "its sight," in 4:8,17. On *ḥāzût* in vs. 8, see NOTE there.

7. *it was enraged.* Literally, "and it embittered itself" (Hebrew *wayyitmarmar*). This hithpalpel form of the root *mrr,* which occurs only here and in 11:11 in the MT, is an Aramaism, perhaps a literal rendering of the underlying Aramaic text.

8. *its big horn.* The translator apparently read Aramaic *qrnh* as *qarnāh=qarnâ=*Hebrew *haqqeren,* "the horn," rather than the probably intended *qarnēh=*Hebrew *qarnô,* "its horn." In any case, English usage demands "its" rather than "the."

four conspicuous ones. Because Hebrew *ḥāzût ʾarbaʿ* is so odd, some exegetes, following the LXX, emend the text to read *ʾăḥērôt ʾarbaʿ,* "four other ones." Others, with Theod. and Vulg., delete *ḥāzût* as an intrusion from vs. 5. Possibly *ḥāzût ʾarbaʿ* might be understood literally as "the conspicuousness of four" (see NOTE on "a conspicuous horn" in vs. 5), and the plural verb with the subject in the singular taken as a *constructio ad sensum.* But more likely the underlying Aramaic was something like *ḥazyān ʾarbaʿ,* "four conspicuous ones," *ḥazyān* being the feminine plural passive participle; and this was mechanically rendered into Hebrew as *ḥazyôt ʾarbaʿ,* which was later corrupted (under the influence of vs. 5?) into *ḥāzût ʾarbaʿ.*

9. *a small horn.* The *ʾaḥat* ("one") in *qeren-ʾaḥat* is used merely as the indefinite article; cf. *ʾayil ʾeḥād* in vs. 3. The horn is "small" in contrast to the "conspicuous" or "big" horn and the four "conspicuous" ones (vss. 5 and 8).

the Lovely One. Palestine. The Hebrew noun *ṣᵉbî,* "a thing of beauty, a jewel, etc.," is used poetically for Palestine in Jer 3:19; Ezek 20:6,14; hence *ʾereṣ haṣṣᵉbî,* "the land of beauty, the lovely land," designates Palestine in Dan 11:16,41. In the present passage, where the term seems inconsistent with the two preceding geographical terms, "the Lovely One" (Palestine) is probably a misplaced gloss on "the south."

10. *the host of the heavens.* The stars, as rightly identified in the gloss (see COMMENT: DETAILED). When the gloss became part of the text, the conjunction *û-,* "and," was prefixed to it for syntactical reasons.

11. *the Prince of the host.* God; see COMMENT: DETAILED.

and defiled the sanctuary and the pious ones. The emended Hebrew text means: "and trampled down the sanctuary and the host." But "the host" here (as distinct from the term in vss. 10*f*) must mean "the pious Jews"; moreover, it is strange that the same verb, "to trample down," should be used both in its literal sense of trampling down the images of the astral deities in vs. 10 and in the figurative sense of persecuting the Jews in vss. 11b,13b. Ginsberg (pp. 52*ff*) has proposed a plausible solution. According to him, the underlying Aramaic at the end of vs. 11 would be: *ûtᵉhappēs miqdāš waḥăsayin,* "and it defiled the sanctuary and the pious ones": *wthps* would have been misread or corrupted into *wtrps* under the influence of the preceding Aramaic *wtrps* (Hebrew *wtrms:* end of vs. 10); *wḥsyn* would have been misread or misunderstood as *wḥyl* under the influence of the preceding Aramaic *ḥyl/ḥyl'* (Hebrew *ṣābā'/haṣṣābā'*), or perhaps the translator vocalized *ḥsyn* as *ḥassîn,* "strong," which he then rendered freely as *ṣābā',* "host," again under the influence of the preceding *ṣābā'.* That *happēs* (haphel of *pss*) can have the meaning of "defile" is clear, e.g. from Targ. Jerush. of Lev 21:7; Aramaic *mapsāh*=Hebrew *ḥălālāh,* "defiled (woman)." Although *ḥăsayin* (emphatic *ḥăsayyâ*), plural of *ḥăsê,* "pious," does not occur in Jewish Aramaic, it is common in Syriac; and it must have been used in Palestinian Aramaic of the Maccabean period, as is clear from the Greek name for the Essenes, *Essēnoi/Essaioi,* which is almost certainly derived from Aramaic *ḥăsayin/ḥăsayyâ.* (Whatever the later history of the Essenes may have been, etymologically speaking, they would have been the same as the Hasideans of I Macc 2:42; 7:13; II Macc 14:6, since the latter term is certainly derived from Hebrew *ḥăsîdîm,* "the pious," which is the exact Hebrew equivalent of Aramaic *ḥăsayin,* "the pious.") The reconstruction of the Aramaic text as given above is admittedly hypothetical. But it receives striking confirmation (see Ginsberg, p. 45) from I Macc 1:46*ff:* included in the anti-Jewish decree of Epiphanes was the order "to defile the sanctuary and the holy ones" (*mianai hagiasma kai hagious*); and the pious Jews were ordered "to sacrifice swine and unclean animals" and thereby "make themselves abominable" (*bdelyxai tas psychas autōn*). See also NOTE on Dan 11:31.

12. *an offense.* The "appalling abomination" of 9:27; 11:31; 12:11, as correctly identified by the gloss on the "offense" in 8:13. See COMMENT: DETAILED on 9:27.

truth. Not truth in an abstract sense, but religious truth, the Torah.

13. *a holy one.* A celestial spirit.

whichever one that spoke. Ginsberg (p. 83) suggests that the strange form, *palmônî,* "so-and-so," which is unique in the MT and seems to be a fusion of *pᵉlōnî 'almōnî,* "so-and-so": I Sam 21:3; II Kings 6:8; Ruth 4:1, may have been caused by the underlying Aramaic, *lipᵉlān man dî mᵉmallēl,* "to so-and-so who spoke," which the translator rendered into Hebrew as *lappalmônî hamᵉdabbēr,* "to the so-and-so speaker."

How long are the events of this vision to last? Literally, "Until when the vision?" Here and in 9:24; 10:14b, Hebrew *ḥāzôn,* literally "vision," refers to the substance of a vision, the things seen in a vision.

the removing of the daily sacrifice, the setting up of an [*appalling*] *offense, and the defiling of the sanctuary and the pious ones.* A summary repetition of the events of the vision described in vss. 11*f.* Since *tēt* is an infinitive, *mirmās* must be taken, not as the noun meaning "trampled down ground" (Isa 5:5; 7:25; 10:6; etc.), but as an Aramaizing infinitive (pᵉʿal infinitive: *miqtal*), and an infinitive (*hārēm* or *hāsēr*) must be supplied after *hattāmîd* (cf. vs. 11). According to the common Aramaic idiom (as influenced by Akkadian, which itself was influenced by Sumerian in this), the noun in the objective case precedes the infinitive—and this order of the words has been mechanically followed by the translator contrary to common Hebrew usage. The underlying Aramaic would be something like: *t^{e}mîdâ lahărāmāh* (or *lahăsārāh*), *w^{e}sorḥān l^{e}mintan, w^{e}qōdeš waḥăsayin l^{e}happāsāh.* On the noun *ḥăsayin* and the verb *l^{e}happāsāh,* see NOTE on vs. 11.

14. *For two thousand and three hundred evenings and mornings.* For 1,150 days, on which 1,150 evening sacrifices and 1,150 morning sacrifices should have been offered on the altar. Note that, since the twenty-four-hour day began for the Jews in the evening, the evening sacrifices are mentioned before the morning sacrifices.

will be purified. The Hebrew verb, *w^{e}niṣdaq* (the only occurrence of the niphal of *ṣdq* in the MT!), should mean "will be justified." But this can hardly be said of the sanctuary. The underlying Aramaic was surely *yidkê,* "will be cleansed, purified," which was corrupted into, or misread by the translator as *yizkê,* "will be victorious, justified."

15. *I beheld a manlike figure standing in front of me.* Literally, "behold, standing in front of me (was) like an appearance of a man." The word used here for "man," *geber* (vigorous young man), is perhaps alluded to in the next verse, where the angel is called "Gabriel" (*geber* of God); cf. 9:21.

16. *at the gate.* The Hebrew phrase *bên 'ûlāi* of the MT can mean only "between the Ulai (River)," which obviously makes no sense. In Theod., the phrase is rendered as *ana meson tou oubal,* "in the middle of the *oubal*"; Greek *oubal* represents Hebrew *'ûbāl,* which, as explained above (see NOTE on vs. 2), should be read as *'ābûl,* "gate." The phrase, "between the gate," is probably to be understood as "between the flanking towers of the gateway," i.e. "within the gateway."

the revelation. Ginsberg (p. 55) appears to be correct in saying that in Daniel, whereas the word for vision is *ḥāzôn,* the word *mar'eh,* besides meaning "aspect, appearance" (e.g. 8:15; 10:6), refers in certain passages (8:16,26a, 27b; 9:23; 10:1) not to what was seen, but to what was heard. For instance, the *mar'eh* of vs. 16 refers back to vs. 13, which tells of what the seer "heard" (*wā'ešm^{e}'āh*) from the angel who spoke (*m^{e}dabbēr, ham^{e}dabbēr*) and "said" something (*wayyō'mer*); and in vs. 26 it is the *mar'eh* "that is uttered" (*'ăšer ne'ĕmar*). The reason for this would be that the underlying Aramaic word was *'aḥwāyāh* (cf. 5:12), which means a "showing, explaining, revealing" of something, whether visibly or audibly; and the translator would have used a Hebrew word (*mar'eh*) that would normally be limited to the meaning of showing something visibly, whereas the context demands a word that means a showing, revealing of something audibly.

17. *I fell prostrate in terror.* Literally, "I was terrified and fell on my face."

man. Literally, "son of man"; see NOTE on 7:13. This form of address, *ben-'ādām,* has been borrowed from Ezekiel, where it is extremely common in passages in which God addresses the prophet as a mere "mortal" (Ezek 2:1,3,6,8; etc.).

18. *I dropped prostrate to the ground.* The Hebrew, if taken literally, would

mean: "I fell into a deep sleep upon my face toward the ground." This is commonly interpreted to mean: "I swooned and fell prostrate to the ground." But nothing in the context implies that the seer was unconscious or even asleep; the angel does not awake him, but merely raises him to his feet. Therefore, it seems probable that the underlying Aramaic verb was *d^{e}mak,* which means both "to lie down" and "to sleep"; the translator apparently understood it wrongly in the second of these two meanings. Cf. also 10:9.

and raised me to my feet. Literally, "and made me stand on my standing"; but cf. Ezek 2:2.

19. *at the last days of the time of wrath.* Literally, "at the latter part of the wrath." The wrath, of course, is Yahweh's.

22. *That it broke off and four other ones rose.* The Hebrew would be literally, "And the broken off one and four rose," which would be unintelligible without recourse to the underlying Aramaic: *w^{e}dî t^{e}bîrat* [cf. *w^{e}dî ḥăzaytāh:* 2:41,43] *wîqûmān 'arba',* "And that it broke off and that four arose." Since in Hebrew the article and a participle can be the equivalent of a relative and a finite verb, the translator made the double equation: Aramaic *dî t^{e}bîrat*= Hebrew *'ăšer nišb^{e}rāh*=Hebrew *hannišberet.* He may have been misled to his participial construction by confusing the Aramaic perfect passive, *t^{e}bîrat,* with the passive participle, *t^{e}bîrāh.*

rose. The use in Hebrew of the verb *'āmad,* "to be standing," as a synonym for *qûm,* "to stand up, to rise," is an Aramaism, which is found also in Mishnaic Hebrew; but see NOTE on 11:17. The form *ya'ămōdnāh* in vs. 22b, with preformative in *y* for the feminine plural imperfect, is not an archaism (cf. Gen 30:38; I Sam 6:12), but a case where the translator thoughtlessly carried over the preformative of the Aramaic *y^{e}qûmān.*

from its midst. The MT *miggôy,* which can only mean "from a nation," does not make sense here. Even if the Hebrew were made to read *miggôyô,* "from his nation," as LXX, Theod., and Vulg. are assumed to have read, it would still not make sense; all the large horns are kingdoms, not kings (see COMMENT: DETAILED). Probably the underlying Aramaic was *mn gwh=min gawwāh,* "from its midst," i.e. from the fourth kingdom; the translator understood *mn gwh* as *miggēwô,* "from its (the he-goat's) back" in the sense of "from its body" (Hebrew *migg^{e}wîyātô*), and his *mgww* was later corrupted into *mgwy.*

23. *when crimes reach their full measure.* Literally, "when crimes are complete." For the same sense, cf. 9:24: "until crime is stopped and sins brought to full measure" (*l^{e}kallēh happeša' ûl^{e}hātēm ḥaṭṭā'ôt*); and also II Macc 6:14*f:* "The Lord waits patiently to punish the other nations until they have reached the full measure of their sins." This concept was traditional in Israel, from Gen 15:16 ("The iniquity of the Amorites will not have run its course until then") to Matt 20:32 ("You fill up the measure of your fathers"). Therefore, the reading *happ^{e}šā'îm* of Syr. and Vulg. (cf. LXX and Theod.) is preferable to the reading *happōš^{e}'îm* of the MT.

24. *he will speak arrogantly.* The MT means literally, "and marvelous things he will destroy" (*w^{e}niplā'ôt yašḥît*). In order to salvage some kind of sense out of this, the feminine plural noun (*niplā'ôt*) has been understood as an adverb, and the phrase rendered as "marvelously he will destroy," or in a free render-

ing, "he shall cause fearful destruction" (*RSV*). However, it should be noted that, on the one hand, a form of the same verb, *yašḥît,* occurs later in the same verse (*w*ᵉ*hišḥît ʿăṣûmîm:* "and he will destroy mighty ones"), so that *yašḥît* looks like a variant of *w*ᵉ*hišḥît* that has dislodged some other verb after *w*ᵉ*niplāʾôt;* and on the other hand, the phrase, *y*ᵉ*dabbēr niplāʾôt,* literally, "he will speak marvelous things," occurs in 11:36—a verse that bears a close resemblance to 8:24*f*. It would therefore not seem improbable that the original phrase in 8:24 was *w*ᵉ*niplāʾôt y*ᵉ*dabbēr* as in 11:36, and that the Aramaic behind both phrases was *m*ᵉ*mallil rabr*ᵉ*bān* as in 7:8,20; the translator may well have tried to imitate the intensive Aramaic *rabr*ᵉ*bān* by Hebrew *niplāʾôt,* "he will speak very big things," i.e. "he will speak arrogantly."

25. *the holy people.* Literally, "people of holy ones" (hend.).

and his treacherous efforts will succeed. Literally, "and he will make treachery succeed in his hand."

Proud of heart. Literally, "and in his heart he will grow big." Possibly there is an intended contrast in Hebrew between *b*ᵉ*yādô,* "in his hand," and *bil*ᵉ*bābô,* "in his heart."

he will suddenly destroy many. The Hebrew term rendered here as "suddenly" is *b*ᵉ*šalweh,* which would ordinarily mean "in contentment, with ease." One might therefore think of rendering the term here as "with impunity." But this would be in contradiction with the next words, "he will be broken." If *b*ᵉ*šalweh* is taken as an Aramaism, it has the meaning of "quietly, unexpectedly, suddenly, immediately." The precise meaning here may depend on the historical event in Epiphanes' actions against the Jews to which the present passage is cryptically referring; see COMMENT: DETAILED.

but not by human hand. Literally, "and in naught of hand." The word, "human," is supplied in English because in the context the contrast is between God and man; cf. the stone cut from the mountain, "without a hand being put to it," that crushed the composite statue in 2:34,45.

26. *for it refers to the distant future.* Literally, "for (it is) unto many days." The same phrase, *l*ᵉ*yāmîm rabbîm,* "unto many days," occurs in Ezek 12:27 ("the vision he is seeing refers to the distant future"). [The expression occurs also in a late seventh-century B.C. Ammonite inscription from Tell Siran: *bywmt rbm;* cf. C. Krahmalkov, "An Ammonite Lyric Poem," *BASOR* 223 (1976), 55–57.]

27. *I, Daniel, was dazed and ill.* The MT means literally, "I, Daniel, became [*nihyêtî*] and I was ill." Obviously, the word *nihyêtî* is either an inner Hebrew corruption or a bungled attempt of the translator to render an Aramaic word that had become corrupt or that the translator did not understand. Ginsberg (p. 59) suggests that the Aramaic word was probably *ʾtwht,* i.e. *ʾettaww*ᵉ*hēt,* "I was astonished, dazed," the ethpaʿal of *twh* (cf. 3:24); the translator would have thought that *ʾtwht* was some reflexive or passive form of *hwh,* "to be," and so he rendered it in Hebrew by the niphal of *hāyāh,* "to be."

and I did not understand it. Literally, "and there was no one understanding it"; see NOTE on vs. 5 ("without touching the ground").

COMMENT: GENERAL

Like the apocalypse of ch. 7, the one of ch. 8 purports to be a preview of the successive kingdoms that would follow the Babylonian one and would end in the Greek kingdom of the Seleucids, the last king of which would persecute the Jews but would ultimately have his power broken by God. Not only in this general way is ch. 8 similar to ch. 7, but also in the particular fact that in both apocalypses the pagan kingdoms are symbolized by strange-looking animals.

But this does not necessarily prove that ch. 8 was written by the author of ch. 7. It could have been written by a different man, who was acquainted with the apocalypse of ch. 7 and modeled his own work in part on it. There are indeed sufficient differences between the two chapters to make it appear probable that the chapters come from different authors. From a literary viewpoint ch. 8 is inferior to ch. 7 and shows a less vivid imagination. The seer of ch. 8 is transported in spirit from Babylon to Susa, where he has his vision; whereas the seer of ch. 7 has his vision in a dream, while at home in Babylon. For the author of ch. 8 the good Jews are "the pious ones" (see NOTE on 8:11) or "the holy people" (8:25). For the author of ch. 7 they are "the holy ones of the Most High" (7:18) or "the people of the holy ones of the Most High" (7:27). [For a full discussion of this group, see Introduction, Part XIII.]

As is the case with ch. 7, certain later insertions into the original apocalypse appear also in ch. 8. What follows on this is based on Ginsberg, pp. 29–38.

It is clear that the dialogue between the two angels in vss. 13–14 interrupts the sequence between vss. 1–12 and vs. 15; the "vision" that Daniel wishes to understand (vs. 15) refers to the vision described in vss. 1–12 and has nothing to do with the conversation of the two holy ones in vss. 13–14, whom he hears speaking but whom he does not see. Moreover, in the basic apocalypse the "holy ones" are the pious Jews (vs. 25), whereas in vs. 13 they are angels. Another secondary intrusion is vs. 16, which logically follows after the inserted vss. 13–14. According to vs. 15 Daniel's dream is over; and fully awake in Babylon, he is trying to understand the vision he had seen in his dream. But according to vs. 16 he is still in spirit at the Ulai Gate in Susa. Besides, in the basic apocalypse the angel who appears to Daniel as a "manlike figure" (vs. 15) and explains to him the meaning of the vision of the ram and the he-goat surely distinguishes himself from the vision as such (vss. 16 and 26b). Since vss. 26a and 27b are concerned with the "revelation" "about the evenings and mornings," they also must be from the same hand that inserted vss. 13–14 and 16 into the basic apocalypse. Inasmuch as the "revelation" consists in foretelling the duration of the religious persecution of approximately three and a half years (vss. 13–14), the conclusion can be drawn that the person who inserted vss. 13–14,16,26a, and 27b is the same one who made the secondary insertions in ch. 7, that is, the author of ch. 9, who climaxed the "prophetic" chronology of his apocalypse by predicting a duration of three and a half years for Epiphanes' persecution of the Jews. An additional reason for assigning these insertions to the author of ch. 9 is the fact that it is the angel Gabriel who makes the revelation about the duration of the persecution both here and in ch. 9. In fact, Gabriel is identified in 9:21 as the angel who had previously appeared to Daniel—obviously a reference to 8:16. The author of ch. 9 therefore made these insertions in ch. 8 for the purpose of establishing a continuity between the two chapters. For the rendering of Hebrew *mar'eh* as "revelation" in these passages, see NOTE on vs. 16.

A different problem is presented by the insertion of vss. 18–19. That these verses have been inserted into the basic apocalypse of ch. 8 is clear for several reasons. According to vs. 17 Daniel falls "prostrate in terror"; but according to vs. 18 he again drops "prostrate to the ground," without having first been raised up. Besides, the introductory words of the angel in vs. 19 seem to be an unnecessary repetition of the introductory words of the angel in vs. 17.

In both passages there is an allusion to Hab 2:3a, although in each passage the words of Habakkuk are applied differently. After Habakkuk asks God how long the wicked are to continue to persecute the just with impunity (Hab 1:12–2:1), God gives him an oracle (*ḥāzôn*), the gist of which is that, though the prophet may not live to see it, God's justice will be done in the end, and therefore the just man must live by faith in God's word (Hab 2:2–4). The pertinent words in Hab 2:3a, *kî ʿēd* [for *ʿôd*] *ḥāzôn lammōʿēd weyāpēaḥ laqqēṣ,* should be translated as "The oracle [no article in Hebrew poetry] is a witness for the appointed time and a testifier for the end (of the period)." [For *ʿēd,* "witness," and *yāpēaḥ,* "testifier," in parallelism, cf. Ps 27:12; Prov 6:19; 12:17; 14:5. For *yāpēaḥ,* see M. Dahood, *Psalms I,* p. 169.] Now, the phrase in vs. 17, *kî leʿet-qēṣ heḥāzôn,* "that the vision refers to the time of the end," takes the word *qēṣ* in the eschatological sense in which it is used in Hab 2:3 (and in which it is understood in 1QpHab, col. 7, line 7: *haqqēṣ hāʾăḥărôn*), even though it takes the word *ḥāzôn* not as an oracle that is about to be given as in Hab 2:3, but as a vision that has just been seen. In vs. 19, however, the word *mōʿēd* is taken to mean not an "appointed time," a "determined date," as in Hab 2:3, but a "fixed period of time," and *qēṣ* is used not in the eschatological sense, but in the general sense of any "end." This is precisely the sense that is imposed on Hab 2:3a in Dan 10:14b; 11:27b,35b (see NOTES on these verses). Therefore, it seems probable that the passage of vss. 18–19 was inserted in ch. 8 by the author of chs. 10–12. This is confirmed by the fact that in 10:9 Daniel drops prostrate to the ground on hearing the angel's voice, just as in 8:18 (and not on seeing him, as in 8:17), and by the strange use of *nirdam* in both 8:18 and 10:9.

The basic apocalypse of ch. 8 was written after Epiphanes' desecration of the temple in December 167 B.C. (cf. vs. 11), but probably not long after this event.

With ch. 8 the language of the book returns to Hebrew after the Aramaic of 2:4b – 7:28. The English translation offered here is based on the assumption that this chapter, like the remaining chapters of the book, has been translated into Hebrew from an Aramaic original. As shown in the NOTES, this assumption leads to a much clearer understanding of the text, even though in this chapter there may not be as clear a case as in 10:3 where the Hebrew translator can be shown with almost absolute certainty to have misunderstood the Aramaic original. On the language of the book as a whole, see Introduction, Part III.

In some places the MT of this chapter is rather corrupt, especially in vss. 10–12. In the textual notes an attempt has been made to restore what is believed to be the original form of the Hebrew translation. But it should be noted that the English translation is based on what is thought to be the original Aramaic that lies behind this corrected Hebrew text, as pointed out in the NOTES. This applies also to chs. 9–12.

COMMENT: DETAILED

The Vision (8:1–2,15,17,26b,27a)

As stated in the COMMENT: DETAILED on *The Four Beasts from the Sea* (7:1–3,17), the purpose of dating each apocalypse is to inspire confidence in its long-term predictions. Since the present chapter was intentionally joined to the preceding one by saying "this vision was after that first one," it is dated in the reign of the same king in which the preceding one is dated (7:1). There is no evident reason why the author picked the "third" year of Belshazzar's reign, which is without any historical value. Perhaps he followed a tradition that gave Belshazzar a three-year reign, so that this apocalypse would be dated in the last year of his reign. This may explain why, unlike ch. 7, this chapter predicts nothing about the Babylonian kingdom and begins its vision with the ram representing the kingdom of the Medes and the Persians.

The author no doubt left the reader to understand that Daniel had his vision in Babylon, where he was in all the preceding chapters of the book. After the vision Daniel resumes his business at the king's court (vs. 27a), which was in Belshazzar's capital (cf. 2:49; 5:29). He was transported to Susa in spirit. Yet at an early date the text was often misunderstood to mean that Daniel was actually in Susa when he had his vision. This is probably the reason why as early as the sixth century A.D. a legendary tomb of Daniel was located in Susa, which is still there today, in the modern village of Shūsh, just west of the ruins of the ancient city. For a seer being transported in spirit from one locality to another our author had as a model Ezekiel's being lifted up by the Spirit of God and brought from the river Chebar to Jerusalem (Ezek 8:3; 11:1). It is hard to say why Susa was chosen as the place of the vision. A possible reason may be the opening scene of the vision concerning the Medes and the Persians, whose winter capital was at Susa; and so Daniel sees the ram, representing the Medo-Persian empire, standing in front of the Ulai Gate at Susa.

While Daniel is trying to fathom the meaning of the vision he had received, an anonymous angel appears in human form before him (vs. 15). Daniel's natural reaction is to fall down in fright. The angel then tells him that the vision has an eschatological meaning (vs. 17): the history of the pagan kingdoms will come to an end when God intervenes to destroy the persecutor of the Jews who dares to desecrate God's Temple in Jerusalem (vss. 20–25). Since Daniel clearly understands the meaning of the vision, it leaves him so overwhelmed with amazement that it is some time before he can return to his regular service at the court of the Babylonian king (vs. 27b).

In keeping with the nature of apocalyptic writing, the account of the vision and its interpretation is presented as having been recorded at the time of Belshazzar; but at the command of the interpreting angel, it is kept a secret until centuries later (vs. 26b). It is presumably discovered and published—of course, by the man who actually wrote the account after Epiphanes desecrated the Temple.

The Ram (8:3–4,20)

The symbolism of the ram and the he-goat is so patent that the reader would have no difficulty in identifying the two-horned ram with the kingdom of the Medes and the Persians, and the one-horned he-goat with the kingdom of Alexander the Great, even if the interpreting angel had not explicitly made the identification (vss. 20–21).

It has been suggested that our author had astrological reasons for choosing a ram and a he-goat as his symbols, because Persia was thought to be under the zodiacal sign of Aries (the ram) and Syria (the part of the Greek empire with which our author was primarily concerned) under the sign of Capricorn (the horned goat). But even if these ideas were known to some ancient astrologers, it is doubtful whether our author knew and made use of them. In any case, his animal symbolism is not nearly as fantastic as that in ch. 7.

Whereas in ch. 2 and ch. 7 there is one symbol for the kingdom of the Medes and another for that of the Persians (2:39; 7:5–6), in ch. 8 there is a single symbol, the ram, for both these kingdoms (8:3–4,20). But this does not mean that the author of ch. 8 is ignorant of the "four kingdom" concept of the rest of the book. On the one hand, both ch. 6 and the Book of Esther treat the Medes and the Persians as kindred peoples in a coalition (Dan 6:9,13; Esther 1:3; 2:14,18; etc.); while on the other hand, ch. 8, in which each of the two large horns of the ram symbolizes a separate kingdom (cf. vs. 20), makes a distinction between the "longer and more recent" horn, Persia, and "the other," Media (vs. 3).

From Susa, Daniel sees the Medo-Persian ram "butting toward the west, the north, and the south" (8:4), that is, into Asia Minor and even Greece (the west), into the lands that lay to the west and south of the Caspian Sea (the north), and into Egypt as far as the first cataract of the Nile (the south). It is rather strange that no mention is made of the extension of the Persian empire to the east. The author of the Book of Esther (1:1) knew that it extended "from India to Ethiopia." The LXX has "to the east, the north, the west, and the south," the four cardinal points given counterclockwise. But Theod. agrees with the MT. Perhaps our author was not interested in the extreme eastern part of the Persian empire because there was no Jewish Diaspora there in his time. The victorious army of the Medo-Persian empire at the height of its power is well symbolized by the two-horned ram; "no beast could withstand it or be rescued from its power. It did as it pleased and became mighty" (8:4).

The He-goat (8:5–8,21–22)

The symbolism of the he-goat coming from the west and overwhelming the ram is so clear that Daniel would hardly have needed the words of the angel to assure him in 8:21 that "the he-goat represents the kingdoms of the Greeks, and the big horn on its forehead is the first kingdom," namely, that of Alexander the Great. The symbolic animals are well chosen; just as a male sheep cannot withstand an attack by a male goat, so the Persian empire was easily overcome by Alexander. For apocalyptic symbolism there is no need to look for any true correspondence in nature or art. While the figure of a one-horned animal can be found in the ancient art of the Near East, where originally it merely portrayed a side view of an animal with its two horns visibly merged as one, there is no such representation of a four-horned animal. For our author the one horn and the four horns are mere symbols for one kingdom and four kingdoms, respectively.

The speed and fierceness with which Alexander vanquished the last Persian king, Darius III Codomannus, is well described in the account of the attack of the angry he-goat on the helpless ram (cf. I Macc 1:1–4). The concept of the he-goat rushing across the land "without touching the ground" (8:5) may have been borrowed from the description of Cyrus' conquest of Babylonia in Isa 41:3: "He does not travel by foot on the road" (so rendered by J. L. McKenzie, *Second Isaiah,* AB 20 [Garden City, N.Y.: Doubleday, 1968], p. 26; but the Hebrew text is uncertain; cf. 1QIsa[a]).

Just as Alexander came to a tragic death soon after conquering the whole Persian empire, so it is said of the he-goat that "at the height of its power, its big horn broke off" (8:8). Although it is historically true that, at the death of Alexander, his empire was divided up among four of his generals—Cassander ruling over Macedonia and Greece; Lysimachus controlling Thrace; Antigonus holding Asia Minor, northern Syria, and the remaining eastern portion of the former Persian empire; while Ptolemy Soter became master of Egypt and southern Syria—our author may not have had this division primarily in mind, for the boundaries and rulers of these regions soon shifted. For him the four Greek kingdoms that took the place of Alexander's single one, as symbolized by the four large horns of the ram that grew up in place of its single one (vs. 22) are rather more generalized as occupying regions "toward the four winds of the heavens" —north, east, south, and west (cf. 11:4).

The Small Horn (8:9–12,23–25)

The name of Antiochus IV Epiphanes, the eighth Seleucid king of Syria, is not mentioned anywhere in this chapter, but there is not the slightest doubt that he is the one meant in the description of the "small horn," whom the angel identifies as a king "brazen-faced and skilled in trickery" (vss. 23–25).

The small horn is pictured as sprouting out of one of the he-goat's four "conspicuous" ones, i.e. it represents Epiphanes as a scion of the Seleucid dynasty, one of the four kingdoms that resulted from the breakup of Alexander's kingdom. In contrast to the four large horns, which symbolize the four Greek kingdoms, this individual king is presented at first as a small horn. But only in this regard is it small. Because of the ambition of the king it symbolizes it soon "grew mightily toward the south" (8:9) by the king's invasion of Egypt in 169 and 168 B.C., and by his attempted invasion of Parthia begun in 166 B.C. As mentioned in the COMMENT: DETAILED on *The Small Horn* in 7:8, all the passages in ch. 7 that concern Epiphanes as the "small horn" were probably inserted in that chapter by a glossator, apparently the author of ch. 9, who borrowed the term from ch. 8.

As the gloss correctly states, "the host of the heavens" are "the stars" (8:10), i.e. "the heavenly bodies, especially as objects of heathen worship and as the celestial rulers of the world" (G. F. Moore, "Daniel viii 9–14," *JBL* 15 [1896], 194). Because Epiphanes, whose name means "(God) made manifest," sought to have himself worshipped as a god, the Jews regarded him as disrespectful even to the pagan gods; cf. 11:36–39. Our author has made Epiphanes resemble the king of Babylon in Isa 14:13, who said, "I will scale the heavens; above the stars of El I will set up my throne. . . . I will be like the Most High." The "Prince of the host" (8:11) is the true God of the Jews, who rules over the heavenly bodies as his creatures; he is "the Prince of princes" (vs. 25) and "the God of gods" (2:47). Even against this God, Epiphanes exalted himself by abolishing the worship of Yahweh in the Temple of Jerusalem and by persecuting the pious Jews who refused to take part in pagan worship. The "stand" (Hebrew *mākôn*) of the daily sacrifice (Hebrew *tāmîd*) is the altar of sacrifice in the Temple, and on this altar Epiphanes set up a statue of Zeus Olympios, here called "an [appalling] offense" (vs. 13) and in 9:27; 11:31; 12:11 "an appalling abomination"; cf. I Macc 1:54; 6:7; II Macc 6:2.

The explanation that the angel gives of the small horn (vss. 23–25) is less specific in describing Epiphanes' persecution of the Jews. But it ends with an important point: ultimately the arrogant king "will be broken—but not by human hand" (8:25; cf. 2:34,45). This is the encouragement that the author wished to give his persecuted compatriots: the destruction of the persecutor would be the work of God himself.

Duration of the Persecution (8:13–14,16,26a,27b)

As shown in the COMMENT: GENERAL on this chapter, all of the passages in ch. 8 that are concerned with the duration of the religious persecution of the Jews by Epiphanes are later insertions, probably made by the author of ch. 9. Daniel, who "was seeking to understand the vision" he had seen (8:15), is told by the interpreting angel, "Understand, O man, that the vision refers to the time of the end" (8:17). The angel then proceeds to give Daniel a lucid explanation of the vision. Therefore, the author of the basic stratum of ch. 8 obviously wished to present Daniel as fully understanding the meaning of the vision. It would serve no purpose to have Daniel told to "keep the vision a secret" (8:26) if he himself did not understand it. On the contrary, the inserted passages, which are concerned not with a vision, but with a revelation about the duration of the persecution, end by saying that Daniel "did not understand it" (8:27).

Could there be clearer evidence to prove that the inserted passages were not written by the same man who wrote the basic apocalypse of ch. 8?

The estimated duration of the persecution that is given here as 1,150 days (see NOTE on vs. 14) is roughly the same as that given in 7:25; 9:27b; and 12:7 as three and a half years or about 1,260 days; see COMMENT: DETAILED on *The Small Horn* in ch. 7 and on 12:11–12.

End of the Time of Wrath (8:18–19)

It was shown in the COMMENT: GENERAL on this chapter that the passage in vss. 18–19 is a later insertion which was probably made by the author of chs. 10–12. The latter, who interpreted Hab 2:3b just as it is interpreted here, presents a rather detailed history, in pseudoprophetic form, of the events that transpired from the time of Cyrus the Great to that of Antiochus IV Epiphanes (11:1–45). He inserted 8:18–19 because he saw in 8:20–25 a pseudoprophecy of historical events similar to his much longer one in 11:1–45. In 8:19, the expression, "the last days of the time of wrath," refers to the period of Epiphanes' persecution of the Jews. The "wrath" is God's "rod of wrath," which in Isa 5:5,15,23–26 refers to Assyria, but is here applied to Epiphanes. The same application of Isaiah 5 is made in Dan 11:36.

IX. REVELATION OF THE SEVENTY WEEKS OF YEARS (9:1–27)

9 1 In the first year of Darius, son of Ahasuerus, of the race of the
Medes, who [a]became king[a] over the realm of the Chaldeans 2 [in the
first year of his reign], I, Daniel, was considering in the Scriptures
the number of the years that, according to the word of Yahweh to the
prophet Jeremiah, were to be completed for Jerusalem's devastation,
namely, seventy years. 3 Then I turned to the Lord God, seeking an
answer from him by earnest prayer with fasting, sackcloth, and ashes.
/ 4 I prayed to Yahweh, my God, and confessed, "Ah, Lord, great
and awesome God, you who loyally keep your covenant with those
who love you and keep your commandments, 5 we have sinned, acted
wickedly, and done evil; we have rebelled and turned aside from your
commandments and your laws. 6 We have not listened to your servants the prophets, who spoke in your name to our kings, our princes,
our fathers, and all the people of the land. 7 Justice is on your side,
Lord; but as for us, even to this day open shame has befallen us—the
men of Judah, the residents of Jerusalem, and all Israel, near and far,
in all the lands to which you have driven them because of the treachery they have committed against you. 8 Yes, Yahweh, open shame
has befallen us, our kings, our princes, and our fathers, because we
have sinned against you. 9 It is for the Lord, our God, to have compassion and forgiveness, since we have rebelled against him. 10 We have
not listened to Yahweh, our God, telling us to live by his teachings
that he gave us through his servants the prophets. 11 All Israel, not lis-
tening to your voice, transgressed your law and went astray; so the
sworn malediction written in the Torah of God's servant Moses has
been poured out upon us, because we sinned against you[b]. 12 God
carried out the threat that he proclaimed against us and against the
rulers who governed us, by bringing upon us a calamity so great, that
the like of what happened in Jerusalem never happened anywhere

[a–a] Read *himlīk* for *homlak;* see NOTE.
[b] Read, with many MSS, *lāk* for *lô*.

else under the heavens. 13 As it is written in the Torah of Moses, this
calamity came upon us in full measure. Since we did not appease
Yahweh, our God, by turning back from our wickedness and recog-
nizing his resoluteness, 14 Yahweh kept watch over the calamity until
he brought it upon us. Yahweh, our God, is just in all that he has
done, for we did not heed his voice.

15 "Therefore, O Lord, our God, you who brought your people
out of the land of Egypt with a strong hand and thus gained renown
for yourself even to this day, we acknowledge the wickedness of our
sins. 16 In keeping with all your vindicating deeds, O Lord, let your
fierce anger be turned away from Jerusalem, your city, your holy
mountain; for on account of our sins and the crimes of our fathers,
Jerusalem and your people have become the reproach of all those
around us. 17 Listen, then, O God, to the earnest prayer of your servant; and [c]for your own sake[c], Lord, deal kindly with your desolate
sanctuary. 18 Incline your ear, O my God, and listen; open your eyes
and see our devastated city, which bears your name; for not on our
own merits but on your great compassion do we rely in presenting our
petition before you. 19 O Lord, hear; O Lord, pardon; O Lord, be at-
tentive and act! For your own sake, O my God, do not delay; for your
city and your people bear your name." 20 While I was occupied with
these prayers, confessing my sins and the sins of my people Israel, and
presenting my petition before Yahweh, my God on behalf of the holy
mountain of my God— /

21 While I was occupied in prayer, the manlike Gabriel whom I had
seen before in vision drew near me, [d]flying like a bird[d], at the time of
the evening sacrifice. 22 He came[e] and spoke with me, saying, "Daniel,
I have now come forth to give you clear understanding. 23 As soon as
you began your petition, its answer was given; so I have come to tell
it [f]to you[f], because you are [g]greatly beloved[g]. Mark, then, the answer
and attend to the revelation.

24 "Seventy weeks are decreed for your people and your holy city,
until crime is stopped, sins brought to full measure, guilt expiated,
everlasting justice introduced, the prophetic vision confirmed, and the
Holy of Holies anointed.

[c–c] Read, with Theod. and vs. 19, *lᵉmaʿankā ʾădōnāy* for *lᵉmaʿan ʾădōnāy*.
[d–d] Perhaps read *mᵉʿôpēp kᵉʿôp wᵉnōgēaʿ* for *mūʿap bîʿāp nōgēaʿ*; see NOTE.
[e] Read, with LXX and Syr., *wayyābōʾ* for *wayyāben*.
[f–f] Insert, with a few MSS and the ancient versions, *lᵉkā* after *lᵉhāgîd*.
[g–g] Insert, with Theod., Vulg., and Syr., *ʾîš* before *ḥămûdôt;* cf. 10:11 and see NOTE.

25 "Know, then, and understand this: from the utterance of the
word regarding the rebuilding of Jerusalem to the coming of an
anointed leader there will be seven weeks. Then during sixty-two
weeks it will be rebuilt, with its streets and moat, but in a time of distress. 26 After the sixty-two weeks an anointed one will be cut down,
when [h]the city[h] is no longer his; and the soldiers of a prince will ruin
the sanctuary. [i]Then the end will come[i] like a flood, and until [j]the end[j]
there will be war[k]. 27 For one week he will make a strong alliance
with many; for half a week he will abolish sacrifice and oblation; and
upon [l]their place[l] will be an appalling abomination[m], until the decreed
ruin is poured out upon the appaller.

[h–h] Read, with a few MSS, *hā'îr* for *w^ehā'îr* and join to the preceding *w^e'ên lô.*
[i–i] Read *ûbā' haqqēṣ* for *habbā' w^eqiṣṣô;* cf. LXX.
[j–j] Read *haqqēṣ* for *qēṣ.*
[k] Omit *neḥĕreṣet šōmēmôt;* dittography from end of vs. 27.
[l–l] Read *kannām* for *k^enap;* cf. 8:11.
[m] Read *šiqqûṣ* as in 11:31; 12:11; partial dittography.

Notes

9:1. *In the first year of Darius.* Literally, "in the year of one to Darius"; for this construction, cf. 8:1; 10:1. According to the chronology of the Book of Daniel this would be 538 B.C.; cf. 5:30 – 6:1.

Ahasuerus. The Hebrew *'ăḥašwērôš* represents the Persian name *khashayârshâ,* which is given in Greek as *xerxēs.* Historically, King Xerxes of Persia was the son, not the father of King Darius I of Persia. Since "Darius the Mede" of the Book of Daniel is not a historical personage (see Introduction, Part VI), the author of ch. 9 invented a father called Xerxes for him, perhaps on the basis of Ezra 4:5–6. Or perhaps MT's *'ăḥašwērôš* stands in some way for Cyaxares (king of the Medes ca. 653–584 B.C.), the father of Astyages, who was the father-in-law of Cyrus the Great of Persia (cf. C. C. Torrey, *JAOS* 66 [1946], 7–8).

became king. The MT has "was made king"; but this would be the only occurrence of the hoph'al, *homlak,* of the root *mlk* in Biblical Hebrew. Most likely, *hmlk,* was originally intended to be read as a hiph'il, *himlīk,* which is either an Aramaism or, more likely, a merely mechanical reproduction by a translator of an original Aramaic *hamlik;* cf. Syriac *'amlek,* "he became king, he reigned."

Chaldeans. See NOTE on 1:4.

2. *in the first year of his reign.* This tautological phrase is not in Theod.; it is

probably a gloss to explain, in shorter form, the preceding cumbersome expression.

I . . . was considering. The Hebrew word *bînôtî* is a hybrid form; originally the root *byn* was used almost always in the hiph'il, *hēbîn,* in the meaning of "to understand" as well as "to give understanding"; since the hiph'il imperfect, *yābîn,* has the appearance of a qal imperfect, a secondary qal perfect was formed from it: *bîn,* "he understood" (10:1); *bînôtî,* "I understood" (9:2). However, such a meaning here is contrary to the whole tenor of the chapter; Daniel needed a revelation precisely because he did *not* understand the sense of Jeremiah's prophecy. Violence is done to the meaning of the verb by translating it as "I tried to understand" (so *NAB*). Nor is it much of an improvement to render it as "I perceived" (so *RSV*). The underlying Aramaic verb may have been *'eśtakkal,* which means both "I understood" and "I considered"; the translator apparently took it wrongly in the former, rather than in the latter sense. See NOTE on 8:5.

the Scriptures. Literally, "the books." But the term is used here in the technical sense of the canonized Sacred Scriptures—the only occurrence in the Hebrew Bible of the use of the term in this sense; cf., however, I Macc 12:9: *ta biblia ta hagia.*

the number of the years . . . seventy years. Literally, "the number of years which (*'ăšer*) was the word of Yahweh to Jeremiah the prophet, to complete (*l^emall'ôt*) for the ruins of Jerusalem: seventy years." The idiom, *'ăšer l-* plus infinitive, is an Aramaism.

3. *Then I turned to the Lord God.* Literally, "Then I turned my face to the Lord God," an idiom based perhaps on the custom of facing Jerusalem's temple in prayer; cf. 6:11.

seeking an answer from him by earnest prayer. In Hebrew, "to seek prayer and supplications." But the verb, *biqqēš,* is used here in the older, technical meaning of "to seek an oracle"; cf. II Sam 21:2; Hosea 5:15. The expression, "prayer and supplication" is a hendiadys for "supplicating prayer"; so also in vs. 17. Cf. *bā'ē' ûmitḥannan* in 6:12—the Aramaic behind the Hebrew here? The adverbial use of these nouns, with no preceding preposition, is an Aramaism, probably caused by a merely mechanical rendering of the original Aramaic; for this idiom in Aramaic, cf. 1QapGen, col. xx, line 8: *dy pm ḥd tlthwn mmllyn,* "for with one accord [literally, mouth] the three of them spoke."

4. *confessed.* The Hebrew verbal root *ydy* is used in the hiph'il (*hôdāh*) in the sense of "to acknowledge God's goodness in grateful praise," and in the hithpa'el (*hitwaddāh*) in the sense of "to acknowledge one's own sins," especially in late Biblical Hebrew (here and in Ezra 10:1; Lev 5:5, 16:21; 26:40; Num 5:7).

Ah. Literally, "Ah, please!" Hebrew *'ānnā'* is a compound of the interjection *'āh* (the *h* with mappiq), "Ah!", and the enclitic particle of entreaty or exhortation, *-nā'*, "please." Here *'ānnā'* anticipates the request in vs. 16: *yāšob-nā' 'app^ekā,* "(please) let your anger be turned away."

who loyally keep your covenant. A hendiadys in Hebrew, literally, "keeper of the covenant (*b^erît*) and loyalty (*ḥesed*)."

who love you and keep your commandments. Literally, "who love him and keep his commandments." The Hebrew idiomatic shift from a second person in a main clause to a third person in a subordinate clause (cf. Ezek 39:3) is contrary to English usage.

5. *and turned aside.* In Hebrew, this is an infinitive absolute, for variety's sake, after four coordinate perfect tenses.

6. *fathers.* Here probably not in the sense of "forefathers" (as in vs. 16), but in the sense of the heads of the various clans (*bêt 'ābôt*), hence, "elders"; so also in vs. 8. We have here a list, in the order of descending dignity, of the rulers of the people.

7. *Justice is on your side, Lord; but as for us, even to this day open shame has befallen us—the men of Judah.* In English, one cannot well imitate the strong contrast of the Hebrew, which is literally: "To you, Lord, (belongs) the justice; but to us (belongs) the open shame as of this very day—to the men of Judah." The English expression, "open shame," is an attempt to render the sense of Hebrew *bōšet happānîm,* literally, "the shame of face," which designates the sense of shame that betrays itself in one's countenance and thus brings on the reproach of others; so also in vs. 8. In modern English, "shamefacedness" ordinarily means "modesty, bashfulness," which obviously would not fit the context here.

11. *the sworn malediction.* Literally, "the malediction and the oath" (hend.).

12. *the rulers who governed us.* Literally, "the judges who judged us." But the term "judges" is used here in the sense of "magistrates" in general, thus including the various classes of rulers mentioned in vss. 6,8; cf. the parallelism of "kings" with "judges" in Ps 2:10 (see NOTE of M. Dahood on the passage in his *Psalms I,* p. 13; and E. A. Speiser's NOTE on Gen 18:25 in his *Genesis,* p. 134).

13. *As it is written in the Torah of Moses.* This is the earliest occurrence of the phrase introducing a citation from Scripture that later became common in the New Testament and the Talmud, even though here it is not followed by a direct citation of a biblical passage. This may explain the strange use of the following *'ēt,* something like English "namely," that begins the next sentence: *'ēt kol-hārā'āh hazzō't bā'āh 'ālênû,* literally, "namely, all the evil that has come upon us."

his resoluteness. [MT has "your resoluteness."] God's *'ĕmet,* "fidelity" to his word, whether (as ordinarily) to his promises of good, or (as here) to his threats of evil.

14. *Yahweh kept watch over the calamity.* The sense of this phrase, taken from Jer 1:12; 31:28; 44:27, is that God kept his eye on the threatened calamity; he did not forget it.

15. *we acknowledge the wickedness of our sins.* Literally, "we have sinned and been wicked" (hend.). In the context, the expression is equivalent to a confession of sin; cf. II Sam 12:13, where David's words to Nathan, "I have sinned," is equivalent to "I confess that I have sinned."

16. *your vindicating deeds.* God's *ṣᵉdāqôt,* "acts of vindication," whereby he shows that he has been right; cf. Judg 5:11; II Sam 12:7; Micah 6:5; Ps 103:6.

fierce anger. Literally, "anger and wrath" (hend.).

17. *deal kindly with your desolate sanctuary.* Literally, "make your face shine on your desolate sanctuary," i.e. with the light of divine favor; cf. Num 6:25; Pss 4:7; 31:17; etc.

18. *our devastated city, which bears your name.* Literally, "our desolation and the city [hend.], upon which your name is called." Jerusalem is called "Yahweh's city" because he has proprietary rights to it; cf. II Sam 12:28: "lest I take the city and my name be called upon it," i.e. "lest it be said that I captured the city and it is mine." So also in Dan 9:19.

merits. Literally, "righteous acts, good deeds."

presenting our petition before you. Literally, "causing our petition to fall before you"; so also in vs. 20. The expression reflects the humble prostration of the petitioner.

20. *I was occupied with these prayers.* Literally, "I was speaking and praying" (*'ănî m^{e}dabbēr ûmitpallēl*). Even in private prayer, the ancients ordinarily prayed aloud; cf. the opposite in I Sam 1:13, where Eli mistook Hannah for a drunken woman because, though her lips moved in prayer, her voice was not heard. On the reason why the sentence is not finished, see COMMENT: GENERAL.

21. *I was occupied in prayer* (*'ănî m^{e}dabbēr batt^{e}pillāh* or *bit^{e}pillāh* [so the variant in the MSS]). Note how this expression differs from the similar one in vs. 20—evidence of two different writers.

the manlike Gabriel. Literally, "the man Gabriel." In 8:16 (a passage from the same author as the one of ch. 9), Gabriel is identified with the anonymous (from a different author!) "manlike figure" (*k^{e}mar'ēh gāber*) who spoke to Daniel (8:15).

before. Literally, "in the beginning"; see NOTE on 8:1.

flying like a bird. MT's *mû'ap bî'āp* can only mean, "wearied with weariness," which is nonsense here. The ancient versions rightly guessed that the Hebrew words were somehow connected with the verb *'ûp,* "to fly." Perhaps the original Hebrew, echoing the *y^{e}'ôpēp* of Isa 6:2 ("it was soaring," said of each seraph), had *m^{e}'ôpēp* here. The participial construction was probably in imitation of the underlying Aramaic. Although the noun, *'ôp,* in classical Hebrew is a collective, "fowl, birds," Mishnaic Hebrew uses it also as a singular, "bird"; cf. *parn^{e}sātô m^{e}'ôpepet lô k^{e}'ôp,* "his sustenance came flying to him like a bird" (Berakoth 63[a]).

at the time of the evening sacrifice. In the late afternoon, the chief time of prayer in Judaism.

22. *come forth.* From heaven.

to give you clear understanding. Literally, "to make you wise (with) understanding." The absolute use of *bînāh,* "understanding," can be construed as an accusative of limitation: "to make you wise as far as understanding (of the problem) is concerned."

23. *its answer was given.* Literally, "a word went forth." In the context, the "word" is the oracle of revelation in answer to Daniel's prayer for enlightenment about the seventy years of Jeremiah's prophecy.

greatly beloved. Literally, "a man of lovableness."

Mark. Or, "Consider." On this meaning of Hebrew *bîn,* see NOTES on 8:5; 9:2.

the revelation. On Hebrew *mar'eh* in the meaning of "revelation," see NOTE on 8:16.

24. *Seventy weeks.* Since Daniel was trying to understand Jeremiah's prophecy about the seventy "years" of Jerusalem's devastation (vs. 2), the meaning of Gabriel's "seventy weeks" is clearly "seventy weeks of years," that is, 490 years. So also in the following verses, a "week" always means "a week of years." The plural *šᵉbû'îm* of *šābûa'*, "week," is peculiar to the Book of Daniel (chs. 9 and 10); it is no doubt caused by a merely mechanical rendering in Hebrew of the Aramaic plural *šabbû'în;* elsewhere in the Bible the Hebrew plural is *šᵉbû'ôt.*

decreed. The root *ḥtk,* primarily meaning "to cut" and then "to decide, to decree," occurs only here in the Hebrew Bible; but it is common in Jewish Aramaic and Mishnaic Hebrew.

until crime is stopped. Literally, "to stop crime"; in all the following phrases the Hebrew has similar active infinitive constructions.

everlasting justice introduced. Literally, "to bring in justice of long ages (*ṣedeq 'ôlāmîm*)"; cf. Qumran's "Apostrophe to Zion" (DJD 4, p. 86, line 13): *ṣdq 'wlmym tśygy,* "May you attain to everlasting justice."

prophetic vision. Hebrew *ḥāzôn wᵉnābî',* literally, "vision and prophet" (hend.). Here "vision" (*ḥāzôn*) has the meaning of "events seen in vision," as in 8:13; cf. Qumran's "Apostrophe to Zion" (DJD 4, p. 87, lines 13–14): *qḥy ḥzwn dwber 'lyk, wḥlmwt nby'ym ttb'k,* "Accept the vision speaking about you, and the dreams of prophets that look for you."

the Holy of Holies anointed. The innermost sanctuary of the Temple reconsecrated after its defilement by Epiphanes. On the anointing with sacred oil in the consecration of various parts of the Mosaic tabernacle, cf. Exod 29:36; 30:26–28; 40:9–11. Instead of "the Holy of Holies," the Hebrew term, *qōdeš haqqŏdāšîm,* can be rendered as "the most holy." But this term is never used (not even in the sometimes alleged passage of I Chron 23:13) of persons; hence the present passage cannot be understood of the anointing of the Messiah, except in an accommodated sense.

25. *the rebuilding of Jerusalem.* Or, in the more literal sense, "the restoring and building of Jerusalem."

the coming of. These words are supplied in English for the sake of clarity; so also in *RSV.*

an anointed leader. Literally, "an anointed one, a leader" (hend.). For the identification of this man, see COMMENT: DETAILED; so also for the identification of the individual persons and events referred to in vss. 26–27.

streets. Literally, the "plaza" (Hebrew *rᵉḥôb*) or wide open space in a city just inside the city gate, used as a market place, forum, place for judicial cases, etc.; here understood for the "streets" of the city in general, as *pars pro toto.*

moat. Literally, the "cut" (Hebrew *ḥārûṣ*), here in the sense of a trench cut into the rock outside the city walls in order to increase the exterior height of the walls. This is the only occurrence in Biblical Hebrew of this word in such a sense; probably an Aramaism (cf. the Aramaic Zakir Inscription from Apis, A

10, where *ḥrṣ* clearly has this meaning; cf. also Akkadian *ḫarīṣu,* which is often used in this sense [*CAD* 6, p. 103b]). By referring to the city's "streets and moat," our author means to say "everything inside and outside the city walls."

26–27. The Hebrew text of these verses is uncertain and obscure in several places; the English translation offered here is merely an attempt to make some plausible sense out of it.

[26. *soldiers.* Hebrew *'am,* which normally means "people, citizens." But here the obvious meaning is "troops, soldiers," as in Judg 5:2 and II Sam 10:13.]

27. *decreed ruin.* Literally, "ruin and decision" (hend.); the Hebrew expression used here is borrowed from Isa 10:23; 28:22.

COMMENT: GENERAL

Whereas the first two (ch. 7 and ch. 8) of the four apocalypses in the second half of the Book of Daniel are symbolic visions in the strict sense, that is, they are real visions in which the appearances of the four monstrous beasts (ch. 7) and the antics of the ram and the he-goat (ch. 8) form the essential elements, with a heavenly being playing merely the role of an *angelus interpres,* the last two "apocalypses" are visions only insofar as a heavenly being appears to Daniel, and this celestial messenger plays a different role, that of an *angelus revelator.*

The primary purpose of the author of ch. 9 is to assure his Jewish compatriots that the religious persecution they are suffering at the hands of Antiochus IV Epiphanes will very soon be brought to an end by their God, who, as the master of history, had long before set the date on which the persecution would end. In order to instill confidence in this prediction, the author offers a novel interpretation of Jeremiah's prophecy on the length of Jerusalem's affliction: Jeremiah's "seventy years" mean seventy weeks of years, i.e. 490 years, and by summarizing history in a rather free manner, the author shows that the end of these 490 years is now at hand. On the details of this *pesher,* "interpretation," of the author, see COMMENT: DETAILED on vss. 1–3,21–27.

If this apocalypse had been left in its original form, it would have been the shortest one in the Book of Daniel. But sometime after its composition, a long Hebrew prayer, by some other writer, was inserted into it, so that ch. 9 was thus brought to approximately the same length as the preceding chapters.

That this prayer (vss. 4–20) is a later insertion into the basic stratum of ch. 9 is clear on several counts. First of all, according to the basic stratum Daniel prays for enlightenment on the meaning of Jeremiah's prophecy (vss. 2–3), and it is in answer to such a prayer that Gabriel explains to Daniel the meaning of the prophecy (vss. 21–27). But the prayer given in vss. 4–20 is of an entirely different nature; it is a prayer of repentance, said in the name of the whole Jewish community, begging for God's forgiveness, so that Jerusalem and its destroyed Temple may be restored.

Moreover, on linguistic grounds the prayer of vss. 4–20 is written in perfectly good Hebrew and does not show the slightest signs (contrary to the rest of the Hebrew in the book) of having been translated from Aramaic. Actually, it is largely composed of bits and pieces borrowed from older passages found in the Hebrew Scriptures. On the contrary, the basic stratum of ch. 9 is written in such Aramaizing Hebrew that there is good reason to believe that, like the apocalypses of ch. 8 and chs. 10–12, it is a Hebrew translation from an Aramaic original.

Finally, whoever inserted the prayer saw fit to add his own introduction (vs. 4a) and conclusion (vs. 20) to it. His introduction is a rather harmless repetition of vs. 3; but his conclusion is not merely an unnecessary duplication of vs. 21; it is such an obvious anacoluthon that the reader cannot fail to recognize the prayer as a later insertion. For the details of this prayer, see COMMENT: DETAILED on vss. 4–20. [B. W. Jones, "The Prayer in Daniel IX," *VT* 18 (1968), 488–493, argues for the authenticity of vss. 4–20 and for the essential unity of the whole chapter. He attempts to show that the unanswered prayer serves as a prop for Gabriel, and that the calamity which had been decreed will come to an end at the appointed time regardless of any prayer or of certain ideas regarding retribution. Cf. also M. Gilbert, "La prière de Daniel, Dn 9,4–19," *RTL* 3 (1972), 284–310, for an excellent study of the structure and background of this prayer.]

COMMENT: DETAILED

Daniel's Puzzlement over Jeremiah's Prophecy (9:1–3)

In two passages of the Book of Jeremiah (Jer 25:11–12; 29:10) the prophet speaks of "seventy years" as the time allotted by God for Babylon's dominion over the various nations of the ancient Near East. According to the translation of John Bright (*Jeremiah,* AB 21, pp. 157 and 205), these passages read: "The whole land shall be an awesome waste, and these nations shall serve the king of Babylon for seventy years. Then, when the seventy years have passed, I will punish [the king of Babylon and] that nation [—Yahweh's word—for their iniquity—that is, the land of the Chaldeans] and will make it a desolation forever" (Jer 25:11–12).

"For this is what Yahweh has said: Only when Babylon's seventy years have been completed will I intervene in your behalf, and fulfill my promise to you to bring you back to this place" (Jer 29:10). The first of these two passages occurs in a prose speech of the prophet dated in the fourth year of the reign of King Jehoiakim of Judah, which is identified with the first year of the reign of Babylon's King Nebuchadrezzar (the older and more correct form of the name that later appears as Nebuchadnezzar), i.e. in the year 605 B.C. It is to be noted that nothing is said here about Jerusalem's destruction or its restoration, although such an implication may be read into the passage. The second passage (Jer 29:10) occurs in a letter written by the prophet in the reign of King Zedekiah of Judah (cf. 28:1), i.e. in the year 594 B.C., to the Jews who had been taken as exiles to Babylonia in 597 B.C. This passage states explicitly that "only when Babylon's seventy years [as previously predicted by the prophet] have been completed" will Yahweh bring back those exiles to Judah. Since the false prophets had been giving the exiles vain hopes of an early return, the "seventy years" was no doubt intended by Jeremiah as meaning a relatively long time, the maximum length of man's life on earth except for a few extremely old men (cf. Ps 90:10). But the number "seventy years" in a genuine prophecy (not a *prophetia post eventum!*) intrigued later biblical writers. In Zech 1:12 it is apparently understood as referring to the period between the destruction of the temple in 587 B.C. and its reconstruction in 520–515 B.C. In II Chron 36:20–23 the prophecy is directly referred to ("to fulfill the word of Yahweh through Jeremiah") as the period between the destruction of Jerusalem in 587 B.C. and Cyrus' edict of 538 B.C. allowing the first Jewish exiles to return to Jerusalem—an interval of much less than seventy years. Actually, if reckoned from the fall of Nineveh in 612 B.C. to the fall of Babylon in 539 B.C., a period of seventy-three years, or if reckoned from the accession year of Nebuchadnezzar (605 B.C.) to the fall of Babylon, a period of sixty-six years, Jeremiah's words about "Babylon's seventy years" of supreme dominion proved to be remarkably close to accuracy.

The author of Daniel 9, however, was not satisfied with any of these explanations for the "seventy years" of Jeremiah's prophecy; he sought the fulfillment of the prophecy in the reconsecration of Jerusalem's Temple after Epiphanes' desecration of it. By means of a free interpretation of Scripture, now well known from the *pesharim* (biblical "interpretations") among the documents of the Qumran sect, written not long after the final compilation of the Book of Daniel, our author took the "seventy years" to mean "seventy weeks of years" or 490 years. Although this is not explicitly stated anywhere in ch. 9, it is clearly implied in the historical summary of the period given to Daniel by his *angelus interpres*. For the shift from "seventy years" to "seventy weeks" of years, see below.

But before Daniel receives this revelation, he first has recourse to prayer and fasting and other forms of bodily penance (vs. 3). In ancient times, fasting was regarded as a proper preparation for receiving a revelation; cf. Exod 34:28. The wearing of rough sackcloth directly next to the skin (cf. II Kings 6:30), over which coarse dirt was first thrown, was also an ancient form of bodily penance often mentioned in the Bible; e.g. Isa 58:5; I Chron 21:16; Neh 9:1; Esther 4:3–4; Matt 11:21; etc.

The Prayer (9:4–20)

The original text of ch. 9 merely said that Daniel prayed, but it did not quote the words of his prayer. This suggested to some later editor the possibility of inserting the words of a prayer here. The inserted prayer was not an *ad hoc* composition; as pointed out in the COMMENT: GENERAL on ch. 9 (see above), the nature and content of the inserted prayer are not at all suited to Daniel's special purpose of asking for enlightenment on the meaning of Jeremiah's prophecy of the "seventy years." Actually, the prayer is much older than the rest of ch. 9; the one who inserted it here found it already made and thought it served his purpose. It is of the liturgical type used since the Deuteronomic age, and may be grouped with those found in I Kings 8:15–53; Jer 32:17–25; I Chron 17:16–27; 29:10–19; II Chron 20:6–12; and especially Ezra 9:6–15; Neh 1:5–11; 9:6–37. Like the prayers in Ezra and Nehemiah, the prayer in Dan 9:4–19 is a mosaic composed of phrases taken either literally or with some freedom from older passages of the Scriptures. This accounts for the seemingly unnecessary repetitions, the strange changes between "I" and "we," and the disconcerting (at least in English) shifts between "you" and "he" in regard to God. For some of the borrowings in this prayer, CF. vs. 4b with Neh 1:5 (based ultimately on Deut 7:9,21); CF. vs. 6 with Jer 7:25; 25:4; 26:5; 29:19; 35:15; 44:4; CF. vs. 7 with Ezra 9:7; Jer 4:4; I Kings 8:26; Lev 26:40; CF. vs. 10 with Neh 9:17; Deut 5:30–31; CF. vs. 11 with Jer 7:20; Deut 29:20 (with reference to Lev 26:14–39; Deut 28:15–68); CF. vs. 12 with Neh 9:8; Jer 35:17; Deut 2:5; CF. vs. 14 with Jer 44:27; Ezra 9:15; CF. vs. 15 with Deut 6:21; Jer 32:20; CF. vs. 16 with Num 25:4; Isa 12:1; Neh 9:2; CF. vs. 17 with I Kings 8:28; Neh 1:6,11; CF. vs. 18 with I Kings 19:16; CF. vs. 19 with I Kings 8:30, 34,36,39.

The closest parallel to the prayer in Dan 9:4–19 is the prayer found in Bar 1:15 – 2:19, which contains many of the phrases that are used in Daniel 9. But the order of the phrases is often different, so that it seems that both prayers come from a common source, probably a synagogal prayer, used in various forms, in the last pre-Christian centuries. Thus, Bar 1:15 – 2:19 would not be a direct borrowing from Dan 9:4–19. [Cf.

C. A. Moore, "Toward the Dating of the Book of Baruch," *CBQ* 36 (1974), 312–320.]

Coming of Gabriel to Daniel (9:21–23)

If the textual emendation on which the translation, "flying like a bird," is correct (vs. 21), this is the earliest reference in the Bible to the now common idea of picturing angels as provided with a pair of wings. Neither the seraphim of Isa 6:2, each of which had three pairs of wings, nor the cherubim on the Mosaic ark of the covenant (Exod 25:18–20) or in Solomon's temple (I Kings 6:23–28), nor the four-winged "living creatures" of Ezekiel's vision (Ezek 1:5–6) were "angels" (Hebrew *mal'ākîm,* "messengers") in the strict sense. The representation of Gabriel with birdlike wings may have been derived partly from the image of the winged cherubim and partly from the ancient portrayal, both in Egypt and in Mesopotamia, of winged genii; cf. the two women "with wings like the wings of a stork" in Zech 5:9. Later Jewish literature (cf. Enoch 61:1) and Christian art, perhaps as a result of Dan 9:21, represented angels as men with feathered wings on their shoulders.

At the very beginning of Daniel's prayer (Hebrew *bitᵉḥillat taḥănûnèkā*), the answer to his prayer was given (Hebrew *yāṣā' dābār,* the "word went forth") by God in the form of an oracle, heard by the angels assisting at the divine throne; and the angel Gabriel was commissioned by God to convey this oracle to Daniel. The author of ch. 9 called this angel "Gabriel" (Hebrew *gabrî'ēl,* "man of God") probably because in his gloss (8:16) on 8:15 he identified him with the unnamed celestial being in the form of a man (Hebrew *kᵉmar'ēh gāber*) of 8:15; see NOTE on 8:15. The name was resumed in later Jewish (e.g. Enoch 9:1–3; 10:9–10) and Christian (Luke 1:19,26) literature. But only in later Christian tradition is Gabriel ranked (like Michael in Jude 9) as an "archangel."

Seventy Weeks of Years (9:24)

One need not take the account of Gabriel's visit to Daniel in the literal sense, as if the interpretation that turned the seventy years of Jeremiah's prophecy into 490 years were a genuinely supernatural revelation. The interpretation could have come solely from the author of ch. 9 himself, albeit convinced that he was led to such an interpretation by divine inspiration. The presentation of a revelation by an angel was a literary device used by apocalyptic writers. [Cf. Introduction, Part X.]

The reader might have expected the angel to explain to Daniel why the latter's hope of seeing Jeremiah's prophecy (as understood by Daniel to mean the complete restoration of Judah's independence as it had been before the Babylonian destruction of Jerusalem) had not been realized in the predicted seventy years. Instead, the reader is told that the expression "seventy years" really means only seventy weeks. But he is soon assured by the quasi-historical, quasi-prophetical explanation of the events of the "seventy weeks" that this really means "seventy weeks of years."

The author of Daniel 9 had good biblical support for his bold interpretation of the "seventy years" meaning "seventy weeks" of years. On the one hand, the author of II Chron 37:21 saw in the seventy years of Jerusalem's desolation a punishment for Judah's "neglect of its sabbaths"; and since the sabbath is the seventh day of each week, one could multiply the seventy years by seven. On the other hand, in Lev 26:18 God threatens to punish his disobedient people, as long as they remain unrepentant, "sevenfold" for their sins—therefore, seven times the seventy years foretold by Jeremiah. Besides, in Lev 26:33–35, the threat is made that, because God's people failed to keep his command concerning the observance of the sabbath years, they will be scattered among the nations, and the land will remain desolate to make up the sabbath years its people failed to observe; and here again, the conclusion could be drawn that the "seventy years" foretold by Jeremiah meant seven periods of sabbath years, or seven times seventy. The author of Daniel 9 is thus using one of the *pesher* methods commonly used by the later Qumran sect and by the rabbinical writers of putting a new interpretation on a Scripture passage by combining it with some other passages of the Scriptures.

The Events of the Seventy Weeks of Years (9:25–27)

One may rightly doubt if the author of Daniel 9 had an accurate knowledge of the chronology of the period. Therefore, his division of the various periods of the early part of his 490-year period cannot be taken too seriously. He is really only concerned with the last "week" of years, the last seven years of the 490-year period. He balances this by making the first section of the 490-year period "seven weeks" or forty-nine years. The long middle section of "sixty-two weeks" of years, or 434 years, is an artificial number, created for the purpose of bringing all three periods to a total of "seventy weeks" of years. In fact, the whole period, which he counts as beginning with "the utterance of the word regarding the rebuilding of Jerusalem," i.e. as beginning with 594 B.C. (see above), and ending with the death of Epiphanes in 164 B.C., amounts to only 430 (not 490) years. Even if the *terminus a quo* for his reckoning would be taken as 605 B.C. according to Jer 25:11–12 (which really does not speak of the rebuilding of Jerusalem at all), the whole period would be only 441 years.

The first section, the first "seven weeks" of years (forty-nine years), is said to last from the utterance of Jeremiah's prophecy to "the coming of an anointed leader" (9:25). This first part of the 490-year period almost certainly refers to the time that ended with the return of the first exiles from Babylonia to Jerusalem in 538 B.C. If the beginning of this period is taken, as it normally would be, as the year 594 B.C., when Jeremiah uttered the prophecy regarding the restoration of Jerusalem, the interval would be fifty-six years; if reckoned from the destruction of Jerusalem in 587 B.C., the interval would be fifty-one years—either figure sufficiently close to the quasi-artificial figure of "seven weeks" of years (Dan 9:25).

Several exegetes have identified the "anointed leader" with Cyrus the Great, who allowed the first Jewish exiles to return to Jerusalem in 538 B.C. Cyrus is indeed called Yahweh's "anointed one" in Isa 45:1; but the author of Daniel 9 is less interested in the political history of Judah than in the history of its religious cult. For the same reason, Zerubbabel, a scion of the Davidic dynasty, who is given messianic titles in Hag 2:21–23, Zech 4:6–10, and Sir 49:11, is a less likely candidate for the "anointed leader" than is his contemporary, Joshua (or, in the Aramaic form, Jeshua) ben Jozadak (or, in the longer form, Jehozadak), who was the first high priest of the restored temple of Jerusalem. Although in the preexilic period the Hebrew term *māšîaḥ,* the "anointed one," was used almost exclusively of kings, at least in the postexilic period the high priest received a solemn anointing with sacred oil on entering his office (cf. Lev 4:3,5,16; 6:15). It seems much more likely, therefore, that the "anointed leader" of 9:25 refers to the high priest, Joshua ben Jozadak. As for the term "leader" (Hebrew *nāgîd*) being applied to a high priest at this time, cf. 11:22, where the high priest Onias III (see below) is called "the prince [Hebrew *nāgîd*] of the covenant." According to Ezra 2:2,36; Neh 7:7,39, Joshua ben Jozadak returned to Jerusalem with the first exiles in 537 B.C. (even though in these passages Zerubbabel is probably confused with his predecessor, Sheshbazzar; see J. M. Myers, *Ezra•Nehemiah,* AB 14, p. 9).

By far the longest section of the 490-year period of our author ("sixty-two weeks" of years, i.e. 434 years) is devoted to a time when Jerusalem was to "be rebuilt, with its streets and moat, but in a time of distress" (vs. 25b). From the Scriptures alone, the only historical events our author could have known about this period would have been from Ezra and Nehemiah. It is to the rebuilding of Jerusalem's walls under Nehemiah, despite the opposition of his hostile neighbors, that our author is referring. During the long interval between the time of Joshua ben Jozadak and that of Antiochus IV Epiphanes there may well have been other times of "distress" for Jerusalem. But it is doubtful if our author knew any more about this very obscure phase of Jerusalem's history than modern historians do. In any case, the 434 years allotted here for this period is much too long; as reckoned even from the earliest possible date for "the coming of an anointed leader" in 538 B.C. to the next mentioned event, when "an anointed one" was "cut down" in 171 B.C. (see below), the period would amount to only 367 years.

The quasi-prophecy that "an anointed one will be cut down, when the city is no longer his" (9:26) refers almost certainly to the murder of the high priest Onias III in 171 B.C. After the death (ca. 195 B.C.) of his father, the high priest Simon II, whose praises are sung in Sir 50:1–21, Onias III became high priest at the Temple of Jerusalem. Accused of pro-Ptolemaic sympathies and even of plotting against Seleucus IV (187–175 B.C.), Onias went to Antioch to defend himself before the king. But before he could do so, Seleucus was murdered by Heliodorus and succeeded by Antiochus IV Epiphanes. On account of the troubled conditions in Jerusalem, Onias remained for a few more years at Antioch. Menelaus, one of the illegitimate claimants for the Jerusalem high priesthood, went to Antioch to buy the office from Epiphanes. Because Onias protested against this, Menelaus had his henchman Andronicus murder Onias near Antioch ca. 171 B.C. (The story of these events is told at length in II Macc 4:1–38, which is substantially historical, even though, to heighten the dramatic effect, some imaginary elements may have been added to it.) Also in Dan 11:22 there is an allusion to the murder of Onias III, who is there called "the prince of the covenant." Since Onias was absent from Jerusalem at the time of his murder, our author adds that at that time "the city [Jerusalem] (was) no longer his."

In 169 B.C., on his return from a successful campaign against Ptolemy VI of Egypt, Epiphanes put down an insurrection at Jerusalem, where he massacred many people and plundered the Temple (I Macc 1:20–28; II Macc 5:11–16). This is referred to in the quasi-prophecy of Dan 9:26: "and the soldiers of a prince will ruin the sanctuary." The reference may be also to the plundering of the Temple in 167 B.C. (I Macc 1:29–35; II Macc 5:22–26). The horrors of Epiphanes' ensuing persecution of the Jews and the numerous battles of the Maccabean revolt against the Syrians are described in a few dramatic words at the end of vs. 26: "Then the end will come like a flood, and until the end there will be war."

The last section of our author's "seventy weeks" of years is devoted to just "one week" (i.e. seven years), during which "he [Antiochus IV Epiphanes] will make a strong alliance with many" of the Jews (vs. 27). The reference is to the pact made between Antiochus and the renegade Jews who favored Hellenistic culture, as described in I Macc 1:11–14.

Beginning with the second "half" of this last "week" of years, "he [Epiphanes] will abolish sacrifice and oblation; and upon their place [the altar of sacrifice in the Temple] will be an appalling abomination." The reference is to the climax of Epiphanes' persecution of the Jews, when he abolished the legitimate sacrifices to Yahweh in the Temple of Jerusalem and set up on its altar of sacrifice the statue of Zeus Olympios, which the

Jews called the "appalling abomination" (cf. I Macc 1:54–59; II Macc 6:1–2).

The Phoenician-speaking Syrians equated the Greek god Zeus Olympios with their ancient god *ba'al šāmēm,* "the lord of the heavens." Just as the scribes substituted the word *bôšet,* "shame," for the word *ba'al* (once legitimately applied to Yahweh) when this word formed part of a personal name—e.g. King Saul's grandson Meribbaal (so still in I Chron 8:34; 9:40) had his name changed by the scribes to Mephibosheth (II Sam 9:6–13; 16:1–4)—so the Jews at the time of Epiphanes substituted *šiqqûṣ,* "detestable (idol)," for *ba'al* (=Zeus). The word *šāmēm,* "the heavens," was intentionally mispronounced as *šômēm* (so in Dan 8:13; 12:11) as a shortened form of the polel participle *m^e^šōmēm* (9:27), "appalling." Thus, whereas in II Macc 6:2 it is stated that the pagan Syrians renamed Yahweh's Temple "the temple of Zeus Olympios" (in Greek, in the genitive, *Dios Olympiou*), in I Macc 1:54 it is said that "they erected a *bdelygma erēmōseōs.*" Although this Greek term was meant to translate the Hebrew term, *šiqqûṣ šômēm,* it was rendered literally in the Latin Vulgate of the I Maccabees passage as *abominandum idolum desolationis,* but in Mark 13:14 and Matt 24:15, where I Macc 1:54 is quoted, as *abominationem desolationis.* From the latter term is derived the English expression, "the abomination of desolation," in the early English versions (*KJV,* Douay, etc.) of Matt 24:15 and Mark 13:14.

Date of Composition

The author of ch. 9 begins his last "week" of years with the murder of Onias III in 171 B.C. At the middle of this seven-year period, i.e. approximately three and a half years after 171 B.C., or ca. 167/166 B.C., he places the profanation of the Temple by Epiphanes, and he expects God to put an end to this profanation after another three and a half years, i.e. ca. 164/163 B.C. Actually, the desecration of the Temple lasted only a few days more than three full years, from the fifteenth day of the month of Chislev in the 145th year of the Seleucid era (I Macc 1:54), which was the sixth of December of the year 167 B.C. in the Julian calendar, until the twenty-fifth day of the month of Chislev in the 148th year of the Seleucid era (I Macc 4:52), which was the fourteenth day of December in the year 164 B.C. of the Julian calendar. Therefore, our author's prediction that the desecration of the Temple would end three and a half years after it had begun was not a *prophetia post eventum,* but a genuine prediction, which slightly overshot its mark. By observing the progress that the Maccabean forces were making in their war against the Syrian armies, our author could foresee that Judas Maccabeus would soon gain control of the Temple area in Jerusalem. Apparently, he expected this to take place in the spring of 163 B.C., but actually Judas gained the Temple area and was able to have the Temple purified of its profanation somewhat sooner than he had expected. The conclusion can therefore be drawn that our author wrote ch. 9 sometime after Epiphanes had profaned the Temple of Jerusalem in 167 B.C., and in fact sometime after he had humbled King Artaxias of Armenia in 166 B.C. (see toward the end of the COMMENT: DETAILED on *The Small Horn* of 7:8,11a,20b–21,24b–25), but sometime before the reconsecration of the Temple on 14 December 164 B.C. As will be shown in the COMMENT: DETAILED on the last of the apocalypses of the Book of Daniel (chs. 10–12), the prediction made there that the persecution of the Jews would last for approximately three and a half years (12:5–10) was most likely inserted there by the author of ch. 9, who made similar insertions in 7:25 and 8:14. He would thus be the final editor of the Book of Daniel (apart from a few still later additions made toward the end of ch. 12).

The date of the prayer in 9:4–20 is difficult to estimate. Although it is a later insertion into the basic stratum of ch. 9, it was originally composed long before the time when the basic stratum of ch. 9 was written. Its general resemblance to the prayers in Ezra and Nehemiah (see above) suggests that this mosaic of phrases from older parts of the Scriptures was put together at about the end of the fifth century B.C. The reference to Yahweh's "desolate sanctuary" (Hebrew *miqdāšᵉkā haššāmēm;* cf. Lam 5:18) in 9:17 might suggest that the prayer was composed during the exile before the rebuilding of the Temple by Zerubbabel and Joshua ben Jozadak. But this term, like so many others in the prayer, was borrowed from the older Scriptures and proves nothing about the time of composition of the whole prayer as such in ch. 9. It may have been this term in the prayer, understood as referring to the desecration of the Temple by Epiphanes, that led to its insertion in ch. 9.

X. THE FINAL REVELATION
(10:1–12:13)

A. The Prologue (10:1–11:1)

10 [1] In the third year of King Cyrus of Persia an oracle was revealed
to Daniel [who had been named Belteshazzar]. The oracle was true.
It concerned much warfare. [a]He paid attention[a] to the oracle, so that
he understood the revelation.

[2] In those days I, Daniel, afflicted myself for three full weeks; [3] I ate
no savory food, I took no meat or wine, and I did not anoint myself
with oil, until the three full weeks were completed.

[4] On the twenty-fourth day of the first month I was on the bank of
the great river [that is, the Tigris]. [5] As I looked up, I saw a man
clothed in linen, with a belt of [b]pure gold[b] around his waist. [6] His
body was like beryl, his face shone like lightning, his eyes were like
flaming torches, his arms and feet had the gleam of burnished bronze,
and his voice sounded like the roar of a multitude. [7] I, Daniel, alone
saw this sight. Although the men who were with me did not see it,
they were overwhelmed with great fear, so that they fled and hid
themselves. [8] When I had been left alone on seeing this great sight, no
strength remained in me, and I turned deathly pale [and I retained no
strength].

[9] Then I heard the sound of his voice; and at the sound of his voice,
I dropped prostrate[c] to the ground. [10] But a hand touched me and
raised me to my hands and knees. [11] "Daniel, greatly beloved," he
said to me, "pay attention to the words I am about to speak to you.
Stand on your feet, for I have now been sent with news for you."
When he told me this, I stood up, trembling. [12] "Don't be afraid,
Daniel," he continued, "from the first day you made up your mind to
gain understanding by afflicting yourself before God, your prayer was

[a–a] Omit *û* before *bîn*, with LXX, Aq., Syr.

[b–b] Read *b[e]ketem ûpāz* for MT *b[e]ketem 'ûpāz;* cf. SoS 5:11. The *aleph* of the MT was perhaps introduced from the variant preserved in a few MSS; *b[e]ketem 'ôpîr*, "gold of Ophir" (cf. Jer 10:9).

[c] Omit *ûpānay*, with LXX, Syr.; dittography (cf. 8:18).

heard; and that is why I started out. 13 But the prince of the kingdom
of Persia was opposing me for twenty-one days, until Michael, one of
the chief princes, came to my aid. The latter was left there with the
[d]prince of[d] the kingdom[e] of Persia; 14 and I have come to make you
understand what [f]is to happen[f] to your people in the last days, for
there is still vision regarding those days."

15 While he was saying this to me, I kept my face turned toward the
ground and remained silent. 16 Then [g]something like a human hand
touched[g] my lips, and I opened my mouth and spoke to the one who
stood before me, saying, "At the sight of you, my lord, I was seized
with pangs and retained no strength. 17 How can my lord's servant
speak to my lord? There is no longer any strength or even breath left
in me." 18 Once more the one who had the appearance of a man
touched me and strengthened me, 19 saying, "Don't be afraid, greatly
beloved; you are safe. Be courageous [h]and strong[h]." As he spoke to
me, I became more courageous; so I said, "Let my lord speak, for you
have given me courage." 20 "Do you know," he asked, "why I have
come to you? I must now go back to fight against the prince of Persia,
and when he departs, the prince of Greece will come. 21 [i]No one supports me against these except Michael, your prince. **11** / 1 "In fact,
[j]since the first year[j] of Darius the Mede I have been [k]standing by[k] to
help and strengthen him. /

B. The Revelation of the Future (11:2–12:4)

2 [l]"But I will tell you what is written in the book of truth. Three
kings of Persia are still to arise, and the fourth will acquire the

[d–d] Insert *śar,* with LXX, Theod., Syr.

[e] Read *malkût,* with 6QDan, two MSS, Theod., for MT *malkê.*

[f–f] Read *yiqreh* with *k^{e}tîb* and some MSS; the *q^{e}rê* of MT (*yiqrā'*) has been influenced by Gen 49:1.

[g–g] Read *kid^{e}mût yad ben 'ādām nāg^{e}'āh;* cf. Theod. (*kid^{e}mût ben 'ādām nāg^{e}'āh*), 6QDan and LXX (*kid^{e}mût yad 'ādām nāg^{e}'āh*), and MT (*kid^{e}mût b^{e}nê 'ādām nôgēa'*).

[h–h] Read *we'ĕmaṣ,* with a few MSS. The *waḥăzāq* of the MT is a dittography of the preceding word, *ḥăzaq*. The ancient versions render the two imperatives by two different, though more or less synonymous verbs.

[i] Transpose *'ăbal 'aggîd l^{e}kā 'et-hārāšûm bik^{e}tāb 'ĕmet* to precede *hinnēh-'ôd š^{e}lōšāh m^{e}lākîm* in 11:2.

[j–j] Read *mišš^{e}nat 'aḥat* for *bišnat 'aḥat* of MT.

[k–k] Read *'ōmēd* for *'omdî* of MT, which has been contaminated by the preceding word, *hammādî.*

[l] Omit *w^{e}'attāh 'ĕmet 'aggîd lāk;* variant dittography of *'ăbal 'aggîd l^{e}kā . . . 'ĕmet* in 10:21 of MT (see textual note [i]).

greatest riches of them all. When he feels strong enough because of
his riches, [m]he will incite the whole kingdom of Greece[m].
3 "Then a mighty king will arise, who will gain dominion over a
vast domain and do as he pleases. 4 But [n]when he has grown strong[n],
his kingdom will be broken up and divided toward the four winds of
the heavens, but not among his descendants or in keeping with the
domain over which he ruled; for his kingdom will be torn asunder for[o]
others, rather than for these.
5 "Then the king of the south will grow strong; but one of his
princes [p]will become stronger[p] than he, and he will gain dominion over
a domain larger [q]than his[q]. 6 After some years they will make an alliance; and the daughter of the king of the south will marry the king of
the north, in order to ensure the peace. But she will not retain [r]her
power[r], and [s]her offspring[s] will not survive; for she and her attendants,
as well as [t]her child[t] and her husband, will be delivered up.
[u]"Later 7 [v]a scion from her own family will arise in his father's place[v];
[w]and he will lead[w] his army and enter [x]the strongholds[x] of the king of
the north, where he will treat them as a conqueror. 8 Even their gods,
with their molten images and precious vessels of silver and gold he
will carry off as booty into Egypt. [y]The king of the north, however,
will again[z] rise up 9 and invade the domain of the king of the south,
even though he will have to return to his own land.

[m–m] Read *yā'ir 'et-kol-malkût yāwān* for *yā'ir hakkōl 'ēt malkût yāwān* of MT.

[n–n] As in 8:8, read *ûke*^{e}*'oṣmô* for *ûk*^{e}*'omdô* of MT, which has been influenced by the preceding *w*^{e}*'āmad*.

[o] Omit *w*^{e} before *la'ăḥērîm;* dittography.

[p–p] Omit the *w*^{e} before *yeḥĕzaq;* dittography.

[q–q] Read *mimmemšaltô* for *memšaltô* of MT; haplography.

[r–r] *Omit hazz*^{e}*rôa'* after *kôaḥ* (cf. 10:8,18: *w*^{e}*lō' 'āzartî kôaḥ*), or read *kôḥāh* for *kôaḥ hazz*^{e}*rôa'; zrw'* of the MT is a dittography of the following *wzr'w*.

[s–s] Read *zar'āh* (for the Hebrew form, cf. Gen 3:5); cf. LXX, Theod., Vulg. The Aramaic suffix *-h* was ambiguous and read by the translator as a masculine, instead of a feminine suffix.

[t–t] Read *w*^{e}*yaldāh* for the *w*^{e}*hayyōl*^{e}*dāh* of the MT; cf. Theod., Sym., Syr., Vulg.

[u] Add *hāhēm* after *bā'ittîm* (cf. 11:14; II Chron 15:5), and join the two words to vs. 7.

[v–v] Read, with LXX (cf. Theod.), *ya'ămōd neṣer miššārāšéhā 'al-kannô* for *w*^{e}*'āmad minnēṣer šārāšéhā kannô* of MT; for *'al-kannô* in the sense of "in his place, in his stead," cf. 11:20,21.

[w–w] Read *w*^{e}*yābē'* for *w*^{e}*yābō'* of MT.

[x–x] Read *b*^{e}*mā'uzzê* for *b*^{e}*mā'ōz* of MT; cf. the following plural suffixes and the *l*^{e}*mā'uzzê* of 11:19.

[y] Read *melek* for *mimmelek* of MT; dittography.

[z] Read *šēnît* for *šānîm* of MT.

10 "But [aa]his son will assemble[aa] a great armed host and come, passing along like a flood, and fight back to the other's stronghold.
11 Enraged at this, the king of the south will go out and fight against
him [against the king of the north], whose assembled multitude will
be given into his hand. 12 [And the multitude will be carried off.] In
the pride of his heart he will lay low tens of thousands, but he will
gain no territory. 13 For the king of the north will muster another
multitude, greater than the previous one, and after some[bb] years he
will advance with this large army and abundant supplies. 14 In those
times many men will rise up against the king of the south, and violent
men of your own people will lift themselves up in fulfillment of vision;
but they will fail. 15 When the king of the north comes, he will throw
up siege works and capture a well-fortified city; for the forces of the
south will not withstand him, [cc]and even his picked troops will not
have the strength[cc] to resist, 16 so that the attacker will do as he
pleases, with no one opposing him. He will occupy the lovely land,
[dd]and all of it[dd] will be in his power. 17 Then he will set himself to
gain control of the other's entire kingdom. [ee]He will make a peace
treaty with him,[ee] [ff]and he will give him his daughter in marriage,[ff] in
order to destroy him. But it will not stand; it will not be[gg]. 18 Afterwards he will direct his attention to the sea lands and capture many of
them. But a magistrate will put a stop to his insolence. [[hh]His insolence will turn back upon him.] 19 Then he will turn his attention back
to the strongholds of his own land, but he will stumble and fall and
disappear.

20 "In his place there will arise one suffering a loss of dominion,
glory, and sovereignty. But in a short time he will be destroyed,
though not openly or in battle.

21 "There will then arise in the latter's place one who had been
spurned and upon whom the royal insignia had not been conferred.
He will slip in suddenly and seize the kingdom. 22 Armed might [ii]will

[aa–aa] Read *ûbenô* (so *ketîb*) *ye'ĕsōp* for *ûbānāyw* (so *qerê*) *yitgārû we'āsepû* of MT; dittography (cf. the *wytgrw* of MT toward the end of the verse).
[bb] Omit *hā'ittîm* of MT; dittography from 11:14.
[cc–cc] Read *ûle'am mibḥārāyw 'ên kôaḥ* for *we'am mibḥārāyw we'ên kôaḥ* of MT.
[dd–dd] Read *wekullāh* for *wekālāh* of MT.
[ee–ee] Read *ûmēšārîm 'immô ya'ăśeh* for *wîšārîm 'immô we'āśāh* of MT; cf. vs. 6.
[ff–ff] Read *ûbittô benāšîm yitten-lô* for *ûbat hannāšîm yitten-lô* of MT. For the underlying Aramaic idiom, see NOTES.
[gg] Omit *lô,* with LXX; dittography. See NOTES.
[hh] Omit *lô biltî* (for earlier *lebiltî*); corrupt dittography.
[ii–ii] Read *hiššāṭōp* for *haššeṭep* of MT.

be completely overwhelmed[ii] before him, [jj]and even the prince of the
covenant will be crushed[jj]. 23 After an alliance is made with him, he
will act treacherously and rise to power with a small party. 24 [kk]With-
out warning he will invade the richest parts of the provinces[kk], and he
will do what neither his near nor his distant ancestors ever did: plunder, spoil, and riches he will lavish on his followers.

"Against the fortified cities he will devise plans, but only for a time.
25 Thus he will rouse up his strength and courage to fight the king of
the south with a great army. The king of the south, in turn, will rise in
opposition to give battle with a very large and powerful army. But he
will not hold his ground because of the plots devised against him
26 by[ll] the members of his court, who will seek to destroy him. His
army [mm]will be overwhelmed[mm], and many will fall slain. 27 The two
kings, their minds set on evil, will sit together at table and exchange
lies. But their alliance will have no success, for there is still a final
phase for the appointed period. 28 The king of the north will then turn
back to his own land with great riches, and his mind will be set
against the holy covenant, as he passes through and returns home.

29 "A year later he will again invade the south, but the second invasion will not be like the first one. 30 When ships of the Kittim come
against him, he will lose heart and retreat. Then he will become
enraged against the holy covenant, as he passes through. But on his
return he will have regard for those who forsake the holy covenant.
31 Armed forces shall be stationed by him, and they will defile the
sanctuary and[nn] the pious ones, abolishing the daily sacrifice and setting up [oo]an appalling[oo] abomination. 32 Those who act wickedly
against the covenant he will make apostatize with flattery, but the
people who are loyal to their God will take strong action. 33 Those of
the people who act wisely will make the multitude understand, but
they will be tested with sword and flames or with exile and plunder
for some time. 34 When, however, they are tested, they will receive a
little help, although many will join them insincerely. 35 Some of those

[jj–jj] Read *w^{e}yiššābēr, gam n^{e}gîd b^{e}rît* for *w^{e}yiššābērû w^{e}gam n^{e}gîd b^{e}rît* of MT.

[kk–kk] Read *ûb^{e}šalwāh b^{e}mišmannê m^{e}dînāh yābō'* for *b^{e}šalwāh ûb^{e}mišmannê m^{e}dînāh yābō'* of MT.

[ll] Omit *w^{e}* before *'ōk^{e}lê pat-bāgô,* and join with the preceding.

[mm–mm] Read, with Syr. and Vulg., *yiššāṭēp* for *yišṭôp* of MT; many MSS have *yišṭōp* (*defective scriptum*).

[nn] Insert *w^{e}* before *hammā'ôz*. On the translator's misunderstanding of Aramaic *ḥsyn,* as if it were to be read as *ḥăsên,* "stronghold," instead of *ḥăsayīn,* "pious ones," see NOTES.

[oo–oo] Read *haššômēm* for *m^{e}šômēm* of MT; cf. 11:27; 12:11.

who act wisely will be tested, to refine, cleanse, [pp]and purify[pp] them[qq],
until the time of the final phase, for there is still the present appointed
period.

36 "The king will do as he pleases. He will exalt himself and make
himself greater than any god, and even against the God of gods he
will speak arrogantly. He will succeed until the time of wrath is completed, for what is decreed must be done. 37 He will have no regard
for the gods of his ancestors; toward the darling of women and toward every other god he will act disrespectfully, for he will make himself greater than all of them. 38 Even the God of the pious ones [rr]he
will despise[rr], and [ss]on that God's stand[ss] he will honor, with gold, silver, precious stones, and costly gifts, a god whom his ancestors did
not know. 39 Into the fortresses of the pious ones he will bring over
soldiers[tt] of a strange god. Whoever acknowledges him he will provide
with great honor, making them rulers over the many and distributing
the land as their wages.

40 "In the time of the final phase the king of the south will come to
grips with him. But the king of the north will sweep over him like a
whirlwind with chariots and cavalry and many ships, invading lands
and passing through them like a flood. 41 As he comes into the lovely
land, myriads[uu] will be tested. But Edom, Moab, and the remnant[vv] of
the Ammonites will be saved from his power. 42 As he extends his
power over the countries, not even the land of Egypt will escape.
43 He will gain control of the treasures of gold and silver and all other
precious things in Egypt; and the Libyans and Cushites will follow in
his train. 44 But as news from the east and the north alarm him, he
will set out with great fury to completely exterminate many. 45 Yet
when he has pitched his palatial tents between the Sea and the lovely
holy mountain, he will come to his end, with none to help him.

12 1 "At that time Michael, the great prince, the protector of your
people, will arise. It will be a time of distress, such as never occurred

[pp–pp] Read *ûl[e]labbēn* for *w[e]lalbēn* of MT. See NOTES.
[qq] For *bāhēm* of MT, read *lāhēm,* the Hebrew translator's mechanical rendering of Aramaic accusative *l[e]hôm.*
[rr–rr] Read *yin'az* or *yibzeh,* which has been lost in the MT by the dittography of *y[e]kabbēd.*
[ss–ss] Transpose *'al-kannô* from before the first (wrong) *y[e]kabbēd* to before the second *y[e]kabbēd.*
[tt] *Read 'am* for *'im* of MT.
[uu] Read, with Sym., *w[e]ribbôt* for *w[e]rabbôt* of MT, for which the feminine plural would have no antecedent.
[vv] Read, with Syr., *ûš[e]'ērît* for *w[e]rē'šît* of MT.

since nations came into being until that time. But at that time your
people will be rescued, every one of them who is found written in the
book. 2 Many of those who sleep in the dirt of the earth will awake;
some will live forever, while others will become everlasting objects of
contempt and abhorrence. 3 But those who act wisely will shine
brightly like the brilliance of the firmament; and those who lead the
multitude to righteousness will shine like the stars forever and ever.
4 As for you, Daniel, keep the words secret and seal the book until the
time of the final phase. Many will apostatize[ww], and evil[xx] will increase."

C. The Epilogue (12:5–13)

/ 5 As I, Daniel, looked on, I saw two others, one standing on this
side of the stream, and the other one on the other side. 6 One of them
said to the man clothed in linen, who was upstream, "How long will it
be until the end of these awful things?" 7 The man clothed in linen,
who was upstream, raised his right hand and his left hand to the
heavens; and I heard him swear by him who lives forever, that it
would be for a year, two years, and half a year; [yy]but that, when the
power of the desecrator of the holy people is brought to an end[yy], all
these things would be accomplished. 8 Although I heard this, I did not
understand it. So I said, "My lord, what is the explanation of this?"
9 "Go your way, Daniel," he answered, "for the words are secret and
sealed until the time of the final phase. 10 The multitude will be
cleansed, purified, and refined. But the wicked will be judged guilty;
none of them will understand it, although those who act wisely will
understand." /

// 11 "From the time the daily sacrifice is abolished and the appalling abomination is set up there will be one thousand two hundred
and ninety days." //

/// 12 "Blessed is the one who has patience and perseveres during
the one thousand three hundred and thirty-five days." ///

/ 13 "As for you, go your way [zz]and take your rest, for you will
rise for your reward at the end of the days." /

[ww] Read *y^{e}śōṭ^{e}ṭû* (pilpel of *śṭṭ*) or *y^{e}śōṭû* (qal of *śûṭ*) for *y^{e}šōṭ^{e}ṭû* of MT; cf. LXX.
[xx] Read *hārā'āh* for *hadda'at* of MT; cf. LXX and I Macc 1:9.
[yy–yy] Read *w^{e}kik^{e}lôt yad nappēṣ 'am-qōdeš* for *ûk^{e}kallôt nappeṣ yad-'am-qōdeš* of MT. For the meaning of *nappēṣ*, see Notes.
[zz] Omit the first *laqqēṣ*, with LXX and Theod.; dittography.

NOTES

10:1. *the third year of King Cyrus.* LXX has "the first year of King Cyrus." But this reading is probably based on an attempt to harmonize 10:1 with 1:21. Although the date is fictitious, it has a bearing on what is implied in the date given in 11:1 (see below).

who had been named Belteshazzar. This clause is probably a later addition, based on 1:7. The apocalypse of chs. 10–12 once circulated as an independent unit before it was annexed, with the other apocalypses of chs. 7–9, to the older stories about Daniel and his companions that now form chs. 1–6 of the book. [Cf. Introduction, Part III.]

oracle. Literally, "word."

It concerned much warfare. This is merely an attempt to give some sense, in the context, to the obscure and possibly corrupt Hebrew of the MT, *w^{e}ṣābā' gādôl,* literally, "and a great army," or possibly "and great service" (or "labor"); cf. Isa 40:2; Job 7:1; 10:17; 14:14.

He paid attention. On this meaning of Hebrew *bîn,* see NOTES on 8:5; 9:2.

so that he understood the revelation. Literally, "and understanding was to him in the revelation." On the use of *mar'eh* in the meaning of "revelation" in certain passages of Daniel, see NOTE on 8:16.

2. *I . . . afflicted myself.* Literally, "I was mourning." But here, as is clear from the context, the emphasis is on the self-affliction that accompanied Hebrew mourning rites for the dead, rather than the mourning or bewailing as such. Cf. Daniel's *hit'annôt,* "self-affliction," in 10:12.

3. *savory food.* Literally, "bread of delightfulness," i.e. delicacies, in contrast to *leḥem 'ōnî,* "the bread of affliction" (Deut 16:3, where it refers to unleavened bread).

I took no meat or wine. Literally, "and meat or wine did not come into my mouth."

and I did not anoint myself with oil. The Hebrew, *w^{e}sôk lō' saktî,* is rendered in all the versions as "I did not anoint myself at all" or by some similar expression, which takes *sôk* as infinitive absolute strengthening the finite verb *saktî.* Although this is perfectly good Hebrew and is, no doubt, what the Hebrew translator of the original Aramaic intended, one may wonder why the author wished to lay such strong stress here on Daniel's complete abstention from self-anointing during his period of penance. Moreover, this is the only occurrence in the Hebrew Bible of the infinitive absolute *sôk.* Besides, in every other occurrence of this verb in a negative phrase, it is always accompanied by the noun *šemen,* "oil": *šemen lō'-tāsûk,* "with oil you will not anoint yourself" (Deut 28:40); *lō'-tāsûk šemen,* "you will not anoint yourself with oil" (Micah 6:15); *'al-tāsûkî šemen,* "don't anoint yourself with oil" (II Sam 14:2); *šemen mišḥat-qōdeš . . . 'al-b^{e}śar 'ādām lō' yîsāk* (read *yûsāk* with Sam.?), "sacred anointing oil shall not be rubbed on the body of any (lay)man" (Exod 30:31–32). Only in positive statements can the word *šemen* be omitted with the verb *sāk* (II Sam 12:20; Ruth 3:3; II Chron 28:15), although even in the positive statement of Ezek 16:9 the word *šemen* is used (*wa'ăsûkēk baššemen,* "and I anointed you with oil"); cf. also Judith 10:3: *echrisato myrō̧ pachei,* "she anointed herself with rich ointment." The unvocalized Syriac text of Dan 10:3 has *wmšḥ' l' msḥt.* Undoubtedly, the Syriac translator, since he was working from the Hebrew text, meant the first word to be read the way it was later vocalized in the Syriac MSS, as *mᵉšāḥâ* "(with) anointing." But this first word could also be vocalized as *mešḥâ,* "with oil." Practically the same phrase occurs in the Aramaic of the Elephantine papyri: *nḥnh . . . mšḥ l' mšḥ(y)n wḥmr l' štyn,* "we . . . with oil did not anoint ourselves, and wine we did not drink" (A. Cowley, *Aramaic Papyri of the Fifth Century,* 30:20; 31:19–20). H. L. Ginsberg (p. 60) is therefore no doubt correct in presenting this passage in Dan 10:3 as a clear example of an instance where the Hebrew of Daniel betrays itself as a translation from an original Aramaic text, which would have read: *wmšḥ l' mšḥt.* Since the translator rightly rendered Aramaic *mšḥt* by Hebrew *skty* (for in Hebrew, *mšḥty* would normally be used only of cultic anointing), he then mistook Aramaic *mšḥ* as a verbal noun, *mᵉšāḥ,* "anointing," and thus rendered it wrongly in Hebrew by the infinite absolute, *swk,* whereas he should have rendered it as *wšmn l' skty,* "with oil I did not anoint myself."

4. *the great river.* Elsewhere this term refers only to the Euphrates (explicitly glossed as such in Gen 15:18; Deut 1:7; Josh 1:4), which is commonly called simply "the River" (*hannāhār:* Gen 31:21; Exod 23:21; Num 20:5; etc.). Apparently the original author of this apocalypse meant Daniel to have the vision near Babylon, which was situated on the Euphrates, since in the rest of the Book of Daniel its protagonist is presented as living in Babylon. Perhaps the glossator had in mind 8:2, where Daniel is pictured as transported to Susa, which was nearer the Tigris than it was to the Euphrates. [Syr. has "the Euphrates" where MT has "the Tigris."]

5. *clothed in linen.* This is the traditional rendering of the Hebrew *lābûš baddîm,* which our author borrowed from Ezek 9:2,3,11; 10:2,6,7. In the latter passages the LXX translated *baddîm* by *podērēs,* "robe reaching to the feet"; hence a sort of alb. The Hebrew singular noun *bad* designates the material, apparently of fine linen, of which various priestly vestments were made (I Sam 2:18; Exod 28:42; Lev 16:4; etc.).

pure gold. The emended Hebrew text contains two terms that seem to refer to two different kinds of gold, "*ketem* gold and *pāz* gold."

6. *beryl.* The exact meaning of the Hebrew word *taršîš,* which designates some kind of precious stone, is uncertain. It is used also in Exod 28:20; 39:13; Ezek 1:16; 10:9; 28:13; Song of Songs 5:14.

shone like lightning. Literally, "was like the appearance of lightning."

feet. The Hebrew word used here, *margālôt,* occurs elsewhere in the MT only in Ruth 3:4,7,8,14, where it means "the place of one's feet" (*raglayim*).

had the gleam of burnished bronze. Literally, "(were) like the eye of lightweight [i.e. smoothed, polished] bronze." The same Hebrew phrase, *kᵉʿên nᵉḥōšet qālāl,* occurs in Ezek 1:7, whence no doubt our writer borrowed it.

7. *sight.* The Hebrew word *mar'āh,* as distinct from Hebrew *mar'eh,* designates here a real, though unusual, external manifestation, and not simply an internal impression of the imagination. If it were merely the latter, and not an external reality, "the prince of the kingdom of Persia" could not have prevented the heavenly visitor from appearing to Daniel for twenty-one days (10:12–13), and Daniel's companions would not have sensed its presence and fled in fear, even though they could not clearly see the nature of the apparition.

and hid themselves. Literally, "in hiding themselves": Hebrew *b^{e}hēḥābē'*. One would expect Hebrew *l^{e}hēḥābē',* "in order to hide themselves"; but the *b* is vouched for in all the ancient versions.

8. *I turned deathly pale.* The Hebrew *w^{e}hôdî nehpak 'ālay l^{e}mašḥît* means literally, "and my splendor was overturned upon me to destruction." As noted by previous commentators (see Ginsberg, p. 41), the Hebrew phrase *w^{e}hôdî nehpak 'ālay* is a mistranslation of the Aramaic *w^{e}zîway yištannôn 'ălay,* which occurs in 7:28 (cf. also 5:9: *w^{e}zîwōhî šānayin 'ălôhî*). In Aramaic, as is also the case with Akkadian *zīmu* (see *CAD* 21, Z, pp. 119–122), from which the Aramaic word is borrowed, *zîw* means, first, "appearance, looks," and secondly, "glow, splendor." The translator of Daniel 10 wrongly took the second meaning, rather than the first.

and I retained no strength. Since the same Hebrew phrase, *w^{e}lō' 'āṣartî kōaḥ,* occurs at the end of 10:16 and since it seems redundant here, it is here probably an accidental dittography or an intentional gloss taken from that verse. The Hebrew phrase, *'āṣar kōaḥ,* occurs elsewhere in the MT only in Dan 11:16; I Chron 29:14; and II Chron 2:5; 13:20; 22:9 and is probably an Aramaism.

9. *I dropped prostrate to the ground.* See NOTE on 8:18, where the same Hebrew phrase occurs. In good classical Hebrew, *wa'ănî hāyîtî* would be pluperfect, "and I had become"; but here it merely reflects the underlying Aramaic, in which such a construction does not put the verb in the pluperfect.

10. *and raised me to my hands and knees.* Literally, "and moved me to my knees and the palms of my hands." For the Hebrew, *watt^{e}nî'ēnî* (hiphil of *nûa'*), cf. II Kings 23:18: *'al-yāna' 'aṣmōtāyw,* "let no one (re)move his bones." An interesting variant reading, *lhny'ny,* "to move me," is found in 6QDan. The translation of the LXX and Theod., *kai ēgeire me,* "and aroused me," which is followed by Vet. Lat., Vulg., and Syr., is merely a rendering *ad sensum* (on the supposition that Daniel had fallen into a deep sleep: *nirdam*) and does not prove that there was a variant Hebrew reading, *way^{e}'îrēnî* (cf. W. Baumgartner's footnote in R. Kittel's *Biblia Hebraica,* 3d ed., Stuttgart: Privilegierte Württembergische Bibelanstalt, 1937).

11. *greatly beloved.* See NOTE on 9:23.

Stand on your feet. Literally, "stand on your standing." See NOTE on 8:18.

I have now been sent with news for you. Literally, "I have now been sent to you." But the verb *šālaḥ* (here is the passive, pu'al) often means "to send a messenger with news."

12. *by afflicting yourself.* The Hebrew text makes this clause coordinate with the preceding one: "and you afflicted yourself." The reference is, of course, to Daniel's fasting that is mentioned in 10:3.

13. *The latter was left.* The reading of the MT, *wa'ănî nôtartî,* is almost cer-

tainly original; but its meaning, "and I was left," is obvious nonsense, since the *angelus revelator* did not stay with the prince of the kingdom of Persia, but with Michael's aid, succeeded in coming to Daniel. On the basis of LXX and Theod., most modern versions correct the Hebrew text to read *we'ōtô hôtartî* or *wehôtartîw* "and I left him." However, neither of these forms is close to the letters of the MT, and the Greek translators were probably merely giving a free rendition of the passage in order to make sense out of it in the context. Ginsberg (p. 60) suggests that the Hebrew translator misread (or had before him a corrupt text that read) in Aramaic, *w'nh 'twtr* (or *'št'r*), "and I was left," in place of the original *wdnh 'twtr* (or *'št'r*), "and this one [the latter] was left." The same misreading of *'nh* for an original *dnh* probably occurs also in 10:20.

14. *there is still vision regarding those days.* Here, as in 8:13 and 9:24, Hebrew *ḥāzôn,* "vision," means "things seen in a vision." Daniel, who is presented here as living in the third year of the reign of King Cyrus of Persia, is warned that many things, now to be revealed to him, must occur before the arrival of "those days," i.e. the eschatological intervention of God for Israel. Instead of *layyāmîm,* "regarding those days," a few Hebrew MSS have *lemô'ēd* (better vocalized as *lammô'ēd,* as in 11:35), "regarding the appointed period," thus keeping closer to the wording of Hab 2:3, from which the present passage is borrowed. Note that the author of the apocalypse of chs. 10–12 applies the Habakkuk passage differently from the way it is used in the basic apocalypse of ch. 8; see COMMENT GENERAL on ch. 8.

16. *I was seized with pangs.* Literally, "my pangs [like those of a woman in childbirth] suddenly overwhelmed me." Our author borrowed his phrase here, *nehepkû ṣîray 'ālay,* from I Sam 4:19: *nehepkû 'ālèhā ṣîrèhā,* "her birth pangs suddenly overwhelmed her."

17. *How.* The MT has the Aramaic *hêk* for Hebrew *'êk.* The only occurrence of this Aramaism in Biblical Hebrew is in I Chron 13:12. The enclitic *zeh* that is used twice in the question can hardly be rendered adequately in English; the sense would be something like: "How can such a servant of my lord speak with such a lord of mine?"

There is no longer . . . in me. Literally, "And as for me, from now on strength does not stay in me, and breath has not remained in me."

19. *you are safe.* The common Hebrew expression, *šālôm lāk,* is usually understood here, in keeping with its common usage elsewhere, as a greeting, "Peace (be) with you!" But if this were the meaning here, one would expect the phrase to be the first words addressed to Daniel; hence, it seems more probable that the phrase should here be understood as a statement of fact: "You have *šālôm,*" i.e. "You are safe."

20. *Do you know . . . ?* H. L. Ginsberg (p. 47) suggests that the original Aramaic may have been *hâ yeda't,* "Behold, you know."

and when he departs. The MT's *wa'ănî yôṣē'* means literally, "and I am departing," i.e. "when I depart." But the context calls for the departure of "the prince of Persia" before "the prince of Greece" can come. Ginsberg (pp. 90–91) suggests that the Hebrew translator misread (or had a copy that wrongly read) Aramaic *w'nh npq* for original Aramaic *wdnh npq.* See NOTE on 10:13.

11:1. *to help and strengthen him.* Literally, "as an upholder and strengthener for him." The Hebrew *m*ᵉ*maḥăzîq ûl*ᵉ*mā'ôz lô* perhaps goes back to Aramaic *lim*ᵉ*gabbēr w*ᵉ*lim*ᵉ*ḥassēn lēh.* If this be so, there may be a play on the name "Gabriel" (see NOTE on 8:15). In any case, the interpolator of the sentence, "In fact, since the first year of Darius the Mede I have been standing by to help and strengthen him," has the anonymous angel of chs. 10–12 identify himself by these words with the angel Gabriel of ch. 9, as will be shown in the COMMENT: DETAILED. The insertion caused the displacement and repetition of the phrases in the MT, which are here corrected in the textual notes. If the original Aramaic had the pa'el participle of *ḥsn* here, which the Hebrew translator rendered by *mā'ôz,* from the root *'wz,* "to be strong," then it is possible, according to the suggestion of Ginsberg (pp. 43–49), that he also mistakenly used the Hebrew root *'wz* when the Aramaic original had *ḥsyn,* "the pious," in 11:31,38,39, as will be shown below.

3. *who will gain dominion over a vast domain.* Literally, "and he will rule (with) a great ruling." The word *mimšāl,* "ruling, domain," which occurs in Hebrew only here and in 11:5 (in I Chron 26:6, *hammimšālîm* should be read as *hammōš*ᵉ*lîm*), is an Aramaism for the normal Hebrew *mimšālāh.*

4. *and divided.* In classical Hebrew the form *w*ᵉ*tēḥāṣ* (modal *waw* before the jussive, apocopated niphal of *ḥāṣāh*) would mean "that it may be divided"; but our writer uses it as if it were a simple connective *waw* with a mere future. Moreover, Hebrew *ḥāṣāh* normally means "to split into two halves"; only in the archaic passages of Judg 7:16; 9:43, where it has a special military sense, is this verb used in regard to dividing a group of men into three parts. In Aramaic, however, the verb *p*ᵉ*lag* means to divide into any number of parts. The Hebrew translator here rendered a presumed original Aramaic *w*ᵉ*titp*ᵉ*lēg* (cf. 2:41) by Hebrew *w*ᵉ*tēḥāṣ* because he was misled by the proportion, Aramaic *p*ᵉ*lag* (7:25): Hebrew *ḥēṣî* (12:7) : : Aramaic *w*ᵉ*titp*ᵉ*lēg* (2:41): Hebrew *w*ᵉ*tēḥāṣ* (11:4); see Ginsberg, p. 61.

will be torn asunder. Literally, "will be plucked up, rooted out."

6. *After some years.* Literally, "And at the end of years" (Hebrew *ûl*ᵉ*qēṣ šānîm*), a phrase designating an unspecified lapse of time, like *miqqēṣ yammîm* in Gen 4:3; I Kings 7:7.

in order to ensure the peace. Literally, "to make straight things." Dynastic intermarriages often followed the making of peace treaties.

and her husband. The Hebrew *ûmaḥăzîkāh* means literally, "and he who took hold of her." But the hiphil of *ḥzq* is not used elsewhere in regard to a man "marrying" a woman. Perhaps, as Ginsberg (p. 47) suggests, the original Aramaic was *wgbrh,* which was to be read as *w*ᵉ*gabrāh* but which the Hebrew translator wrongly read as *um*ᵉ*gabb*ᵉ*rāh;* see NOTE on 11:1.

will be delivered up. In Hebrew, *tinnātēn.* But this usage of *ntn* in the sense of "to deliver up to death" is unique in Hebrew; one would expect it to be followed by *lammāwet,* "to death," as in Ezek 31:14. Perhaps the original Aramaic verb used here was *msr,* which besides meaning "to hand over," can also mean "to betray."

Later. Literally, according to the emended Hebrew text, "in those times."

7. *a scion from her own family will arise in his father's place.* Literally, ac-

cording to the emended Hebrew text, "a shoot from her roots will arise on his place." In the context, the "his" must refer back to "the king of the south" mentioned in 11:5,6a; hence, for the sake of clarity, "his" is freely rendered here as "his father's."

his army. The Hebrew *'el-haḥayil* would be literally, "to the army." The translator mistook the Aramaic *l*, which is here the exponent of the direct object, as a preposition, Hebrew *'el*, "to"; and the final *h* of the Aramaic personal pronoun suffix (*l*ᵉ*ḥêlēh*) as the sign of the emphatic state (*l*ᵉ*ḥêlāh*), hence Hebrew *haḥayil*.

the strongholds. The original Aramaic for Hebrew *mā'uzzê* was most likely *ḥisnê*; so also in 11:10b,12,19 the translator rightly rendered the Aramaic root *ḥsn* by the Hebrew root *'wz*. But this misled him in 11:31,38,39 to connect Aramaic *ḥsyn*, "the pious ones," with the same Hebrew root *'wz*.

he will treat them as a conqueror. Literally, "he will deal with them and prevail" (hend.). The use of Hebrew *w*ᵉ*heḥĕzîq*, in the meaning of "and he will prevail" is either an Aramaism (cf. II Chron 26:18) or an attempt to translate Aramaic *wîgabbēr*, which can have this meaning.

8. *The king of the north, however, will again rise up*. The emended Hebrew text would be literally, "And he again will rise up, (namely) the king of the north." However, the original Aramaic almost certainly began with *wh'*=*w*ᵉ*hâ*, "And behold," which the translator mistook for *w*ᵉ*hû'*, "And he."

10. *passing along like a flood*. The Hebrew *w*ᵉ*šāṭap w*ᵉ*'ābār*, (literally) "and he will overflood and pass along," is taken from Isa 8:8; cf. also Dan 11:22,31, where the imagery of an invading army coming on like an overwhelming flood is likewise taken from Isa 8:8.

the other's stronghold. Literally, "his stronghold"; but the "his" refers here to the king of Egypt. Again, Hebrew *mā'uzzô* represents Aramaic *ḥisnēh*.

12. *And the multitude will be carried off*. This is apparently a gloss or a variant reading on the preceding phrase, "whose assembled multitude will be given into his hand," based on 2:35.

In the pride of his heart he will lay low tens of thousands. Literally, "and his heart will become high [cf. 5:20], and he will cause tens of thousands to fall."

but he will gain no territory. The Hebrew, *w*ᵉ*lō' yā'ôz*, would be literally, "and he will not be strong"; but behind the Hebrew lies Aramaic *w*ᵉ*lâ yaḥsēn*, and on the haphel of Aramaic *hsn* as meaning "to gain possession," see 7:18,22.

14. *in fulfillment of vision*. The Hebrew, *l*ᵉ*ha'ămîd ḥāzôn*, would be literally, "to make vision stand." But the allusion is very obscure. Montgomery (p. 439) calls attention to Ezek 13:6, where the false prophets are said to wait for Yahweh "to fulfill the word" (*l*ᵉ*qayyēm dābār*).

16. *the lovely land*. The land of Israel; see NOTE on 8:9.

and all of it will be in his power. The unemended MT means literally, "and destruction will be in his hand."

17. *to gain control of the other's entire kingdom*. The Hebrew, *lābô' b*ᵉ*tōqep kol-malkûtô*, is so ambiguous that various interpretations of it are possible. If *b*ᵉ*tōqep* is taken as a phrase in the construct state, the sense may be, "to come into the power of all his own kingdom." But it seems to fit the context better to

make *malkûtô* the direct object of *lābô'* and understand the "his" of "his kingdom" as referring to the king of the south; thus the whole phrase would be literally, "to enter with power his [the Egyptian king's] kingdom."

and he will give him his daughter in marriage, in order to destroy him. As long ago as 1892, Bevan (p. xii) wrote that the Hebrew, *ûbat hannāšîm yittenlô lehašḥîtāh* (literally, "and the daughter of women he will give him in order to destroy her"), is based on an Aramaic original that probably read, *wbrth bnšyn yntn lh lḥblwth,* and that *bnšyn yntn* means "he will give in marriage," just as the Syriac idiom, *yab beneššē',* means "he gave in marriage." The Hebrew translator mistook *wbrth bnšyn* to mean "the [the final *h* of *wbrth* as the exponent of the emphatic state] daughter among women," and he mistook the final *h* of *lḥblwth* as the feminine (Aramaic *-āh*) rather than the masculine (Aramaic *-ēh*) personal pronoun suffix.

But it will not stand; it will not be. This is a quotation from Isa 7:7. But whereas the MT of Isa 7:7 has *lō' tāqûm welō' tihyeh,* our author has *welō' ta'ămōd welō' tihyeh,* which shows that he is translating (correctly enough) the phrase from the Aramaic and not quoting the passage directly from the Hebrew text of Isaiah. In the Hebrew parts of the Book of Daniel the verb *qûm* occurs only in 8:27; elsewhere Hebrew *'āmad* (in keeping with late Hebrew) is always used to represent Aramaic *qûm,* which in Aramaic means not only "to stand up," but also merely "to stand, to be standing."

18. *the sea lands.* The Hebrew term, *'îyîm,* literally "islands," is used of any place that can be reached by ship in the Mediterranean Sea. No doubt it refers here to the regions of western Asia Minor and Thrace (see COMMENT: DETAILED).

a magistrate. The Hebrew word, *qāṣîn* (related to Arabic *qaḍî,* "judge"), which is an archaic and poetic synonym for *šōpēṭ,* "judge," as a military leader (Josh 10:24; Judg 11:6,11; Isa 1:10; 3:6,7; etc.), is well chosen here to designate a Roman "consul"; see COMMENT: DETAILED.

19. *to the strongholds of his own land.* Note once more the use of Hebrew *lemā'uzzê 'arṣô* for Aramaic *leḥisnê 'ar'ēh.*

and disappear. The same Hebrew phrase, *welō' yimmāṣē',* literally, "and will not be found," occurs also in the same sense, "and disappear," in Ps 37:36; Job 20:8.

20. *one suffering a loss of dominion, glory, and sovereignty.* The Hebrew, *ma'ăbîr nôgēś heder malkût,* literally, "one sending over an exactor [or, slave driver] of splendor of kingdom," although most likely the reading of the Hebrew translator, is sheer gibberish. Following F. Zimmermann (*JBL* 57 [1938], 265–266) and Ginsberg (p. 42), the translation offered here is based on the supposition that the Hebrew translator misunderstood the original Aramaic, *mh'dy šlṭn yqr wmlkw* (=*meha'day šolṭān yeqar ûmalkû*). The translator mistook *mh'dy* for an active (cf. 5:20) instead of a passive participle haphel of *'dy,* and *šlṭn* for *šilṭōn* (cf. 2:3) instead of for *šolṭān* (cf. 3:33; 4:19,31; 6:27; 7:6,14,26,27). Especially enlightening for the Aramaic idiom, *šlṭn 'dy,* is 7:14. The translator may have been misled into his faulty rendering of the Aramaic by interpreting the passage in connection with the events narrated in II Macc 3:1–40; see COMMENT: DETAILED.

not openly. The natural meaning of the Hebrew, *lōʼ beʼappayim,* would seem to be "not in anger" (for the singular, *ʼap,* "anger," cf. Exod 15:8; Prov 30:33); Vulg. has *non in furore*. But more likely the Hebrew expression represents a merely mechanical rendering of the Aramaic idiom, *beʼappîn* (cf. Syr. *baʼpē*), literally, "in the face," then, "in public." On the death of this king, see COMMENT: DETAILED.

21. *one who had been spurned*. The Hebrew *nibzeh* may mean either "despised" or "despicable." But here the writer was probably referring objectively to the lowly origin of this king rather than subjectively to the lowly opinion held of him by the Jews.

He will slip in suddenly. Literally, "He will come in with suddenness and slipperiness." On *bešalweh* meaning "suddenly," see NOTE on 8:25. On *ḥălaqlaqqôt* meaning "slipperiness," cf. Jer 23:12; 35:6. The expression, "to come in with slipperiness," is taken here as a hendiadys for "to slip in."

22. The masculine plural of the verb (*yiššāṭepû*) with a feminine plural subject (*zerōʻôt*) before it is common in Mishnaic Hebrew; but here it could be regarded as a *constructio ad sensum* (cf. the word with a masculine plural ending, *zerōʻîm,* in the sense of "armed forces," 11:31).

the prince of the covenant. The high priest at Jerusalem, who is here called *negîd berît,* "leader of the covenant" (see NOTE on 11:25) because in the post-exilic period the high priest was frequently called *negîd bêt hāʼĕlōhîm,* "the prince of God's house" (Neh 11:11; I Chron 9:11; II Chron 31:13) or simply *negîd habbayit,* "prince of the temple" (II Chron 28:7). The term "covenant" is used here and in 11:30,33 almost in the sense of "the covenanted people" (cf. Isa 42:6: *berît ʻam*).

23. *After an alliance is made*. Literally, "and from allying themselves." The form of the hithpaʻel infinitive that is used here, *hitḥabberût,* is either an Aramaism in late Hebrew (cf. *lehašmāʻût* in Ezek 24:26, where, however, the text is probably corrupt) or has been lifted bodily from the original Aramaic of the passage.

and rise to power. Literally, "and he will go up and he will become powerful" (hend.).

with a small party. This is probably the meaning of the rather barbarous Hebrew *bimeʻat gôy,* literally, "in a little of a nation."

24. *the richest parts of the provinces*. The Hebrew *mišmannê medînāh* is probably an echo of *mišmannê hāʼāreṣ* (Gen 27:28,39). The singular *medînāh* is used here as a collective in keeping with good Semitic idiom.

what neither his near nor his distant ancestors ever did. Literally, "what his fathers or the fathers of his fathers did not do," which obviously cannot be rendered literally into English, since he had only one father.

plunder. The noun *bizzāh* (also in 11:33) is an Aramaism, occurring only in late Hebrew (Esther 9:10,15,16; Ezra 9:7; Neh 3:36; etc.).

he will lavish. In Hebrew, *yibzôr*. Apart from its archaic use in the piʻel in Ps 58:31, the verbal root *bzr* occurs only here in Hebrew. It is an Aramaism for the normal Hebrew *pāzar,* "to scatter." The regular Aramaic root is *bdr* (which the Syriac version has here), occurring in the paʻel in Dan 4:11. This shows that the root in proto-Semitic was *bḏr,* as in Arabic.

on his followers. Literally, "to them"; but the only possible antecedent can be the "small party" mentioned in 11:23.

the fortified cities. Of Egypt. The Hebrew word, *mibṣārîm,* translated here as "fortified cities," is not the same as Hebrew *mā'uzzîm,* which is translated above (11:1,7,10,11,19) as "strongholds" (Aramaic *ḥisnîn*). A new paragraph is begun here with the last words of 11:24, which are regarded as giving an introductory summary of the Syrian king's first Egyptian campaign, as described more in detail in 11:25–28 (see COMMENT: DETAILED).

25. *courage.* Literally, "heart."

25–26. *because of the plots devised against him by the members of his court, who will seek to destroy him.* Literally, "because the partakers of the royal menu [see NOTE on 1:5] will devise plots against him and break him."

27. *The two kings.* The expression in the MT, *ûšᵉnêhem hammᵉlākîm,* literally, "and the two of them, the kings," can hardly be said to be good Hebrew; it is merely a mechanical rendering of the good Aramaic idiom, *ûtᵉrēhôn malkayyâ* (cf. the Syr. here, and the Aramaic *tᵉlāttēhôn* in 3:23).

their alliance will have no success. Literally, "it [feminine, impersonal] will not prosper."

there is still a final phase for the appointed period. An allusion to Hab 2:3, as in the MT (with *'ôd,* not *'ēd*) and as in Dan 10:14b. See NOTE there, and COMMENT: GENERAL on ch. 8.

28. *The king of the north.* In Hebrew, merely "he," but in English he must be identified for the sake of clarity.

as he passes through. The Hebrew translator misread, or had a faulty copy that read, Aramaic *wy'br* as *wy'bd;* hence his nonsensical *wᵉ'āśāh,* "and he will do." The same misreading occurs also in 11:30 (cf. 11:39). Only in 11:10,40 did he read *wy'br* correctly, because of the implicit quotation from Isa 8:8 in these verses.

29. *A year later.* The Hebrew *lammô'ēd* is usually translated as "at the appointed time." But the original Aramaic probably had *'iddān* here, which besides having the meaning of "time, period, season" (Hebrew *mô'ēd*), is also used in the sense of "year" in 4:13,20,22,29; 7:25. In 12:27, Hebrew *mô'ēd* almost certainly represents Aramaic *'iddān* in the sense of "year," and so also probably in the present verse. See NOTE on 4:13.

30. *the Kittim.* Although Hebrew *kittîm* referred originally to the inhabitants of the island of Cyprus, thus named after the chief Phoenician colony of Kittion on this island (Gen 10:4; Isa 23:1,12; etc.), in Jer 2:10 it probably refers to the peoples of the islands and coastlands of the Mediterranean in general. In I Macc 1:1; 8:5, it is used to designate the Macedonians. But here it refers to the Romans (as correctly rendered by the LXX). So also for the Qumran writers the Kittim (Hebrew *kittī'îm*) are the Romans (see F. M. Cross, *The Ancient Library of Qumran,* rev. ed., p. 82, note 46; p. 124, note 28). In the present verse, the author of chs. 10–12 offers a free interpretation (a *pesher* in the Qumran sense) of the passage in Num 24:24. Although the form of this passage as now preserved in the MT and as apparently read by our author had suffered corruption from its original form (cf. W. F. Albright, "The Oracles of Balaam," *JBL* 63 [1944], 207–233), the passage may be translated: "Ships

will come from Kittim, and they will afflict Assur, and they will afflict Eber." Our author interpreted this to mean: "Ships will come from Rome [or, Italy], and they [the Romans] will afflict the Seleucid Syrians, and the latter will afflict the Hebrews."

he will lose heart. In Hebrew, *w^e^nik'āh,* the niphal of a root **kā'āh,* which occurs only here in the MT; it is probably an Aramaism (cf. Syr. *k'',* "to rebuke, intimidate").

as he passes through. The Hebrew *w^e^'āśāh,* "and he will do," is based on Aramaic *wy'bd,* a misreading of Aramaic *wy'br,* "and he will pass through"; see NOTES on 11:28,39.

31. *the sanctuary and the pious ones*. The Hebrew, *hammiqdāš hammā'ôz,* means "the sanctuary, the stronghold." As pointed out above (see NOTE on 11:1), the original Aramaic had words from the root *ḥsn,* "to be strong," in 11:1,7,10,19, which the Hebrew translator correctly rendered by words from Hebrew *'wz*. But misled by this, he wrongly rendered Aramaic *ḥsyn,* "pious ones," by words from the same Hebrew root, *'wz* in 11:31,38,39. Our present passage refers to the same anti-Jewish decree of Epiphanes that is mentioned in I Macc 1:46: Epiphanes ordered his pagan soldiers "to defile the sanctuary and the holy ones" (in Greek: *mianai hagiasma kai hagious*). See NOTE on 8:10.

32. *he will make apostatize*. The Hebrew hiphil of **ḥānap* means elsewhere (Num 35:33; Jer 3:2,9) "to pollute" (the land). But here it is probably a denominative hiphil from the common adjective *ḥānēp,* "alienated from God, apostate" (Isa 9:16; 10:6; 33:14; etc.).

with flattery. Literally, "with slipperiness." That the reading of the MT, *baḥălaqqôt* is correct here and not to be emended to *baḥălaqlaqqôt* (as it is in 11:21,34, and in a few MSS here) is confirmed by the phrase, *dwršy hḥlqwt,* "seekers of flattery," in 4QpNah, where the term is borrowed directly from our present passage (see Cross, *Ancient Library of Qumran,* p. 91, note 25).

will take strong action. Literally, "will make strong and act" (hend.).

33. *the multitude*. Literally, "the many (*lārabbîm*)," a term often used in the Qumran documents in reference to the ordinary members of the community as distinct from its leaders. The *l* is merely the Aramaic sign of the direct object.

but they will be tested. The Hebrew, *w^e^nikš^e^lû,* means "and they will be tripped up," i.e. they will stumble. But in 11:35, *yikkāš^e^lû,* must mean in the context, "they will be tested"; therefore the same meaning is probable also in 11:33–34. In Aramaic, *hitt^e^qēl* (or, *'itt^e^qēl*) means both "to be weighed" and "to be tested" (so in Jewish Aramaic and Syriac). Since the Hebrew translator correctly rendered the passive of Aramaic *tql* by the niphal of Hebrew *kšl* in 11:14,19, he mechanically, but incorrectly, rendered it in the same way in 11:33–35,41. See Zimmermann, *JBL* 57 (1938), 266.

34. *insincerely*. Literally, "in slipperiness."

35. *and purify*. The MT vocalizes *wllbn* as a Hebrew aphel (!) infinitive, *w^e^lalbēn*. However, outside of the Book of Daniel in the MT the Hebrew denominative hiphil, *hilbîn,* always means literally "to become white" (Isa 1:18; Joel 1:7; Ps 51:9). Clearly the Hebrew translator, following his original Aramaic, intended *wllbn* to be read as a pi'el, *ûl^e^labbēn,* which is common in

Mishnaic Hebrew with the meaning, not only "to make white," but also "to polish, to purify"; cf. the passive hithpa'el, *yitlabb*^{e}*nû*, "they will be purified," in 12:10.

until the time of the final phase, for there is still the present appointed period. See Notes on 11:27 and 8:17.

36. *he will speak arrogantly.* See Note on 8:24.

38. *the pious ones.* See Note on 11:31.

on that God's stand. The literal, "on his stand," would be ambiguous in English. For Epiphanes' desecration of Yahweh's altar, cf. 8:11–12, and see Comment: Detailed on 8:9–12.

39. *he will bring over.* The Hebrew translator, with his *w*^{e}*'āśāh*, "and he will make," read Aramaic *wy'bd* instead of original Aramaic *wy'br*, just as he did in 11:28,30. Here, however, Aramaic *wy'br* should have been read as an aphel, *w*^{e}*ya'ăbēr*.

soldiers. Here, as frequently in the Hebrew Bible, *'am*, though normally meaning "people," is used in the military sense of "soldiers."

as their wages. Literally, "in price," i.e. for their services.

40. *passing through them like a flood.* Literally, "he shall overflow and cross over" (hend.).

41. *the lovely land.* The land of Israel, as in 11:16; see Note on 8:9.

will be tested. See Note on 11:33.

But Edom, Moab, and . . . from his power. Literally, "And these will be saved from his hand: Edom, Moab, and . . . the Ammonites." Although this sentence is written in correct enough Hebrew, there seems to be no reason for the first term, *w*^{e}*'ēlleh*, "and these." Perhaps the Aramaic original was *'ellâ*, "but," and the *w*^{e} before it came by dittography from the end of the preceding word (*yikkāšēlû*). The conjunction *'ellâ*, from earlier Aramaic *'im lâ*, "if not," is common in Mishnaic Hebrew, though ordinarily used after a preceding negative.

43. *treasures.* The *hapax legomenon* in Biblical Hebrew, **mikmannîm*, is an Aramaism; the root *kmn*, "to be hidden," is of frequent occurrence in Jewish Aramaic and Syriac.

44. *to completely exterminate.* Literally, "to destroy [*l*^{e}*hašmîd*] and to devote to utter destruction [*ûl*^{e}*haḥărîm*, i.e. to make *ḥerem*, doom]"; hend. The same two infinitives, but in inverse order, *l*^{e}*haḥărîm ûl*^{e}*hašmîd*, occur in II Chron 20:23.

45. *Yet when he has pitched.* Literally, "and he will plant" (Hebrew *w*^{e}*yiṭṭa'*). The ordinary Hebrew word for "pitching" a tent is *nāṭāh*, literally, "spreading out" the (more or less) flat roof of the bedouin cloth dwelling (e.g. Gen 12:8). Therefore, some have suggested emending *w*^{e}*yiṭṭa'* here to *w*^{e}*yiṭṭeh*. However, the MT may be correct, if the writer thought of driving the tent pegs into the ground (cf. Eccles 12:11), or he may have been influenced by the MT of Isa 51:16, where *linṭōa'*, "to spread out" the heavens like a tent, is generally corrected, with the Syriac, to *linṭôt*.

his palatial tents. Literally, "the tents of his palace." The *hapax legomenon* in Biblical Hebrew, *'appadnô*, "his palace," is an Aramaism, coming ultimately from the Old Persian word, *appadāna*, "colonnaded audience hall," which was borrowed both into Late Babylonian (see *CAD* 1, Part II, p. 178) and into so-called Imperial Aramaic (see M. Wagner, *Die lexikalischen und grammatikalischen Aramaismen im alttestamentlichen Hebräisch,* p. 28).

the Sea. The Mediterranean. Here the word is in the plural and without the article, *yammîm,* in keeping with archaic poetic usage (e.g. Judg 5:17; Deut 33:19).

the lovely holy mountain. Mount Zion, literally, "the mountain of loveliness of holiness" (see NOTE on 7:9, and cf. 11:16,41).

12:1. *Michael, the great prince.* Since "prince" (Hebrew *śār*) is used in chs. 10–12 in reference to an angel whom God has appointed the "guardian angel" over a nation (10:13,20), Michael, whom God has made the "guardian angel" of Israel (10:21), is the greatest of these "guardian angels." Therefore, he is called in Jude 9 *ho archangelos,* "the archangel." The concept of each nation having its own "guardian angel" is already witnessed to in Deut 32:8 (as emended according to 4QDeut 32 and LXX), where, however, Yahweh himself, and not an angel, is Israel's special guardian; cf. also Sir 17:(14)17. The concept, no doubt, goes back to Canaanite mythology, in which each nation has its own protecting deity; the Bible has eliminated the polytheistic element by making "the sons of El" into angels. [Cf. COMMENT: DETAILED on 10:13.]

the protector of your people. Literally, "he who stands over the sons of your people." For the late Hebrew idiom, *'āmad 'al,* literally, "to stand over," in the sense of "to protect, to defend," cf. Esther 8:1; 9:16.

the book. The document in which the divine decrees for the future are written (cf. Ezek 2:9–10; 3:1–3; Zech 5:1; Pss 41:8; 139:16)—similar in concept to the Babylonian "tablets of fate." Although the idea of "the book" may be connected here with that of "the book of life (or, of the living: Hebrew *seper haḥayyîm*)," in which God keeps listed the names of all who are alive on earth, the outlook in the present context is toward eschatological life (cf. Isa 4:3: "every one marked down for life").

2. *those who sleep.* A late Hebrew euphemism for "the dead," found already in Ps 22:30 (see M. Dahood, *Psalms I,* AB 16, p. 143) and of frequent occurrence in the New Testament (Matt 9:24; 27:52; John 11:11; Acts 7:60; I Cor 11:30; 15:20; etc.).

the dirt of the earth. The Hebrew phrase, *'admat 'āpār,* is usually rendered as "the dust of the earth"; but the Hebrew word for "dust" or "fine ashes" is *'eper,* not *'āpār,* which, as used here and elsewhere, means "dirt, clay." The present expression, *'admat 'āpār,* literally, "ground [or, earth] of clay," is taken from Gen 3:19, where Adam is condemned to return to "the ground" (*hā'ădāmāh*) and to "clay" (*'āpār*), because his body had been molded by God out of "the clay from the ground" (*'āpār min-hā'ădāmāh:* Gen 2:7).

will become everlasting objects of contempt and abhorrence. Literally, "will be for contempt, for abhorrence of eternity." Since the Hebrew word *dērā'ôn,* "abhorrence," is used elsewhere in the Hebrew Bible only in Isa 66:24, the word *ḥărāpôt,* "contempt," may be a gloss here on the rare term *dir'ôn 'ôlām,* "abhorrence of eternity," i.e. everlasting abhorrence. Note the absence in Hebrew of the conjunction *û,* "and," between the two terms.

3. *and those who lead the multitude to righteousness.* The Hebrew here, *ûmaṣdîqê hārabbîm,* is an echo of Isa 53:11: *yaṣdîq ʻabdî lārabbîm* [omit *ṣaddîq* as dittography], "my servant will bring righteousness to the many." On *hārabbîm,* literally, "the many," in the sense of "the multitude," see NOTE on 11:33.

4. *Many will apostatize, and evil will increase.* The MT is generally rendered something like "Many shall run to and fro, and knowledge shall increase" (so *RSV*). But this hardly makes any sense. The meaning given to it here is based on an emended text (see textual notes [ww] and [xx]).

5. *two others.* Two other angels.

6. *One of them said.* Literally, "And he said." The indefinite singular implies that Daniel does not recognize or does not wish to state which one of the two angels asked the question. Changing the MT's *wayyō'mer* to *wā'ōmer,* "and I said," on the basis of the Greek versions (so *RSV*), misses the point; as in 8:13–14,16, so here also Daniel overhears the conversation between the angels, but he himself does not take part in it.

the man clothed in linen. The angel spoken of in 10:5; see NOTE there.

who was upstream. Literally, "who was higher up on the waters of the stream," on the bank of which Daniel was standing (10:4). This seems to imply that the two other angels were farther down on the banks of the stream. The Hebrew word *hay*^{e}*'ôr* rendered here as "stream" is used elsewhere only of the Nile (except in Isa 33:21 and Job 28:10, where the plural, *y*^{e}*'ōrîm,* means "canals, channels").

these awful things. Literally, "the wondrous things" (*happ*^{e}*lā'ôt*); but the reference here is to the arrogant deeds (*niplā'ôt*) of Epiphanes (see NOTE on 8:24).

7. *a year, two years, and half a year.* As in 7:25, three and a half years. On Hebrew *môʻēd* as the equivalent of Aramaic *ʻiddān* in the sense of "year," see NOTES on 4:13; 11:29.

the desecrator. The Hebrew *nappēṣ* (infinitive piʻel of *npṣ*) is literally, "the shattering." However, as Ginsberg (pp. 83–84) suggests, *nappēṣ* is here a mistranslation from the original Aramaic, which had *mps* (*mappes=m*^{e}*happes*), "desecrator." See NOTE on 8:10. The translator understood *mps* as *mippas* (Aramaic infinitive p^{e}ʻal of *pss*), which in Jewish Aramaic can mean "to break up, divide, distribute," and hence he rendered it as Hebrew *nappēṣ,* "to shatter."

8. *the explanation.* The Hebrew word, *'aḥărît,* means "the latter part, the issue" (so *RSV*). But most likely the original Aramaic was *'ḥwyt* (*'aḥăwāyat,* "explanation," as in 5:12), which the translator misread (or found in his *Vorlage*) *'ḥryt* (*'aḥărît*), which does occur in the Aramaic of 2:28.

9. *secret and sealed.* Although these words are borrowed here from 12:4, where they have their natural, literal sense, in the present context they are given the meaning of "obscure, mysterious"; see COMMENT: DETAILED.

10. *cleansed, purified, and refined.* These words are taken from 11:35, where, however, they occur in a somewhat different form and order.

13. *reward.* Literally, "lot, allotted portion."

COMMENT: GENERAL

Although the apocalypse in ch. 7 is the core of the Book of Daniel, chs. 10–12, which form a single and final apocalypse, are by far the most important for historical information. As indicated in the COMMENT: GENERAL on ch. 9, the present apocalypse portrays a vision only in the sense that a heavenly being appears to Daniel and acts as *angelus revelator*. The apocalypses of chs. 7 and 8, however, are real visions in which various symbolic beasts appear and act, but the angel performs the function merely of interpreter. There are three dramatic parts to this narrative which is the longest and most intricate of the book's five apocalypses: *The Prologue* which describes the angel's appearance to Daniel and the opening conversation (10:1–11:1); *The Revelation of the Future* which provides a historical survey from the beginning of the Persian period down to the time of Antiochus IV (11:2–12:4); and *The Epilogue* which contains a concluding scene and the angel's final words to Daniel (12:5–13).

The Prologue. Daniel prepares himself by a fast of "three full weeks" for an oracle which was revealed to him "in the third year of King Cyrus of Persia" (10:1–3). Upon seeing a celestial being in the form of a man of dazzling appearance, Daniel becomes duly terrified (10:4–8). At the sound of the angel's voice Daniel falls prostrate to the ground. The angel touches him and reassures him that all is well. Still trembling, Daniel stands up. Then the angel tells about the war in heaven between the prince of the kingdom of Persia and himself, and how Michael, "one of the chief princes," comes to his aid (10:9–14). Despite the angel's reassurances, Daniel remains dumbstruck by what is happening to him. The angel touches him again, this time on the lips, a symbolic action that enables the seer to speak. A third touch finally restores Daniel's courage, and he urges the angel to speak on (10:15–11:1).

The Revelation of the Future. The angel informs Daniel that what he is about to hear "is written in the book of truth." There follows a select survey of history as it affects the fortunes of the Jews. Four Persian kings will arise; the fourth "will acquire the greatest riches of them all" and will stir up "the whole kingdom of Greece" (11:2). Alexander the Great (336–323 B.C.) will then arise, but his vast domain will be divided up (11:3–4). The conflicts of the Ptolemies and Seleucids are described as prelude (11:5–20) to the detailed account of the disastrous reign of the archvillain of the book, Antiochus IV Epiphanes, who "will succeed until the time of wrath is completed." Antiochus will blaspheme not only the true God but also his ancestral gods (11:21–45). But despite his ingenious schemes to subvert the true faith and its practices, God's people "will be rescued, every one of them who is found written in the book," thanks to the efforts of Michael, "the great prince" (12:1–3). The angel then gives Daniel a final exhortation (12:4).

The Epilogue. When asked by one of the two other angels who now appear in Daniel's vision how long these "awful things" will last, the *angelus revelator* answers, "a year, two years, and half a year" (12:5–10). Later glosses have 1,290 days (12:11) and 1,335 (12:12). The book ends with the consoling remark that Daniel "will rise for [his] reward at the end of the days" (12:13).

This last apocalypse is, in a sense, the climax of the book. Abundant details—some artificial, others of historical interest—are given that fill out the first four enigmatic apocalypses (chs. 2, 7, 8, 9) that also deal with the destiny of the Israel of faith at the end of the present evil age. As in the case of the earlier apocalypses, the vision here has the form of prophetic predictions of the future course of history. But actually what is found here, except for a few verses near the end, is a narrative account of selected events prior to and including the lifetime of the author, who undoubtedly lived during the reign of Antiochus IV. The chief purpose of the author was to demonstrate by means of these *vaticinia ex eventu* that the God of Israel is Lord of history, and that regardless of the severity and scope of the vicious persecutions initiated by Antiochus those Jews who remain loyal to the Covenant will be vindicated and rewarded at the end of the present age.

This apocalypse is modeled to some extent on the one in ch. 8. Both apocalypses, for example, have Hab 2:3a as theme, although in each the words of Habakkuk are applied differently; cf. COMMENT: GENERAL on ch. 8 and NOTES on 10:14; 11:27,35. Nevertheless, it is more probable to recognize with Ginsberg (pp. 35–37) that the author of the original apocalypse here is different from the author of the core apocalypse in ch. 8. The date of the present apocalypse can be ascertained on the basis of 11:40–45, a section which attempted, unsuccessfully, to predict the death of Antiochus IV. In these verses, the author, who is otherwise quite well informed as regards the career of Antiochus, shows no familiarity at all with the eastern campaign the tyrant began in 165 B.C., or with the rededication of the Temple on 14 December 164, or with the king's death in November or December 164. Hence, it is generally agreed that chs. 10–12 were composed in 165 or possibly early in 164 B.C., at the height of the Syrian persecution of the Jews who refused to become Hellenized.

Four glosses have been added to the work, the first two by the author of ch. 9, who was also the final redactor of the book. The first is 11:1, which attempts to identify the unknown *angelus revelator* of this apocalypse with the angel Gabriel in ch. 9. The second is the appendix (12:5–10,13) which has as its principal purpose to console the seer and to inform him that the persecution will last three and a half years, the same duration given in 7:25 and 9:27, all of which texts were written by the same author. The third and fourth glosses (12:11 and 12, respectively) are further attempts at specifying the length of time God's People will be subjected to adversity.

COMMENT: DETAILED

The Prologue (10:1–11:1)

Introduction (10:1). As indicated in the NOTE on 10:1, "the third year of King Cyrus," or 536 B.C., is a fictitious date, the latest in the book, to provide the setting for the *vaticinium post eventum* which is to follow. According to II Chron 36:32; Ezra 1:1 and 6:6, the Babylonian Exile came to an end in the first year of King Cyrus, or 538 B.C., the first year of his hegemony over the Jews—not the first year of his reign as king of Persia, ca. 550 B.C. The first year of Cyrus is also the date given in Dan 1:21 as being the apparent *terminus ad quem* of Daniel's ministry. No contradiction is necessarily involved in the dates in 10:1 and 1:21. In 1:21, the author merely states that Daniel was still active in the Babylonian court when Cyrus began his rule over the Jews in 538; nothing is said about Daniel's demise. It may be suggested, moreover, that "the third year" of Cyrus, or 536 B.C., was deliberately written here so that the years of Daniel's ministry, which began in 606 ("the third year of . . . Jehoiakim"; see NOTE on 1:1), would total the biblically perfect number seventy. If this suggestion be correct, then it could also be said that Daniel's "perfect" (i.e. most significant and extensive) vision took place in the seventieth or "perfect" year of his ministry.

The phrase, "in the third year," and the names, "King Cyrus" and "Belteshazzar," all of which appear here and in 1:1,7,21, may be viewed as instances of deliberate *inclusio* connecting the last narrative of the book with the first. This rhetorical device is common in biblical literature. In 10:1, the author speaks of Daniel in the third person, as in 7:1 and in the stories of chs. 1–6. Cyrus' being called "king of Persia," if meant as an official title, is anachronistic in the author's fictional 536 B.C. setting, as many commentators have noted (e.g. Driver, p. 152; Montgomery, p. 405; Charles, pp. 254–255; Jeffery, p. 500; Porteous, p. 150; Delcor, p. 205; Lacocque, pp. 151–152). Cyrus was indeed "king of Persia" and was so designated *before* he conquered Babylon in 538 B.C., but after the conquest he was known as "king of Babylon," "the king" (as in 1:21), "the great king," "king of kings," "king of the lands," or the like (often in combination). Cyrus was again called "king of Persia" but only in Hellenistic times. Cf. Driver, *Introduction,* pp. 545–546, and Linder, pp. 429–430. In 10:1, the author clearly implies that Daniel did not go back to Palestine with the first wave of returnees after Cyrus' Edict of Restoration; see vs. 4. "An oracle [Hebrew *dābār,* literally 'word, matter, thing'] was revealed [Hebrew *niglāh*]." The Hebrew verb *gālāh,* "to reveal," has a rich meaning in Second Isaiah (40:5; 47:2; 53:1; 56:1). Lacocque (p. 152) is of the opinion that the present apocalypse is a midrash on Isaiah, and that the midrash begins here with the verb *niglāh.* He points out that the noun *dābār* has become practically a synonym for "mystery," particularly when used in conjunction with the verb *gālāh.* In 9:2, *dābār* has a similar meaning. "The oracle was true": the author affirms that what is written in this apocalypse is absolutely trustworthy; a similar affirmation is made in 7:26. If the translation, "It concerned much warfare," is correct (see NOTE), reference is most likely being made to the human and angelic conflicts detailed in the narrative to follow. The sentence, "He paid attention to the oracle, so that he understood the revelation" (Hebrew *bîn 'et-haddābār ûbînāh lô bammar'eh*), recalls the words of 9:23, "Mark, then, the answer and attend to the revelation" (Hebrew *ûbîn baddābār w^{e}hābēn bammar'eh*). As will be indicated below, there are several other parallels between ch. 9 and the present unit.

Daniel's Fast and Penance (10:2–3). The motive for these ascetical practices is not stated here. But 10:12 suggests that by means of prayer and fasting Daniel prepared himself for understanding the divine revelation (10:1) he is about to receive; cf. 9:2–3,21–23. Similar spiritual preparations are described in Ezra 8:21; Esther 4:16; II Chron 20:3; Jer 36:9; II Esd 5:13,20; 6:31,35; 9:24–26; 12:51; II Baruch 5:7; 9:3; 12:5; 21:1; 47:2; Ascension of Isaiah 2:10–11; and Test. of Reuben 1:9–10. Since in II Esd 6:35 a fast of three weeks is also mentioned, quite probably the number "three" has symbolic value, denoting the idea that the fast was perfect; cf. M. H. Pope, "Number, Numbering, Numbers," *IDB* 3, p. 564. The expression, "three full weeks" is literally "three weeks *of days,*" and is probably used to differentiate from the phrase "weeks *of years*" that is clearly implied in ch. 9. Gen 41:1 has a similar phrase, "two years of days," and Deut 21:13, "a month of days." Daniel's fast did not involve abstention from all food and drink, but consisted rather in a kind of bread and water diet. Meat and wine were the food and drink of the prosperous or of those who were rejoicing (cf. Isa 22:13); 10:3 implies that Daniel, because of his position and status, had been accustomed to such provisions prior to his fast. Because anointing oneself with oil was considered a luxury (cf. Amos 6:6) and a sign of joy, it was omitted during periods of mourning (II Sam 14:2; Isa 61:3; Eccles 9:8; Judith 10:3) and fasting (Matt 6:17).

Daniel's Vision (10:4–8). In keeping with one of the usual conventions of apocalyptic literature (cf. Introduction, Part X) a precise date is assigned to Daniel's vision—"the twenty-fourth day of the first month" (10:4). "The first month," which corresponds approximately to mid-March to mid-April of our calendar, was also called "Abib" (a Canaanite word meaning "ears of barley," cf. Exod 9:31) prior to the Exile (cf. Exod 13:4; 23:15; 34:18; Deut 16:1), and "Nisan" (a Babylonian word probably meaning "first month" or "month of sacrifice") after the Exile (cf. Neh 2:1; Esther 3:7). These names, however, never achieved widespread acceptance in the biblical period; the most commonly employed system was naming the months by number, as in 10:4 (cf. S. J. De Vries, "Calendar," *IDB* 1, p. 486). If it may be assumed that "the twenty-fourth day" marked the end of Daniel's period of fasting, then the seer was doing penance during the Passover, on the fourteenth day of the same month, and the Feast of Unleavened Bread, which began the next day and continued to the twenty-first. Thus, Daniel's vision occurred three days after the close of the latter festival. The detail of "the great river" (see NOTE regarding the gloss, "that is, the Tigris") apparently is borrowed from Ezekiel (1:1), as indeed are many other features of the vision to follow. The river here is undoubtedly the same one referred to in 12:5–7.

When Daniel looked up he saw "a man"—not a human being, but, as is clear from what is said of him, an angelic being in human form (10:5). The angel is "clothed in linen" (see NOTE); the angelic being in Ezek 9:2,3,11; 10:2,6,7 is also dressed in a linen garment which distinguishes him from the six others whom he accompanied. Linen, considered a ritually pure fabric, was also worn by the priests in the Old Testament (cf. Lev 6:10), and in the Book of Revelation by the angels (Rev 15:6), the Lamb's Bride (Rev 19:8), and the armies of heaven (Rev 19:14). The angel is given no name, but is often identified with Gabriel because of the likenesses between 10:11,13–14,19,21 on the one hand and 8:15–16; 9:21–23 on the other. But the identification is far from certain. Charles (p. 257), who does not agree with this identification, aptly observes: "Not only does the description of this unnamed angel transcend immeasurably that of Gabriel in chapters 8 and 9, but the effect of his appearance on the Seer is far more profound." Jeffery (p. 502), following the lead of Charles, writes: "The description given here . . . suggests some supernatural being superior to Gabriel and Michael and carefully distinguished by the writer from them. Early Christian commentators saw in this figure the Messiah Jesus." The dazzling description of Jesus in Rev 1:13–16 and 2:18, which contain remarkable similarities with Dan 10:5–6,9, undoubtedly suggested this identification. "A belt of pure gold" was part of the costume of the wealthy and royal classes in the ancient Near East (cf. I Macc 10:89; 11:58). In Rev 1:13, Jesus also is adorned with such a belt or sash.

In 10:6, there is a description of the angel's body. Here the author relies heavily on Ezekiel 1 where the four living creatures or cherubim (cf. Ezek 10:20–22) are described. In 10:1, *gewîyāh,* an unusual word for "body," is exactly the Hebrew word used of the bodies of the cherubim in Ezek 1:11,23. Usually, however, *gewîyāh* means "corpse" (Judg 14:8–9; I Sam 31:10,12; Nahum 3:3). The Tarshish-stone, here translated "beryl" (see NOTE), is borrowed from Ezek 1:16, where it is used to describe the sparkling appearance of the wheels underneath each of the cherubim. Tarshish is probably derived from Tartessus in Spain whence the stone was reputed to be exported. The phrases, "his face shone like lightning, his eyes like flaming torches," are modeled on Ezek 1:13: "In among the living creatures something like burning coals of fire could be seen; they seemed like torches, moving to and fro among the living creatures. The fire gleamed, and from it came forth flashes of lightning." The expression, "his arms and feet had the gleam of burnished bronze," calls to mind the description of the cherubim in Ezek 1:7 (cf. NOTE). "His voice sounded like the roar of a multitude" is a reminiscence of Ezek 1:24. Hebrew *hāmôn,* here rendered "multitude," is a general word applying to any deep or loud sound —the roar of the sea (Jer 51:42); the tumult of the peoples (Ps 65:8); the rumble of an immense crowd (Isa 13:4); the noise of chariot-wheels (Jer 47:3); the sound of songs (Ezek 26:13), of shouting (I Sam 4:14), and of rain (I Kings 18:41). The author of the Book of Revelation employs many of the images found in 10:5–6 in his description of the exalted Jesus (Rev 1:13–16).

Although Daniel is in the company of several other men, only he sees the "great sight" (10:7). Apparently, however, his companions sense that something supernatural has happened (cf. NOTE). Terror-stricken, they flee the scene and go into hiding. This episode has some parallels in the two different accounts (Acts 9:7 and 22:9) of what Saul's companions experienced when he saw the vision of Jesus Christ on the road to Damascus. Daniel, now alone, is drained of strength and says, "I turned deathly pale" (10:8), Hebrew *wehôdî nehpak 'ālay lemašḥît* (cf. NOTES). The last Hebrew word is taken from Isa 52:14 which has a slightly different form, *mišḥat* (the verb root in both cases is *šḥt*). Second Isaiah uses the term to describe the disfigurement of the Servant of Yahweh. Cf. Lacocque, p. 155.

The Angel's Opening Address (10:9–14). Verses 9–11 are modeled on 8:16–18 and 9:21–23. At the sound of the angel's voice Daniel falls prostrate to the ground (cf. NOTE on 8:18), as does Saul during his dazzling experience of Jesus for the first time (Acts 9:3–4; 22:6–7). Falling face to the ground seems to be the usual gesture when one witnesses a theophany or angelic appearance (cf. 8:16–18; Josh 5:14; Ezek 1:28; Rev 1:17; I Enoch 24:24). Apparently, such a gesture is based on the Old Testament belief that for sinful man to see God is to die (cf. Exod 3:6; 19:21; 33:18–20; Isa 6:5). The appearance of Gabriel in 8:17–18, though it too terrified Daniel, was not quite so shocking an experience. Nevertheless, Daniel calls the sight "great" (10:8), doubtless with reference to the singular splendor and majesty displayed (cf. Keil, p. 414). Its effect on him was so powerful that he requires more celestial first-aid and supportive therapy than in ch. 8: "a hand touched me and raised me to my hands and knees" (10:10); " 'Daniel, greatly beloved,' he said to me '. . . Stand on your feet' " (10:11); " 'Don't be afraid, Daniel' " (10:12); "Then something like a human hand touched my lips" (10:16); "Once more the one who had the appearance of a man touched me and strengthened me, saying, 'Don't be afraid, greatly beloved; you are safe. Be courageous and strong' " (10:18–19). The phrase "Don't be afraid," repeated twice (10:12,19), is the usual expression of extraterrestrial visitors to allay the terror of the people to whom they appear; cf. Gen 15:1; 21:17; 26:24; Tobit 12:17; Luke 1:13,30. In the Old and New Testaments the phrase is also a formula of revelation introducing an oracle of salvation. Likewise it is the priestly response to an individual lament as in Lam 3:52–57 (cf. Lacocque, p. 155).

There is no convincing reason to assume that the hand in 10:10 belongs to anyone other than the celestial being first mentioned in 10:5 (cf. Jeffery, pp. 504–505). The angelic hand raised Daniel merely to all fours (cf. NOTE). Apparently, the seer now has enough strength restored to stand on his own two feet when the angel urges him to do so in 10:11. Daniel is affectionately called "greatly beloved" in 10:11 and 19, exactly the title he received from Gabriel in 9:23. The injunction, "stand on your feet" (cf. NOTE), implies that being upright is the normal position for a human being to be in when God reveals himself either directly or, as here, through an angel; cf. 8:18; Ezek 2:1–2. The "now" in 10:11 refers to the three-week delay mentioned in 10:13. The Hebrew verb *šālaḥ,* here translated "I have been sent with news" (cf. NOTE), and Greek *apostellō* in the LXX and Theod., are technical terms "for the sending of a messenger with a special task; the messenger himself does not have to be named. In other words, the emphasis rests on the fact of sending in conjunction with the one who sends, not on the one who is sent" (K. H. Rengstorf, *TDNT* 1, p. 400). Thus, despite the use of the verb *šālaḥ* in the first person singular, the unnamed angel calls attention not to himself but to God who sent him with the message. Although Daniel can stand up by himself now, thanks to the therapeutic touch he received in 10:10, he is still shaking all over. The purpose of the seer's ascetical practices in 10:2–3 is now explicitly stated: "to gain understanding" (10:12), presumably of what the angel is about to tell him. It was Daniel's prayer and penance that occasioned the angel's starting out from heaven in the first place. Despite the commission from God, however, the angel was deterred from going to Daniel immediately because "the prince of the kingdom of Persia" opposed him "for twenty-one days" (10:13), precisely the duration of Daniel's fast (10:2). But "Michael, one of the chief princes" came to the rescue and "was left [cf. NOTE] there with the prince of the kingdom of Persia" (10:13).

"The prince of the kingdom of Persia," mentioned twice (cf. Textual Notes [d–d] and [e]) in 10:13, and called simply "the prince of Persia" in 10:20 is not King Cyrus of 10:1 or a corporate person representing as a group the kings of Persia, as Calvin and most of the reformers thought, but is rather the tutelary spirit or guardian angel of the Persian kingdom, as the rabbis and most Christian commentators have rightly acknowledged (cf. Keil, p. 416; Jeffery, pp. 506–507). In like manner, Michael is the guardian angel of the Jewish people (cf. also I Enoch 20:5) and so is called "one of the chief princes" in 10:13, "your prince" in 10:21, and "the great prince, the protector of your people" in 12:1. The name "Michael" (Hebrew *mîkā'ēl,* "Who is like God?") is a theophoric name like Micaiah (Hebrew *mîkāyāh,* "Who is like Yahweh?") in Neh 12:35. It used to be thought that the name "Michael" in Daniel is a survival and a deliberately altered form of the name Mikal, a Canaanite god, that is found on some Canaanite inscriptions. Mikal appears unvocalized as *mkl,* probably from the verb root *ykl* which means "to be powerful"; hence, the name can be interpreted as "Powerful One" or "Conqueror." Cf. Delcor, pp. 210–211, for details. Now, however, we know for certain that the original name behind Hebrew *mîkā'ēl* is *mi-kà-il* ("Who is like Il, or god?"), a name that appears in the recently discovered Ebla documents written in Old Canaanite ca. 2400 B.C.; cf. G. Pettinato, "The Royal Archives of Tell Mardikh-Ebla," *BA* 39 (1976), 50. The use of the term "prince" in these verses probably depends on Josh 5:14–15 where the angel-commander of the army of Yahweh is also so named. What is implied here is that Israel has a powerful protector in the heavenly court, its tutelary spirit being Michael, one of the foremost angels. Thus, although the Chosen People may be of little significance in terms of political acumen, military capability, or economic resources, they will never be destroyed by any other nation, no matter how strong it may be. In Jude 9, Michael is designated "archangel," a title also given him in I Enoch 9:1 and 71:3; "archangel" corresponds to "great prince" in Dan 12:1. In Rev 12:7–9, Michael appears as leader of the angels battling against the huge dragon and his angels. In Daniel 8, God is referred to as "Prince of the host" and "the Prince of princes" (8:25); cf. COMMENT: DETAILED on 8:9–12,23–25.

The belief in guardian angels for nations is a survival of an ancient polytheistic theology which held that each city-state or nation or empire had a tutelary god who was in a particular way its protector, enjoying in return special status and cultic recognition. As in former times the patron-god looked after the interests of the nation in his charge, so in orthodox monotheistic circles the guardian angel was thought to be commissioned by the one God to see to it that the affairs of state ran smoothly. If anything went wrong in the nation, then the guardian angel could be blamed for lack of wisdom or skill. In this way, God would be excused from any charge of mismanagement or neglect. To preserve the basic Israelite tenet of monotheism, guardian angels were made subject to God's supreme authority, exercising their functions either by defying the divine will (as apparently the angels of Persia and Greece have done in Daniel 10–12), or by acting explicitly as God's agents (as Gabriel did in chs. 8 and 9 and the unnamed angel as well as Michael in chs. 10 and 12).

Echoes of an older Israelite theology that admitted the existence of other gods can be found in the Old Testament itself: Deut 4:19; 32:8 (but reading *b^e^nê 'ĕlôhîm,* "sons of God" as in 4QDeut^q^, instead of "sons of Israel" as in MT; cf. P. W. Skehan, *JBL* 78 [1959], 21); Josh 24:15; Judg 5:19–20; Isa 24:21; and Psalm 82. Deut 4:19; 32:8; and Psalm 82 seem to be the most immediate biblical sources from which the belief in a guardian angel for each nation evolved. In this development, the guardian angel replaced the tutelary god. But the time and circumstances of this transformation of belief remain uncertain. For a brief history of the doctrine of guardian angels for nations, cf. D. S. Russell, *The Method and Message of Jewish Apocalyptic,* pp. 244–249. A similar development can be traced in the belief of guardian angels for individual persons; cf. T. H. Gaster, *Myth, Legend, and Custom in the Old Testament,* pp. 212–214.

By the second century B.C. when the present apocalypse was composed, belief in tutelary angels for nations must have been widespread and perfectly orthodox; cf. Sir 17:17; Jub 15:31–32; I Enoch 20:5; 89:59–67. It is true that Psalm 82 and Isa 24:21 show traces of the tradition of heavenly battles between angelic beings, but that is all. The tradition achieves clear expression only in the Book of Daniel and in the later apocalyptic literature. The usual Old Testament scenario portrays Yahweh and his heavenly host fighting against human enemies on earth (cf. Judg 5:19–20 and Hab 3:12–13). Outside the Bible, the cosmic myths of Canaan and Mesopotamia depict in livid color heavenly battles fought by divine beings —e.g. the Enuma Elish (The Creation Epic), *ANET,* pp. 60–72, and the

Ugaritic Baal Epics, *ANET,* pp. 129–142. Cf. P. D. Miller, *The Divine Warrior in Early Israel,* HSM 5 (Harvard University Press, 1973). In the ancient Near Eastern myths the heavenly battle was what really mattered, the earthly counterpart being a mere by-product. By returning the locale to the heavens, the author of the present apocalypse seems to reflect a world structure similar to the one found in the ancient myths; so J. J. Collins, "Apocalyptic Eschatology as the Transcendence of Death," *CBQ* 36 (1974), 32–33; "The Mythology of Holy War in Daniel and the Qumran War Scroll: A Point of Transition in Jewish Apocalyptic," *VT* 25 (1975), 597–603.

Our author here assumes his readers are familiar with not only guardian angels but also the conflicts these angels engage in with one another as they go about their business of seeing to the best interests of their respective client-nations. It is not stated in 10:13,21 whether the conflict is a legal or military one. In II Macc 5:1–4, however, there is a graphic and dramatic account of a vision in which presumably angelic horsemen charge in mid-air, "companies fully armed with lances and drawn swords." This passage suggests that warfare does take place in heaven, but on a much larger scale than in Dan 10:13 where only the guardian angel of Israel opposes his Persian and, in 10:20, his Greek counterparts. The idea of a heavenly conflict between Michael and the Persian and Greek angels is transformed in Rev 12:7–9 to a large-scale battle between good angels and bad angels.

The purpose of the angel's mission is now stated explicitly: "I have come to make you understand what is to happen to your people in the last days" (10:14). The Hebrew phrase *bᵉʾaḥărît hayyāmîm,* "in the last days," is clearly eschatological; cf. NOTE on 2:28. The "last days" are those of Antiochus IV, during whose infamous reign the present work was written to encourage the Jews to remain faithful in the face of bitter persecution.

Daniel's Reaction and the Angel's Response (10:15 – 11:1). At the angel's announcement of new revelations to come (10:14), Daniel, though comforted and encouraged in 10:10–12, is again stunned into silence (10:15; cf. 8:17–18). But his terror is soon allayed by a touch on the lips. The "something like a human hand" (10:16) that does the touching belongs presumably to the angel whose first appearance is of "a man clothed in linen" (10:5). Isaiah and Jeremiah received their prophetic vocation by means of a touch (Isa 6:6–9; Jer 1:9–10). Here Daniel simply receives back the power of speech after being dumbstruck. Speaking for the first time to the angel, Daniel merely says he is overwhelmed with pain like birthpangs (10:16, cf. NOTE) and devoid of strength. He is deprived even of "breath," Hebrew *nᵉšāmāh* (10:17), without which life is impossible. In Gen 2:7, man, formed "out of the clay of the ground," becomes a living being only after God "blew into his nostrils the *nᵉšāmāh* of life." Four times (10:16,17[twice],19) Daniel calls the angel "my Lord" (Hebrew *'ădônî*), a title of great respect; cf. I Sam 1:15,26; 22:12. The angel touches the seer a third time, thus restoring his full strength (10:18). The angel's reassuring words, "You are safe" (cf. NOTE), soothe and encourage Daniel so much that he now invites the angel to speak on (10:19). In 10:10–19, the angelic touches, the twofold repetition of the phrases, "Don't be afraid" and "greatly beloved," and the other comforting words are artistic embellishments to highlight the awesomeness of the angel's appearance and the extraordinary significance of the revelation about to begin.

In 10:20, the question—"Do you know why I have come to you?" (cf. NOTE)—may be rhetorical, because back in 10:12,14 the angel has already informed the seer of the purpose of his visit; so Driver (p. 161), Jeffery (p. 509), and Rinaldi (p. 140). But it may also be suggested that the author uses this question as a dramatic device to emphasize that Daniel was too frightened or overwhelmed (cf. 10:15–17) to comprehend what had been said in 10:12,14. Delcor (p. 214) thinks the angel's question has as its purpose to call Daniel to attention; cf. the similar procedures in Zechariah 1–6 and Rev 7:13.

The Hebrew text of 10:20b–21 and 11:1 is jumbled (cf. NOTES). The present translation (cf. the Textual Notes) attempts to put some order into these verses; most commentators try to do the same thing. Because the angel is in a hurry "to go back to fight against the prince of Persia" (10:20b), he implies that he will be rather brief in giving Daniel the revelation. He begins by presenting a mini-summary of the "future" that will come to pass, a "future" he will explain in great detail in chs. 11 and 12. After the prince of Persia departs, i.e. after the Persian empire comes to an end, the prince of Greece will come, i.e. the empire of Alexander the Great and the kingdoms of the Ptolemies and Seleucids will arise (10:20c). Only Michael, the guardian angel of the Chosen People ("the best part of mankind," according to I Enoch 20:5), supports the angel against these princes (10:21). Instead of "Michael, your prince" of the MT, Papyrus 967 of the LXX reads: *Michaēl ho aggelos ho stratēgos ho dynatos ho hestōs epi tōn huiōn tou laou,* "Michael the angel, the powerful commander [or general], who has been placed [or stands] over the sons of the people." As pointed out in the NOTE, 11:1 is a later interpolation (hence the slashes given in the translation) which attempts to identify the anonymous angel of the present apocalypse with the angel Gabriel of ch. 9. The final redactor of the book, who wrote the bulk of ch. 9 (cf. COMMENT: DETAILED on 9:27), added this gloss in an attempt to provide a clear identity to the unnamed angel of ch. 10. Being specific as to dates and names is one of the characteristics of apocalyptic literature (cf. COMMENT: DETAILED on 10:4). Darius the Mede (11:1), as in 9:1, is not a historical person (cf. Introduction, Part VI).

The Revelation (11:2–12:4)

This is the lengthiest section of the present work. Like the dream in ch. 7 and the vision in ch. 8, the present vision or revelation purports to be a prophetic prediction "written in the book of truth" (11:2), of events that are to happen. It begins with the Persian age and culminates in the Maccabean age, becoming more and more specific and vivid as the godless rule of Antiochus IV Epiphanes approaches. The reign of terror of this villainous tyrant is described with the greatest precision and detail—another indication that this apocalypse was composed during his lifetime. In keeping with the fiction assumed in the book, Daniel is still in Babylon; but for this vision he is placed in time near the beginning of the Persian hegemony over that part of the world (10:1). Because the survey of world kingdoms from Cyrus the Great to Antiochus IV is popular and non-scientific history, there are some notable omissions as well as interesting, not to say tendentious, interpretations of the events alluded to. Montgomery appositely remarks (p. 421): "The writer gives the historian no new data until he reaches his own age, and even then his history is so veiled that all possible secular help is required for its interpretation; . . . his 'apocalypse' is chiefly valuable historically for its presentation of inner currents of Judaism in that age." The modern reader must employ utmost caution in utilizing the allusive language of the Book of Daniel as a historical source. The revelation comes to an end with a prediction, properly so called, that the righteous will ultimately triumph when God comes to their rescue (12:1–4). R. J. Clifford, "History and Myth in Daniel 10–12," *BASOR* 220 (1975), 23, writes "that in Dan 11:2b–35, where the author was bound by the historical record, he selected and structured historical details to give a profoundly original interpretation of Antiochus IV, which stemmed from his own Danielic party. In Dan 11:36–12:3, where he was not bound by Seleucid history, he re-used OT traditions and transformed Canaanite mythic material to the same purpose."

Outline of this section (11:2–12:4)

A. The Persian age (11:2).
B. Alexander the Great (336–323 B.C.) and the breakup of his empire (11:3–4).
C. The battles and fortunes of the earlier Seleucids and Ptolemies (11:5–20):
    1. Ptolemy I Soter (323–285) and Seleucus I Nicator (312/11–280) (11:5).

2. The intrigues of Ptolemy II Philadelphus (285–246) and Antiochus II Theos (261–246) (11:6).
3. The revenge of Ptolemy III Euergetes (246–221) for the death of his sister Berenice, and his overrunning the kingdom of Seleucus II Callinicus (246–226) (11:7–9).
4. The long and eventful reign of Antiochus III the Great (223–187) (11:10–19).
5. Seleucus IV Philopator (187–175) (11:20).

D. The infamous reign of Antiochus IV Epiphanes (175–164) and his bitter presecution of the Jews (11:21–45).
E. The final victory of God's chosen ones (12:1–4).

From the Persian Age to Antiochus IV (11:2–20). Now comes the revelation of the future course of events affecting the Jewish people. "*What is written* in the book of truth" (11:2)—the verb here (Hebrew *rāšûm,* qal passive participle of *ršm,* a loanword from Aramaic occurring only once in the MT) has the technical meaning of inscribing or registering decrees (cf. 5:24,25), or signing a document (cf. 6:9,11). "The book of truth" is God's infallible record of past history and of future events. Elsewhere God's book is said to be a ledger also of an individual's behavior and destiny; cf. Exod 32:32–33; Mal 3:16; Tobit 12:12; Pss 40:8; 56:9; 139:16; I Enoch 81:1–2. In Jub 5:12; 23:30–32; and 30:21–22, tablets are mentioned in which future events are recorded. T. H. Gaster, *Myth, Legend, and Custom,* p. 764, has shown that the concept of a "Book of Fate" was not uncommon in the ancient Near East. In Dan 12:1, reference is made to those "found written in the book." Whether "the book of truth" is a literary convention or theological datum is of peripheral significance. What the author clearly implies here is that the unfolding of history comes about under the sovereign sway of the Lord of history. Come what may, God's will shall be done, and his faithful ones, regardless of adversity and persecution, shall be vindicated.

The identification of the Persian kings is not commonly agreed upon by commentators. There is argument even over the number being referred to in 11:2. Presumably, Cyrus the Great is the first king; he is to be followed by three others. If "the fourth" refers to the fourth in the series, then there are only four kings. But if the fourth refers to a king after the three "still to arise," then there are five kings. For an excellent survey, with bibliography, of the opinions of the older commentators as to the identity of these four or five kings, see Montgomery, pp. 423–424. For more recent views, cf. Plöger, pp. 157–158; Delcor, pp. 218–219; Lacocque, pp. 160–161. The assumption is made here that the author of this apocalypse was familiar with the text and interpretation of ch. 7, in vs. 6 of which the Persian empire is described as a leopard with four heads symbolizing four kings whom the author knew from the Old Testament (e.g. Ezra 4:5–7) to be Cyrus, Ahasuerus (Xerxes), Artaxerxes I, and Darius II, called "Darius the Persian" in Neh 12:22 (cf. COMMENT: DETAILED on 7:6). Montgomery (p. 423), who is followed by Lacocque (p. 161), has Darius III Codomannus as the fourth king. There will probably be no consensus among scholars as to who these four or five kings are. It may be appropriate to recall here Montgomery's perceptive remark (p. 422) on ch. 11 in general: "The commentator must steer cautiously between the Scylla and Charybdis of over-insistence upon the chapter's worth as a historical document and depreciation of it. Many problems of interpretation must therefore be left *sub iudice*."

That Darius II, the fourth king, as suggested above, was not the richest of Persia's rulers—"the fourth will acquire the greatest riches of them all" (11:2)—does not necessarily argue against this interpretation. Xerxes, in fact, was the king particularly noted for his fabulous wealth; see Herodotus vii 20–21. The author of this section, quite in keeping with the type of epic panorama of history given here, may simply be attributing to the last Persian king the greatest riches as a sort of dramatic detail to highlight the wealth of Persia's kings as a whole, a wealth that amazed the ancient world and incited the greed of Alexander.

There is universal agreement as to the identity of the "mighty king" in 11:3. Alexander the Great, the he-goat with the big horn in 8:5–8,21, did indeed carve out the largest empire the world had known to that time. Although Alexander could "do as he pleases" because of his enormous success, he could still do nothing about the brevity of his rule, which lasted a mere twelve years and eight months. At the height of his power (cf. 8:8) he was dramatically laid low in Babylon by a death-dealing fever at the age of thirty-three. After his death, his empire was broken up and divided among four of his generals: Lysimachus, Cassander, Antigonus, and Ptolemy Soter. Cf. COMMENT: DETAILED on 8:8. Power struggles began almost immediately, and it was not until the decisive battle of Ipsus (Ipsos) in Phrygia in 301 B.C., more than twenty years after the initial breakup of Alexander's empire, that the political situation stabilized: Lysimachus was in control of Thrace and Asia Minor, Cassander of Macedonia and Greece, and Ptolemy Soter of Egypt, Palestine, and Phoenicia, while Seleucus replaced Antigonus in Babylonia and Syria. "The four winds of the heavens" (11:4), as in 8:8, refer most likely to the four regions of the compass (north, south, east, and west) rather than to the four major political divisions that emerged after 301. In the remainder of ch. 11 the author, it should be noted, refers to the particular Ptolemy being discussed as "the king of the south," and to the respective Seleucid as "the king of the north." None of Alexander's relatives or descendants succeeded in gaining control over any part of his vast empire. His ambitious generals gradually put each of them out of the way—his dim-witted half-brother Philip Arrhidaeus in 317; his posthumous son by Roxane in 311; and his illegitimate son Herakles in 309.

Now the author's attention concentrates on the struggles between the Ptolemies to the south and the Seleucids to the north for control of Phoenicia and Palestine. Indeed, it is only these two dynasties that directly concerned Jewish history. In 11:5, "the king of the south" is Ptolemy I Soter (323–285), son of Lagus, who became master of Egypt at Alexander's death but assumed the title of king only in 306. Seleucus I Nicator, who obtained the satrapy of Babylonia in 321, was forced to flee his domain in 316 in order to escape from Antigonus. Seleucus offered his services to Ptolemy (hence the phrase "one of his princes," 11:5) and together they defeated Demetrius, the son of Antigonus at Gaza in 312. Seleucus then recovered Babylonia and later northern Syria and the other eastern provinces of Alexander's empire. After the battle of Ipsus in 301, Seleucus was able to consolidate his power, and, except for Egypt and Palestine, he gained a huge empire extending from the Punjab to Asia Minor and across the Hellespont into Europe, thus satisfying his long-cherished ambition. He did indeed "gain dominion over a domain larger than [Ptolemy's]" (11:5)—this translation does not quite capture the alliterative paronomasia found in the Hebrew: *ûmāšāl mimšāl rab mimmemšaltô* (cf. textual note [q–q]).

In ca. 250 B.C., "after some years" (11:6), Ptolemy II Philadelphus (285–246), "the king of the south," attempted an ill-fated alliance with his archrival Antiochus II Theos (261–246), "the king of the north," by giving him in marriage his daughter Berenice. The conditions of this alliance practically assured tragedy for most of the individuals involved in the subsequent intrigues. Antiochus II had to divorce his wife and half-sister Laodice and had to exclude his two sons by her (Seleucus and Antiochus) from succession. Only a son of Berenice could succeed to the throne. After Ptolemy's death, however, Antiochus II violated the pact and put aside Berenice. He effected a reconciliation with his former wife Laodice, and they began living together again. This time 'round, however, Laodice took no chances and had Antiochus poisoned. Thus did she avenge the gross insult of the divorce. "Heaven has no rage like love to hatred turned, / Nor hell a fury like a woman scorned" (Wm. Congreve, *The Mourning Bride* III viii). Laodice also sent agents to murder the infant son of Berenice and later Berenice herself together with many of her Egyptian attendants. Thus did Laodice arrange to have her own sons put right back in line for succession to the Seleucid throne. All this calamitous history is summarized allusively in 11:6.

While these bloody events were taking place in the north, the son of Ptolemy II, Ptolemy III Euergetes (246–221), brother of Berenice, hence called "a scion of her own family" (11:7, cf. NOTE), was leading his army and fleet from the south to Seleucia and Antioch, "the strongholds of the king of the north" (11:7), and, though he subdued these cities, he was too late to save his sister. He did, however, avenge her brutal murder by putting Laodice to death. "The king of the north," Seleucus II Callinicus (246–226), son of Laodice, could offer no effective resistance against the Egyptian forces; so Ptolemy also conquered large portions of Upper Asia as far as Bactria. But for reasons which are not quite clear (St. Jerome suggests there was a sedition in Egypt) Ptolemy left the territory he had vanquished, thereby failing to make the most of his victory. When he returned to Egypt, however, he was in possession of enormous war spoils. St. Jerome relates that Ptolemy brought back with him forty thousand silver talents and twenty-five hundred precious vessels and images of gods, among which were included the very idols Cambyses had plundered from Egypt and carried off to Persia in 525 B.C. (cf. Linder, p. 450). It was for this good deed that the Egyptians gave Ptolemy III the title "Benefactor," Greek *Euergētēs*. Jerome's information is confirmed by the Canopus Decree (238 B.C.), in which Ptolemy is praised for having "restored the holy images carried out of the country by the Persians" (cf. Montgomery, p. 431). According to Josephus, Ptolemy "instead of sacrificing to the gods of Egypt in thanksgiving for his success, came to Jerusalem, and there, after our manner, offered numerous sacrifices to God, and dedicated votive gifts appropriate to such a victory" (*Against Apion* ii 5 [vol. 1, pp. 310–313, in the LCL edition]). "Even their gods, with their molten images and precious vessels of silver and gold he will carry off as booty into Egypt" (11:8)—carrying away the images of the gods of a subjugated land was common practice in the ancient Near East; cf. Isa 46:1–2; Jer 48:7; 49:3. "Egypt" in 11:8 is the first explicit mention of the country designated elsewhere in this section (except for 11:42–43) as "the south." Curiously, the LXX substitutes "Egypt" wherever the MT has "the south." Because Ptolemy's victory was not decisive, Seleucus II was able to "again rise up and invade the domain of the king of the south" (11:8b–9a). This reference is to the Syrian campaign in Egypt that began in 242 and ended disastrously in 240 when Seleucus was forced to return to Antioch (11:9b) with a decimated army (cf. Jeffery, p. 517).

Seleucus II was succeeded first in 227 B.C. by his elder son Seleucus III Ceraunus, who was murdered in 223, and then by his second son Antiochus III (223–187), about whose fortunes and incessant wars 11:10–19 are concerned. Because the author of this apocalypse almost certainly lived during part of the long reign of Antiochus III, he writes here on the basis of first-hand knowledge. After Antiochus consolidated his position by defeating certain treacherous aspirants to his throne, he began operations to fulfill the long-cherished dream of his house—the conquest of Phoenicia and Palestine or southern Syria, known as "Coele-

Syria," to distinguish it from northern Syria, or "Syria Seleucia" (the river Eleutherus was the boundary).

His Egyptian opponent was the morally flabby Ptolemy IV Philopator (221–203). Antiochus opened his campaign in 219 by recapturing Seleucia, the port of Antioch. Next came systematic and vigorous attacks against Palestine, the army's advance being described here as "passing along like a flood" (11:10a; cf. NOTE). In 217, Antiochus pressed a massive assault against Raphia, "the other's stronghold" (11:10b), on the Palestinian border but was met by a determined Egyptian force commanded by Ptolemy himself (11:11) and his sister-wife Arsinoe. According to Polybius (*Histories* v 79), Ptolemy's army consisted of seventy thousand foot soldiers, five thousand cavalry, and seventy-three elephants (the tanks of ancient warfare). Antiochus' "assembled multitude" (11:11) numbered some seventy thousand men, of which he lost seventeen thousand (cf. Montgomery, p. 433) when he suffered an ignominious defeat at the hands of Ptolemy (11:12), the erstwhile weakling and voluptuary. The words in brackets in 11:11 are simply an explanatory gloss. Ptolemy gained "no territory" (11:12; cf. NOTE), because once again he became too preoccupied with his playboy activities to capitalize on his spectacular victory (cf. Linder, p. 452). Ptolemy merely repossessed Coele-Syria and made peace with Antiochus.

The peace lasted about fourteen years, during which time Antiochus gained great fame by his eminently successful campaigns in Asia Minor and Persia up to the frontiers of India. For his brilliant recapture of the eastern part of the old Seleucid empire Antiochus won for himself the title "the Great." With his old confidence and power thus restored, Antiochus decided once again to settle matters with Egypt. Ptolemy IV had died in the meanwhile and was succeeded by his infant son Ptolemy V Epiphanes (203–181). There could be no better time to wage war on Egypt. Thanks to an alliance, Antiochus was able to enlist the help of Philip V of Macedon in a joint attack on Egypt. The Egyptian troops were under the command of Scopas, a highly competent Aetolian general. But the massive forces alluded to in 11:13 proved to be too much for Scopas who was roundly defeated in 199 at Paneas (later known as Caesarea Philippi), near the sources of the Jordan River. 11:14 is a parenthesis: the "many men [who] will rise up against the king of the south" are Egyptian insurgents reacting against the oppressive measures of Agathocles, the regent of the infant king, as well as the soldiers of Philip of Macedon. The "violent men of your own people [who] will lift themselves up" (11:14) belong most likely to a Jewish, pro-Seleucid party anxious for the overthrow of Egyptian sovereignty in Palestine; cf. Josephus *Antiquities* xii 3, 3–4 (vol. 7, pp. 64–79, in the LCL edition). What is being referred to in the phrase "in fulfillment of vision" (11:14; cf. NOTE) is difficult to say. Possibly because the phrase recalls the severe condemnation of the false prophets in Ezek 13:6, the allusion may be to an attempt on the part of some or all of these Jews to seek legitimation for their pro-Syrian activity by appealing to a made-to-order prophetic vision one of them is reputed to have experienced. "But they will fail" (11:14)—may be a reference to an anti-Egyptian uprising Scopas put down, as Jeffery (p. 520) suggests on the basis of a statement in Polybius (*Histories* xvi 39, 1). The sacred author condemns these Jews also because they supported Antiochus III, the father of the despicable tyrant Antiochus IV.

The narrative now resumes with 11:15, which is a continuation of 11:13, 11:14 being as stated above a parenthesis; hence, the repetition of the subject "the king of the north." After Scopas was defeated at Paneas, he led his battered troops to the Egyptian fortress of Sidon. Antiochus laid siege to the city and took possession of it in 198 B.C., when famine compelled Scopas to surrender. The "picked troops" are either Scopas' own well-trained Aetolian mercenaries, or special forces sent from Egypt to relieve him. Antiochus was now firmly in control of Coele-Syria, "with no one opposing him" (11:16a). Thus all of "the lovely land" (11:16a) became part of the Seleucid empire. "The lovely land," meaning Palestine (cf. NOTE on 8:9), is an expression that is found also in I Enoch 89:40 and 90:20. Prompted by his dazzling successes in Phoenicia and Palestine, Antiochus "set himself to gain control of the other's kingdom" (11:17; cf. NOTE). In 197, he seized three areas on the southern coast of Asia Minor—Cilicia, Lycia, and Caria, all of which had been under Egyptian rule—thereby further weakening his enemy while at the same time consolidating his control over his newly conquered territories. Antiochus did not, however, attack Egypt proper, for he feared intervention on the part of Rome. Instead he made "a peace treaty with" Ptolemy V and sealed it by giving "him his daughter in marriage" (11:17; cf. NOTE). The woman's name was Cleopatra, Egypt's first. According to St. Jerome, the formal betrothal took place in 197, and the marriage in 193 at Raphia. Antiochus had hoped to manipulate Ptolemy through Cleopatra "in order to destroy him" (11:17). But the scheme failed completely, or as the author puts it, "it will not stand; it will not be" (11:17; cf. NOTE). Marriage alliances between Seleucids and Ptolemies just did not fulfill the great expectations of their initiators; see COMMENT: DETAILED on 11:6. Cleopatra proved to be perfectly loyal to her new husband and homeland, even urging an alliance of Egypt with Rome, which would turn out to be a calamity for Antiochus and his cherished dreams of achieving a mighty empire like Alexander's.

In 197 B.C. or shortly thereafter, Antiochus resumed his incursions into the "sea lands" (11:18; cf. NOTE) of Asia Minor, overrunning many Egyptian cities, despite the peace treaty. The Macedonian towns were also easy prey, thanks to setbacks suffered by Philip of Macedon. Antiochus then crossed the Hellespont to claim the Thracian Chersonese, former satrapy of Lysimachus; he was now in a position to attack Greece itself. Insolently ignoring the warnings of the Romans to keep his hands off Greece, he went ahead with his invasion in 192, only to be defeated soundly by the Romans at Thermopylae a year later. Then in 190, the Romans drove him also out of Asia Minor, crushing his forces in a decisive battle at Magnesia near Smyrna. This overwhelming victory marked the end of Antiochus' power west of the Halys River and Taurus Mountains. The "magistrate" of 11:18 (cf. NOTE) is evidently Lucius Cornelius Scipio who ruined Antiochus at Magnesia, thus earning for himself the title Asiaticus. The words in brackets in 11:18 are a gloss rephrasing the last words of the previous sentence; presumably, the editor responsible for the gloss wanted to emphasize that the colossal insolence and insufferable *hybris* of Antiochus were adequately requited by Scipio who forced him to submit to humiliating peace terms, which included the payment of a huge indemnity to Rome. Now despoiled of his western territories, Antiochus had no choice but to "turn his attention back to the strongholds of his own land" (11:19a). In 187 B.C. at Elymais he stumbled and fell and disappeared (11:19b; cf. NOTE), i.e. he was assassinated while attempting to sack the treasury of Bel, one of his own gods, in order to meet his payments of tribute to Rome. In this ignominious manner ended the career of Antiochus III who had once earned the title, the Great.

The lackluster reign of Seleucus IV Philopator (187–175), son of Antiochus, is given brief, almost sarcastic, notice in 11:20. His reign of twelve years is described as "a short time" relative to the lengthy, thirty-six-year rule of his father. Inheriting his father's enormous financial burdens, the weak and ineffective Seleucus had as first priority the raising of money, hardly a task befitting a king. Because of this unattractive necessity he could do nothing to win back the domains lost by his father's misadventures. Hence, the sacred author characterizes him as "one suffering a loss of dominion, glory, and sovereignty." If this translation is correct (cf. NOTE on 11:20), the verse says nothing directly about Seleucus' sending his foster brother and finance minister Heliodorus on a mission to Jerusalem to pillage the treasury of the Temple, a story dramatically narrated in II Macc 3:1–40. Seleucus was assassinated in 175 B.C., the victim of a conspiracy planned by the same Heliodorus and possibly abetted by Seleucus' younger brother Antiochus IV who was on his way back to Syria after being held hostage in Rome since 190. It is because of this furtive plot that the destruction of Seleucus is said to have occurred "not openly [cf. NOTE] or in battle" (11:20). In other words, even his death was inglorious and unbecoming a king. Montgomery (p. 448) writes: "He was killed, but not 'with his boots on,' a disgrace to a king; *cf.* Saul's death."

The Reign of Antiochus IV (175–164 B.C.) (11:21–45). The notorious Antiochus IV Epiphanes receives the lion's share of space in ch. 11. The reason is not hard to understand. The sacred author, who doubtless composed this apocalypse some time before the tyrant's death late in 164 B.C., had personally lived and suffered through the diabolical and systematic persecution depicted here. The purpose of this chapter and indeed of the rest of the book was to urge on his fellow Jews continued fidelity to their religious heritage. As pointed out in the COMMENT: GENERAL, the author skillfully employs the device of fictional prophecy (*prophetia post eventum*) to convey to the recipients of the book the solemn and infallible assurance that history and its outcome fall under the sovereign and almighty sway of "him who lives forever" (12:7). Notwithstanding immediate victories of the forces of evil (11:36), God will ultimately prevail and will vindicate his faithful people (12:1–3). If apocalyptic can be defined as resistance literature (cf. Introduction, Part X), here is an illustration of it at its best. This section of ch. 11 is divided into the following: Antiochus' usurpation of the throne and early rule (11:21–24c); his first war with Egypt (11:24d–28); his second war with Egypt and its aftermath (11:29–35); his blasphemous behavior (11:36–39); an imaginative prediction of his death (11:40–45).

Antiochus IV's Usurpation of the Throne and Early Reign. After the battle of Magnesia in 190 B.C. Antiochus IV, the younger son of defeated Antiochus the Great, was taken as hostage to Rome where he lived for fourteen years in royal splendor rather than as a prisoner. Then for reasons which are far from clear, his brother Seleucus IV shortly before his assassination sent his own elder son Demetrius to replace Antiochus in Rome. On the way home Antiochus lived in Athens for a while and got himself elected to the chief magistracy of that still famous city, so great was his charm and the political acumen he had acquired while in Rome. When news of the murder of Seleucus IV reached him in Athens he left immediately for Antioch. Demetrius, now hostage in Rome, was of course the legitimate heir to his murdered father's throne; but Heliodorus, chief of the conspirators responsible for the death of Seleucus, was busy at another conspiracy to seize power under the pretext of acting as regent of the younger son of Seleucus. But thanks to some outside help on his arrival in Antioch, Antiochus was able to move swiftly to nullify the conspiracy. Heliodorus fled; Antiochus "who had been spurned and upon whom the royal insignia had not been conferred" (11:21) usurped the throne and murdered his young nephew the puppet king. So cunning and thorough had Antiochus been that he was able to gain control of the kingdom almost immediately. His sly machinations and rapid climb to power are summarized in 11:21 (cf. NOTES).

The panoramic view of Antiochus' reign given in 11:22 does not violate chronology. The first half of the verse implies that Antiochus had to put down armed opposition to his takeover of the Seleucid throne. He was able, however, to undo any attempts on his power. As pointed out in the NOTE, "the prince of the covenant" (11:22b) is the Jerusalem high priest, who would "be crushed" because of Antiochus' wicked interference in the high priestly office. Recent commentators agree that the man in question is Onias III who was firmly opposed to the Hellenizing policies of Antiochus. Shortly after his accession in 175 B.C. Antiochus was approached by Onias' brother Jason who in exchange for the high priestly office was willing to offer the monarch a generous bribe of "three hundred and sixty talents of silver, as well as eighty talents from another source of income" (II Macc 4:8). Jason, moreover, not only agreed to the Hellenization of Judaism but would himself take positive measures to promote this policy (cf. II Macc 4:9–19). Not being one to pass up a good deal, Antiochus graciously accepted Jason's bribe and deposed Onias. In ca. 172, Menelaus approached Antiochus and outbid Jason for the high priesthood by three hundred talents of silver (II Macc 4:23–24). Now it was Jason's turn to be deprived of office. Some time later, when Onias learned that Menelaus had stolen some gold vessels from the Temple, he made a public protest and to ensure his own safety fled to the sanctuary of Daphne. In 170, Menelaus had Onias treacherously murdered outside that sanctuary (cf. II Macc 4:32–34).

Commentators are not in agreement as to the events referred to in 11:23–24. Some of the older commentaries understand 11:22–24 as allusions to Antiochus' devious associations with Egypt's rulers, translating *n^{e}gîd b^{e}rît* not as "the prince of the covenant" but as "a prince allied to him," i.e. Ptolemy VI Philometor (181–146 B.C.), son of his sister Cleopatra; cf. Linder, pp. 459–462. Most modern exegetes, who accept the interpretation of 11:22 given above, think that 11:23–24 refer to Antiochus' activities in Syria-Palestine during the earlier part of his reign. The treachery and double-dealing of Antiochus in consolidating his power and influence were quite well known; 11:23 merely gives an impressionistic mini-précis of his rise to power and his other shady operations. The mention of his invading "the richest parts of the provinces" (11:24a) is undoubtedly, as Montgomery points out (p. 452), a reference to his "ability in seizing by hook and crook the wealth of the provinces, in advance of the attack upon Egypt." 11:24b–c alludes to Antiochus' extravagant and senseless squandering of plunder, spoil, and other stolen riches upon his friends and supporters; cf. Introduction, Part VI. I Macc 3:20 states explicitly that Antiochus gave gifts "with a more liberal hand than the preceding kings." Josephus *Antiquities* xii 7, 2 (vol. 7, p. 151, in the LCL edition), speaks of Antiochus as "being munificent and liberal with gifts."

Antiochus' First War with Egypt (11:24d–28). Against which "fortified cities" of Egypt (11:24d; cf. NOTE) Antiochus devised plans is not clear. Most likely, however, one of them was the frontier fortress and key city of Pelusium which he in fact seized in 169 on his campaign into Egypt. Whatever the case, this brief summary (11:24d) of the first Egyptian war concludes with the calm and firm assurance that Antiochus would prevail, "but only for a time" (Hebrew *wᵉʿad-ʿēt,* literally "but up to a time"). Regardless of his wealth and power, his military prowess and cunning, Antiochus would not exceed the limits allotted him by the Lord of history (cf. 11:27).

A few selected details of the Syrian-Egyptian war are supplied in 11:25–28. The causes of the war are not given, but it is known from other sources that the unwise advisers of Ptolemy VI Philometor actually provoked Antiochus to attack. Antiochus' sister Cleopatra had been the intelligent and enterprising regent of Egypt while her sons Ptolemy VI and Ptolemy VII Euergetes II Physcon were minors. When she died in 172 B.C., Philometor was technically king, but was actually a puppet of two ambitious advisers—the eunuch Eulaeus and the Syrian Lenaeus, who foolishly urged the young king to recapture Syria and Palestine, which had been possessions of Egypt years before. In 169, Antiochus met and crushed the invading Egyptian army, and then proceeded to capture the key border fortress of Pelusium and later the city of Memphis. His army thoroughly routed, Philometor was persuaded again by his unwise counselors to flee, but Antiochus caught up with him and took him captive. The account of this campaign is also found in I Macc 1:16–19. The disastrous defeat of Philometor's forces is attributed to "the plots devised against him by the members of his court, who will seek to destroy him" (11:25–26). The allusion is most likely to the singularly stupid advice given by Eulaeus and Lenaeus indicated above.

The two kings in 11:27 are, of course, Antiochus and his nephew and prisoner Ptolemy Philometor. When Antiochus attempted to subdue Alexandria he failed. There powerful nobles had crowned Philometor's brother as Ptolemy VII Euergetes II Physcon. This act gave Antiochus a good pretext for masquerading as protector of Philometor's interests and crown. Antiochus and Philometor apparently became allied against Physcon—an alliance Antiochus had high hopes of using to weaken Egypt by strengthening the rivalry between his two royal nephews. The sacred author suggests here that Philometor himself, despite his youth, was no stranger to double-dealing. What he was plotting, however, is not stated, nor is it known from other sources. "The two kings . . . will sit together at table and exchange lies"—the author severely indicts both kings for the grossness of their treachery because each was guilty of violating a solemn principle of ancient Near Eastern ethics, plotting evil against a table companion (cf. Ps 41:10; John 13:18). "Their alliance will have no success" not only because Antiochus' scheme to drive a wedge between his two nephews was thwarted when the two Ptolemies were later reconciled by their sister Cleopatra II and agreed to a joint rule, but also, and more importantly from the author's religious perspective, because "there is still a final phase for the appointed period" (cf. NOTE); i.e. the end of Egyptian power will come not by human designs but only when the period appointed by God has run its course. Thus, as in 11:24, the inspired author stresses here the theological datum that God is Lord of history.

In 11:28, mention is made of Antiochus' return "to his own land with great riches" (cf. I Macc 1:19). Several reasons prompted his leaving Egypt with only part of his plans accomplished. One of the reasons was turmoil in Jerusalem. It seems a rumor got started that Antiochus had been killed in action in Egypt. Jason, who had been deposed as high priest after being outbid by Menelaus (cf. COMMENT: DETAILED on 11:22), seized the opportunity to try to reinstate himself in office. To ensure success Jason also murdered many of the supporters of Menelaus. When Antiochus heard of these activities he became enraged. He invaded Jerusalem, and as punishment for Jason's revolt massacred many Jews. Then with the reinstated Menelaus acting as guide, he looted the Temple and carried its treasures back to his capital Antioch. A detailed and somewhat imaginative account of this shameful episode is found in II Macc 5:5–21; a condensed account in I Macc 1:20–24. The highhanded and barbaric actions of Antiochus in Jerusalem resulted from his mind being "set against the holy covenant" (11:28). The Hebrew phrase *bᵉrît qōdeš* (also in 11:30), literally, "the covenant of holiness," means the true (i.e. Jewish) religion. Theod. has here *diathēkē hagia,* an expression which is taken over in I Macc 1:15,63 with the same meaning. Antiochus reacted swiftly and brutally to reinstate Menelaus because in his mind what was at issue was not religion but rather his authority, which Jason had attempted to undermine. In the purview of the sacred author, however, Antiochus was fighting against God himself when he interfered with the practice of the Jewish faith and desecrated the Temple.

Antiochus' Second War with Egypt and Its Aftermath (11:29–35). Shortly after Antiochus left Egypt to settle matters in Jerusalem, he received word from Egypt that Philometor and Physcon had been reconciled by their sister and were now reigning conjointly. They also agreed to join forces against their Syrian uncle. Furious at this unexpected turn of events, Antiochus invaded Egypt in 168 B.C., just about a year (cf. NOTE) after his first successful campaign there. "But the second invasion will not be like the first one" (11:29), because "ships of the Kittim" (11:30; cf. NOTE) will come against him, carrying a Roman delegation headed by Gaius Popillius Laenas. It was this gentleman who in the name of Rome ordered Antiochus to leave Egypt forthwith. When Antiochus tried to temporize, Popillius, adding insult to injury, drew a circle around Antiochus and demanded a decision before the king stepped outside it. Antiochus, of course, dared not disobey, and so with knuckles sharply rapped and pride deeply wounded, he returned home, or as our author has it, "he will lose heart and retreat" (11:30). For further details and references to the ancient sources, cf. Schürer, pp. 151–152. The haughty and impudent Antiochus finally received some of his own medicine. His power play for control of Egypt had been totally neutralized by mighty Rome.

Cowed, frustrated, and enraged, Antiochus decided to strengthen his hold on Palestine. Some years before, his policy of Hellenization had been instigated primarily as a unifying factor in his domain, and even in the Holy Land he had succeeded in recruiting many Jews who went along with his basically pagan programs (cf. Introduction, Part VI). As mentioned above, the high priestly office itself was purchased first by Jason and then by Menelaus, both of whom were energetic supporters of Hellenistic culture and religion. 11:30b–35 tell how Antiochus, passing through Judea on his way from Egypt to Antioch, vented his feelings of rage on pious Jews particularly in Jerusalem who opposed his Hellenizing activities. But renegade Jews (the *paranomoi,* "lawless ones," of I Macc 1:11) who went along with him he left alone (11:30b). Bitter and bloody persecution lasted from 167 to 164 B.C. It is not known whether on this occasion Antiochus intervened personally in Jerusalem as he did after the first Egyptian campaign (cf. 11:28); cf. Schürer (pp. 152–154) for details as to the contrasting views of scholars on this question. What seems certain, however, is that after Antiochus' appearance in Jerusalem following the first Egyptian war in 169, he had stationed "Philip, a Phrygian by birth, and in character more cruel than the man who appointed him" (II Macc 5:22), as a royal governor in Jerusalem, and Andronicus as governor in Samaria. It was the responsibility of these royal appointees to further the policy of Hellenization. Evidently, the opposition to that policy in Jerusalem was too great for Philip and his troops to handle effectively. Consequently, according to II Macc 5:23–26 and I Macc 1:29–35, in 167 B.C. Antiochus sent Apollonius, the brutal commander of his Mysian mercenaries, at the head of a large force to teach Jerusalem a lesson. "When this man arrived in Jerusalem, he pretended to be peacefully disposed and waited until the holy day of the sabbath; then, finding the Jews refraining from work, he ordered his men to parade fully armed. All those who came out to watch, he massacred, and running through the city with armed men, he cut down a large number of people" (II Macc 5:25–26). "He plundered the city and set fire to it, demolished its houses and its surrounding walls, took captive the women and children, and seized the cattle. Then they built up the City of David with a high, massive wall and strong towers, and it became their citadel" (I Macc 1:31–33). The citadel mentioned here was called the Akra and was manned by Syrian troops, "the armed forces . . . stationed by him [i.e. Antiochus]" in 11:31a. For a period of twenty-five years the Akra stood as a loathsome symbol of pagan domination. In it were garrisoned Gentiles (I Macc 3:45; 14:36) and apostate Jews (I Macc 6:21–24; 11:21) whose principal aim was to harass loyal Jews and to strengthen the cause of Hellenization (I Macc 6:18); for a brief history of the Akra, cf. Abel, pp. 121–124.

As regards "the sanctuary and the pious ones" in 11:31, see NOTE. I Macc 1:44–50 contains a detailed list of anti-Jewish regulations that Antiochus issued in Jerusalem and other cities of Judah. Among these is the prohibition of "holocausts, sacrifices, and libations in the sanctuary" (I Macc 1:45), the "daily sacrifice" of Dan 11:31c. The "appalling abomination" (11:31c) was the altar and/or image of *Ba'al Shāmēn* ("Ba'al [Lord] of the heavens") or *Zeus Olympios* in Greek (cf. II Macc 6:2). As to whether there was an altar or an image or both, cf. H. H. Rowley, "Menelaus and the Abomination of Desolation," in *Studia Orientalia Ioanni Pedersen* (Copenhagen: Einar Munkegaard, 1953), pp. 303–315. The "abomination" was set up in early December 167 B.C., according to I Macc 1:54; cf. NOTES and COMMENT: DETAILED on 8:11–12 and 9:27. Antiochus also forced the Jews to take part in the sacrifices offered at the monthly celebration of his birthday, and to march in procession wearing wreaths of ivy during the festival of Dionysus (Bacchus), god of the grape harvest and wine (cf. II Macc 6:7).

"Those who act wickedly against the covenant" (11:32a) are doubtless the same group mentioned in 11:30c. The Hebrew expression used to describe these people in 11:32a, *maršî'ê berît,* is found also in the Dead Sea Scrolls (1QM 1, 2) to designate, as here, the renegade Hellenizers. These reprobates were induced to apostatize by "flattery" (11:32a; cf. NOTE)—a method used unsuccessfully on the stalwart Mattathias in I Macc 2:17–18. "But the people who are loyal to their God [literally, the people who know their God] will take strong action" (11:32b); i.e. they will remain firm in the practice of their faith, ready to endure suffering and death (cf. I Macc 1:60–63). "Those . . . who act wisely," Hebrew *hammaśkîlîm* (11:33a), are the Jewish leaders of the anti-Hellenistic resistance, who are later called in Greek *Hasidaioi,* usually transcribed Ḥasidim, from Hebrew *ḥăsîdîm,* "pious ones" (I Macc 2:42; 7:13; II Macc 14:6). Cf. Introduction, Part VII, on the Ḥasidic origin of the Book of Daniel. The loyal, hence wise, Jewish leaders made "the multitude [Hebrew *hārabbîm*] understand" (11:33a) what needed to be done, for the ordinary Jew was confused by the tumultuous events he had to live through and was undecided whether he should go along with Hellenization as even some of the high priests had done. With fidelity to the covenant would come the test of "sword and flames," exile and loss of property (11:33b). As Jeffery points out (p. 533), four types of persecution are mentioned, not because the Syrian oppressors used only four, but because it is characteristic of this sacred author to gather related items into groups of four. Details of these bloody persecutions and cruel afflictions are found in I Macc 1:30–32,60–63; 2:6–12,27–38; 3:38–41; II Macc 6:6–11,18–31; 7:1–41; cf. Heb 11:36–38. The testing will last, however, only "for some time," literally, "for (some) days" (11:33b) because God will not permit the oppression to exceed its allotted measure. The association of *ham-maśkîlîm* and *hārabbîm* in 11:33a is a clear reminiscence of Isa 52:13–53:12, one of the Suffering Servant Songs. H. L. Ginsberg, "The Oldest Interpretation of the Suffering Servant," *VT* 3 (1953), 400–404, presents a good case that the inspired author has identified the Servant with the *maśkîlîm,* who like the Servant will justify the many, *hārabbîm;* cf. also 10:8 and 12:3.

The desperate plight of the faithful Jews was alleviated somewhat—"will receive a little help" (11:34a)—by the first relatively modest successes of the Maccabean resistance movement under Mattathias and his son Judas (I Macc 2:15–28,42–48; 3:10–26; 4:1–25). But the sacred author appears unenthusiastic about such military measures; hence, his expression "a little help." On the origin of the Book of Daniel as a pacifistic manifesto, cf. Introduction, Part VII. Overzealous in championing the cause of their religion, Mattathias and Judas dealt harshly and swiftly with renegade Jews (I Macc 2:44–46; 3:5–8). They even forcibly circumcised any boys found in the territory of Israel (I Macc 2:46). Because of such brutal measures, many Jews who had previously renounced the practice of their faith for the security and comforts of Hellenistic culture and religion, joined in the resistance movement to save their necks: "many will join them insincerely" (11:34b). But as soon as the opportunity presented itself, such Jews again abandoned their faith (I Macc 9:23).

In 11:35, the author speaks again of the wise leaders of the Jews first mentioned in 11:33 and later in 12:3,10; here the purpose of their being "tested" is stated explicitly, "to refine, cleanse, and purify them." The Deuteronomic theology of retribution (Deuteronomy 28) did allow the possibility of adversity serving as a test of fidelity or as a means of purification, as here; cf. Job 5:17–18; Judg 2:22–3:6; Prov 3:11–12; Sir 2:1–2,5. Cf. A. A. Di Lella, "Conservative and Progressive Theology: Sirach and Wisdom," *CBQ* 28 (1966), 143–145. Our author may have had some feeling for the Maccabean revolt, but his true sympathies lay with those engaged in non-violent resistance. It was their suffering love unto death that would "refine, cleanse, and purify" the nation and vindicate the principles of true religion which no human power can crush. Montgomery (p. 459) calls attention to this verse as being the earliest expression of the thought that "the blood of martyrs is the seed of the Church." As in 11:24 and 27 (cf. NOTES and COMMENT: DETAILED), the persecution will last only as long as God allows it.

Antiochus' Blasphemous Behavior (11:36–39). The inspired author's survey of history as interpreted from a uniquely theological viewpoint was brought up to his own day in 11:35. The next section provides a description and evaluation of the conduct of the supercilious and contemptible Antiochus; cf. also 8:9–12 where his shameless activities are summarized. That the tyrant "will do as he pleases" (11:36a) should come as no surprise, for after all Alexander (11:3) and Antiochus the Great (11:16) are said to have done the same; cf. also 8:4. Nor is it extraordinary that Antiochus exalted himself (11:36b; cf. Isa 10:15) by assuming divine honors. Indeed Alexander and his Hellenized successors all were given such honors. What was especially pretentious and obnoxious to the pious Jew is that Antiochus IV took very seriously the honorific titles as well as the acclaim attached to them. He also considered himself "greater than any god" (11:36b,37c) in his empire—an appalling impiety even for the monotheistic author of these lines. Antiochus was the first to arrogate to himself the appellation Theos, "God," on his coins, and the addition of Epiphanes, "(God) Manifest" (almost in the sense of "Incarnate"), to his name shows the extent of his self-identification with the godhead. Also on his coins he had his portrait made to look like that of Zeus Olympios. It was for such consummate arrogance, among other things, that many of the people called Antiochus not Epiphanes but Epimanes, Greek for "mad man." Tcherikover (pp. 176–177) supplies other instances of Antiochus' peculiar and erratic behavior. As in 2:47, "the God of gods" (11:36c) is the one true God of Israel (cf. Deut 10:17). In Semitic idiom, the phrase "God of gods" expresses the superlative degree (hence, the most divine God), as do such combinations as "king of kings" (Ezek 26:7; I Tim 6:15), "Lord of lords" (Deut 10:17; Ps 136:3; I Tim 6:15), "holy of holies" (Exod 26:33–34), and "Song of songs" (Song of Songs 1:1). Except for 11:36c, there is no record of any particular blasphemy spoken by Antiochus against the God of Israel; but his conduct being what it was, it is highly probable that the first recipients of this apocalypse were aware of some instances when the tyrant committed this heinous sin. Antiochus will succeed in his gross villainy only until "the time of wrath" decreed by God has been fulfilled (11:36d); cf. COMMENT: DETAILED on 8:19.

The next section (11:37–39) amplifies, almost by way of synonymous parallelism, what was stated in brief compass in 11:36. It is not certain how Antiochus was disrespectful to "the gods of his ancestors" (11:37a), i.e. the gods usually worshipped by the other Seleucids. Heaton writes (p. 238) that Antiochus in his efforts to unify his empire (I Macc 1:41–42) tried to absorb or suppress local and lesser deities like Apollo (whose image no longer appears on coins, being replaced by Zeus) and the fertility god Tammuz (or Adonis), called "the darling of women" (11:37b) because of his feminine devotees (cf. Ezek 8:14). On the fertility myths involved here, cf. Lattey, p. 104. Montgomery adds (p. 461) that this replacement of gods, which was quite contrary to ancient Near Eastern sentiment (cf. Jer 2:11), may suffice to explain the author's caustic comment. It may be further suggested that because Antiochus used to plunder the temples of his own gods (so Polybius xxxvi 4, 10) when his treasury needed to be replenished, he could be judged guilty of making himself "greater than all of them" (11:37c).

On the stand (i.e. altar) of "the God of the pious ones" Antiochus honored "with gold, silver, precious stones, and costly gifts, a god whom his ancestors did not know" (11:38), i.e. Zeus Olympios. This verse makes reference to the "setting up an appalling abomination" (cf. COMMENT: DETAILED on 11:31) which is also mentioned in ch. 8 (cf. COMMENT: DETAILED on 8:11–12). Although the Seleucids before Antiochus IV venerated Zeus Olympios (his image was inscribed on some of their coins), the historic god of the dynasty was Apollo who was pictured on coins seated upon the Cyprian omphalos (cf. Montgomery, p. 461, for references to the pertinent literature). This being the case, it could be said that Zeus Olympios was a god whom Antiochus' ancestors did not know, in the sense that they did not recognize him to be their chief god; Apollo had that distinction. If this interpretation is correct—most other commentators translate and understand 11:38 quite differently—the inspired author intended a double indictment of Antiochus, first for abominably desecrating the Temple with the altar and/or image of Zeus Olympios, and secondly (here our author is being sarcastic) for setting up the worship of Zeus, the god who was not even acknowledged as principal deity of the Seleucids. Abel (pp. 124–129) gives a fine historical account of the efforts of Antiochus to promote the cult of Zeus Olympios.

In 11:39a, "the fortresses of the pious ones" are the strongholds and fortified cities of Judea (cf., for instance, I Macc 5:9,26–27). It was quite natural for Antiochus to garrison his own soldiers in these fortresses to enforce his will on the local populace. Perhaps the author also had in mind the Akra in Jerusalem, a fortress indeed built by Antiochus and manned by his own troops (cf. COMMENT: DETAILED on 11:31). But if this conjecture be correct, the Akra was considered by loyal Jews ("the pious ones") as belonging to themselves because it was located in their holy city Jerusalem. Doubtless, Antiochus was lavish to those who went along with his policies (11:39b). In the touching story of the martyrdom of the faithful and fearless Jewish mother and her seven sons, there is this statement: "As the youngest brother was still alive, [Antiochus] appealed to him, not with mere words, but with promises on oath, to make him rich and happy if he would abandon his ancestral customs: he would make him his Friend [a royal favorite in Hellenistic courts] and entrust him with high office" (II Macc 7:24; cf. also I Macc 2:18).

As a postscript to this section it may be added that 11:36–39, despite occasional obscurities, refer certainly to the biography of Antiochus, and so say nothing at all of a future Antichrist, as many of the older commentators used to believe (e.g. Keil, pp. 461–467). The Antichrist interpretation of these verses is exegetically witless and religiously worthless.

An Imaginative Prediction of Antiochus' Death (11:40–45). The fictional prophecy begun in 11:2 concludes in 11:39. The present section contains no historical information at all, but purports rather to be a genuine prediction of events to happen after this apocalypse was composed and presumably circulated among the faithful. The trouble is that nothing in these verses matches the actual course of history as it is known from other sources. This untoward situation has caused believers through the centuries great difficulty. And unusual interpretations, however well intentioned and prompted as they were by deep faith in Sacred Scripture, were put forward in a misguided attempt to salvage the inerrancy of the biblical text. Although the apparent literary form of this passage is prediction, it is best to view these verses as the sacred author's imaginative expectation of what would happen in the final days of Antiochus' career. That the expectation does not correspond to the known data of history in no way detracts from the author's confident faith and sure hope that the Lord of history holds unquestioned control also over such powerful men as Antiochus IV Epiphanes. Cf. Introduction, Part XIV.

In addition to this exegesis of 11:40–45, which is shared by most modern authors except the fundamentalists, three other hypotheses have been offered by commentators: (1) 11:40–45 refer to a third war against Egypt after 168 B.C.; (2) these verses contain a succinct recapitulation of Antiochus' affairs and predict in a general way his death; and (3) the entire section, 11:36–45, deals not with Antiochus but with the future Antichrist and his death. Linder (pp. 471–474) explains each of these interpretations and provides detailed bibliography.

In 11:40, "the time of the final phase" which was alluded to in 11:27 and specifically mentioned in 11:35, has finally arrived. The day of recompense is at hand. Antiochus, "the king of the north," will again be provoked by Ptolemy Philometor, "the king of the south," into waging another war, but this time the Syrian tyrant will overwhelm Egypt "like a flood." Antiochus will attack by land and by sea, presumably because only in this way will he be able to subdue Alexandria which had eluded his grasp before. Except for the allegation of a post-168 B.C. Egyptian campaign (which would have been the third) attributed by St. Jerome (*PL* 25, col. 572) to Porphyry, there is no mention at all in the extant ancient sources for the war predicted in 11:40. In fact, after the ultimatum Antiochus received from the Roman legate Popillius in 168 (cf. COMMENT: DETAILED on 11:30) it appears extremely unlikely that the tyrant would return to Egypt, thereby risking military intervention by Rome. Porphyry's testimony is based on Dan 11:40, as most historians now agree; hence, it is worthless as a historical source. Cf. Driver, p. 197; Rinaldi, p. 148; and Delcor, pp. 246–247.

As Antiochus comes south "into the lovely land" of Israel (11:41; cf. NOTE), tens of thousands of faithful Jews will be tested (cf. NOTE). It is not altogether clear why our author predicts that "Edom, Moab, and the remnant of the Ammonites will be saved from his power" (11:41). Commentators offer three principal theories: (1) during the pogroms the Edomites and Ammonites were hostile to the Jews, and according to I Macc 4:61 and 5:1–8 they were friendly to Antiochus, who consequently spared them on this latest adventure of his; (2) because the Moabites, a people who had long before disappeared from history, also are mentioned, the author merely wished to state that the invasion will include only the land between the Mediterranean and the Jordan River, whereas the domains east of the Jordan and the Dead Sea (i.e. Ammon, Moab, and Edom) will be spared; and (3) Edom, Moab, and Ammon, although related to Israel by descent, were the hereditary enemies of the Chosen People (cf. Ps 83:7–8; II Chron 20:1–2) and so are taken here as terms of reproach applied to the apostate Jews who will not suffer from Antiochus' assumed onslaught.

As Antiochus marches south, no country will be able to resist; "not even the land of Egypt will escape" (11:42), as happened when Rome intervened to save Ptolemy Philometor in 11:30. Antiochus had plundered Egypt on his first campaign there (11:28); this time he will carry away "the treasures of gold and silver and all other precious things in Egypt" (11:43). The sacred author imagined that Antiochus who was constantly short of funds would now loot Egypt's fabulous hidden treasures (cf. NOTE on 11:43)—something he was unable to complete on his first expedition (cf. COMMENT: DETAILED on 11:28). In 11:43b, "the Libyans," whose land was west of Egypt, and the "Cushites" (i.e. Ethiopians), who were south of Egypt, represent the traditional limits of the Egyptian empire, as Dan and Beersheba represent the limits of biblical Israel (cf. Judg 20:1, etc.). What is meant here, therefore, is that Antiochus will subdue Egypt completely.

But as happened before (11:28), Antiochus will receive alarming "news from the east and the north" (11:44a) and will be compelled to abandon his newly acquired territory. "He will set out with great fury to completely exterminate many" (11:44b). As a matter of historical record, Antiochus spent the last months of his life campaigning against the

Parthians who were in the eastern part of the Seleucid empire, and the Armenians who were located to the north. It may have been possible for the sacred author when he wrote these lines to have surmised correctly that Antiochus would eventually have to deal with these peoples. On his way north from Egypt Antiochus will again "exterminate" faithful Jews, the most obvious meaning of "many" (Hebrew *rabbîm*); cf. 11:33 and 12:2–3.

The death of Antiochus is forecast in 11:45. After he has set up his headquarters—"pitched his palatial tent"—between the Mediterranean and Mount Zion, "the lovely holy mountain," he will meet his end, "with none to help him." Daniel 8 predicts that Antiochus "will be broken—but not by human hand" (cf. COMMENT: DETAILED on 8:25). For the locale of Antiochus' death the inspired author selected the hill country to the west of Jerusalem, because in the last days the final enemies of God's people would fall on "the mountains of Israel" (cf. Ezek 38:14–39; Rev 20:7–9), or be judged in the vicinity of Jerusalem (Joel 3:2,12–15; Zech 14:2–12). Moreover, in our author's view, the worst crimes of Antiochus were perpetrated in the Holy Land; hence, it was singularly appropriate that the tyrant be cut down near the center of that land. It is a matter of historical record, however, that Antiochus died in Persia between 20 November and 19 December 164 B.C.; cf. Lacocque, p. 172. Being as usual hard-pressed for funds, he sought to pillage the rich temple of Artemis in Elymais but was repulsed by the enraged citizens. Discouraged and humiliated, he withdrew to Tabae, near Isfahan in Persia, where he was felled by a mysterious disease and came to a miserable end (I Macc 6:1–16); cf. Schürer, pp. 165–166. As was pointed out in the COMMENT: GENERAL, critics are in general agreement that this apocalypse was composed in 165 or 164 B.C., because in 11:40–45 the author is unaware of Antiochus' real-life eastern campaign in 165, or of the rededication of the Temple in December 164, or of the tyrant's death late in 164 in Persia.

The Ultimate Victory of the Righteous (12:1–3). The first four verses of ch. 12 contain the final words of the angel's revelation which began in 10:20. In 12:1–3, the author conveys his profound beliefs—and presumably the beliefs of the Jewish community of his day—as to the final outcome of the conflict of the forces of evil against the upright who remain steadfast in their faith. These verses have received various interpretations, which are conveniently surveyed by B. J. Alfrink, "L'idée de résurrection d'après Dan., XII, 1.2," *Bib* 40 (1959), 355–362. It is probably best to understand 12:1–3 as continuing the prediction of 11:40–45. Hence, the timeframe intended by the author is the period after Antiochus' death. Because resurrection of the dead is, however, the subject matter being dealt with, the Jews long after Antiochus and still later the Christians, who both accepted the Book of Daniel as sacred and canonical, reread 12:1–3 as pertaining to the eschatological future when there would be a dramatic intervention of the Lord of history in the life of the believing community or, as the verses would even later come to be interpreted, of the individual believer. The primary audience addressed is, therefore, the loyal group of Jews who suffered cruel persecution under Antiochus IV. These stalwart men, women, and children will be vindicated by God and will be rewarded for their fidelity not here on earth but beyond the grave. It is significant that the locus of retribution is placed in the afterlife where neither proof nor disproof is possible by empirical means. Faith alone in the goodness and justice of God who has revealed himself to the Chosen People enables the believer to accept without scientific validation or confirmation the consoling truth of resurrection.

In 12:1, the twice repeated phrase "at that time" (Hebrew *bāʿēt hahîʾ*), though it is one of the usual eschatological phrases, refers to the time of the miserable death of Antiochus IV, and not to some distant time in the future. To be sure, the sacred author most likely was of the opinion that the definitive intervention of God would take place when Antiochus had received his due recompense. This being the case, "Michael, the great prince" (12:1a; cf. NOTE), the guardian angel or "protector of your people," i.e. the Israel of blood, "will arise" to defend the cause of the upright. That "it will be a time of distress, such as never occurred since nations came into being until that time" (12:1b), comes as no surprise. In biblical literature, the end period when God steps into human history more directly to set things right is characterized by great alarms and upheavals in nature; cf. Jer 30:7; Exod 9:18; Joel 2:1–2; Mark 13:19; Matt 24:29–31; Rev 16:18. Despite the extraordinary distress, "every one of them who is found written in the book" (12:1c), Hebrew *kol-hannimṣāʾ kātûb bassēper,* will be rescued. In 4QDibHam, 6, 12–14, published by M. Baillet, *RB* 68 (1961), 210–211, a similar expression occurs: "(Deliver your people) . . . every one who is written in the book of life (or of the living)," Hebrew *kol hakkātûb bᵉsēper haḥayyîm.* This Qumran document containing a rather lengthy prayer dates from after the final redaction of the Book of Daniel. "The book of life (or of the living)" is mentioned also in Isa 4:3 and Ps 69:29. In the New Testament "the book of life," Greek *biblion* or *biblos tēs zōēs,* in which are inscribed the names of those who are to be saved, is mentioned in Philip 4:3; Rev 3:5; 13:8; 17:8; 20:12,15; 21:27 (cf. Luke 10:20). In I Enoch, "the book of life" occurs in 108:3, and "the books of the living" in 47:3; in 81:1–2, reference is made to "heavenly tablets" and "the books of all the deeds of mankind," and in 103:2, similar expressions are found. In Dan 12:1, although the archangel Michael is protector of the whole Israel of blood, only the Israel of faith, i.e. the remnant who have persevered despite the threat of punishment and death, will be delivered so that they may enjoy the reward of their constancy and loyalty in the Kingdom of God.

Now comes the most discussed statement of the whole book: "Many of those who sleep in the dirt of the earth will awake; some will live forever, while others will become everlasting objects of contempt and abhorrence" (12:2). The Hebrew phrase *'admat 'āpār,* "the dirt of the earth," can also be translated "the country of the dirt." In either case, the grave is meant as well as Sheol, the underworld abode of the dead; cf. Job 7:21; 17:16. A similar expression referring to Sheol occurs in Isa 26:19: "(Awake and sing) you who dwell in the dirt" (Hebrew *šôkᵉnê 'āpār*). The rest of Dan 12:2 likewise echoes Isa 26:19, of which our author is giving an inspired midrash.

Much depends on the interpretation of "many," Hebrew *rabbîm,* in 12:2. Does it mean "not all but simply many," or is the word a Semitism for "all"? In Mark 14:24 and Matt 26:28, the blood of Jesus is said to be poured out "in behalf of many" (Greek *pollōn*). Explaining the Marcan text, V. Taylor, *The Gospel according to St. Mark* (London: Macmillan, 1963), p. 546, writes: "The use of *pollōn* is . . . Semitic; its meaning is not 'some, but not all', but 'all in contrast to one.'" This exegesis receives corroboration from I John 2:2: "He [Jesus] is an offering for our sins, and not for our sins only, but for those of the whole world." A.-M. Dubarle, "Prophètes d'Israël: Daniel," *DBSup,* vol. 6, cols. 755–756, also points out that the text here could refer to a general resurrection because in Isa 52:14 and 53:12 as well as in the Qumran documents *rabbîm* or *hārabbîm* (with the definite article), "(the) many," are virtually the multitude, the community, the totality. Thus it is possible that *rabbîm* in 12:2 also means "all," i.e. Jews and Gentiles alike. This view, however, is not probable, because after the word *rabbîm* the Hebrew preposition *min* in the expression *mîyᵉšēnê* is most naturally understood as partitive; hence, the translation "(many) of those who sleep." LXX, Theod., and Vulgate offer the same interpretation. In the Syriac Peshiṭta, however, the partitive idea is lost: *saggî'ê 'aylên dᵉdamkîn,* "many who sleep," and could lend some outside support to those commentators who would take *rabbîm* to mean "all."

It seems more plausible to assume, however, that our author is not particularly concerned about the lot of all the dead, but only of the Jews—on the one hand, the stalwart men, women, and children who suffered martyrdom rather than obey the wicked decrees of Antiochus IV (I Macc 1:60–62; II Macc 6:10–11,18–31; Daniel 7); and on the other hand, the cowardly apostates who submitted to the impious tyrant. The loyal Jews, "every one of them who is found written in the book" (12:1), are the "some" who will awake to experience everlasting life in the resurrection, but the renegade Jews, when they awake, are the "others" who "will become everlasting objects of contempt and abhorrence" (12:2). In the realm of the afterlife, each person will receive from God the recompense he or she deserves. Resurrection here is not a matter of national restoration as in Hosea 6:1–2; Ezek 37:1–14; Isa 26:19; Pss 80:19–20; 85:6–7; but it is rather something that each individual will achieve on the basis of his or her response to God, and not on the basis of race or nation. Thus, God will do justice to the courageous Jewish martyrs as well as to the pusillanimous apostates. In this interpretation, the "many" who awake from the sleep of death includes "all" the Jews, the pious and the impious; so Plöger, p. 171. Non-Jews are not even taken into account. G. W. E. Nickelsburg, *Resurrection, Immortality, and Eternal Life in Intertestamental Judaism,* HTS 26, p. 19, writes: "For Daniel resurrection is *a means* by which both the righteous and the wicked dead are enabled to receive their respective vindication or condemnation." Charles (p. 327) holds a similar view.

In my judgment, the best interpretation of 12:1–2 is the one offered by B. J. Alfrink, "L'idée de résurrection," *Bib* 40 (1959), 362–371. On the basis of solid evidence as to the meaning of the twofold *'ēlleh,* usually translated as here "some . . . others," as well as the ancient Israelite doctrine of retribution which held that God will give life to the upright but death to the wicked (confer, e.g. Deuteronomy 28), Alfrink suggests that the "many" who awake and receive eternal life in the resurrection refers only to "these" (Hebrew *'ēlleh*) faithful Jews who are rescued in 12:1. The renegades are "those" (again Hebrew *'ēlleh*) who will not awake, but "will become everlasting objects of contempt and abhorrence" (Hebrew *dērā'ôn*), never to rise but destined to rot away "in the dirt of the earth" (12:2), totally devoid of any kind of life worthy of the name. Our author uses the Hebrew word *dērā'ôn* to call attention to the very last verse of the Book of Isaiah (66:24)—the only two places where the word occurs in the whole MT—"[All mankind] shall go out and see the corpses of the men who rebelled against me; their worm shall not die, nor their fire be extinguished; and they shall be abhorrent [*dērā'ôn*] to all mankind." In 12:1–2, therefore, resurrection is a prerogative bestowed by God as a free gift only on the faithful Jew; it is not given to all men and women irrespective of their religious and moral uprightness. Nor did the doctrine of the resurrection in the Book of Daniel derive from Iranian sources, as it was once fashionable to believe. Much less is resurrection viewed here as an anthropological or philosophical necessity that is due to the very nature of the human person. For a fuller discussion of these issues, cf. W. Eichrodt, *Theology of the Old Testament,* vol. 2 (1967), pp. 515–526; and Lacocque, pp. 172–180.

The inspired author of 12:1–2 is the first Old Testament writer to affirm unambiguously the truth of eternal life after death for at least some individuals, viz. the righteous Jews. Prior to the time of our author, the normative doctrine of retribution was simply this: faithful observance of the Law brought prosperity in the present life and length of days to nation and individual; sin brought adversity and early death (cf. Deuteronomy 28). Rewards and punishments after death were not even thought of. Because after death all men and women—saints and sinners alike—went to Sheol, the abode of the dead, and because the dead were believed not to rise again (Job 14:12), Sheol cannot be understood as a place of retribution. In Sheol, all the dead, regardless of their loyalty or disloyalty to the Covenant, shared alike a dark, listless, dull subsistence separated from God. Cf. A. A. Di Lella, "The Problem of Retribution in the Wisdom Literature," in *Rediscovery of Scripture: Biblical Theology Today*, pp. 109–112.

Although, as already indicated, the extent of resurrection in 12:1–2 is not absolutely clear—opinions ranging from universal resurrection to resurrection of only the Jewish martyrs and no one else—our author must be credited with giving the first sure teaching on life beyond the grave. The doctrine of resurrection for the faithful is also found in II Macc 7:7–23; 12:38–46; 14:45–46; but the wicked are excluded from being raised to life. Cf. F.-M. Abel and J. Starcky, *Les livres des Maccabées, SBJ*, 3d ed., p. 21. Only in the Wisdom of Solomon, composed about the beginning of the first century B.C., does retribution in the afterlife take place for both the virtuous and the wicked; cf. A. A. Di Lella, "Conservative and Progressive Theology," *CBQ* 28 (1966), 150–154.

In 12:3, our author makes mention of a particular class of loyal Jews who will receive special glory in the resurrection. Although it is possible that the verse refers to two different classes of heroes—"those who act wisely" and "those who lead the multitude to righteousness"—a view favored by Charles (p. 330) and Jeffery (p. 543), it seems more plausible that in view of 11:33,35 and the present context only one specific group is meant under two different images (so Montgomery, p. 471; Plöger, p. 171; Heaton, p. 248; and Delcor, pp. 255–256). In 12:3a, this group is described as "those who act wisely," the same designation they receive in ch. 11; cf. COMMENT: DETAILED on 11:33 and 35. These wise leaders of the Jewish non-violent resistance will be distinguished from the rest of the faithful because "they will shine brightly like the brilliance of the firmament" (cf. Exod 24:10). The LXX has here "will shine like the lights [Greek *phōstēres*] of heaven," an idea taken up in Matt 13:43: "The saints will shine like the sun in their Father's kingdom"; cf. Rev 2:28; 22:16. In 12:3b, this group is special also because they "lead the multitude [Hebrew *hārabbîm*] to righteousness" (cf. NOTE), i.e. by their own teaching and upright example. Because they have given of themselves generously and enthusiastically, they "will shine like the stars forever and ever" (cf. Wisd Sol 3:7), eternally admired by the ordinary folk they have instructed in the ways of the Lord. The stars here, as in Job 38:7, may symbolize the angels; if so, this group of stalwarts are said to share in the splendor of the angels.

J. J. Collins, "Apocalyptic Eschatology as the Transcendence of Death," *CBQ* 36 (1974), 33–35, has argued from the angelic host ideology evidenced in ch. 10 that in 12:3 the final vindication and victory of the righteous are described as elevation to the ranks of the angels. This interpretation, he says, receives support from contemporary literature. In I Enoch 104:2, the upright "will shine as the stars of heaven," and in 104:6, "will become companions to the hosts of heaven." Also in the Similitudes of Enoch 39:5, the righteous are said to dwell with the holy angels. A similar idea, Collins notes, is found in Matt 22:30, "When people rise from the dead, they neither marry nor are given in marriage but live like angels in heaven." One immediate objection that can be raised against these views, which Collins repeats in "The Son of Man and the Saints of the Most High in the Book of Daniel," *JBL* 93 (1974), 55–58, is that some of the evidence he alleges can hardly be classified as contemporary with Daniel. For instance, J. T. Milik, "Problèmes de la littérature hénochique à la lumière des fragments araméens de Qumrân," *HTR* 64 (1971), 373–378, dates the Similitudes or Parables of Enoch to A.D. 270. And the Gospel of Matthew cannot be adduced as a parallel for interpreting the Book of Daniel which is more than two hundred years earlier. A more serious objection is that Collins misunderstands the intent of 12:3, which he translates as follows: "the wise will shine like the splendor of the firmament and those who lead the many to justice will be like the stars forever." In his argument he lumps together the faithful in general, "the many" (Hebrew *hārabbîm*) of 12:2,3 with the special class of the faithful in 12:3. It is only the latter who can be said to have part in the glory of the angels, symbolized by the stars. Of the large number of faithful Jews in 12:2 it is simply stated that they "will awake . . . and will live forever"; i.e. they will experience resurrection from the dead. Nothing is said about their being elevated to the ranks of the angels.

The Final Exhortation to Daniel (12:4). The present apocalypse originally ended with 12:4. Because Daniel prayed and did penance (10:2–3,12) and is "greatly beloved" by heaven (10:11,19), he has been made privy to the secrets of the future which are "written in the book of truth" (11:2). There is no reason to assume that Daniel did not understand what the angel said to him (compare with the gloss in 12:8). In fact, now that the angel has finished his revelation of the future course of history and has given solemn assurance of the ultimate victory through resurrection of the faithful, he orders Daniel to "keep the words secret and seal the book until the time of the final phase" (12:4a). As in 8:26, this injunction is necessary and typical of such works of *vaticinia ex eventu;* otherwise the fiction of attributing the prophecy to some ancient worthy without its contents being known in the intervening centuries would not be acceptable, much less credible. Evidently, the sealing of a scroll or book was taken very seriously (cf. Isa 29:11), and the breaking of the seal could be accomplished only by an authorized person (cf. Rev 5:1–5). "The book" to be sealed is evidently the entire book and not just the present apocalypse (chs. 10–12). As in 11:35, "the time of the final phase" is the author's own time, a time of religious crisis and persecution. Now that the final phase has arrived, the book may be opened so that the suffering Jew who strove mightily to remain steadfast in faith may receive encouragement, strength, and consolation from the truth that what he is now experiencing during the reign of Antiochus IV Epiphanes is all part of God's preordained but inscrutable plan of history, which, according to the author's inspired literary convention of fictional prophecy, was revealed to Daniel in the Persian period some three hundred and fifty years earlier. The MT of 12:4b is corrupt; cf. NOTE. The first audience to read or hear the Book of Daniel in the period of Antiochus was painfully aware of the fact that many Jews apostatized and that evil was on the increase.

Epilogue (12:5–13)

The angel's long discourse concludes in 12:4 with the command that Daniel is to "seal the book." As indicated earlier, 12:4 was the conclusion of the present apocalypse; so Ginsberg, pp. 30–31. There are two basic opinions regarding the Epilogue that now follows: (1) it is a series of later glosses or additions made by different hands (so Ginsberg, pp. 30–38); and (2) it is an authentic supplement to this lengthy apocalypse (so Montgomery, p. 474, followed by Lacocque, pp. 181–183).

The view is taken here that this section contains material from three different people. In the translation these additions are indicated by one, two, and three slashes, respectively. As indicated in the COMMENT: DETAILED on 9:27, the section comprising 12:5–10,13 was added by the writer responsible for the core material of ch. 9. This same person put the Book of Daniel into its present form, except for 12:11 and 12:12 which are still later glosses composed by two other hands.

Duration of the Persecution (12:5–12). Two other angels besides the heavenly being who, first introduced in 10:5, acted as narrator of the revelation in chs. 10–12, now appear for the final solemn scene (12:5). As Hitzig has suggested (cited by Keil, p. 487), the reason for the extra two angels is to be found in 12:7—an oath required two or three witnesses (Deut 19:15; cf. Deut 4:26; 30:19; 31:28), and apparently since the oath is made by an angel, angelic witnesses are called for. "The stream" (Hebrew *hay*^{e}*'ôr;* cf. NOTE on "who was upstream" in 12:6) is the same body of water first mentioned in 10:4, viz. the Tigris. Two angels also appear in conversation in 8:13–14, another passage most probably composed by the writer of the core apocalypse in ch. 9, who was also responsible for 12:5–10,13. One of the angels said (cf. NOTE) "to the man clothed in linen," i.e. the *angelus revelator* first appearing in 10:5 and later implicitly identified as Gabriel (cf. COMMENT: DETAILED on 11:1), "How long will it be until the end of these awful things?" (12:6). The "awful things" (Hebrew *happ*^{e}*lā'ôt;* cf. NOTE) are presumably the wicked deeds of Antiochus IV detailed in ch. 11, or more specifically the *niplā'ôt* (see NOTE on 8:24) that Antiochus perpetrated in 8:24 and 11:36. Cf. Delcor, p. 257; and Lacocque, p. 182. The *angelus revelator,* who was farther upstream from the two newly arrived angels, now raises not only his right hand, the customary one in swearing an oath (Gen 14:22; Deut 32:40; Isa 62:8; Ezek 20:5; Rev 10:5–6), but also his left in order to add greater solemnity to the oath (12:7a). In Daniel's hearing the angel swears by "him who lives forever" (12:7b); the same phrase is found in 4:31 (in Aramaic) and in the Greek of Sir 18:1 (the Hebrew text of this verse is not extant in the Cairo Geniza fragments or in the Qumran scrolls or in the Masada MS of Sirach). See also Rev 10:6; cf. Deut 32:40. The usual introduction to an oath was "As Yahweh lives" (Judg 8:19; I Sam 14:39,45; 19:6; 20:3,21; 25:26,34, etc.). What the *angelus revelator* swears in answer to the question addressed to him is that it would be "for a year, two years, and half a year" (12:7b), the identical expression used in 7:25. In 9:27, the time span is exactly the same, "half a week," i.e. of years, or three and a half years. In 8:14, however, the duration of the villainy is "two thousand and three hundred evenings and mornings," or 1,150 days, a period of time that only approximates the three and a half years given in 7:25; 9:27; and 12:7. For the exegesis cf. COMMENT: DETAILED on 7:25 and 9:27. The last clause of 12:7 is obscure in the MT; the translation here is based on an emended Hebrew text; cf. Textual Note [vv–vv]. "The desecrator of the holy people" (12:7c) is Antiochus IV whose power would be "brought to an end" after the three and a half years have elapsed, when "all these things" prophesied in ch. 11 "would be accomplished."

Baffled by what he hears, Daniel politely addresses the *angelus revelator* as "my lord," a title of respect used by the seer also in 10:16,17,19, and then asks the angel to explain the conversation (12:8; cf. NOTE). Daniel, who had previously been granted understanding of the revelation because of his prayers and penance (10:2–3,12), was instructed in 12:4 to "keep the words secret and seal the book"; cf. COMMENT: DETAILED on 12:4. But now in 12:8, he appears confused and in need of an explanation. Doubtless, this ploy is used by the glossator to heighten the sense of mystery given in the prediction made here as well as in 7:25; 8:14; and 9:27. But the angel gives Daniel little satisfaction, merely reminding him that "the words are secret and sealed until the time of the final phase" (12:9), something the seer should have been already aware of from the instructions he received in 12:4. In other words, since the words of the revelation are now sealed, no new information can be given. As Ginsberg rightly points out (p. 31), the words "hidden (or secret) and sealed," borrowed from 12:4, have acquired in 12:9 the figurative sense of "obscure and mysterious." Thus, 12:8–9 can be viewed as further evidence that the present section (12:5–10,13) was composed by the glossator and not by the author of the apocalypse which began in 10:1 and ended in 12:4.

"The final phase" will be a time when "the multitude will be cleansed, purified, and refined" (12:10a). Here again "the multitude," Hebrew *rabbîm,* appear as in 11:33,44 and 12:2–3, and accordingly it seems wisest to take *rabbîm* as referring to the pious Jews who are or will be subjected to tribulation under Antiochus IV. In 11:35, only the wise leaders of the people were said to be tested "to refine, cleanse, and purify them"; note the different order of the verbs. Now the process of purgation will extend to all the faithful; cf. COMMENT: DETAILED on 11:35. "But the wicked will be proved wicked," i.e. they will fill up the measure of their wickedness; cf. Rev 22:10. There is chiastic order in the Hebrew words of the last part of 12:10: *lōʾ yābînû kol-r*^{e}*šāʿîm w*^{e}*hammaśkîlîm yābînû,* literally, "They shall not understand (it), all the wicked, but those who act wisely will understand." Most likely, what is meant here is that the renegade Jews will not understand the significance of the events occurring "in the time of the final phase," whereas the wise Jews of the loyal opposition to Antiochus will have a profound understanding of these realities. Although the phrase "those who act wisely," Hebrew *hammaśkîlîm,* refers only to the faithful leaders of the people in 11:33,35 and 12:3, it appears quite plausible that here in 12:10 the expression also includes all the common folk, "the multitude," Hebrew *rabbîm,* mentioned at the beginning of the verse, who "will be cleansed, purified, and refined" by persecution and adversity.

It is commonly admitted by exegetes that 12:11–12 are successive glosses, the purpose of which is to add a few more days to the 1,150-day period predicted in 8:14 as the duration of the time when the daily sacrifice, Hebrew *tāmîd,* would be suspended and the Temple would be defiled by "the appalling abomination" (8:13). The theory is that when those 1,150 days came and went without the Temple being cleansed, some zealous and holy Jew changed the number (12:11) to 1,290 days (the marginal reading in Syh. has 2,290 days!). Then when nothing happened on the 1,290th day, another equally concerned Jew upped the number to 1,335 days (12:12), a duration of time that also appears in Ascension of Isaiah. The new calculation is prefaced with the pious remark, "Blessed is the one who has patience and perseveres" (a reminiscence of Isa 30:18). The trouble with this theory is that according to I Maccabees, the Temple was defiled on 6 December 167 B.C. (I Macc 1:54) and rededicated by Judas Maccabeus on 14 December 164 B.C. (I Macc 4:52), a period of three years and eight days in the Julian calendar, or a sum of 1,103 days —$(365\times3)+8$—somewhat less than the 1,150 days predicted in 8:14, and the three and a half years or 1,260 days (forty-two months, each of thirty days), predicted in 7:25; 9:27; and 12:7; cf. COMMENT: DETAILED on 7:25 and 9:27. In view of these circumstances, it seems best to admit that what the glossators had in mind as happening at the end of the 1,290 days in 12:11 and 1,335 days in 12:12 simply cannot be ascertained with any confidence. Only guesses are possible. Nevertheless, since none of the predicted numbers in 7:25; 8:14; 9:27; and 12:7 were meant to be understood as being mathematically precise, it appears plausible that the calculations in 12:11 and 12:12, whatever the respective *terminus ad quem* may refer to, were also intended only as round numbers. For a fine survey of commentators' attempts at explaining these numbers, cf. Linder, pp. 489–494; a more recent study was attempted by C. Schedl who appropriately entitles his article "Mystische Arithmetik oder geschichtliche Zahlen (Dan., 8, 14; 12, 11–13)," *BZ* 8 (1964), 101–105. Whether or not it has any significance at all, it may be noted that 1,290 days (12:11) equal forty-three months of thirty days each (cf. 6:8,13), and that 1,335 days (12:12) equal forty-four and a half such months. At this point the reader should be reminded that it is not unusual for numbers in the Bible to be used, disconcertingly, for purposes other than precise counting. A number may be given exclusively for its symbolic value; e.g. "four" signifies the world (which was thought to have four corners), "six" imperfection, "seven" perfection or totality, "three and a half" gross imperfection (the predicted duration in years of the persecution in 7:25; 9:27; and 12:7; cf. also Rev 11:2 where this same duration of adversity is predicted), "twelve," the tribes of Israel, "thousand," immensity. Unfortunately, the symbolism of some numbers, undoubtedly obvious to the biblical writers and their original audiences, eludes today's readers completely.

Final Words to Daniel (12:13). As already suggested above, this verse originally came after, and was written by the same author of, 12:5–10. Daniel the seer, whom the pseudonymous second-century B.C. author of this apocalypse fictionally situated in 536 B.C. (10:1), is now told by the *angelus revelator* to take his rest, i.e. in the grave (Isa 57:1–2) with the saints (Wisd Sol 3:3; 4:7; Rev 14:13). The grave, however, will not be Daniel's permanent resting place, for the angel assures him that he will rise for his "reward at the end of the days." The word for "the days" here is Hebrew *yāmîn,* with the Aramaic masculine plural ending *-în* in place of the normal Hebrew ending *-îm;* this phenomenon is another indication that the Hebrew parts of Daniel were translated from Aramaic, as was pointed out in the Introduction, Part III. Nowhere else in the Hebrew Bible is *yāmîn* spelt this way. Hebrew *gôrāl,* here translated "reward," but literally, "lot, allotted portion, assignment," is employed in the spiritual sense also in Jer 13:25 where the word means "destiny"; cf. also Micah 2:5; Ps 125:3; Col 1:12 (so Montgomery, p. 478). The "reward at the end of the days" is resurrection unto glory in God's Kingdom; cf. Isa 26:19.

On this peaceful and hopeful note the Book of Daniel comes to a close. As M. Stuart appositely observes (cited in Montgomery, p. 478), this conclusion is "an assurance full of comfort to him, who was now very far advanced in life; and full of comfort to all who walk in his steps, and are animated by his spirit."

Appendix

Susanna

13: 1 In Babylon there lived a man
named Joakim, 2 who married a very
beautiful and God-fearing woman, Susanna, the daughter of Hilkiah; 3 her
pious parents had trained their daughter according to the law of Moses.
4 Joakim was very rich; he had a
garden near his house, and the Jews
had recourse to him often because he
was the most respected of them all.

5 That year, two elders of the people were appointed judges, of whom
the Lord said, "Wickedness has come
out of Babylon: from the elders who
were to govern the people as judges."
6 These men, to whom all brought their
cases, frequented the house of Joakim.
7 When the people left at noon, Susanna used to enter her husband's
garden for a walk. 8 When the old
men saw her enter every day for her
walk, they began to lust for her. 9 They
suppressed their consciences; they
would not allow their eyes to look to
heaven, and did not keep in mind just
judgments. 10 Though both were enam-
ored of her, they did not tell each
other their trouble, 11 for they were
ashamed to reveal their lustful desire
to have her. 12 Day by day they
watched eagerly for her. 13 One day
they said to each other, "Let us be off
for home, it is time for lunch." So
they went out and parted; 14 but both
turned back, and when they met again,
they asked each other the reason.
They admitted their lust, and then
they agreed to look for an occasion
when they could meet her alone.

15 One day, while they were waiting
for the right moment, she entered the
garden as usual, with two maids only.
She decided to bathe, for the weather
was warm. 16 Nobody else was there
except the two elders, who had hidden themselves and were watching
her. 17 "Bring me oil and soap," she
said to the maids, "and shut the garden doors while I bathe." 18 They did
as she said; they shut the garden doors
and left by the side gate to fetch what

she had ordered, unaware that the
elders were hidden inside.

19 As soon as the maids had left, the
two old men got up and hurried to
her. 20 "Look," they said, "the garden
doors are shut, and no one can see us;
give in to our desire, and lie with us.
21 If you refuse, we will testify against
you that you dismissed your maids
because a young man was here with
you."

22 "I am completely trapped," Susanna groaned. "If I yield, it will be
my death; if I refuse, I cannot escape
your power. 23 Yet it is better for me
to fall into your power without guilt
than to sin before the Lord." 24 Then
Susanna shrieked, and the old men
also shouted at her, 25 as one of them
ran to open the garden doors. 26 When
the people in the house heard the
cries from the garden, they rushed in
by the side gate to see what had happened to her. 27 At the accusations by
the old men, the servants felt very
much ashamed, for never had any such
thing been said about Susanna.

28 When the people came to her husband Joakim the next day, the two
wicked elders also came, fully determined to put Susanna to death. Before
all the people they ordered: 29 "Send
for Susanna, the daughter of Hilkiah,
the wife of Joakim." When she was
sent for, 30 she came with her parents,
children and all her relatives. 31 Susanna, very delicate and beautiful,
32 was veiled; but those wicked men
ordered her to uncover her face so as
to sate themselves with her beauty.
33 All her relatives and the onlookers
were weeping.

34 In the midst of the people the two
elders rose up and laid their hands on
her head. 35 Through her tears she
looked up to heaven, for she trusted
in the Lord wholeheartedly. 36 The
elders made this accusation: "As we
were walking in the garden alone, this
woman entered with two girls and
shut the doors of the garden, dismiss-
ing the girls. 37 A young man, who
was hidden there, came and lay with
her. 38 When we, in a corner of the
garden, saw this crime, we ran toward
them. 39 We saw them lying together,
but the man we could not hold, because he was stronger than we; he
opened the doors and ran off. 40 Then
we seized this one and asked who the
young man was, 41 but she refused to
tell us. We testify to this." The assembly believed them, since they were
elders and judges of the people, and
they condemned her to death.

42 But Susanna cried aloud: "O
eternal God, you know what is hidden
and are aware of all things before they
come to be: 43 you know that they
have testified falsely against me. Here
I am about to die, though I have done
none of the things with which these
wicked men have charged me."

44 The Lord heard her prayer. 45 As
she was being led to execution, God
stirred up the holy spirit of a young
boy named Daniel, 46 and he cried
aloud: "I will have no part in the death
of this woman." 47 All the people
turned and asked him, "What is this
you are saying?" 48 He stood in their
midst and continued, "Are you such
fools, O Israelites! To condemn a
woman of Israel without examination
and without clear evidence? 49 Return
to court, for they have testified falsely
against her."

50 Then all the people returned in
haste. To Daniel the elders said,
"Come, sit with us and inform us,
since God has given you the prestige
of old age." 51 But he replied, "Separate these two far from one another
that I may examine them."

52 After they were separated one
from the other, he called one of them
and said: "How you have grown evil
with age! Now have your past sins
come to term: 53 passing unjust sen-
tences, condemning the innocent, and
freeing the guilty, although the Lord
says, 'The innocent and the just you
shall not put to death.' 54 Now, then, if
you were a witness, tell me under what
tree you saw them together." 55 "Under a mastic tree," he answered.
"Your fine lie has cost you your
head," said Daniel; "for the angel of
God shall receive the sentence from
him and split you in two." 56 Putting
him to one side, he ordered the other
one to be brought. "Offspring of
Canaan, not of Judah," Daniel said
to him, "beauty has seduced you, lust
has subverted your conscience. 57 This
is how you acted with the daughters
of Israel, and in their fear they yielded
to you; but a daughter of Judah did
not tolerate your wickedness. 58 Now,
then, tell me under what tree you
surprised them together." 59 "Under
an oak," he said. "Your fine lie has
cost you also your head," said Daniel;
"for the angel of God waits with a
sword to cut you in two so as to make
an end of you both."

60 The whole assembly cried aloud,
blessing God who saves those that
hope in him. 61 They rose up against
the two elders, for by their own words
Daniel had convicted them of perjury.
According to the law of Moses, they
inflicted on them the penalty they had
plotted to impose on their neighbor:
62 they put them to death. Thus was
innocent blood spared that day. 63 Hilkiah and his wife praised God for
their daughter Susanna, as did Joakim
her husband and all her relatives, because she was found innocent of any
shameful deed. 64 And from that day
onward Daniel was greatly esteemed
by the people.

Bel

14: 1 After King Astyages was laid
with his fathers, Cyrus the Persian succeeded to his kingdom. 2 Daniel was
the king's favorite and was held in
higher esteem than any of the friends
of the king. 3 The Babylonians had an
idol called Bel, and every day they
provided for it six barrels of fine flour,
forty sheep, and six measures of wine.
4 The king worshiped it and went every
day to adore it; but Daniel adored
only his God. 5 When the king asked
him, "Why do you not adore Bel?"
Daniel replied, "Because I worship
not idols made with hands, but only
the living God who made heaven and
earth and has dominion over all mankind." 6 Then the king continued,
"You do not think Bel is a living
god? Do you not see how much he
eats and drinks every day?" 7 Daniel
began to laugh. "Do not be deceived,
O king," he said; "it is only clay inside and bronze outside; it has never
taken any food or drink." 8 Enraged,
the king called his priests and said to
them, "Unless you tell me who it is
that consumes these provisions, you
shall die. 9 But if you can show that
Bel consumes them, Daniel shall die
for blaspheming Bel." Daniel said to
the king, "Let it be as you say!"
10 There were seventy priests of Bel,
besides their wives and children.

When the king went with Daniel into the temple of Bel, 11 the priests of Bel said, "See, we are going to leave. Do you, O king, set out the food and prepare the wine; then shut the door and seal it with your ring. 12 If you do not find that Bel has eaten it all when you return in the morning, we are to die; otherwise Daniel shall die for his lies against us." 13 They were not perturbed, because under the table they had made a secret entrance through which they always came in to consume the food. 14 After they departed the king set the food before Bel, while Daniel ordered his servants to bring some ashes, which they scattered through the whole temple; the king alone was present. Then they went outside, sealed the closed door with the king's ring, and departed. 15 The priests entered that night as usual, with their wives and children, and they ate and drank everything.

16 Early the next morning, the king came with Daniel. 17 "Are the seals unbroken, Daniel?" he asked. And Daniel answered, "They are unbroken, O king." 18 As soon as he had opened the door, the king looked at the table and cried aloud, "Great you are, O Bel; there is no trickery in you." 19 But Daniel laughed and kept the king from entering. "Look at the floor," he said; "whose footprints are these?" 20 "I see the footprints of men, women, and children!" said the king. 21 The angry king arrested the priests, their wives, and their children. They showed him the secret door by which they used to enter to consume what was on the table. 22 He put them to death, and handed Bel over to Daniel, who destroyed it and its temple.

The Dragon

23 There was a great dragon which the Babylonians worshiped. 24 "Look!" said the king to Daniel, "you cannot deny that this is a living god, so adore it." 25 But Daniel answered, "I adore the Lord, my God, for he is the living God. 26 Give me permission, O king, and I will kill this dragon without sword or club." "I give you permission," the king said. 27 Then Daniel took some pitch, fat, and hair; these he boiled together and made into cakes. He put them into the mouth of the dragon, and when the dragon ate them, he burst asunder. "This," he said, "is what you worshiped."

28 When the Babylonians heard this, they were angry and turned against the king. "The king has become a Jew," they said; "he has destroyed Bel, killed the dragon, and put the priests to death." 29 They went to the king and demanded: "Hand Daniel over to us, or we will kill you and your family." 30 When he saw himself threatened with violence, the king was forced to hand Daniel over to them. 31 They threw Daniel into a lions' den, where he remained six days. 32 In the den were seven lions, and two carcasses and two sheep had been given to them daily. But now they were given nothing, so that they would devour Daniel.

33 In Judea there was a prophet, Habakkuk; he mixed some bread in a bowl with the stew he had boiled, and was going to bring it to the reapers in

the field, [34] when an angel of the Lord
told him, "Take the lunch you have
to Daniel in the lions' den at Babylon." [35] But Habakkuk answered,
"Babylon, sir, I have never seen,
and I do not know the den!" [36] The
angel of the Lord seized him by the
crown of his head and carried him by
the hair; with the speed of the wind,
he set him down in Babylon above
the den. [37] "Daniel, Daniel," cried
Habakkuk, "take the lunch God has
sent you." [38] "You have remembered
me, O God," said Daniel; "you have
not forsaken those who love you."
[39] While Daniel began to eat, the angel
of the Lord at once brought Habakkuk back to his own place.

[40] On the seventh day the king came
to mourn for Daniel. As he came to
the den and looked in, there was
Daniel, sitting there! [41] The king cried
aloud, "You are great, O Lord, the
God of Daniel, and there is no other
besides you!" [42] Daniel he took out,
but those who had tried to destroy
him he threw into the den, and they
were devoured in a moment before his
eyes.

INDEX OF AUTHORS

INDEX OF SUBJECTS

INDEX OF BIBLICAL REFERENCES

(Order of books, including deuterocanonical, as in *NAB*)

INDEX OF PSEUDEPIGRAPHA, QUMRAN, AND RABBINIC LITERATURE

Pseudepigrapha

Ascension of Isaiah 2:10–11 278

II Baruch 5:7 278
9:3 278
12:5 278
21:1 278
47:2 278

I Enoch 9:1 70, 282
1–3 249
10:9–10 249
20:5 282, 283, 285
24:24 281
37–71 88
39:5 310
46–48 88
46:1, 3 88
47:3 88
48:2–6 88
61:1 249
71:3 70, 282
81:1–2 287
83–90 92
86:1–6 92
6 93
87:2–3 93
89:1 92, 93
6 93
13 92
40 292
59–65 93
59–67 283
66 93
68 92
72 93
2–4 92
90:2 93
9–16 92
13 93
103:2 306
104:2 310
6 310
108:3 306

I Esd 3:1 – 4:63 55, 60
3:2 198
9 198
10–12 60
4:14 60
14–32 60
35 60
40 60
42 60
43–63 61
58 199

II Esd 5:13 278
20 278
6:31 278
35 278
9:24–26 278
12:51 278
13:1–3, 25–26 88

Jub 4:20 8
5:12 287
15:31–32 283
19:8 130
23:30–32 287
30:21–22 287

Testament of Twelve Patriarchs, Joseph 2:7 130
3:4 130

Testament of Twelve Patriarchs, Reuben 1:9–10 278

Qumran Literature

Rabbinic Literature

KEY TO THE TEXT

Chapter	*Verses*	*Section*
1	1–21	I
2	1–49	II
3	1–30	III
3	31	IV
4	1–34	IV
5	1–30	V
6	1	V
6	2–29	VI
7	1–28	VII
8	1–27	VIII
9	1–27	IX
10	1–21	XA
11	1	XA
11	2–45	XB
12	1–4	XB
12	5–13	XC